Law and Power

# Impact of Empire

ROMAN EMPIRE, C. 200 B.C.–A.D. 476

*Edited by*



VOLUME 49

The titles published in this series are listed at *brill.com/imem*

# Law and Power

*Agents of Social and Spatial Transformation in the Roman West*


*Edited by*

Emilia Mataix Ferrándiz
Antonio López García
Anthony Álvarez Melero
Diego Romero Vera



BRILL

LEIDEN | BOSTON

Cover image: Roman road found near the ancient city of Acci (Guadix, Granada, Spain).
Copyright Antonio López García.

Library of Congress Cataloging-in-Publication Data

Names: Mataix Ferrándiz, Emilia, editor.
Title: Law and power : agents of social and spatial transformation in the Roman West / edited by Emilia Mataix Ferrándiz, Antonio Lopez García, Anthony Álvarez Melero, Diego Romero Vera.
Description: Leiden ; Boston : Brill/Nijhoff, 2024. | Series: Impact of empire, 1572-0500 ; 49 | Includes bibliographical references and index.
Identifiers: LCCN 2023045410 (print) | LCCN 2023045411 (ebook) | ISBN 9789004685727 (hardback) | ISBN 9789004685734 (ebook)
Subjects: LCSH: Municipal corporations (Roman law) | City planning and redevelopment law—Rome.
Classification: LCC KJA3090 .L39 2023 (print) | LCC KJA3090 (ebook) | DDC 342/.09—dc23/eng/20231002
LC record available at https://lccn.loc.gov/2023045410
LC ebook record available at https://lccn.loc.gov/2023045411

Typeface for the Latin, Greek, and Cyrillic scripts: "Brill". See and download: brill.com/brill-typeface.

ISSN 1572-0500
ISBN 978-90-04-68572-7 (hardback)
ISBN 978-90-04-68573-4 (e-book)
DOI 10.1163/9789004685734

# Contents

**PART 3**
## *Interconnectedness*

# Acknowledgements

This book grew out of an international conference entitled "Law and Imperial Power: Agents of Transformation of the Territorial and Urban Landscapes in Roman Hispania" and organised in Helsinki in October 2019 and funded by Universidad de Sevilla's VI Own Plan for Research and Knowledge Transfer (PPIT-US). The workshop was co-organized by the research project Law, Governance and Space: Questioning the Foundations of the Republican Tradition (SpaceLaw), funded by the European research council (grant agreement: 771874) together with Dr. Diego Romero Vera from the University of Seville (Spain). We would like to thank Professor Kaius Tuori (Spacelaws' PI) for hosting the event at the University of Helsinki and funding part of it. Emilia Mataix Ferrándiz would like to thank the financing of the European Union-Next generation EU, which has supported her María Zambrano fellowship of the University Basque country. Antonio López García has received funding from the Next Generation framework of the European Commission through the programme María Zambrano for the attraction of international talent at the University of Granada. This book is also is part of the R&D&I project PID2022-138873NB-I00, funded by MCIN/AEI/10.13039/501100011033/ and 'ERDF. A way of making Europe'. Likewise, this volume was conceived under the umbrella of the project "Italica Adrianea: la *Nova Urbs*. Análisis arqueológico del paradigma urbano y su evolución, y contrastación del modelo" (Ref. PID2020-114528GB-I00), funded by Ministry of Science and Innovation and the State Research Agency of the Government of Spain. On behalf of the team of this volume, we thank the amazing, supportive, and highly professional administration of the university of Helsinki, who encouraged and assisted with the organisation of the conference. We are very grateful to the editor of the Impact of Empire Series, Oliver Hekster, as well as to Giulia Moriconi and Lucas Faessen from Brill and for their steadfast and dedicated support of our project. And last but not least, we express our deep gratitude to all the contributors of this volume for their excellent research and fruitful collaboration.

# Figures and Table

## Figures

## Table

# Notes on Editors and Contributors

*Anthony Álvarez Melero*

(Brussels, Belgium, 1981), educated at the Free University of Brussels (ULB) with a Ph.D. in History, Art, and Archaeology (2010), is now associate professor at the University of Seville. His research concentrates most on epigraphy, Latin onomastics, prosopography, women in ancient Rome and Roman social history, and he is the author of several books on these topics, such as *Matronae equestres. La parenté féminine des chevaliers romains originaires des provinces occidentales sous le Haut-Empire romain* (*I*er–*III*e *siècles*) (Brepols 2018). He has also published works in English, French and Spanish in journals and books in prestigious scholarly publishing houses in Spain, Belgium, France, the Netherlands, the United States, Italy, Poland, Germany, Austria, Switzerland and the United Kingdom. In addition, he is part of the team working on the publication of the new volume of inscriptions, CIL II$^2$/4, as well as a member of several international research groups, such as ORDO and *Conditio feminae*, funded by the Spanish Ministry of Science and Innovation.

*Daniel Becerra Fernández*

developed his doctorate with a pre-doctoral contract corresponding to the projects of Excellence of the Junta de Andalucía and in 2019. He obtained his Ph.D. with the thesis entitled *Los materiales marmóreos del* Traianeum *de* Italica, under the direction of doctors P. León and J. Beltrán, who deserved the qualification of outstanding cum laude and the international distinction. In 2020, he enjoyed a postdoctoral contract from the Junta de Andalucía and since January 2021 he is a postdoctoral researcher "Juan de la Cierva-Formación" at the University of Córdoba. He has obtained a contract from the University of Málaga for the incorporation of doctors with an excellent research career. In 2022 he obtained the accreditation as Profesor Contratado Doctor (ANECA) and has carried out funded research stays at the University of Oxford, Sapienza University of Rome and at the German Archaeological Institute also in Rome. He has carried out most of his scientific activity in the field of Classical Archaeology, specifically in the study of marble in Antiquity, mainly in its characterisation, exploitation, use, dissemination and reuse.

*Francisco Cidoncha Redondo*

graduated in History from the University of Seville in 2012. Ph.D. in Ancient Histoy in the same university institution. Furthermore, he has also been a visiting researcher in the University of Oxford and the Escuela Española de Historia y Arqueología in Rome. He is currently a professor in Ancient History in the

University of Seville. He has published several researches on Roman Family, mainly on the role of Roman women and other members of families such as slaves and freedmen. He is the author of one monograph El concubinato y el contubernio en la sociedad romana (siglos I a.C. – III d.C.).

*Cristina de la Escosura Balbás*
is a Ramón y Cajal Researcher at the Complutense University of Madrid. After graduating from Sapienza University of Rome (Italy) and Complutense University of Madrid (Spain), de la Escosura obtained her Ph.D. from Autónoma U. of Madrid and Complutense. She has worked for the University of Zaragoza as a Juan de la Cierva Postdoctoral Fellow. Her research focuses on the Roman colonisation during the Republic. De la Escosura has a special interest in epigraphy, onomastics, and interactions between Romans and the local population. Her monography on *Carthago Nova*'s population won the Géza Alföldy Prize awarded by AIEGL.

*Sergio España-Chamorro*
is a Marie Skłodowska-Curie Fellow at the Dipartimento di Scienze dell'Antichità of the Sapienza University of Rome and Associate Fellow of the Institut Ausonius, UMR 5607 CNRS-Bordeaux-Montaigne University. His main fields of research are Roman roads and milestones, connectivity processes, landscape archaeology, and Latin epigraphy in Africa, Hispania, and Italy.

*David Espinosa Espinosa*
Ph.D. in Ancient History by the Complutense University of Madrid. Postdoctoral fellow at the University of Santiago de Compostela and the University of Vienna. Assistant Professor in Ancient History at the University of Oviedo and the Complutense University of Madrid. With a wide track record in international mobility, he focuses on the granting of Latin rights in the western Roman provinces, the Roman civil wars during the Republic, and Roman epigraphy. He has among his publications the books *Plinio y los* 'oppida *de antiguo Lacio'. El proceso de difusión del* Latium *en* Hispania Citerior (Oxford 2014) and *Epigraphy in the Digital Age. Opportunities and Challenges in the Recording, Analysis and Dissemination of Inscriptions* (Oxford 2021, along with I. Velázquez Soriano).

*Javier Herrera Rando*
Javier Herrera Rando (Málaga, 1986). He graduated in History from the University of Málaga and obtained a Ph.D. in Ancient History from the University of Zaragoza. His main lines of research are the Romanization and linguistic Latinization of the Iberian Peninsula, the relationship between Roman and indigenous epigraphic cultures in the Western Mediterranean,

and the publication of epigraphic novelties. He has participated in the international projects *Ancient European Languages and Writings* (AELAW) or *El Nacimiento de las culturas epigráficas en el Occidente Mediterráneo* among others and has carried out research stays in Oxford, Rome, and Geneva. Currently, he is an FCT postdoctoral researcher at the University of Lisbon.

*Daniel León Ardoy*
graduated in History from the University of Seville in 2018 and completed the master's degree in advanced Historical Studies (Itinerary in Ancient History) at the same university in 2019, obtaining in both degrees several awards, from public and private institutions, for the best academic record of the promotion. Since the end of 2019, Daniel has been working on his doctoral thesis project on female participation in political conspiracies during ancient Rome through a FPU pre-doctoral contract. In recent years he has carried out research stays at the Spanish School for History and Archaeology in Rome and at the Sapienza University of Rome.

*Antonio López García*
(Granada, Spain, 1986) is a María Zambrano Fellow at the department of Prehistory and Archaeology at the University of Granada, where he directs a research project on the landscapes of the ancient colony of Acci. He is specialized in Roman archaeology and topography. He is affiliated with the ERC-funded *SpaceLaw Project* at the University of Helsinki, where he leads a subproject on the transformation of administrative space in the city of Rome. He obtained a Ph.D. in history and archaeology of the ancient world from the University of Florence, a master's degree in architecture for archaeology from the Sapienza University of Rome, and a degree in history from the University of Granada. Previously, he has been a fellow of the Royal Academy of Spain in Rome. As a field archaeologist, he has participated in numerous international projects in Italy, Spain, and the United Kingdom and directed two archaeological excavations in Spain. During his career he has been a visiting researcher at the University of California Berkeley, the École française de Rome, the Finnish Institute of Rome, the German Archaeological Institute of Rome, and the Italian School of Archaeology at Athens, among others.

*Emilia Mataix Ferrándiz*
is a María Zambrano Fellow at the department of Roman Law at the University of the Basque Country. She has a Ph.D. in Roman law (University of Alicante and Faculty of Law of Palermo) and a second Ph.D. in Roman archaeology

(University of Southampton and Lumière-Lyon 2). She has hold research positions in Helsinki, Belgium and in Germany. She has published extensively on Roman law and its maritime focus. She is the editor of two volumes, *Roman law and Maritime Commerce* (EUP 2022) and *Seafaring and Mobility in the Late Antique Mediterranean* (Bloomsbury 2022). She is also the author of one monograph *Shipwrecks, Legal Landscapes and Mediterranean Paradigms: Gone under Sea* (Brill 2022). She is currently working on her new monograph: *Ports, Law and Material Culture in the Roman World. Negotiating Commercial Practice* (OUP). He has also been a visiting researcher at many institutions, such as the University of Pavia, the University of Ghent, the French and British Schools at Rome or the Finnish Institute of Rome, among others.

*Diego Romero Vera*

received his bachelor's degree in history from the University of Seville. He continued his training at the University of Córdoba where he acquired a master's degree in Archeology and Historical Heritage. In 2012, he obtained a University Teaching Fellowship for the realization of a Ph.D. degree, which was defended in 2016. He had the opportunity to benefit from research stays at the University of Florence, at the German Archaeological Institute of Rome, the Institute of Archaeology of the University of Coimbra and the University of Oxford. He has completed his postdoctoral training at the Ausonius Centre of the University of Bordeaux-Montaigne and at the Department of Prehistory and Archaeology of the University of Seville, where he currently works as a Lecturer. His research has been mainly focusing on the urban evolution of the Roman cities in Iberia during Antonine Age and on the dynamism of these cities from the study of Epigraphical Sources. Other centers of interest are the study of the Epigraphic habit and the funerary associations in ancient *saltus Tugiensis* (Jaén), the analysis of the empty spaces or vacant areas located in the interior of the Hispano-roman cities, as well as the imperial properties in Hispania.

*Anna-Maria Wilskman*

She currently working on her Ph.D. in the project *Law, Governance and Space: Questioning the Foundations of the Republican Tradition.* Her background is in Latin Language and Roman Literature with a strong emphasis on Classical Archaeology and Museum Studies. Her upcoming dissertation concentrates on the ways especially young Roman magistrates utilised material culture in their political ambitions. Teaching, research, art, and cultural heritage are constant sources of inspiration for her.

CHAPTER 1

# Introduction

*Emilia Mataix Ferrándiz and Anthony Álvarez Melero*

Cic. *Leg.* 3.1.3. *Nihil porro tam aptum est ad ius condicionemque naturae (quod cum dico, legem a me dici intellegi volo) quam imperium; sine quo nec domus ulla nec civitas nec gens nec hominum universum genus stare nec rerum natura omnis nec ipse mundus potest; nam et hic deo paret, et huic oboediunt maria terraeque, et hominum vita iussis supremae legis obtemperat.*

There is nothing so consonant with the justice and structure of nature – and when I say that I want you to understand that I am speaking of the law – as the power of command, without which no home or state or nation or the whole race of humankind can survive, nor can nature or the world itself. The world obeys God, land and sea obey the world, and human life follows the commands of the supreme law. (Cicero, *On the Commonwealth and On the Laws*. Edited by J. E. G. Zetzel. (Cambridge 1999), 157–158).

Sometime around the decade of the 40's BC, Cicero wrote his book three of *De legibus*, in which he provided a philosophic answer to the crisis of the *Res publica*. The third book of the treatise contains the fragment included above of which we will not develop a detailed philosophical analysis (as other scholars have done before us),[1] but instead, we will use it as basis to explain what our book is about. In the text, Cicero claims that law is the force that governs

1 This treatise has been interpreted mostly in two ways: that Cicero looked for the organisation of *leges humanae* according to the *natura hominis*, see: K. M. Girardet, *Die Ordnung der Welt. Ein Beitrag zur philosophischen und politischen Interpretation von Ciceros Schrift* De legibus (Wiesbaden 1983), Cicero searched for the essence of natural law, see e.g. J. W. Atkins, *Cicero on Politics and the Limits of Reason. The Republic and Laws* (Cambridge 2013); B. Straumann, *Roman Law in the State of Nature. The Classical Foundations of Hugo Grotius' Natural Law* (Cambridge 2015), 30.

 | DOI:10.1163/9789004685734_002

and organises societies and their environments. Perhaps because in this book, Cicero was more concerned about the philosophical essence of law rather than on how law performed in contact with human activities, the statement is enthusiastic and bold, but fails to reflect the impact of law on human life. As our book studies how law and legal thought affected and transformed territories and the lives of the peoples who populated the Roman west, the different cases presented will take Cicero's assertion forward, to test the impact and influence of law on societies and their environments.

The different examples from the chapters forming the volume will demonstrate that law is something that people do, a living institution that is continuously being tested, negotiated, created, and recreated within a given society.[2] Our study is firmly set within recent studies on the societal, political, and economic importance of legal regulations and institutions. In that sense, we want to point out that, apart from any material effects resulting from particular laws, the act of legislating, and perhaps particularly the act of legislating private life, is meaningful in and of itself, and influences people, their behaviour, and surroundings. Law, therefore, is a medium of representation, and concretely, a channel by which governments display their authority. What counts, in fact, is the possession by the Roman government of attributions, which determine the effectiveness of their action and the obedience of those who execute it and relay it.[3] Law creates social meaning, and in that sense, it has a landscape, even independent of what their inhabitants might think that landscape is.[4] Law, like a wall, may serve to either unify or divide, and in that sense, it constitutes a way of construing the abstract workings of political institutions as real-world phenomena, a way of emphasizing the material effects, good and bad, of what may seem to be small ideological interventions, which affect societies at a very high level.[5]

---

2 See e.g.: J. W. Cairns and P. J. du Plessis (eds.), *Beyond Dogmatics. Law and Society in the Roman World* (Edinburgh 2007); P. J. du Plessis (ed.), *New Frontiers. Law and Society in the Roman World* (Edinburgh 2013); J. J. Aubert and B. Sirks (eds.) *Speculum Iuris. Roman Law as a Reflection of Social and Economic Life in Antiquity* (Ann Arbor 2002); T. A. J. McGinn, '*Cui bono?* The True Beneficiaries of Roman Private Law', in *Ancient Law, Ancient Society*, ed. D. P. Kehoe and T. A. J. McGinn (Ann Arbor 2017), 133–166; D. Johnston, *Roman Law in Context* (Cambridge 2022).

3 *Imperium* is a determining factor here. See e.g. J. Richardson, '*Imperium Romanum*: Empire and the Language of Power', *JRS* 81 (1991), 1–9; 'The Meaning of *imperium* in the Last Century BC and the First AD', in *The Roman Foundations of the Law of Nations. Alberico Gentili and the Justice of Empire* ed. B. Kingsbury and B. Straumann (Oxford 2010), 21–29.

4 A. Russell, *The Politics of Public Space in Republican Rome* (Cambridge 2016); D. J. Gargola, *The Shape of the Roman Order. The Republic and its Spaces* (Chapel Hill 2017), 189.

5 K. Milnor, 'Augustus, History, and the Landscape of the Law', *Arethusa* 40, no. 1 (2007), 7–23.

In the Roman world, landscapes become legal and institutional constructions, being at the core of social, political, religious, and economic life. The built environment becomes the axis of the legal, administrative, sacred, and economic system and the main element of dissemination of imperial ideology. During the past decades, the use of this approach in different fields of study has increasingly emphasized the importance of spatiality in understanding the history of the human being and of its relationship with the environment.[6] The latter demonstrates that space is no longer a neutral concept and cannot be considered independent from that which it contains, or immune to historical, political, and aesthetic changes.

Until very recently, legal scholars neglected the importance of the spaces where law was put into practice and likewise, of the impact of legal institutions in space.[7] This emerged from the idea that Roman law merely reflected the concerns, ways of thinking, and values of a small *stratum* of society that belonged to those who created the law and those who should use it.[8] This approach has isolated juristic literature from the material evidence reflecting the practicalities of trade and those who were involved in their performance. Furthermore, it does not provide an understanding of the spatial of the Romans from the actor's perspective. While never ignoring the fact that we are temporally bound beings, during the past few decades, the use of this approach in different fields of study – including the study of the ancient past – has increasingly emphasised the importance of spatiality in understanding the history of the human being and of its relationship with the environment.[9] This sort of approach can help set forth more nuanced theories regarding the relation between social systems and their environment, using case studies and methods applied in different disciplines such as sociology, anthropology, literary analysis, or history.

6 For the Roman world, see: D. Spencer, *Roman Landscape: Culture and Identity* (Cambridge 2010); M. Scott, *Space and Society in the Greek and Roman Worlds* (Cambridge 2012); Russell 2016, op. cit., 16–24, including a complete bibliography on the different uses of the spatial turn on classical studies.

7 L. Capogrossi Colognesi, *Law and Power in the Making of the Roman Commonwealth* (Cambridge 2014); Russell 2016, op. cit.; Gargola 2017, op. cit.

8 A. Watson, *The Spirit of Roman Law* (Athens, GA 1995); *contra* J. A. Crook, *Law and Life of Rome* (Ithaca, NY 1967). As a response to that, several scholars – also stretching over previous work – have promoted through their works the rapport of Roman law with its social, economic, religious, cultural, and intellectual context, see references in n. 2.

9 L. Thommen, *An Environmental History of Ancient Greece and Rome* (Cambridge 2012); A. Wilson, 'The Mediterranean Environment in Ancient History: Perspectives and Prospects', in *The Ancient Mediterranean Environment between Science and History*, ed. W. V. Harris (Leiden 2013), 259–276.

Thus, the study of landscapes and how they reflect their belonging to the Roman world has been studied under different angles, sometimes focusing on the whole of the Roman world,[10] others on more particular case studies or geographical areas.[11] In 2021, Horster and Hächler's published a work, which focused mainly on the ways in which Rome's dominance influenced, changed, and created landscapes, and in which ways (Roman) landscapes were narrated and symbolised.[12] This book succeeds and complements that volume, bearing in mind that the relationship of landscapes with changes in the legal and institutional apparatus that supported (or hindered) the social and territorial landscapes of the Roman world has not been satisfactorily integrated into the wider historical narrative. The volume targets the relation between law, landscapes, built structures, and the individuals populating them. It follows the approach that Romans developed ambitious urban transformations, seeking to equate civic monumentality and legal status.[13] Rulers and legal scholars in response to perceived interests modified legal institutions: political, social, or economic. On their turn, these institutions had an impact on landscapes and human environments in general, which are characterised by the human acting and reacting within a given space and in different periods.

Roman law was once considered a key instrument of imperial rule, as it was thought to have been used by Rome in an effort to integrate and organise the many and varied subject communities of the Roman Empire.[14] How Roman law adapted to different contexts, was integrated into diverse cultures, or transferred into practices and built environments are issues that have been targeted

10 B. Antela-Bernárdez and T. Ñaco del Hoyo (eds.), *Transforming Historical Landscapes in the Ancient Empires. Area of Research in Studies from Antiquity Universitat Autònoma de Barcelona Proceedings of the First Workshop – December 16–19th 2007* (Oxford 2009); J. Salmon and G. Shipley (eds.), *Human Landscapes in Classical Antiquity. Environment and Culture* (London-New York 1995); M. Flohr (ed.), *Urban Space and Urban History in the Roman World* (London 2020).

11 R. Witcher, D. P. Tolia-Kelly and R. Hingley, 'Archaeologies of Landscape: Excavating the Materialities of Hadrian's Wall', *Journal of Material Culture* 15, no. 1 (2010), 105–108; T. V. Franconi (ed.), *Fluvial Landscapes in the Roman World* (Portsmouth 2017).

12 M. Horster and N. Hächler (ed.), *The Impact of the Roman Empire on Landscapes. Proceedings of the Fourteenth Workshop of the International Network Impact of Empire (Mainz, June 12–15, 2019)* (Leiden 2021).

13 E.g. P. Houten. *Urbanisation in Roman Spain and Portugal: Civitates Hispaniae in the Early Empire* (London 2021).

14 K. Verboven and O. Hekster, 'Introduction', in O. Hekster and K. Verboven (eds.), *The Impact of Justice on the Roman Empire* (Leiden 2017), 1–17.

by scholars focusing on the impact of legal plurality in the Roman world.[15] How would these individuals benefit from legal dispositions that enabled them to deal with daily problems? What was the impact of these practices on the social and physical construction of their environments? The latter raises issues such as the self, and the identity or the personhood of the individuals associated with their spaces of interaction.[16]

In addition, there is the problem of change, whether of personal status, historical period, or location, and how that was addressed in, the legal language and taxonomies used to deal with daily problems.[17] The latter have also a translation onto their landscapes, expressing the reception of law and the government it represented in a myriad of ways.[18] One key conceptual starting point of the book is that it resists attempting to bring together all the evidence to capture the supposed 'true nature' of Roman Imperial social and territorial landscapes.[19] Rather, acknowledging that both law and landscapes are complex phenomena, this volume has an interest in exploring and analysing the relationship between imperial social and institutional traits as depicted in law and juristic writings and the material evidence and associated spaces.

## 1 Law and Landscape in the Roman World

The role of law in connecting and shaping landscapes of the Roman world is one of the more central themes of this book. Land has a legible history of law and politics, that has been sometimes violently, and others not, inscribed

---

15 E.g. K. Czajkowski, B. Eckhardt and M. Strothmann (eds.), *Law in the Roman Provinces* (Oxford 2020); K. Czajkowski and B. Eckhardt, 'Law, Status and Agency the Roman Provinces', *P&P* 241 (2018), 3–31.

16 E. Mataix Ferrándiz, *Shipwrecks, Legal Landscapes and Mediterranean Paradigms. Gone under Sea* (Leiden 2022), 2–8.

17 K. Czajkowski, B. Eckhardt and M. Strothmann 2020, op. cit., 157–183; 462–485.

18 C. Ando, 'Law and the Landscape of Empire', in *Figures d'empire, fragments de mémoire. Pouvoirs et identités dans le monde romain impérial (II^e s. av. n. è.–VI^e s. de. n. è.)*, ed. S. Benoist, A. Daguet-Gagey and C. Hoët-van Cauwenberghe (Lille 2011), 25–47.

19 Thus, the discourse of Romanity targeted in the previous book of impact of empire, see: N. Hächler and M. Horster, 'Le regard du vainqueur?', in *The Impact of the Roman Empire on Landscapes. Proceedings of the Fourteenth Workshop of the International Network Impact of Empire (Mainz, June 12–15, 2019)*, ed. M. Horster and N. Hächler (Leiden 2022), 3–17.

through territorial lines, borders, and divisions,[20] institutional definitions,[21] or social meanings.[22]

In addition, the legal aspect of being Roman had important consequences on the landscape as well, since personal statuses influenced political participation, social standing, legal protection, and economic opportunities.[23] Thus, this volume will deal with the unavoidable and reciprocal relation between landscapes and the people who populated them. In the Roman world, the basic legal tenet was that law applied to people based on a personality principle (in other words, the community to which one belongs) not to an area principle, as is common in modern states (for example, laws applied to those living in Judea or in Egypt).[24] The latter means that landscapes were a sort of white canvas in which individuals from different legal statuses moved along, interacted, and especially – how it would be appreciated through some of the volume's contributions – aimed to leave a mark, to indicate who they were and what was their status inside the society that populated a given landscape. Evidently, not everyone expressed their belonging to a certain status in the same way, while some decided to express it through inscriptions, in some other cases that can be perceived through onomastics, others leaved messages in their epitaphs for after they were gone.

Studying the ways institutional agents and privates decided to represent themselves on the landscape can be done from a wider or narrower perspective, providing different results, what underlines the complexity of the issues

---

20 See e.g. H. Elton, *Frontiers of the Roman Empire* (London 1998); T. Kaizer and O. Hekster (eds.), *Frontiers in the Roman World. Proceedings of the Ninth Workshop of the International Network Impact of Empire (Durham, 16–19 April 2009)* (Leiden 2011); C. Cortés Bárcena, *Epigrafía en los confines de las ciudades romanas. Los Termini publici en Hispania, Mauretania y Numidia* (Rome 2013); S. L. Dyson, *The Creation of the Roman Frontier* (Princeton 2014).

21 S. T. Roselaar, *Public Land in the Roman Republic. A Social and Economic History of* Ager Publicus *in Italy, 396–89 BC* (Oxford 2010); G. Kantor, 'Property in Land in Roman Provinces', in *Legalism: Property and Ownership*, ed. G. Kantor, T. Lambert and H. Skoda (Oxford 2017), 55–74.

22 E.g. E. Muñiz Grijalvo and F. Lozano Gómez, 'Imperial Cult Processions and Landscape in the Greek Cities of the Roman Empire: The Case of the *Demosthenia* of *Oenoanda*', in *The Impact of the Roman Empire on Landscapes. Proceedings of the Fourteenth Workshop of the International Network Impact of Empire (Mainz, June 12–15, 2019)*, ed. M. Horster and N. Hächler (Leiden 2022), 249–262.

23 E.g. P. Garnsey, *Social Status and Legal Privilege in the Roman Empire* (Oxford 1970); F. Millar, *The Crowd in Rome in the Late Republic* (Ann Arbor 2002); Russell 2016, op. cit.

24 K. Tuori, 'The Savage Sea and the Civilizing Law: The Roman Law Tradition and the Rule of the Sea', in *Thalassokratographie: Rezeption und Transformation antiker Seeherrschaft*, ed. H. Kopp and C. Wendt (Berlin 2018), 201; Mataix Ferrándiz 2022, op. cit., 3.

studied.[25] Taking a general perspective over a given area, Javier Herrera Rando analyses the epigraphic landscape of *Baetica*, studying the phenomenon of local ruling groups controlling public spaces and competing for their visibility. Otherwise, David Espinosa Espinosa and Anna-Maria Wilskman's contributions study the epigraphic marks left by magistrates in or from *Hispania*, focusing on the meaning and importance of these inscriptions in both the political and personal spheres affecting these subjects. Thus, these chapters focus on institutional elements of the Empire, providing an image of how the Roman government and the instruments used to represent their identity were implemented in concrete provincial contexts. However, does that mean that these media of representation speak for the population inhabiting these areas and their identities? Studies on Roman onomastics have for the most part assumed that every individual bearing a Latin onomastic is a Roman citizen, or at least someone pretending to be one.[26] The chapter by Cristina de la Escosura Balbás reviews the uses and abuses of onomastics, points out the problems with the traditional theories, and explains how the *iura* of the Latin communities could explain the onomastic patterns in *Hispania* during the Republic. With her study, she demonstrates how the assumption that a Latin name indicated citizenship compromises the progress of research by distorting our perception of the Iberian Peninsula during the Republic.

In addition, there are the natural acts derived from the mere interaction among peoples: how different groups aligned themselves in a society, how do they organise to have an impact and influence to achieve their goals. All these different behaviours shape not only the structure from a society, but also its associated landscapes. For example, the case study of funerary landscapes (a topic in itself),[27] is addressed in this volume by Francisco Cidoncha-Redondo,

---

25 Concerning epigraphic landscapes, see: A. Ruiz Gutiérrez, 'El paisaje epigráfico de la ciudad romana: concepto y perspectivas de estudio', in *Paisajes epigráficos de la Hispania romana. Monumentos, contextos, topografías*, ed. J. M. Iglesias Gil and A. Ruiz Gutiérrez (Rome 2013), 13–28.

26 E. Badian, *Foreign* Clientelae (*264–70 BC*) (Oxford 1958); P. A. Brunt, *Italian Manpower, 225 B.C.–A.D. 14* (Oxford 1971); R. C. Knapp, 'The Origins of Provincial Prosopography in the West', *AncSoc* 9 (1978) 187–222 and S. L. Dyson, 'The Distribution of Roman Republican Family Names in the Iberian Peninsula', *AncSoc* 11–12 (1980–1981) 257–300; M. Jehne and F. Pina Polo (eds.), *Foreign* Clientelae *in the Roman Empire. A Reconsideration* (Stuttgart 2015).

27 E.g. E.-J. Graham, 'The Quick and the Dead in the Extra-Urban Landscape: the Roman Cemetery at *Ostia/Portus* as a Lived Environment', in *TRAC 2004: Proceedings of the Fourteenth Annual Theoretical Roman Archaeology Conference, Durham 2004*, ed. J. Bruhn, B. Croxford and D. Grigoropoulos (Oxford 2005), 133–143; S. Cormarck, 'The Tombs at *Pompeii*', in *The World of* Pompeii, ed. P. Foss and J. J. Dobbins (London 2007), 585–606;

who analyses the case of the necropolis of *Ostia* and *Portus*, and how women, both for themselves and for their relatives and loved ones often promoted their construction. Through their decisions and actions, these women contributed to the configuration of the landscapes of the necropoli located on the outskirts of the city.

Yet another way to measure how the individuals from a society align themselves in it is through their consumption patterns, since this was one way in which Romans expressed their identities.[28] Aspirations to elite status were reflected in the use of luxury materials such as marble, as Daniel Becerra Fernández explains for the case of *Italica* from the Augustan era until Late Antiquity. The widespread use of *marmora* in this Baetican city, for public as well as for private buildings, shows how these high-valued stone materials were used as indicators of social status and imperial propaganda, as well as to reaffirm *Italica*'s place in the Empire. Marble is a key case study that can be also appreciated in other areas of the Empire,[29] what indicates the impact of globalisation in the Roman Empire, as well as a decline on the use of distinctive material attributes that acted as markers of regional identities.[30] Both public and private uses of marble constituted actions driven by the city and its inhabitant's self-esteem: a way to represent what they had become.[31]

The landscapes of the Roman world also had a life of their own, if one can put it that way. Landscape forms arose and were sustained by local resources and constraints of the natural environment, commerce, customs and beliefs, rituals and religion, self-awareness, language, and local traditions. This local or

---

G. Ciampoltrini, *Munere Mortis. Complessi tombali d'età romana nel territorio di Lucca* (Pisa 2009); D. Francisci, 'Le sepolture come indicatori di centuriazione. Due casi di studio dal Trentino-Alto Adige/Südtirol (Italia)', in *Sistemi centuriali e opere di assetto agrario tra età romana e primo medioevo. Atti del convegno Borgoricco (Padova) – Lugo (Ravenna), 10–12 settembre 2009*, ed. P. L. dall'Aglio and G. Rosada (Pisa–Rome 2010), 283–288; N. Brundrett, 'Roman Tomb Gardens: the Construction of Sacred Commemorative Landscapes', *The Brock Review* 11, no. 2 (2011), 51–69; S. Déderix, 'Funerary Landscapes and GIS Applications: a Review', in 3rd ARCH_RNT Proceedings Archaeological Research and New Technologies, ed. N. Zacharias (Kalamata 2014), 21–30.

28 P. Zanker, *The Power of Images in the Age of Augustus* (Ann Arbor 1990); J. P. Walsh, *Consumerism in the Ancient World: Imports and Identity Construction* (London 2014).

29 R. M. J. Isserlin, 'A Spirit of Improvement? Marble and the Culture of Roman Britain', in *Cultural Identity in the Roman Empire*, ed. R. Laurence and J. Berry (London–New York 1998), 125–155; E. Öğüş, 'Columnar Sarcophagi from Aphrodisias: Construction of Elite Identity in the Greek East' (Ph.D. diss., Harvard University, 2010).

30 M. Pitts and M. J. Versluys (eds.), *Globalisation and the Roman World: World History, Connectivity and Material Culture* (Cambridge 2014), 161–206.

31 G. Woolf, *Becoming Roman: The Origins of Provincial Civilization in Gaul* (Cambridge 1998), 170–171.

individual involvement (in the case of an artist or author) was incorporated into the Roman framework and made a legal, social, religious, ritual, economic landscape. In sum, Roman landscapes are shaped by the lives of its inhabitants and these lives where on their turn shaped by the legal conceptions that structured the interactions of the different members forming a society. The chapters of Daniel León Ardoy and Diego Romero Vera from two different angles address these topics: the first devoted to the study of the impact of matrons' activities in monarchic and republican Rome,[32] while the second studies the widespread phenomenon of evergetism focusing on the concrete case of *Italica*.

On the one hand, the public interventions of matrons have been described in the works of classical authors such as Livy or Gellius (among others), which mostly focus on their collective political actions, which sometimes were key for Rome's survival. The distinctiveness of this chapter lies on the fact that, while other authors have focused on the Roman urban landscapes frequented by matrons,[33] this chapter focuses on the key role of these women in shaping the social landscape of Rome, from their households to the public and political spheres of the city.[34] These women would act in a group, led by one of them who acted from the marginal position where law placed them, except perhaps in the religious sphere.[35]

On the other hand, Diego Romero Vera focuses his attention on the Roman city of *Italica* and the phenomenon of evergetism, as a form of gift-exchange between the emperor Hadrian and his city/community of fellow citizens.[36] The study of the main archaeological and epigraphic documents from the city's late Antonine and early Severan phases bear witness of the urban vitality sought by the emperor for his hometown. However, these materials also reveal whether the city experienced an early urban crisis caused, at least in part, by the maintenance of excessive monumental apparatus. As this chapter demonstrates, evergetism reflected, and helped to propagate, a new status definition

32 See also, S. A. Takács, *Vestal Virgins, Sibyls, and Matrons: Women in Roman Religion* (Austin 2008); and E. A. Hemelrijk, *Matrona Docta. Educated Women in the Roman Elite from Cornelia to Julia Domna* (London–New York 1999).

33 A. K. Strong, *Prostitutes and Matrons in the Roman World* (Cambridge 2016), 142–170.

34 See also F. Rohr Vio, *Powerful Matrons. New Political Actors in the Late Roman Republic* (Seville–Zaragoza 2022), 19–32.

35 Cf. C. E. Schultz, *Women's Religious Activity in the Roman Republic* (Chapel Hill 2006); N. Boëls-Janssen, *La vie religieuse des matrones dans la Rome archaïque* (Rome 1993).

36 A. Zuiderhoek, *The Politics of Munificence in the Roman Empire. Citizens, Elites and Benefactors in Asia Minor* (Cambridge 2009), 6.

of the civic community and their place in the Empire, but as can be appreciated in the case study analysed, it did not come without consequences.[37]

This volume follows the modern trend of a multicultural, legally plural, multi-layered Roman world, but at the same time reduces its complexity. It views 'Roman law' not only in the sense of power politics or citizenry, but also in a cultural context, and in this way, the individuals appear in scene. It highlights 'landscapes' and puts into the shadow important administrative and legal structures, i.e., individuals *viz.* local and imperial members of the elites living in cities, which ran the Roman world.[38] However, the contributions included in this book break beyond the limits of focusing on cities and lives of the elite and use different evidence to also understand the role of other actors in Roman history. Some examples are the cases of women (as the cases of Francisco Cidoncha-Redondo and Daniel León Ardoy summarised previously), or the impact of law and Empire in rural landscapes (such as the chapters by Sergio España Chamorro and Antonio López García indicated below). Altogether, these contributions will help draw a more complete portrait of the Roman world, bearing in mind the mosaic of peoples and environments that formed it, under the unitary focus of its legal and institutional framework.

## 2 Landscapes in Roman Culture and Its Associated Identities

Landscapes are shaped by humans acting and reacting in each space in different periods. Thus, they appear as the scenarios where people from different statuses interacted, influenced each other, and left a mark (such as epigraphic, territorial, or monumental). In the Roman imagination, frontiers and boundaries were used to divide humanity into different spheres: us and the others (foreigners).[39] In the aftermath of Roman expansion, individuals and jurists came to view these differentiations not solely in spatial terms,

37 This ambiguity is very well reflected by A. Zuiderhoek, 'The Ambiguity of Munificence', *Historia* 56, no. 2 (2007), 196–213 and D. Johnston, 'Munificence and *Municipia*: Bequests to Towns in Classical Roman Law', *JRS* 75 (1985), 125.

38 On the topic of the city and rural integration, see for example: T. C. A. de Haas and G. Tol (eds.), *The Economic Integration of Roman Italy: Rural Communities in a Globalising World* (Leiden–Boston 2017); C. Ando, 'Local Citizenship and Civic Participation in the Western Provinces of the Roman Empire', in *Civic Identity and Civic Participation in Late Antiquity and the Early Middle Ages*, ed. C. Brélaz and E. Rose (Turnhout 2021), 39–64.

39 D. Slootjes and M. Peachin (eds.), *Rome and the Worlds beyond its Frontiers* (Leiden 2017); M. Symonds. *Protecting the Roman Empire. Fortlets, Frontiers, and the Quest for Post-Conquest Security* (Cambridge 2017).

but also as historical, geopolitical, and civilizational ones.[40] Bearing that in mind, this volume will tackle the topic of jurisdiction and adjudication (the role of *imperium*,[41] the importance of municipal rules)[42] and their impact on landscapes.[43] As mentioned previously, law mirrors the government from which it is enacted, and on its turn, it is represented by the boundaries it sets, clearly demarcating a line between ones (Roman citizens) and the others (peregrines). These broad issues are explored in two contributions of this volume, being one by Antonio López García and the other by Sergio España Chamorro.

In his contribution, Sergio España Chamorro focuses on the transformation of land management and road networks from *Mauretania* and *Numidia*, since the strategy employed by Rome's territorial administration can be observed along these boundaries. The main issue of España Chamorro's article is to provide a chronological vision of the construction of the border between these two provinces and to make more valuable the social and economic aspects that influence in their fixation. The contribution reveals a far from casual constitution of their jurisdictions, even though at certain points there is a lack of data to understand the choice of layout. The latter does not imply that their organisation was random, but rather that their study allows for a historical understanding of their territorial and administrative development. In sum, the way in which the spaces were laid out was not exclusively the result of strategic considerations of political nature, but also of social and economic choices from the individuals populating these areas.

Differently, Antonio López García examines the administrative border between the provinces of *Hispania Baetica* and *Hispania Tarraconensis* at one of its most critical points: the southeastern part of the Iberian Peninsula. Between the end of the Roman Republic and the beginning of the imperial era, several adjustments were made to the eastern border of *Hispania Ulterior* province, specifically in the area between the current provinces of Granada and Jaén. The relationship between Roman boundaries and their economic and administrative development is a perfect example of how pre-existing

40 C. R. Whittaker, *Frontiers of the Roman Empire: A Social and Economic Study* (Baltimore–London 1994), 60–97; D. Cherry, *Frontier and Society in Roman North Africa* (Oxford 1998); S. Guédon, *La frontière romaine de* l'Africa *sous le Haut-Empire* (Madrid 2018a).

41 See references n. 3.

42 Such as the *Lex Malacitana* (*CIL* II, 1964) or the *Lex Irnitana* (*CILA* Se 4, 1201).

43 E.g. F. de Angelis, *Spaces of Justice in the Roman World* (Leiden 2010); B. Stolte, 'Jurisdiction and the Representation of Power, or the Emperor on Circuit', in *The Representation and Perception of Roman Imperial Power. Proceedings of the Third Workshop of the International Network Impact of Empire (Roman Empire, c. 200 B.C.–A.D. 476), Rome, March 20–23, 2002*, ed. P. Erdkamp, O. Hekster, G. de Kleijn, S. T. A. M. Mols and L. de Blois (Leiden 2003), 261–268.

structures, topographical characters, individual decisions, all interact and contribute to shaping the landscape and determining the influence and representation of the central government in the landscape.[44]

Despite the rhetoric of unity of legal orders, of harmony of all Romans, of maintaining traditions, of the good old values or *mos maiorum*, and of dogmatic characterisations of ownership and personal status,[45] the Roman world was highly dynamic. The contributions included in this book shift the focus to developments and transitions and thematise the broader geographical framework than the Roman world and of the dynamics within the Roman world and changing perceptions of Roman identity.[46] They reflect on materials, and they apply different approaches and premises to discuss the impact of law and institutional frameworks on landscape without risking falling into the stumbling blocks of the debate on the term and the underlying concept of 'romanisation' as a one-way road.[47]

In that sense, another major issue addressed in this book is that of law and its social and cultural context. Even if the Roman legal framework defined the Empire's rights and duties, it is necessary to be aware of Rome's legal and cultural plurality.[48] Legal pluralism – two or more legal systems operating in the same social field – is prevalent in nearly all large premodern societies, typically struggling with weak formal institutions and lack of enforcement capabilities, relying heavily therefore on the co-optation and adaptation of imposed formal institutions to pre-existing local practices and rulings. We need to keep in mind that 'Roman' is an umbrella term that encompasses great regional variety, as well as ethnically diverse cultures.[49] As the Roman world was composed of a

44 S. Benoist, 'Penser la limite : de la cité au territoire impérial', in *Frontiers in the Roman World. Proceedings of the Ninth Workshop of the International Network Impact of Empire (Durham, 16–19 April 2009)*, ed. T. Kaizer and O. Hekster (Leiden 2011), 31–48.

45 Kantor 2017, op. cit., 55–74.

46 As underlined also by B. Eckhardt, 'Law, Empire, and Identity between West and East: The Danubian Provinces', in *Law in the Roman Provinces*, ed. K. Czajkowski, B. Eckhardt and M. Strothmann (Oxford 2020), 417–435 also using the focus of law and Empire.

47 As underlines in the work of K. Czajkowski, *Localized Law: The Babatha and Salome Komaise Archives* (Oxford 2017), focusing on law and using the term 'localised law' to indicate the hybridity existing between Roman and local law.

48 For example, some key works on the topic of legal plurality in the Roman world are: K. Tuori, 'Legal Pluralism and the Roman Empire', in *Beyond Dogmatics: Law and Society in the Roman World*, ed. J. W. Cairns and P. J. du Plessis (Edinburgh 2007), 39–52; C. Ando, 'Legal Pluralism in Practice', in *The Oxford Handbook of Roman Law and Society*, ed. P. J. du Plessis, C. Ando and K. Tuori (Oxford 2016), 283–296; Czajkowski, Eckhardt and Strothmann 2020, op. cit.

49 Mataix Ferrándiz 2022, op. cit., 2.

wide variety of far-flung regions, what needs to be stressed is that while a legal text or an inscription could be an individual manifestation of a local mentality, it still reflects a conception of the landscape that can help establish common traits and differences to arrive at a broader view. Javier Herrera Rando's study of *Baetica*'s epigraphic landscapes exemplifies how the area became a model of Romanity. After suffering the Civil Wars, southern *Hispania* was subjected to intense processes of municipalization and the establishment of colonies during the second half of the first century BC, which reinforced the already dense urban network and spread Roman ideological and legal models. This was accompanied by strong economic growth due to the export of agricultural, fishing, and mining products as well as the early and swift integration of some notable local people into imperial power circles.

As Javier Herrera Rando indicates, the diffusion of epigraphic practice at the beginning of the Empire was general throughout the Roman provinces, although each region had its own characteristics depending on the different geographical areas and underlying cultures. Provincial societies began to possess a new symbolic and cultural language with which to express themselves and interact. The latter had a definitive drawback on landscapes, as people decided to conduct themselves following the legal, historical, and political trends from the moment. The fluidity of these practices contrasts with dogmatic presentations of Roman law, which tend to offer taxonomic definitions about the individuals interacting in Roman society (e.g. the son-in-power, the slave).[50] However, Roman texts, and especially when read in relation to the material culture and spaces with which these are associated, highlight the idea of motion; that is, the change of status boundaries, or moving between different legally designated spaces.[51] If we think of law and landscape as dynamic, then one can see a picture of cultural fluidity, variety, richness, and of change in the self-perception of the peoples populating the Roman world, traits that permeate all the contributions forming this volume.

50 An issue debated and presented in, T. S. Taylor, 'Social Status, Legal Status and Legal Privilege', in *The Oxford Handbook of Roman Law and Society*, ed. P. J. du Plessis, C. Ando and K. Tuori (Oxford 2016), 349–361.

51 C. Ando, 'Self, Society, Individual, and Person in Roman Law', in *Self, Self-Fashioning, and Individuality in Late Antiquity. New Perspectives*, ed. M. R. Niehoff and J. Levinson (Tübingen 2019), 375–392.

## 3 Individuals, Law, and Institutional Agents: Impact on the Landscape and on the Emergence of a General Roman Order

Law and institutions cannot be separated from the organisations and collectives that generate, monitor, and enforce them. In sum, that we cannot separate law from the society that produced and employed it.[52] Nevertheless, both law and institutions come in many guises, and find their expression in manifold ways. The major divide is between formal or designed institutions and organisations, and informal or non-designed institutions and collectives.[53] Formal or designed institutions and organisations are the visible forms of governance – the institutions are laws, decrees, statutes, etc, and the organisations are official bodies endowed with the authority to formulate, interpret, and enforce institutions. Both have been intentionally created (usually) to protect perceived interests. Designed institutions are relatively easy to spot in the material and textual evidence. Informal, implicit, or social institutions and collectives are the implicit, largely invisible forms of governance.

The institutions here are social norms, conventions, customs, or religious rituals; the collectives supporting them are for instance families, villages, and neighbourhoods, closed groups such as *collegia*, and religious associations.[54] They have a moral authority to formulate, interpret and enforce rules inside the communities that endorse them but no official power to provide validity to them for the whole of the Roman world.[55] One clear example in this volume would be the case of the collective organisations of matrons described by Daniel León Ardoy. Their activities and organisation were not institutionally created nor supported by the state, but are bound up with cultural beliefs, both descriptive of world views, which produce normative consequences in society, such as the creation of values.

This book is a story in which the state appears not as the sole purveyor of authority but as one actor among many, in a multi-vocal and plural legal environment where a diversity of religious laws, customs and legal cultures intersected, and competed. The latter had an imprint on epigraphic culture (e.g. Francisco

52 See biblio n. 2. *contra* Watson 1995, op. cit.

53 As with the case of trust among merchants, as described by S. Johnstone, *A History of Trust in Ancient Greece* (Chicago 2011) and T. T. Tersptra, *Trading Communities in the Roman World: A Micro-Economic and Institutional Perspective* (Leiden 2013); *Trade in the Ancient Mediterranean: Private Order and Public Institutions* (Princeton 2019).

54 J. G. Manning, *The Open Sea. The Economic Life of the Ancient Mediterranean World from the Iron Age to the Rise of Rome* (Princeton–Oxford 2018), 173–215.

55 The phenomenon is described form a bird-eye view by K. Verboven, 'Professional *Collegia*: Guilds or Social Clubs?', *AncSoc* 41 (2011), 187–195.

Cidoncha-Redondo, Javier Herrera Rando, Anna-Maria Wilskman, David Espinosa Espinosa), monumental landscape (e.g. Diego Romero Vera and Daniel Becerra Fernández); roads and boundaries (Sergio España Chamorro and Antonio López García), personal onomastics (Cristina de la Escosura Balbás) or women (Daniel León Ardoy). By making this shift, we can learn a story of the Roman world through provincial, subaltern actors and local authorities as legal actors who shaped the ancient world.[56] More importantly, this perspective invites to consider the ways in which encounters in the Roman world have not only shaped our conceptions of Roman landscapes but our very ideas of law, order, sovereignty, and power.

## 4 Final Reflections

How can we evaluate the impact of law and power in Roman landscapes? There is more than one answer to this question, depending on time, scale, or location. For this volume, we have decided to use several cases devoted to the study of the Roman west, and specially, for many of them, the case of Hispania. The latter does not indicate a lack of interest on the impact of law and power on eastern landscapes. However, we thought that providing several case studies from areas located closely to the imperial axis of power, Rome, will give a better idea of the impact of the central state over some of its provinces. However, we wanted to acknowledge that gap and bear in mind the interest of studying similar issues to the ones addressed in this volume but focusing on the eastern provinces.

Law and power have been labelled in this volume as 'agents of transformation' of imperial landscapes, but what is left to say from that labelling is that these agents can be perceived in a more elusive or notorious way on landscapes. On the one hand, elements such as monuments, public laws,[57] munificence granted to municipal cities, roads, or boundaries, are blatant demonstrations of state power, and no one can deny that these had an impact on landscapes and the people populating them. However, no one could predict what would be the extent of that impact, or how would individuals react to these manifestations of authority, reason why the different case studies gathered in

56 This is the approach taken by R. Mawani, *Across Oceans of Law. The Komagata Maru and Jurisdiction in the Time of Empire* (Durham–London 2018).

57 Another example for Roman Africa is quite well described by C. Ando, 'Public Law in Roman North Africa', in *Law in the Roman Provinces*, ed. K. Czajkowski, B. Eckhardt and M. Strothmann (Oxford 2020), 346–357.

this book provide some answers to these complex issues. On the other hand, law could also manifest in less flagrant ways, through social constructions or norms, hierarchies, systems of trust, etc. Many times, these rulings or norms are not enforced by the authority but by social sanctions (from shunning and gossip to boycott). Even in contexts governed by not institutionally enforced rulings, norms create a powerful cultural frame and a cognitive template that allowed the prevention and handling of social conflicts in relatively peaceful ways. These socially legitimised norms established frameworks of behaviour and shaped expectations people had from them. In sum, what is important to underline is the effectiveness with which law and justice successfully integrated culturally and socially different groups with sometimes opposing interests into a single empire that in cultural terms outlasted even the political institutions that formed it.[58] We believe that this book will contribute to a better understanding of how this phenomenon was possible.

58 Hekster and Verboven 2017, op. cit., 14.

# PART 1

## *Integration*

CHAPTER 2

# Imperial Ideology and the Making of Baetican Epigraphic Landscapes

*Javier Herrera Rando*

## 1 Introduction

Around the turn of the Era, the province of *Hispania Ulterior Baetica* decided to erect a statue in Rome honouring Augustus, who was responsible for the care and pacification of the province. The gift in itself was impressive: a one-hundred-pound gold statue of which, obviously, only the pedestal remains.[1] A few years later, in AD 25, an embassy from the same province arrived in the *Urbs* to ask for Tiberius' permission to build a temple in his honour. Although shortly before the city of *Smyrna* in Asia Minor had done the same, this time Tiberius chose to deny permission.[2]

Both episodes exemplify Baetica's conversion into a model of Romanity. After suffering the Civil Wars, southern Hispania was subjected to intense processes of municipalisation and the establishment of colonies during the second half of the 1st century BC, which reinforced the already dense urban network and spread Roman ideological and legal models. This was accompanied by strong economic growth due to the export of agricultural, fishing, and mining products as well as the early and swift integration of some notable local people into imperial power circles.[3]

One of the consequences of the material and legal urbanisation process was the appearance of what is known as an 'epigraphic landscape'. This is understood as the environment generated by inscriptions as publicly displayed texts, together with visual and material elements like the type of letters, the iconography, and, in short, everything that sought to generate a visual impact on the audience and facilitate the transmission and duration of the message. The diffusion of epigraphic practice at the beginning of the Empire was general

1 *CIL* VI, 31267 (= *ILS* 103) = *EDR*100525.
2 Tac. *Ann.* 4.37–38.
3 Without aiming to be exhaustive, see A. T. Fear, *Rome and Baetica* (Oxford 1996); E. W. Haley, Baetica Felix. *People and Prosperity in Southern Spain from Caesar to Septimius Severus* (Austin 2009); J. Remesal Rodríguez, *La Bética en el concierto del imperio Romano* (Madrid 2011).

 | DOI:10.1163/9789004685734_003

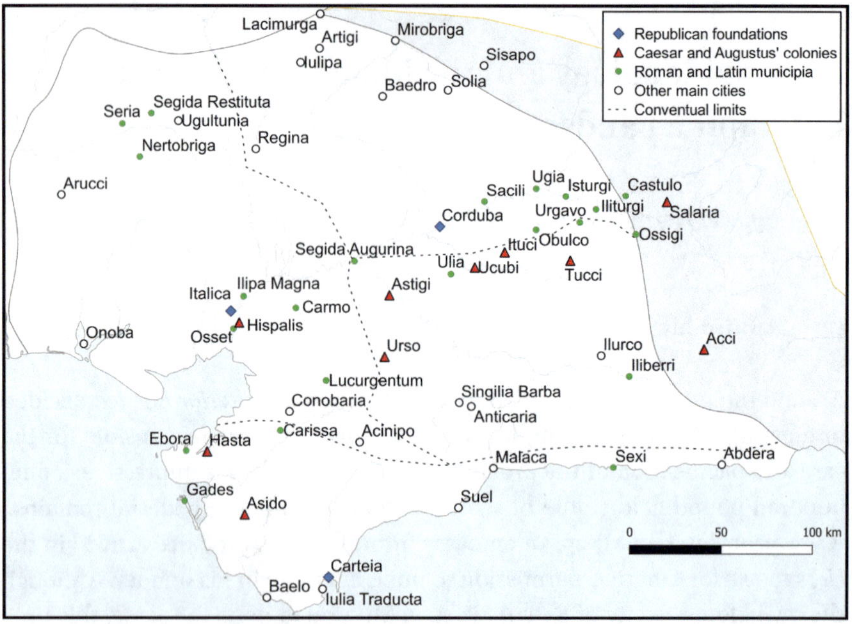


FIGURE 2.1 A political map of early-Roman *Baetica*
© THE AUTHOR

throughout the Roman provinces, although each region had its characteristics depending on the different geographical areas and underlying cultures. Provincial societies began to possess a new symbolic and cultural language with which to express themselves and interact.[4]

Undoubtedly, there is a direct relationship between the appearance of these epigraphic landscapes and the extensive monumentalisation processes in Baetican cities, including the construction of new buildings and public spaces, the erection of statues, and even the introduction of changes in funerary habits.[5] The latter aims to say that the period's growing social desire for visibility and durability acquired a useful tool in epigraphy. However, the

4 G. Woolf, 'Monumental Writing and the Expansion of Roman Society in the Early Empire', *JRS* 86 (1996), 22–39; A. Ruiz Gutiérrez, 'El paisaje epigráfico de la ciudad romana. Concepto y perspectivas de estudio', in *Paisajes epigráficos de la Hispania romana. Monumentos, contextos, topografía*, ed. J. M. Iglesias Gil and A. Ruiz Gutiérrez (Rome 2013), 13–28; F. Beltrán Lloris, 'The "Epigraphic Habit" in the Roman World', in *The Oxford Handbook of Roman Epigraphy*, ed. C. Bruun and J. Edmondson (Oxford 2015), 131–151.

5 J. Beltrán Fortes, 'Monumentalizzazione urbana nella *Baetica* augustea: esempli e modelli' in *Augusto e la Campania. Da Ottaviano a Divo Augusto. 14–2014 d.C.*, ed. C. Capaldi (Naples 2020), 497–508.

concept should not be limited only to monumental inscriptions, but it must also include two such highly symbolic forms of expression as numismatics and legal epigraphy, which, in the case of the West, was mainly recorded on bronze.

From a socio-political point of view, epigraphic landscapes represented the authentic staging of the cities' power, with the local ruling groups trying to control this public space and competing for visibility. In this way, they tended to reproduce the established ideology and emphasise dominant values.[6] Thus, it is not surprising that imperial ideology played an essential role in the birth of epigraphic landscapes. The ever-changing concept of *Romanitas* now had one of its new pillars in public adherence to the Imperial House, and epigraphy provided a new tool in this regard. Emperors and their families became the object of collective and individual dedications and, directly or indirectly, their presence became common in provincial public spaces, imitating in a certain way what was happening in the city of Rome.[7]

All these factors, together with the richness and variety of its epigraphic material, make *Baetica* an ideal territory to study the impact of imperial ideology on the birth of provincial epigraphic landscapes during the Early Empire and the reasons behind this process. Abandoning the dichotomy that distinguished between imposition and spontaneity and which has proven to be excessively simplistic,[8] we will opt for an interpretation that emphasizes the dialectical relationship between the imperial centre, the local communities, and individual agency. We will therefore focus on the epigraphic record of the Julio-Claudian period (including numismatics and bronze epigraphy) and on the different parties' incentives and conditioning factors that made adherence to the emperors a defining cultural trait of Baetican cities.

---

6 L. Revell, 'The Written City: Political Inscriptions from Roman *Baetica*', in *Written Space in the Latin West, 200 BC–AD 300*, ed. G. Sears and P. Keegan (London 2013), 229–332; C. Ando, 'Colonialism, Colonization: Roman Perspectives', in *The Oxford Handbook of Literatures of the Roman Empire*, ed. D. L. Selden and P. Vasunia (Oxford 2015), 27–34.

7 G. Alföldy, 'Augusto e le iscrizioni: tradizione ed innovazione. La nascita dell'epigrafia imperiale', *Scienze dell'Antichità* 5 (1991a), 573–600. A more recent reedition of the original text in German in G. Alföldy, 'Augustus und die Inschriften: Tradition und Innovation. Die Geburt der imperialen Epigraphik', in *Die epigraphische Kultur der Römer*, ed. A. Chaniotis and C. Witschel (Stuttgart 2018), 73–102. On the Augustan epigraphic impact in the city of Rome, see also the studies collected in G. Alföldy, *Studi sull'epigrafia augustea e tiberiana di Roma* (Rome 1992).

8 F. Lozano Gómez, 'El surgimiento y desarrollo de la adoración imperial: la dicotomía explicativa imposición-espontaneidad', in *Jerarquías religiosas y control social en el mundo antiguo. Actas del XXVII Congreso Internacional GIREA-ARYS*, ed. L. Hernández Guerra and J. Alvar (Valladolid 2002), 433–439.

## 2 The Role of Local Communities: Civic Coinage

The propagandistic use of coinage had been growing during the Republic, and Augustus turned it into another ideological tool of his new regime. Coining by imperial-controlled mints coexisted with other issues carried out by civic communities, which lasted until the mid-1st century in the western provinces and the mid-3rd century in the eastern ones. We will focus on Baetican civic coinage.

Introduced in southern Hispania by ancient Phoenician colonies such as Gadir or Malaka, the monetary economy was consolidated after the Roman conquest, with around fifty local mints operating in Republican times until the period of the Civil Wars. Republican issues were extremely heterogeneous with a notable presence of local features. After the emergence of the Principate, civic issues were resumed but with a smaller number of mints. *Gades*, *Abdera*, and *Carteia*, which had produced coinage in Republican times, reactivated their output; the same happened in *Corduba*, which had experienced the settlement of the *colonia Patricia*. *Italica*, *Hispalis* (*colonia Romula*), *and Iulia Traducta* minted for the first time.[9] All of them were short-lived, with their activity ending, this time definitively, around the middle of Tiberius' reign. Based on studies of dies and monetary circulation, the volume of coinage struck was generally low, on bronze or orichalcum, and its main economic function was to satisfy local demands for small transactions, while imperial mints supplied the higher value currency, to whose metrological system the civic issues adapted.[10]

The decision to issue currency fell to the communities and, although the main Spanish cities did strike issues, other important centres such as *Astigi* (*colonia Augusta Firma*) or *Urso* (*colonia Iulia Genetiva*) in *Baetica* did not see the need to mint their own coinage. This autonomy was to some extent relative: communities that lacked a previous tradition had to request permission from the emperor, which was reflected in the legends by the expressions *perm*(*issu*) *Caes*(*aris*) *Aug*(*usti*) or similar ones that appear in *colonia Patricia*, *colonia Romula*, *Italica* and *Iulia Traducta*. Although the degree of control exercised by the central power continues to be the subject of historiographical discussion,[11] there is no doubt that the issuing communities had a certain degree of freedom when choosing iconographic motifs, which can be

9 The mints of *Irippo*, *Osset* and *Laelia*, with a chronology linked to the Triumviral period and, furthermore, with serious problems of interpretation, are not taken into consideration.

10 P. P. Ripollès, *Las acuñaciones provinciales romanas de Hispania* (Madrid 2010), 20–21.

11 Ripollès 2010, op. cit., 16–19.

divided between those within the Roman cultural aesthetic and the 'pseudo-autonomous' ones of local inspiration.[12]

There is no doubt that the most emblematic of all the Baetican local motifs is the *Heracles-Melkart* of *Gades*. It is a constant image on the coinage of this city throughout its long history and, furthermore, it extended to other cities in the south of the Peninsula during the Republican era (fig. 2.1). Sesterces and *dupondii* were issued with their obverses presenting this deity, together with other series commemorating Agrippa's patronage of the city and the reign of Tiberius. *Carteia* also used characteristically traditional local types such as the dolphin or the figure of a fisherman, whose origins date back to the first issues of the city in the 2nd century BC.[13]

This iconographic conservatism should not be interpreted as a political statement. First, the 'pseudo-autonomous' types do not monopolise the iconography of these cities: in addition to the busts of different imperial family members such as Agrippa, Augustus, or Tiberius, *Gades* uses the *acrostilium* and the *sympula* or sacrificial instruments. In addition to its traditional motifs, *Carteia* also shows the bust of a *Tyche*. Second, whether in iconography or legend, the *Domus Augusta* is present on the issues, so these traditional motifs cannot be separated from the new imperial reality.

An extreme case of the combination of traditional and imperial iconographies can be found in *Abdera*'s asses from the Tiberian period (fig. 2.2). On the obverse, Tiberius' bust is presented with his imperial title as a legend, while on the reverse contains a tetrastyle temple. Two of the columns of the temple are tuna fishes, a motif used in regional republican coinage, which alludes to the fishing activity of this community. In the tympanum of the temple, there is a Punic legend with the name of the city, which in some issues appears together with the Latin one. It constitutes a very late case of bilingualism, at a time when Latin had already spread widely throughout *Baetica*, and the evidence of indigenous languages is limited to some ceramic graffiti.[14] In this way, language, iconography, and imperial image came together to express a new civic identity. The Phoenician tradition of *Abdera* was now a value: opposition to the new imperial regime was not sought but, on the contrary, was utilised to

12 M. Horster, 'Coinage and Images of the Imperial Family: Local Identity and Roman Rule', *JRA* 26 (2013), 245.

13 For *Gades'* Agrippa issues: *RPC*, no. 74–83; for the *Heracles-Melkart* ones: no. 91–94. For *Carteia*'s ones: no. 116–118 and 120–121. On their symbolic value, see F. Machuca Prieto, *Una forma fenicia de ser romano: identidad e integración de las comunidades fenicias de la Península Ibérica bajo poder de Roma* (Seville 2019), 294–298.

14 M. J. Estarán Tolosa, *Epigrafía bilingüe del Occidente romano: el latín y las lenguas locales en las inscripciones bilingües y mixtas* (Zaragoza 2016), 468–470.

FIGURE 2.2 A) *Sestertius* from *Gades* (RPC, nº 78). B) *As* from *Abdera* (*RPC*, nº 125). C) *Dupondius* from *Italica* (RPC, nº 66)


highlight a prestigious position, based on a past reputation that had its roots in Phoenician colonisation. As F. Machuca has recently studied, this strategy of 'accommodation' was common to the communities of Phoenician origin in *Hispania*. Throughout the Republican and Julio-Claudian periods (and even earlier, with the Carthaginians) these cities maintained a marked local identity, reworked to place themselves within the imperial reality.[15]

This process of public expression of *Romanitas* was widespread. The cities that lacked iconographic precedents (here we must include *colonia Patricia*, established on the site of republican *Corduba*, which had minted currency) generally resorted to Roman-inspired motifs: the civic crown (*colonia Romula*, *colonia Patricia*, and *Iulia Traducta*), legionary *signa* (*colonia Patricia* and *Italica*), sacrificial elements (*colonia Patricia* and *Italica*) or even the Capitoline Wolf, the *Genius Populi Romani* and the representation of Rome in *Italica*. All of them serve to highlight the origin (also ideological) of these communities.

However, one of the defining features of *Romanitas* was adherence to the imperial family. We have already mentioned that Augustus and Tiberius were present in one way or another in these issues. The greater freedom in the choice of local types in comparison with imperial issues is manifested in the

15 Machuca Prieto 2019, op. cit.

significance of the imperial family, generally absent from the latter, but which played a notable role in provincial issues. Livia, the first emperor's wife and the second's mother, is represented in *colonia Romula* and *Italica*. In the latter, she appears enthroned and with a sceptre (fig. 2.2), a model that was not included in the imperial coinage until Claudius.[16] Also interesting is the representation of Augustan succession policy, with several issues by *Gades* and *Iulia Traducta* dedicated to the grandsons of Augustus and others by *Carteia*, *colonia Romula*, and *Italica* to Germanicus and Drusus, the frustrated potential successors of Tiberius.[17]

Baetican monetary workshops closed in the course of the reign of Tiberius, within a general process that occurred in the western provinces. In the rest of *Hispania*, the last local emissions date to the time of Claudius, while the rest of the western local coinage ended during the reign of Nero. As in the Republican era, currency fulfilled an identity-definition mission but in a new context in which local elites sought to show their adherence to the new imperial regime. Even the closing of the mints has been interpreted, among other factors, as a display of fidelity to the emperor, with their bronze currency being replaced by the pieces struck in the imperial mints.[18]

## 3 The Role of Local Communities: Civic Dedications to the Imperial Family

Statues honouring living rulers and leaders was a practice with Hellenistic roots that was slowly introduced in Rome because of contact with these areas. Although there were some late republican precedents, Augustus took this practice to a new level, monopolizing the control of public space in the city of Rome and, at the same time, becoming a role model for the imperial and provincial elites in Italy and the provinces.[19] In a short time, erecting statues (with their corresponding inscribed pedestals) as a way to honour individuals

16 *RPC*, no. 66–67; *RIC* I, Claudius no. 17–18.

17 *Gades*: *RPC*, no. 96–97; *Iulia Traducta*: no. 107; *Carteia*: no. 123; *colonia Romula*: no. 74–75; *Italica*: no. 68–71. On the significance of the imperial family as a motif in Spanish local coinage, see also F. Beltrán Lloris, 'Identidad cívica y adhesión al príncipe en las monedas municipales hispanas', in *Religión y propaganda en el mundo romano*, ed. F. Marco Simón, F. Pina Polo and J. Remesal Rodríguez (Barcelona 2002), 159–189. A general approach in J. A. Mellado Rivera, Princeps Ivventvtis. *La imagen monetaria del heredero en la época Julio-Claudia* (Alicante 2002).

18 Ripollès 2010, op. cit., 34–35.

19 See W. Eck, 'Emperor and Senatorial Aristocracy in Competition for Public Space', in *The Emperor and Rome. Space, Representation and Ritual*, ed. B. C. Ewald and C. F. Noreña (Cambridge 2010a), 89–110, with abundant bibliographical references.

became popular in the urban areas of the Empire, a practice described by Pliny the Elder as *humanissima ambitio* (*NH*. 34.17), which decidedly marked public spaces, especially the *fora*. Dedications to the imperial family were essential in this rise.[20]

In southern *Hispania*, Republican examples of homage to the Roman provincial authorities are few in number, limited to two pedestals from *Italica* and *Carissa Aurelia* (Espera, Cádiz).[21] The first civic honours to Augustus and his family were linked to the institution of imperial patronage over communities. This was a legal figure that came from the Republic and which the Princeps integrated into the new political system so that the cities obtained a representative of their interests within the imperial government. Obviously, the imperial household or individuals very close to it became a primary object of attention for these communities.[22]

Augustus himself served as the patron of *Ulia Fidentia* (Montemayor, Córdoba). An indigenous city that started to mint coinage in the republican era, during the Civil Wars *Ulia* aligned itself with the Caesarian side, so it was rewarded with the status of *municipium civium Romanorum* with the epithet of *Fidentia*.[23] The *fidelitas* shown during the fight against the Pompeian party must have generated an opportunity for this city to gain prestige through its connection with the Imperial House. Thanks to the epigraphic record we know that in addition to the first emperor, Agrippa, Lucius Caesar, and the young Tiberius were patrons of *Ulia Fidentia*. The four received homage from the city as its patrons within a propagandistic programme that included the erection of a statue dedicated to a son of Agrippa (*Pupus Agrippa M. f.*) whose name is not mentioned.[24]

The case of *Ulia* is certainly peculiar in terms of the staggered accumulation of patrons. Agrippa's inscription must be dated between 19 and 18 BC; Lucius Caesar's dedication could be placed around 2 BC, the year when he not only received the *toga virilis* but was also presented to the Senate and appointed *Princeps iuventutis*; and that of Tiberius probably between 11 BC, after his marriage to Julia, and AD 4. It is more difficult to date the inscription

20 Beltrán Lloris 2015, op. cit., 131–136.

21 B. Díaz Ariño, *Epigrafía latina republicana de Hispania* (Barcelona 2008), U.3 and U.7 respectively.

22 At a general level, on civic patronage see J. Nichols, *Civic Patronage in the Roman Empire* (Leiden 2014); for *Hispania* specifically: E. Melchor Gil, *El patronato cívico en la Hispania romana* (Seville 2018).

23 Caes. *Bell. Alex*. 61; Caes. *Bell. Hisp*. 3–4; Plin. *NH*. 3.3.10.

24 Augustus: *CIL* II$^2$/5, 486; Agrippa: *CIL* II$^2$/5, 488; Lucius Caesar: *CIL* II$^2$/5, 487; Tiberius: *CIL* II$^2$/5, 490; Agrippa's son: *CIL* II$^2$/5, 489.

to Augustus, but the number of dedications to him began to increase from 9 BC onwards, so the last decade of the 1st century BC is a suitable *terminus post quem*.[25] Although probably not deliberate, the result was the realisation of a sculptural and epigraphic ensemble with an enormous visual impact in the heart of *Baetica*. It is not difficult to imagine the effect it would have had on a spectator entering the forum in this provincial city, probably of some importance, but which was not even the capital of a juridical *conventus*.

Without reaching the level of *Ulia Fidentia*, other Baetican cities also adopted members of the *Domus Augusta* as patrons. Agrippa has already been mentioned appearing on some monetary issues of *Gades*, in which he is designated as *municipii parens* and *patronus*. The formalisation of this patronage must have taken place during his visit to the south of the Peninsula between 19 and 18 BC when he was able to participate in the institutional reorganization of the city.[26] As for Tiberius, he exercised his patronage over the city of *Italica*, recorded on a highly fragmentary marble plaque that must have been part of a pedestal.[27] As has been seen, this city also minted coins with the effigy of the second emperor. Outside *Baetica*, Augustus was honoured as the patron of *Emporiae* (Ampurias, Gerona), as well as Agrippa and Caius or Lucius Caesar. There are also epigraphic records of Agrippa and Tiberius as patrons of *Carthago Nova* (Cartagena, Murcia) and of Augustus' grandchildren in *Augusta Emerita* (Mérida, Badajoz) and *Salaria* (Úbeda, Jaén).[28]

The weight that Agrippa and his sons had in the overall set of imperial dedications, a common phenomenon in the three Spanish provinces, is interesting. It should not be forgotten that, in addition to being Augustus' deputy, Agrippa visited the Iberian Peninsula on several occasions, which made it logical for local communities to have a particular interest in establishing a tie with him through civic patronage.[29] It is not a mere coincidence that these individuals were potential successors of Augustus (we must also remember the appearance of both Caius and Lucius as well as Drusus and Germanicus on local coinage), but there are three complementary readings. First, the immediate

25 Melchor Gil 2018, op. cit., 64.

26 *RPC*, no. 74 and 77–83. On the patronage over *Gades*, see É. Cardon, 'Le patronat municipal en Bétique et en Tarraconaise sous les premiers Julio-Claudiens. Un exemple de loyalisme dynastique', in *Hispanité et romanité*, ed. J. M. André (Madrid 2004), 39–58. The same author thinks that Agrippa's patronage of *Ulia Fidentia* was formalized around the same date.

27 *CIL* II, 1113 = *CILA* Se 2, 364.

28 *Emporiae*: *AE* 1990, 662; *IRC* III, 24 and *AE* 1990, 663 respectively; *Carthago Nova*: *AE* 1979, 366 and *CIL* II, 5930 (= *ILS* 144); *Augusta Emerita*: *HEp* 18, 2009, 40–41; *Salaria*: *CIL* II, 5093 = *CILA* Ja 2, 357.

29 J. M. Roddaz, 'Agripa y la Península Ibérica', *Anas* 6 (1993), 111–126.

political relevance: trying to win the support of those who were destined to govern in the future was a logical strategy for communities. Second, the ideological implications. These dedications fixed civic memory in the epigraphic landscape of cities; at the same time, that memory was clearly linked to the future, taking for granted the survival of the Empire and the peaceful succession to power. In this sense, the Roman understanding of 'memory' not only as a vision of the past but as an instrument for the construction of the future should be emphasized, and that character of permanence was very present in the iconographic language of the early years of the Empire, including the phenomenon of statuary homage itself.[30] The desire for continuity was even more relevant when considering that the memory of the Civil Wars was still fresh and must have been especially intense in *Baetica*. Third, the possibility of ideological guidelines being communicated by imperial power centres (in this case the succession of Augustus), not through laws and regulations, but via other categories of channels. The simple imitation of models does not explain the phenomenon by itself: let us recall the representations of the *Domus Augusta* in coin iconography, absent from imperial coinage but frequent on local issues. We will return to this question later.

After Augustus' death, evidence referring to imperial civic patronage in *Hispania* declines drastically, ultimately disappearing during Tiberius' reign.[31] Even though civic patronage continued to exist during the High Empire as an instrument through which communities obtained representatives in the imperial elite, the Imperial House lost interest in this respect.[32]

The statues dedicated to civic patrons are part of a much larger series of dedications decreed by cities, very active during the Early Empire, and given material expression by the erection of statues. During the reign of Augustus, 14 cases are recorded in *Baetica* (including those indicated above), five of which were dedicated to the emperor himself[33] and the other nine to his relatives.[34] The figure is considerably lower under his successor, Tiberius: a single civic

30 See E. Orlin, 'Augustan Reconstruction and Roman Memory', in *Memory in Ancient Rome and Early Christianity*, ed. K. Galinsky (Oxford 2016), 115–144.

31 Epigraphically, only Tiberius is mentioned as the *patronus* of *Aquae Calidae* (Caldes de Montbui, Barcelona) in *IRC* I, 40 and his son Drusus Caesar in *Metellinum* (Medellín, Badajoz) in *CIL* II, 609.

32 Melchor Gil 2018, op. cit., 74–75.

33 For the identification of imperial inscriptions as civic, we follow F. J. Navarro, 'La presencia del emperador en las ciudades de la Hispania romana', in *De Augusto a Trajano. Un siglo en la historia de Hispania*, ed. F. J. Navarro (Pamplona 2000), 40. For Augustus they are *CIL* II$^2$/5, 72, 198 and 7* (*Tucci*); *CIL* II$^2$/7, 253 (*Corduba*), *CIL* II$^2$/7, 70 (*Urgavo Alba*).

34 Civic dedications to Agrippa: *CIL* II$^2$/5, 488 and 489 (*Ulia Fidentia*). To Caius and/or Lucius: *CIL* II$^2$/7, 140 and 141 (*Epora*); *CIL* II$^2$/5, 487 (*Ulia Fidentia*); *CIL* II$^2$/7, 71 (*Urgavo*

dedication to his person and three more to his relatives (his mother Livia and his son Drusus).[35] There are no testimonies of civic homage to Caligula in *Baetica*; his short rule and the *damnatio memoriae* to which he was subjected explain this fact. However, it is curious that two honorific inscriptions have survived, presumably by civic initiative, dedicated to his sister Agrippina and another to his mother Antonia.[36] With Claudius only one civic tribute and another to Britannicus, his son, are recorded,[37] while for the last emperor of the dynasty, Nero, there is also no record of honours by the cities of *Baetica*, probably the result of the effectiveness with which the *damnatio memoriae* was applied.

If we consider the set of 58 civic tributes carried out in Julio-Claudian *Baetica*,[38] the *Domus Augusta* turns out to have been the object of 24 of them, 41% of the total, which makes them the main group of recipients. This weight is even greater if we consider the homage paid to members of the senatorial and equestrian orders, which, with eleven cases, represent 18% of the total. This trend may well have been an entry point for the epigraphic honorific habit in these communities, acting as a model for local elites. Returning to the case of *Ulia Fidentia*, in addition to the five inscriptions to the Imperial House, another series of four dedications to various local magistrates carried out by the *municipes et incolae* comes from this Andalusian community, as well as two other private dedications to members of the imperial family.[39]

## 4 The Role of the Imperial Centre

It has already been mentioned that the propagandistic exploitation of epigraphy by Augustus in the city of Rome became an example to follow for both the imperial and local elites. Beyond providing a model, certain direct and indirect interventions by the imperial centre helped spread the imperial ideology, leaving a record in provincial epigraphic landscapes. Although the role

*Alba*); *CIL* II, 1305 (*Asido Caesarina*). Civic dedications to Tiberius before his accession to the throne: *CIL* II, 1113 = *CILA* Se 2, 364 (*Italica*); *CIL* II$^2$/5, 490 (*Ulia Fidentia*).

35 Civic dedications to Tiberius as emperor: *CIL* II$^2$/5, 747 (*Anticaria*); *CIL* II$^2$/5, 592 (*Ipagrum*). Civic dedications to Livia after Augustus' death: *CIL* II$^2$/7, 73 (*Urgavo Alba*); *CIL* II$^2$/5, 73 (*Tucci*). Dedication to Drusus Caesar: *CIL* II$^2$/5, 440 (*Ucubi*).

36 Civic dedications to Agrippina: *CIL* II$^2$/5, 4 (*Mentesa*); *CIL* II, 963 = *CILA* Hu, 2 (*Arucci*). To Antonia: *CIL* II$^2$/5, 533 (found in Montilla, Córdoba).

37 *CIL* II$^2$/5, 994 (*Ostippo*); *AE* 1988, 728 (*Baelo Claudia*) respectively.

38 J. Herrera Rando, *Cultura epigráfica y romanización en la Hispania meridional. La epigrafía pública entre la república y el imperio* (Vitoria 2020), 352–370.

39 *CIL* II$^2$/5, 491; 495; 497; 498; 499 and 511.

of the provincial authorities in the introduction of the imperial cult appears quite clear in the last regions to be conquered, as was the case of northwestern *Hispania*, the information is less well defined in more urbanised and integrated provinces, such as *Baetica*.[40]

One of these means of intervention was the financing of public works. In his *Res Gestae*, the first emperor celebrates having granted benefits and donations to his colonies of veterans[41] and, indeed, there is an epigraphic record of the evergetic involvement of Augustus in cities such as *Augusta Emerita* or *Pax Iulia*.[42] Despite the importance of settlements housing former military personnel, this kind of donation is absent in *Baetica*; the only testimonies of imperial buildings are those related to the road network.[43] Nor is there any noteworthy epigraphic activity on the part of the provincial governors, with only one possible Julio-Claudian testimony: an altar from Martos, Jaén, dedicated to *Hercules Victor*, which suffered the erasure of several lines of the text. G. Alföldy proposed that the donor should be identified as *Q. Granius Marcianus*, proconsul of *Baetica* in AD 33–34, who shortly afterwards suffered *damnatio memoriae*.[44]

By contrast, southern *Hispania* has been extraordinarily prolific in normative bronze documents, with a concentration unrivalled in other parts of the Empire, both as regards its quantity and variety, which have significantly helped define the relationships between the imperial centre and the provinces.[45] As an example, the recently published Tiberius' *senatus consultum* of AD 14, probably coming from colonia *Genetiva Iulia* at *Urso* (Osuna, Seville). In it, the

40 See F. Marco Simón, 'Los inicios del culto imperial en la *Hispania* augustea', *Gerión* 35, no. 1 (2017), 773–789, with abundant bibliography.

41 R. Gest. 3.3, 10.2 and 28. Suetonius (*Aug.* 46) also echoes it.

42 *AE* 1959, 28 (*Augusta Emerita*); *AE* 1989, 368 (*Pax Iulia*). On imperial building activity, see M. Hörster, *Bauinschriften römischer Kaiser: Untersuchungen zu Inschriftenpraxis und Bautätigkeit in Städten des westlichen Imperium Romanum in der Zeit des Prinzipats* (Stuttgart 2011). For the specific case of *Hispania*, see also Navarro 2000, op. cit., 33–55.

43 See S. España Chamorro, '*Corpus Milliariorum Baeticae*. Miliarios y política viaria en la *Hispania Ulterior Baetica* en época imperial', *ArchClass* 70, no. 9 (2019), 397–450.

44 *CIL* II$^2$/5, 65; G. Alföldy '*Epigraphica Hispanica* VIII. Eine kaiserliche Widmung in der Stadt *Tucci*', *ZPE* 59 (1985), 189–199.

45 For a detailed introduction to the question, see A. Caballos Rufino, 'Publicación de documentos públicos en las ciudades del Occidente romano: el ejemplo de la Bética', in *Selbstdarstellung und Kommunikation. Die Veröffentlichung staatlicher Urkunden auf Stein und Bronze in der römischen Welt*, ed. R. Haensch (Munich 2009), 131–172; A. Caballos Rufino, '*Monumenta fatiscunt*. Meaning and Fate of Legal Inscriptions on Bronze: The *Baetica*', in *Literacy in Ancient Everyday Life*, ed. A. Kolb (Berlin 2019a), 289–318.

recently promoted emperor points out the need to increase taxes in order to fulfill the commitments of his predecessor and adoptive father.[46]

The writing of legal texts on durable supports was not the norm and this decision implied a special wish to disseminate the terms and make them last. As occurred in the Hellenistic East with the use of marble, in the western provinces bronze was the preferred support for this task, making the *tabulae aeneae* part of epigraphic landscapes. For example, consider the foundational law of *colonia Genetiva Iulia* (improperly known as *Lex Ursonensis*), collected on eleven bronze tablets intended for public exhibition, which would have been laid out over a length of 15 or 16 metres. The motive behind this cumbersome public display was not functional (there would have been more manageable copies in local archives), but symbolic. For the potential audience, the association between text content and material provided a symbolic image of power that connects perfectly with the concept of epigraphic landscape.[47]

The relationship of bronze documents with Roman power and the provincial authorities started in the first moments of the Roman presence in southern *Hispania*. In fact, the first Latin epigraphs found in the region are the *tabulae Lascutana* and *Alcantarensis*, two bronze tablets collecting decrees of republican provincial governors in the 2nd century BC.[48] This link is maintained throughout the High Empire.

An early example is the one known as *ius iurandum* from *Conobaria* (Las Cabezas de San Juan, Seville). It is an oath of allegiance to Augustus, the young Caesars *Caius* and Lucius, and Agrippa Postumus, carried out by the *senatus et populus Co*[*nobariensium*] between 6 and 5 BC and recorded on a bronze

46 A. Caballos Rufino, 'Un senadoconsulto del año 14 d. C. en un epígrafe bético', *ZPE* 219 (2021), 305–326; D. Martínez Chico and A. González García, 'Análisis metalográfico e isotópico del « bronce de Tiberio », epígrafe jurídico bético del año 14 d. C.', *CPAM* 48, no. 2 (2022), 183–204.

47 C. Williamson already proposed that bronze as a material must have had a symbolic value by itself as a demonstration of state power: C. Williamson, 'Monuments of Bronze: Roman Legal Documents on Bronze Tablets', *ClAnt* 6, no. 1 (1987), 160–183. Both F. Beltrán and A. Caballos have criticised this assumption, which does not reflect the frequent reuse that these pieces experienced. It was the legal text itself which gave value to the epigraph and not the material, and what made bronze be associated with the display of norms of special significance in the West: F. Beltrán Lloris, 'Inscripciones sobre bronce: ¿un rasgo característico de la cultura epigráfica de las ciudades hispanas?', in *XI Congresso Internazionale di Epigrafia Greca e Latina* (Rome 1999), 23–25; Caballos Rufino 2009, op. cit., 144–146.

48 Díaz Ariño 2008, op. cit., U.1 and U.2. On these and other Republican examples from Hispania, see B. Díaz Ariño, 'Epigrafía y gobernadores provinciales en *Hispania* durante la República romana', *Chiron* 41 (2011), 149–179.

tablet recovered in the 1980s.[49] The text opens with a mention of the proconsul of *Baetica*, *P. Petronius Turpilianus*, and his quaestor, *M. Alfius Laches*, followed by a series of local magistrates in charge of swearing the oath. The two Roman magistrates appear as the eponymous dating of the document, without specifying their role in its execution. The date coincides with the public presentation of the young Caius, when other samples of collective adhesion were also made, such as the oath to the Imperial House by the Greek city of Samos or the one made by the Jews when Herod the Great ordered them to ally with Augustus.[50] Although there is no direct evidence of official instruction, an overall tendency to honour the potential successors of Augustus can be detected. In this respect, we must remember the monetary issues of *Gades* and *Iulia Traducta* dedicated to Caius and Lucius.

Years later, in AD 37, when the reign of Caligula had just begun, the inhabitants of the Lusitanian town of *Aritium* (Aronches, Portugal) made another collective oath to the emperor, the other one recorded in *Hispania*. Despite some variations in its vocabulary, the content is similar to the Andalusian bronze: the people of *Aritium* committed themselves to fight against the enemies of the new emperor, using an oath taken by several local magistrates, and sanctioned by the senate and the community.[51]

Although the degree of initiative on the part of the provincial authorities in these collective adhesions cannot be determined, it does seem apparent that there was a clear harmony with the local ones. In this context, the provincial governors could have acted as conductors of these acts, guiding the desire to show collective adherence to such a well-known Roman legal formula as the loyalty oaths.[52]

Other pieces of considerable significance belong to the set referring to Germanicus' funerary honours and the trial and sentence of his murderer. In AD 19, Germanicus, nephew of Tiberius and a potential rival in the succession planned for his son, Drusus Caesar, died in *Syria* under strange circumstances.

49 *AE* 1988, 723; see J. González Fernández, 'The First Oath *pro Salute Augusti* Found in *Baetica*', *ZPE* 72 (1988), 113–127.

50 P. Herrman, *Der römische Kaisereid: Untersuchungen zu seiner Herkunft und Entwicklung* (Göttingen 1968), no. 6; Jos. *Ant.* 17.42. *Cf.* J. González Fernández, 'El origen del culto imperial en la Bética según la documentación epigráfica', in *Culto imperial: política y poder*, ed. T. Nogales Basarrate and J. González Fernández (Mérida 2006), 186–187.

51 *CIL* II, 172 (= *ILS* 190) = *IRCPacen* 647; Herrman 1968, op. cit., no. 1.

52 González Fernández 2006, op. cit., 186–187. Recently, in his study about imperial governors, R. Olmo López has minimised the role of local communities in these loyalty manifestations in favour of the initiative of the imperial authorities: R. Olmo López, *El centro está en la periferia. Las competencias de los gobernadores provinciales romanos en Hispania durante el Principado* (Zürich 2018), 485–493.

The possibility that the emperor himself was involved in the event triggered a deep political crisis that forced Tiberius to intervene through a series of Senate decrees: first, ordering magnificent funeral services and honours for Germanicus in Rome and the provinces, and second, organizing a trial against the governor of *Syria, Cnaeus Calpurnius Piso*, close to the emperor and charged with murdering his nephew. Although the accused committed suicide before the trial came to an end, the Senate decreed a series of measures against him.[53]

The funerary honours were laid out in what is known as the *lex Valeria Aurelia*,[54] of which several fragments have survived in *tabulae aeneae*. The two from *Baetica* stand out: the *tabula Carissiana* and, above all, the *tabula Siarensis*, which allowed most of the text of the law to be reconstructed.[55] The first piece, a very small fragment, comes from *Carissa Aurelia*, a Latin municipality near *Gades*, while the *tabula Siarensis* was found in an archaeological context in the town of El Coronil (in the province of Seville), identified as the ancient community of *Siarum*. The *lex* itself included provisions about its distribution: the consuls had to transcribe and send it to the *coloniae* and *municipia* of Italy and the colonies in the provinces, and the provincial governors were also expected to exhibit the decrees in the most frequented place possible. In addition to the immediate political solution to the crisis generated by Germanicus' death, the decrees present a clear ideological programme, based on consensus (*consensus universorum civium*) and the unity of all levels of Roman society (*omnium ordinum*), with Tiberius and the *Domus Augusta* acting as the backbone of society.[56]

The existence of the Baetican copies proves that the *lex* was actually distributed in the provinces; in fact, with greater intensity than ordered. Pliny reports that *Carissa Aurelia* was a *municipium Latinorum*, while he does not

53 On the events related to Germanicus' death, including a comparison of Suetonius' account with the epigraphic record, see J. González Fernández, *Tácito y las fuentes documentales*. SS.CC. De honoribvs Germanici decernendis (Tabula Siarensis) *y* de Cn. Pisone patre (Seville 2002).

54 M. Crawford, *Roman Statutes* (London 1996), 507–543.

55 *AE* 2000, 725 and *AE* 1983, 515 respectively. Since its appearance four decades ago, much has been written about the *tabula Siarensis*. The edition used here is A. Sánchez-Ostiz. Tabula Siarensis. *Edición, traducción y comentario*, Pamplona 1999, with an exhaustive historical, legal and philological study. More recently and systematising the previous bibliography, see J. González Fernández, '*Monumenta Memoriae Germanici Caesaris*', in Monumenta et memoria. *Estudios de epigrafía romana*, ed. J. M. Iglesias Gil and A. Ruiz-Gutiérrez (Rome 2017), 117–142.

56 G. Rowe, *Princes and Political Cultures. The New Tiberian Senatorial Decrees* (Ann Arbor 2005), 64–66.

mention the legal status of *Siarum*.[57] As H. Galsterer pointed out, regardless of the reasons for distinguishing between colonies and municipalities in Italy and only colonies in the provinces, the regulation does not expressly prohibit municipalities or peregrine cities from making and exhibiting copies of the law.[58] We will return to this idea when discussing the following documents.

As mentioned previously, in AD 20 and after his trial and suicide, the Senate decreed a series of symbolic measures against Piso, collected in the *Senatus consultum de Cn. Pisone patre*. In 1996, two bronze tablets recovered in southern Spain, along with four more small fragments, were edited and published, allowing the reconstruction of the text of the law and proving the existence of at least six copies in *Baetica*.[59] The provenance of the larger fragments is uncertain. One of the copies may come from *Irni* (El Saucejo, Seville), a site that was extensively looted in the last century and one from which the Flavian *lex Irnitana* would also have come. For the second large fragment, both the sites of *Olaurum* (Lora del Río, Seville) and Benamejí, Córdoba, have been proposed. In any case, they are all places of relatively minor importance, which ultimately guaranteed the survival of the bronzes and that they were not melted down, the usual fate for this type of piece. The four smaller fragments entered into the Archaeological Museum of Seville without any information about their origin.

Focusing on the provisions of the text itself for its dissemination, it is ordered that in the city of Rome Tiberius should choose the place to exhibit the decree, and that, engraved in bronze, the same must be done in the busiest city of any province. There, it should be placed in the busiest place (*in* (…) *celeberruma urbe eiusque in urbis ipsius celeberrimo loco*); besides that, it had to be displayed in the winter barracks of the legions. Assuming that in most cases the busiest city would correspond to the provincial capital (doubtless *Corduba* in the case of *Baetica*), the existence of several copies in centres of lesser importance indicates that the text sent from Rome was reproduced in many cities beyond the provisions of the law. As an explanation, the first factor is the attitude of the local communities. Faced with the open crisis in the imperial regime, the elites of the Baetican cities showed their support by making copies that reproduced

57 Plin. *NH*. 3.3.11 and 15.

58 H. Galsterer, 'The *Tabula Siarensis* and the Augustan Municipalization in *Baetica*', in *Estudios sobre la* Tabula Siarensis, ed. J. González Fernández and J. Arce (Madrid 1988), 61–62.

59 Two editions of the document have been published, in Spanish and German: A. Caballos Rufino, W. Eck and F. Fernández Gómez, *El Senadoconsulto de Gneo Pisón padre* (Seville 1996); W. Eck, A. Caballos Rufino and F. Fernández, *Das Senatus Consultum de Cn. Pisone patre* (Munich 1996). See also the 1999 special issue dedicated to the question by the *American Journal of Philology*.

the text displayed in *Corduba*. After all, there were no limitations on this. In the same way, the desire for emulation among cities may also have further stimulated the process.[60]

Was the reaction of the Baetican communities very spontaneous? As with the *Tabula Siarensis*, the role of the provincial governor must be considered; in this case, this was the proconsul *N. Vibius Serenus*, the governor in AD 20–21 or 21–22, who was responsible for the text exhibited in the busiest city of *Baetica*, as is reflected in the title of the decree. Regarding this individual, Tacitus points out that he is known to have been close to Tiberius and a person of debatable behaviour in order to please the emperor.[61] The editors of the *senatus consultum* themselves pointed out that *Vibius Serenus* could have instigated the production of the multiple Baetican copies.[62] As an example, they cite the copy of Diocletian's *Edictum de pretiis* from *Aizanoi*, in the province of *Caria-Phrygia*: the provincial governor ordered the communities to display the imperial decree for its preservation in perpetuity (which, given the number of copies preserved, must have been a general and effective provision). From this point of view, *Vibius Serenus* either ordered or in some way encouraged the making of local copies. The process must have occurred in other provinces, although probably with less intensity. It has proved possible to identify a small bronze fragment found during excavations in Roman *Genava* (Genève, Switzerland) as a new copy of the Senate decree, so far, the only one that has appeared outside *Baetica*, in *Gallia Narbonensis*.[63] It is possible that the piece originally came from the nearby *colonia Iulia Equestris* at *Noviodunum* (Nyon, Switzerland) in *Germania Superior* and moved to Genève, together with other materials, after its destruction in the 3rd century. Neither the 1st-century *Genava*, then a small *vicus* dependent of Vienne, nor the aforementioned colony could be considered the 'busiest cities' of their provinces. Therefore, everything points to the fact that local copies were also made beyond the provisions of the *senatus consultum*.[64]

60 Beltrán Lloris 1999, op. cit., 28–29; Herrera Rando 2020, op. cit., 317–319.

61 Tac. *Ann.* 2.30; 4.13; 4.29 and 4.37; also, Suet. *Tib.* 25. See *PIR*² V 575; G. Alföldy, Fasti Hispanienses. *Senatorische Reichsbeamte und Offiziere in den spanischen Provinzen des römischen Reiches von Augustus bis Diokletian* (Wiesbaden 1969), 149.

62 Caballos Rufino et al. 1995, op. cit., 139–141. The same positions in Sánchez-Ostiz, op. cit., 320–321; Olmo López 2018, op. cit., 509–510.

63 *AE* 1997, 1065 = *ILN* V/3, 869 = *AE* 2009, 839.

64 J. Bartels, 'Der Tod des Germanicus und seine epigraphische Dokumentation: Ein neues Exemplar des *senatus consultum de Cn. Pisone patre* aus Genf', *Chiron* 39 (2009), 1–9. Although the Nyon provenance is more feasible, it is clear that if the bronze was originally exhibited in Genève, it belonged to *colonia Iulia Vienna*, an important and well-connected city in Gaul.

Initiatives undertaken by local authorities and governors are not mutually exclusive but, on the contrary, complementary. Within the dialectic between centre and periphery, it was logical for the interests of local elites wishing to show their adherence to the Imperial House and those of a provincial governor who sought to further his credentials in his political career to meet. Of course, other local conditions favoured the proliferation of bronze inscriptions in southern *Hispania*: the abundance of raw materials, the existence of a substantial urban network, the presence of artisans, and a traditional link between the publication of normative texts in bronze and the Roman authority.[65] Ultimately, the proliferation of these documents helped spread the ideological views of the imperial centre on a massive scale and link the collective memory of the communities with the *Domus Augusta*.

## 5 The Individual's Role in the Reception of Imperial Ideology

The third factor in this study is the individual agency, that is, the behaviour of each subject in the face of ideological and legal conditions generated by both the imperial authorities and local communities. Beyond the conduct of the elites as civic collectives, their members competed for prestige, political power, and public visibility. The epigraphic landscape of the High Imperial Roman *civitas* became a space of struggle in which individuals tried to represent themselves in the eyes of society. For this purpose, they used the symbolic language that the diffusion of the epigraphic habit and imperial ideology had provided.[66]

The imperial cult is one of the facets in which this individual role is most evident.[67] Traditionally, it has been considered that the creation of provincial priesthoods in *Baetica* was the work of Vespasian, but, at the local level and in a

65 Herrera Rando 2020, op. cit., 294–296.

66 A. U. Stylow, 'Las estatuas honoríficas como medio de autorrepresentación de las élites locales de Hispania', in *Élites hispaniques*, ed. S. Demougin, M. Navarro and F. Des Boscs-Plateaux (Bordeaux 2001), 142–144; E. Melchor Gil. 'Las élites municipales hispanorromanas a fines de la República y en el Alto Imperio: ideología y conductas sociopolíticas', in Hispaniae. *Las provincias hispanas en el mundo romano*, ed. J. Andreu Pintado, J. Cabrero Piquero and I. Rodà de Llanza (Tarragona 2009a), 393–394.

67 Besides Fishwick's monumental work on the imperial cult and Étienne's classic volume focused on *Baetica*, we will only mention two recent works of synthesis, with ample bibliographies and references: F. Marco Simón, 'Los inicios del culto imperial en la *Hispania* augustea', *Gerión* 35, no. 1 (2017), 773–789; C. Alarcón Hernández, 'Una aproximación al culto imperial en Hispania: avances interpretativos', *Revista de Historiografía* 28 (2018), 183–212.

FIGURE 2.3 Inscription from the Theatre of Italica (*CILA* Se 2, 382)
© THE AUTHOR

somewhat disorganised way, there had been local priesthoods in the province since the reign of Tiberius, which provided magnificent platforms for competition between elites.[68]

For example, in *Italica*, the building of the theatre at the beginning of the Era allowed some of the *pontifices primi creati Augusto* to carry out (and show) large-scale evergetic donations. *L. Blattius Pollio* and *C. Traius Pollio* built "the orchestra, the proscenium, the paths, the altars and the statues", a generous donation that was recorded in a no less magnificent inscription. The text was put on a series of slabs forming a twelve-metre-long grandstand in front of the theatre's proscenium and visible, thanks to 18-cm-high letters, to a large part of the audience.[69] Less monumental but also relevant is the marble plaque that commemorated the construction, also in the theatre, of some arches and porticoes by the priest *L. Herius* (fig. 2.3).[70] The three persons indicate that they were the first to occupy those priesthoods, combined with high magistracies of the municipality.

Interestingly, the presence of early local imperial priesthoods in some peregrine communities shows that the organisation of the emerging imperial cult did not necessarily follow a legal framework.[71] The series of pedestals

68 For the earliest manifestations of the imperial cult in *Baetica*, see González Fernández 2006, op. cit., 175–189.

69 *CILA* Se 2, 383.

70 *CILA* Se 2, 382.

71 See J. A. Delgado Delgado, *Élites y organización de la religión en las provincias romanas de la Bética y las Mauritanias: sacerdotes y sacerdocios* (Oxford 1998).

made in *Anticaria* (Antequera, Málaga) stands out: the two dedicated by the *pontufex Caesarum M. Cornelius Proculus* to Tiberius and Livia once divinized, and the one by the priest *Cornelius Bassus* to Drusus Caesar. To these must be added a fourth pedestal, seemingly dedicated by the city itself.[72] By contrast, the *seviri Augustales* are later, and the first testimonies date from well into the second half of the 1st century.[73]

The control of public space by local authorities limited individual initiative, although this never reached the level of an absolute monopoly and did not affect dedications made in a private sphere. Among the private individuals who made dedications to the Julio-Claudian emperors, we find that four held priesthoods (in addition to other civic magistracies), four were local magistrates, and 19 were private individuals who do not record the positions they held. It must be considered that, of the 59 inscriptions dedicated to the first imperial dynasty, 24 were of civic initiative, individuals promoted 19, and in 16 cases, the promoter is unknown.[74]

This difference between individual and civic activity should not be understood in terms of opposition: indeed, some cases show a clear convergence between the two. An obvious example is found in a statue from Castro del Río, Córdoba, paid for by the freedman *Optatus* and dedicated to the emperor Claudius. Although the result of an individual initiative, the local senate ultimately declared the statue part of the public property in perpetuity.[75]

## 6 Conclusions

In a recent study, the British academic G. Woolf argued for a vision of imperial power as a network of interpersonal relationships arranged from the centre and with the provincial elites acting as direct recipients of these relationships.[76] The signs of adherence to the imperial regime, whether collective through the action of the *civitas* or individual, allowed the engagement of that power to be shown publicly in its different facets (ideological or political). Take as an example the dedications to civic patrons, some of whom, as has been seen,

72 *CIL* II$^2$/ 5, 749; 748; 750 and 747 respectively.

73 See C. Castillo García, 'Sevirato y augustalidad: un estamento intermedio en la vida ciudadana', in *Sociedad y economía en el Occidente romano*, ed. C. Castillo García (Pamplona 2003), 73–90.

74 Herrera Rando 2020, op. cit., 273–276.

75 *CIL* II$^2$/5, 394.

76 G. Woolf, 'The Rulers Ruled', in *Reconsidering Roman Power*, ed. K. Berthelot (Rome 2020), 76–99.

were members of the imperial family. From this point of view, both sides had incentives: the local elites could show their relationship with the regime and, ultimately, with power, while these expressions became materialisations of imperial control over their subjects, a subtle (or perhaps not so subtle) reminder to local ruling groups that their position ultimately depended on the imperial government's favour.

Part of the success of the Roman Empire as a political system was the ability to integrate and balance the interests between the centre, represented by the emperor together with the higher classes, and the elites of the provincial peripheries. The imperial ideology was a key instrument in that process, providing a new symbolic language in relation to power. The ample local scope for action allowed the integration of local traditions into this system; the coin iconographies of *Gades* and *Carteia* constitute good Baetican examples, although there are many different cases throughout the Empire.

The epigraphic landscape of the *civitas* became the stage on which to exhibit those demonstrations of adherence to the political regime and official memory, both imperial and local. Furthermore, local elites, especially in the most urbanised provinces such as *Baetica*, tried to imitate the occupation of public spaces that Augustus inaugurated in Rome, being one of the factors that stimulated the development of honorific epigraphy during the High Empire. This fed the ideological process: as G. Alföldy noted,[77] apart from the direct dedications to the *Domus Augusta*, the presence of magistracies and priesthoods bearing his name (*legati Augusti, pontifices Caesarum, …*) or the devotions to the Augustan deities ultimately made Augustus' figure omnipresent in the epigraphic landscapes of Early Imperial cities. The province of *Baetica* during the first decades of the Empire is a good example of this.

77 Alföldy 1991a, op. cit., 592–593; Alföldy 2018, op. cit., 94–95.

CHAPTER 3

# Gone with the Law: the Survival of Latin Onomastics in a *Peregrinorum Hispania* during the Republic

*Cristina de la Escosura Balbás*

## 1 Uses and Abuses of Onomastics

When considering the processes of "Romanisation", onomastics allows us to measure the prevalence and various forms of the adaptation of indigenous elements.[1] However, the risk of losing sight of the specific context of each element is high, and "acculturation et statut civique ne doivent pas être confondus".[2] Moreover, any study based on onomastics presents a particular methodological challenge for this historical period, for which the surviving documentation depends largely on Epigraphy. As pointed by Le Roux, there are two major methodological complications to consider. First, onomastic lists should not be used without the proper perspective since the presence of a name proves nothing on its own. Second, and more importantly, that a chronological framework is essential, and any seemingly probative testimony, even if spread over many centuries, should not lead to long-term quantitative or qualitative assumptions.[3] In the field of Roman Republican studies, it must be pointed out that the available onomastic data can be used to draw conclusions about *gentes*, but only rarely about families and individuals.[4] The appearance and disappearance of a certain *gens* will not exclusively depend on the problems of conservation and transmission inherent to epigraphy, but on possible

1 G. Bandelli, *Ricerche sulla colonizzazione romana della Gallia Cisalpina: le fasi iniziali e il caso aquileiese* (Rome 1988), 125.

2 M. Dondin-Payre and M. T. Raepsaet-Charlier (eds.), *Noms, identités culturelles et romanisation sous le Haut-Empire* (Bruxelles 2001), 198.

3 P. Le Roux, 'L'émigration italique en Citérieure et Lusitanie jusqu'à la mort de Néron', in *Roma y el nacimiento de la cultura epigráfica en Occidente*, ed. F. Beltrán Lloris (Zaragoza 1995), 86 [= P. Le Roux, *Espagnes romaines. L'Empire dans ses provinces. Scripta varia II* (Rennes 2014), 64].

4 F. Pina Polo, 'Generales y clientelas provinciales: ¿qué clientelas?', in *Romanización, fronteras y etnias en la Roma Antigua: el caso hispano*, ed. J. Santos Yanguas, G. Cruz Andreotti, M. Fernández Corral and L. Sánchez Voigt (Vitoria 2013), 76.

 | DOI:10.1163/9789004685734_004

migrations, ascents or descents on the social and economic ladder, communal or individual legal changes, and so on.

To date, studies on Roman population have been mainly approached from the perspective of prosopography, which looks for the common elements within a collective rather than the exceptional aspects of individuals. Although such an approach is well grounded, attempts to apply it to such a specific collective as the provincial population of the Republican period encounters a severe problem in the scarcity of data, especially considering the impossibility of establishing a ratio between the numbers of preserved and lost inscriptions. The debate on the usefulness of prosopography is like that on the use of the statistical-epigraphic method. The solution at the methodological level lies in determining the representativeness of the *r* letter that has reached us, and the overall validity of such generalisations in the face of the restricted amount of data. Therefore, I will use the term 'onomastic' instead of Prosopography in this chapter.

The analysis of the data faces the difficult problem of determining how 'Romans', '*Latini*', and '*peregrini*' can be distinguished from each other. It seems clear that, for Romans, a name was not simply a narrative utterance, neither human nor divine.[5] The legal condition inherent in Roman onomastic structures with two or three elements (what we call *duo/tria nomina*) is not automatically transferred to those populations in the same environment, and in which similar onomastic structures are to be expected, especially during the first centuries of contact and formation. At least for some time, the onomastic formula consisting of a name followed by a patronymic would not only be characteristic of *peregrini*, but also of *Latini*, and even of Romans.[6] We also cannot determine when the Roman *duo/tria nomina* fully acquired its condition as a legal identifier.[7] Throughout Roman history we have examples of how it was used fraudulently,[8] which indicates that it was indeed a legal identifier, as otherwise there could be no cases of it being used illegally. The prohibition on the use of *tria nomina* by non-citizens has led authors like Mommsen to

---

5 M. Salvadore, *Il nome, la persona. Saggio sull'etimologia antica* (Genoa 1987), 100.

6 S. Panciera, *Epigrafi, epigrafia, epigrafisti: scritti vari editi e inediti* (1956–2005) *con note complementari e indici* (Rome 2006), 1412.

7 Nicolet made an interesting survey of the Republican history of the *duo/tria nomina and* proposed that the appearance of its status as a "état-civil" should be fixed at the end of the 4th century BC at the latest. cfr. C. Nicolet, 'L'onomastique des groupes dirigeants sous la République', in *L'onomastique latine*, ed. H.-G. Pflaum and N. Duval (Paris 1977), 45–61.

8 Perhaps the clearest example is the decree of Claudius in Suet. *Claud.* 25: *Peregrinae condicionis homines vetuit usurpare Romana nomina dum taxat gentilicia. Civitatem R(omanam) usurpantes in campo Esquilino securi percussit.*

argue that non-Roman could not make use of it.[9] Part of the French academy has adopted the same approach, mainly following the work of A. Chastagnol, who maintains that "quand un personnage, dans sa cité, porte les *tria nomina* (ou les *duo nomina* lorsque l'usage du prénom se perd) cela veut dire qu'il est citoyen romain".[10] However, Cherry already pointed out the possibility of Roman names being usurped, as a general explanation of the scarce evidence for the actual possession of Roman citizenship versus the incidence of the appearance of *tria nomina*.[11] Häussler, almost one decade later, is categorical: "*tria nomina* cannot be a sign of Roman citizenship".[12] In any case, there is a risk in onomastic studies of falling into the trap of employing exceptions as patterns.[13]

According to the requirements of the census referred to in the *tabula Heracleensis*,[14] *tria nomina* included *nomina, praenomina, patres aut patronos, tribus* and *cognomina*; but Cicero already warned that a record in the census is not proof of citizenship, but rather of 'acting' as a citizen.[15] However, the epigraphic data, beyond that pertaining to elements of the elite, usually identifies *praenomina, nomina, patres aut patronos* and *cognomina*. Only occasionally will inscriptions mention the *tribus* and some form of *origo* (understood in a broad, rather than a narrow/technical, sense). This greatly hampers our ability to distinguish a full-fledged Roman citizen in the record, since I

9 T. Mommsen, *Römisches Straatsrecht* III[3] (Leipzig 1887), 213.

10 A. Chastagnol, 'L'onomastique de type pérégrin dans les cités de la Gaule Narbonnaise', *MEFRA* 102, no. 2 (1990), 576. In 2001, M. Dondin-Payre and M. T. Raepsaet-Charlier (2001, op. cit.) stated that "absolument rien n'autorise à mettre en doute l'affirmation claire et argumentée d'A. Chastagnol".

11 D. Cherry, 'The Minician Law Marriage and the Roman Citizenship', *Phoenix* 44, no. 3 (1990), 256, 263.

12 R. Häussler, 'Writing Latin – from Resistance to Assimilation: Language, Culture and Society, in N. Italy and S. Gaul', in *Becoming Roman, Writing Latin? Literacy and epigraphy in the Roman West*, ed. A. E. Cooley (Portsmouth 2002), 71.

13 Solin explained it clearly through the cases of imperial freedmen bearing the *nomina* of emperors who lived before them, as well as the auxiliary cohorts of the army with *tria nomina*. cfr. H. Solin, 'Abuso dell'onomastica nella ricerca epigrafica', in *Usi e abusi epigrafici. Atti del Colloquio Internazionale di Epigrafia Latina*, ed. M. G. Angeli Bertinelli and A. Donati (Rome 2003), 286.

14 *CIL* I[2], 593, vv. 146–17 = M. H. Crawford (ed.), *Roman Statutes, Institute of Classical Studies* (London 1996), 335–391, n. 24 = *ILS* 6085.

15 Cic. *Arch.* 5.11: [...] *census non ius civitatis confirmat ac tantum modo indicat eum qui sit census ita se iam tum gessisse pro cive.*

subscribe to the theory that the *Latini* promoted after 338 BC[16] were entitled to bear *tria nomina*. Furthermore, I accept, along with most researchers, the (not unproblematic) theory that *peregrini* were *a priori* characterized by the use of a single name plus the filiation, which could be expressed in different ways according to local traditions and their adaptation to Latin (patronymics, matronymics, formations that function as a single word, combinations, etc.).

Alföldy was one of the first to defend the relationship of Latin status with any kind of onomastic structure.[17] This flexibility would be one of the distinguishing features of Latinity. Their organisational autonomy and onomastic usages would be recognized as being in accordance with the law after the granting of *ius Latii*. This *variatio* would disappear after the promotion to Roman citizenship and the adaptation of the consequent rigid onomastic. Considering the documentation from Hispanic communities after the Flavian period, especially in *Baetica*, *Latini* apparently did not fall under the prohibition of the use of *duo/tria nomina* by non-Romans. For García Fernández, this general authorisation (not requirement) to use *tria nomina* was the cause of the expansion of every type of Roman onomastics throughout *Hispania*.[18] Where the local onomastic tradition was more deeply rooted, their structures would prevail against the Roman ones, with tensions and adjustments.[19]

Therefore, we have Latin communities where *Latini* are invisible, or, perhaps more accurately, indistinguishable within the onomastics contained in the epigraphic record. This is what García Fernández defines as "the Latinity paradox", that is, the existence of over abundantly documented Latin communities in all the western provinces where not a single inhabitant who enjoys this status can be identified.[20] We must bear in mind that although Latin colonies or *municipia* had common characteristics, they were autonomous communities that could express their own particularities, whether pre-Roman or

16 This year saw the disappearance of the Latin League proper and the emergence of an understanding of Latinity as an abstract set of rights that could exist outside the geographical and cultural framework of *Latium*, see A. N. Sherwin-White, *The Roman Citizenship* (Oxford 1973), 101; H. Galsterer, *Untersuchungen zum römischen Städtewesen auf der Iberischen Halbinsel* (Berlin 1971), 80.

17 G. Alföldy, 'Notes sur la relation entre le droit de cité et la nomenclature dans l'Empire romain', *Latomus* 25 (1966), 56.

18 E. García Fernández, 'Sobre la condición latina y su onomástica. Los ediles de *Andelo*', *ETF(hist)* 25 (2012), 428.

19 Alföldy 1966, op. cit.; Dondin-Payre 2001, op. cit. for central Gaul; García Fernández 2012, op. cit. for *Andelo*.

20 E. García Fernández, *El municipio latino. Origen y desarrollo constitucional* (Madrid 2001), 125.

resulting from their contact with Rome. Therefore, just as we have many provincial 'latinities',[21] we will also find a wide variety of onomastics that will tend to converge into a single type of *tria nomina*.

Only an analysis carried out *civitas* by *civitas* would allow comparative studies to made between them and enable us to appreciate the possible local variations. Data drawn from areas where we predominantly find *civitates liberae*, such as Greece, allows us to document how individuals from non-promoted communities (neither Roman nor Latin) were not allowed to make use of a Roman onomastic structure with two or three elements. In these regions, the record shows individuals bearing purely Greek names whose filiation is a full Roman *tria nomina* structure.[22]

This question is not only influenced by the lack of ancient sources on the type of onomastic formations that *Latini* could bear, but also by our ignorance about the mechanisms of the composition of *tria nomina* in certain categories of individuals who legally became Roman citizens through different paths. Progress in this field may facilitate the work on *Latini*. However, we are still not certain about the process of forming *tria nomina* that was associated with the individual grants of Roman citizenship to *peregrini*. Their situation has been equated with that of freedmen, who took their *praenomen* and *nomen* from their owners and used their slave's name as their new *cognomen*. However, the paradigmatic (and not unique)[23] case of *L. Cornelius Balbus* (who was a client of *C. Iulius Caesar* and promoted by *Cn. Pompeius Magnus*), as studied by Pina Polo,[24] reveals that the two situations are not comparable.

---

21 E. García Fernández, 'Ni ciudadanos ni extranjeros: la condición jurídica de la población provincial', in *Ciudadanos y extranjeros en el mundo antiguo: segregación e integración*, ed. J. Mangas Manjarrés and S. Montero Herrero (Madrid 2007), 233–234.

22 A. J. N. Wilson *Emigration from Italy in the Republican Age of Rome* (Manchester 1966); J-L. Ferrary, 'L'onomastique dans les provinces orientales de l'Empire à la lumière du dossier des mémoriaux de délégations de Claros', *CGG* 19 (2008), 246–278; E. García Fernández, 'Movilidad, onomástica e integración en *Hispania* en época republicana: algunas observaciones metodológicas', in *Viajes y cambios de residencia en el mundo romano*, ed. J. M. Iglesias Gil and A. Ruiz Gutiérrez (Santander 2011), 47–66 and E. García Fernández, 'Client Relationships and the Diffusion of Roman Names in *Hispania*. A Critical Review', in *Foreign* Clientelae *in the Roman Empire. A Reconsideration*, ed. M. Jehne and F. Pina Polo (Stuttgart 2015b) 107–118.

23 Badian already identified some cases; see E. Badian, *Foreign* Clientelae (*264–70 B.C.*) (Oxford 1958), 302–308. See also Alföldy's (1966, op. cit.) systematic work on this subject, focusing on *Dalmatia, Noricum* and *Pannonia*. Also on this subject, Pina Polo 2015, op. cit.

24 F. Pina Polo, 'Los Cornelio Balbo: clientes en Roma, patronos en *Gades*', in *Identità e autonomie nel mondo romano occidentale. Iberia-Italia, Italia-Iberia III*, ed. A. Sartori and A. Valvo, (Faenza 2011), 335–354.

Another aspect to consider is the capacity for change and adaptation that we saw in frontier epigraphy, which is also reflected in onomastics. This is the case with the mausoleum of Torreparedones (Baena, Córdoba, Spain). In less than a generation, the members of this family had removed almost all traces of their indigenous origins from their names, demonstrating how quickly onomastics can change even within the same family group.[25] The bilingual Latin-Gaulish inscriptions studied by Langslow can also serve as an example.[26] Some individuals chose to keep the same onomastic form, while others tried to translate it to an equivalent Roman form (without constructing *duo/tria nomina*). New Roman citizens created their *tria nomina* with a *nomen* derived from their father's name and their own anthroponym as a *cognomen*. On the other hand, on Hispanic coins, the use of Latin in individual names precedes its use in toponyms.[27]

Today, the available data allows us to appreciate how contact with both Roman and Latin culture enabled their local counterparts to create new or modified forms of expression. Conversely, we cannot rationalize a model to determine the common features in the onomastics of *Latini*, or in the relationship between the names of *peregrini* and Roman citizens. Then again, to what extent can onomastics reveal civic status? This is why onomastics alone, as a succession of names, cannot provide useful data to help determine the legal status of the *civitas* in which its citizens lived.

Everything illustrated so far leads us to consider that we can identify manifold different combinations in the onomastics of each territory, due to their internal characteristics and their ways of relating with newcomers (whether Roman-Italics or not), without necessarily having to fit them into the strict binomial of 'full-fledged Roman citizen' or '*peregrini*'. We can thus introduce the category of 'Latin citizen'.

---

25 B. Díaz Ariño, *Epigrafía latina republicana de Hispania* (Barcelona 2008), 53–54. In the five oldest examples, individuals show peregrine onomastics and indigenous names: *Ildrons Velaunis f.; Igalghis Ildronis f.; Vegana; Sisean Bahannonis f.; Gracchi*. The seven remaining inscriptions show Romanized onomastics, and in only two cases have the indigenous anthroponym been preserved as a *cognomina*: *M. Pompeius Q.f. Gal. Icstnis IIvir; Fabia M.f. Aninna; M. Pompei Q.f.; Iunia L.f. Insghana; Pompeia Q.f. Nannae; Q. Pompei Q.f. Sabini; Q. Pompeius Q.f. Velaunis / Cn. Pompeius Cn.f. Gal. Afer aed. IIvir.*

26 D. R. Langslow, 'Approaching Bilingualism in Corpus Languages', in *Bilingualism in Ancient Society. Language Contact and the Written Word*, ed. J. N. Adams, M. Janse and S. Swain, (Oxford 2002), 23–51. Lowe observes the same phenomenon in Republican Iberia. However, in contrast to Langslow, Lowe refers to the *usurpatio*, see B. Lowe, 'Bilingualism and Language Contact in Republican Iberia', *Epigraphica* 76 (2014), 113.

27 A. Burnett, 'Latin on Coins of the Western Empire', in *Becoming Roman, Writing Latin? Literacy and Epigraphy in the Roman West*, ed. A. E. Cooley (Portsmouth 2002), 38.

## 2 Why Were There So Many *tria nomina* in Hispania during the Republic?

As noted above, studies on Roman onomastics have been marked, largely, by the automatic assumption that every individual bearing a Latin name is a full-fledged Roman citizen, or at least someone who pretends to be so. This assumption has compromised the progress of research by distorting our perception of the Iberian Peninsula during the Republican period. At the root of the problem is the unexpectedly large number of onomastic structures with two or three elements of an apparent Latin nature that can be dated to the Republican period. Deriving mostly from epigraphic documentation, the more than 210 *duo/tria nomina* in the *corpus* elaborated by Díaz Ariño can be considered an extensive body of evidence on its own, and even more so if we add the numerous inscriptions identified from coins.[28] In conclusion, the large number of individuals with Latin onomastics poses a challenge with controversial solutions.

Historians who have dealt with the issue have traditionally opted for one of four theories, or a combination of some of them, to explain the phenomenon: Italic immigration, grants of Roman citizenship *ob honorem* or to *clientelae*, and *nomina* by *imitatio*. Even simplifying the traditional assumptions as much as possible, probably the most influential work in this debate has been *Foreign Clientelae* by Ernst Badian.[29] This works defends the existence of a connection between Republican provincial governors and local *nomina* until the Principate, ruling out the possibility that they were Italic emigrants. Brunt further elaborated on his conclusions by arguing that the ancestors of those provincials now bearing Latin names need not have come from the Republican period, but could also have come from the Principate.[30] For his part, Knapp criticized Brunt because the Roman names taken were never of Republican origin, but were rather Imperial, and argued that there was a relationship between the percentage of years of service of Republican governors and the percentage of associated *nomina* in *Hispania*.[31] Based on Badian's idea, Dyson established a relationship between the names adopted by indigenous individuals from their patrons as a token of loyalty.[32] More recently, Amela Valverde

28 Díaz Ariño 2008, op. cit., 361–366.

29 Badian 1958, op. cit.

30 P. A. Brunt, *Italian Manpower, 225 B.C.–A.D. 14* (Oxford 1971).

31 R. C. Knapp, 'The Origins of Provincial Prosopography in the West', *AncSoc* 9 (1978), 187–222.

32 S. L. Dyson, 'The Distribution of Roman Republican Family Names in the Iberian Peninsula', *AncSoc* 11–12 (1980–1981), 257–300.

has considered this as an interesting but unprovable theory, while pointing out that natives would have to keep changing their names to maintain the custom, which was neither practical nor possible.[33] Today, there is a growing number of historians who believe that the model created by Badian needs to be abandoned, both in its methodological aspects and in its fundamental conclusions.[34] Even so, the explanations for Latin onomastics keep focusing on the emigration of Italics, grants of citizenship, *clientelae* connections, and *imitatio*, without introducing the option of considering colonial centres, as Bandelli does for *Gallia Cisalpina*.[35]

### 2.1 *Italic Immigration*

The first half of the 2nd century BC is a period of exceptional, unprecedented, and not to be repeated population mobility.[36] Trade relations in the Mediterranean, whose routes were fully integrated with the peninsular coasts, were of great importance in laying the foundations for post-conquest acculturation. Studies on onomastics and trade have determined that a considerable quantity of Italics settled in various Mediterranean ports. Initially, the point of origin of most of the Italic settlers in the Hispanic Southeast was identified as *Apulia* and *Campania*,[37] while those from the Northeast were believed to have come from the Tyrrhenian region. Subsequently, the number of immigrants from Northern Italy increased, while the number of people arriving from the South decreased.[38]

This extensive migratory movement is not clearly reflected in the number of tribes mentioned in individual onomastics: one would expect a greater variety beyond the *Sergia*, the *Galeria*, and the *Quirina* that dominate in the Iberian

33 L. Amela Valverde, 'El *nomen Pompeius* en Hispania: algunos aspectos críticos', *Emerita* 69, no. 2 (2001), 247.

34 García Fernández 2011, op. cit.; Pina Polo 2013, op. cit., 78; M. Jehne and F. Pina Polo (eds.), *Foreign* Clientelae *in the Roman Empire. A Reconsideration* (Stuttgart 2015).

35 Bandelli 1988, op. cit., 55.

36 F. Pina Polo, 'Las migraciones en masa y su integración en el Imperio romano', in *Pluralidad e integración en el mundo romano*, ed. F. J. Navarro (Pamplona 2010), 63.

37 M. Stefanile, *Dalla Campania alle* Hispaniae. *L'emigrazione dalla Campania romana alle coste mediterranee della Penisola Iberica in età tardo-repubblicana e proto-imperiale* (Napoli 2017); C. Domergue and C. Rico, 'Les itinéraires du commerce du cuivre et du plomb hispaniques à l'époque romaine dans le monde méditerranéen', in *La Corse et le monde méditerranéen des origines au Moyen-âge: échanges et circuits commerciaux, Actes du colloque de Bastia* (Bastia 2014) 135–168; M. J. Madrid Balanza and J. M. Noguera Celdrán, '*Carthago Nova*: fases e hitos de monumentalización urbana y arquitectónica (siglos III a.C.–III d.C.)', *ETF(arqueol)* 7 (2014), 13–60.

38 Le Roux 1995, op. cit., 93 [= Le Roux 2014, op. cit., 74–75].

Peninsula and have traditionally been associated with the legal promotions of Caesar, Augustus, and the Flavians respectively.[39] To explain this scarcity, Stylow has suggested the hypothesis that the new immigrants were assigned to the *Sergia*.[40] The only place in Hispania that reflects an amalgamation of tribes associated with a strong migratory flow of Italic peoples is *Carthago Nova*, which registered up to eleven different examples.[41] Without questioning the importance that migratory movements had in the diffusion of Roman culture and the settlement of non-*peregrini* in Hispanic communities, these movements had, at first sight, little legal status. However, the lack of legal status for a non-collective emigration, such as those that took place for the most part in Hispania, should not prevent us from seeing the importance of the clues it provides. Thus, a single Roman or Italic emigrant (or his freedmen) who landed in an unpromoted indigenous site would be just another foreigner, and their history would die with him. Instead, if they landed along with a community with *conubium*, the possibility of him perpetuating his presence and of us following the trail of his activities and descendants over time would increase considerably. Due to the peculiarities of the documentation, we cannot determine what part of the Latin onomastics of the Iberian Peninsula is attributable to Italic immigration. Its importance is undoubted, but it is not sufficient by itself to explain the volume of recorded examples, especially if we consider that the existence of promoted communities that possessed the *ius conubii*, as seems to be the case for *Latini*, is not usually accepted.

39 This statement by Kubitschek ("*Sergiam in Hispanis oppidis ad liberae rei publicae tempora recedere, Galeriam ad Augustum, Quirinam ad Vespasianum*", J. W. Kubitschek, *Imperium Romanum tributim discriptum* (Roma 1972), 169) has in recent years been the subject of an appeal for caution by Fasolini, who considers that it should be applied literally in all cases, see (D. Fasolini, 'La compresenza di tribù nelle città della Peninsola Iberica: il caso della *Tarraconensis*', in Hispania *y la epigrafía romana. Cuatro perspectivas*, ed. J. F. Rodríguez Neila (Faenza 2009), 179; D. Fasolini, 'L'ascrizione tribale delle comunità iberiche: il caso della Tarraconense', in *Le tribù romane. Atti della XVI$^{e}$ Rencontre sur l'épigraphie*, ed. M. Silvestrini (Bari 2010), 10–11, 89; D. Fasolini, *Le tribù romane della* Hispania Tarraconensis. *L'iscrizione tribale dei cittadini romani nelle testimonianze epigrafiche* (Milan 2012), 10).

40 A. U. Stylow, 'Apuntes sobre las tribus romanas en *Hispania*', *Veleia* 12 (1995) 105–124. F. C. Tweedie, 'The *Lex Licinia Mucia* and the *Bellum Italicum*' in S. T. Roselaar (ed.), *Processes of Integration and Identity Formation in the Roman Republic* (Leiden–Boston 2012), 117–118.

41 M. C. de la Escosura Balbás, *La población de* Carthago Nova *de la conquista al Principado. Epigrafía y onomástica* (Barcelona 2021).

### 2.2 *Grants* ob honorem

The status of 'Roman citizen' was not unambiguous and monolithic, nor did the rights associated with them belong only and exclusively to 'citizens'. The necessity and predisposition of Romans either to grant Roman citizenship (fully or with restrictions), or to grant foreigners or foreign communities some rights belonging to 'citizens', transformed foreigners into the driving force of the development of the legal system and, therefore, the state ideology.[42] Rome's experiences associated with its Mediterranean expansion led it to maintain and develop this type of attitude towards the granting of Roman citizenship, even though it retained its privileged character until very late in the Empire. Before the beginning of the Mediterranean expansion, archaic Roman law was not generous to 'foreigners', who were defined by the same word as the enemy, *hostis*, as seen in the Law of the Twelve Tables. However, as we move forward in time, we can observe how the categories of 'citizen' and 'foreigner' changed. They become more nuanced as new laws or situations appeared that changed their content and their use, both legally and in their practical application to social, commercial, or political realities.[43]

Individual grants of Roman citizenship have generated much controversy since ancient times. This is demonstrated, for example, by the court case against *L. Cornelius Balbus* from the Republican period, as recorded by Cicero in *Pro Balbo*, or the later correspondence between Pliny the Younger and the emperor Trajan that deals with a request for Roman citizenship for the doctor of the then *propraetor* of *Bithynia*.[44] For whom, how, and under what circumstances these grants were carried out are still questions to which researchers cannot find unanimous answers. Some have argued that Roman colonial law gave the *triumviri* a broad capacity to offer citizenship and land, and to register settlers.[45] Other authors have reasoned that, in the late Republican era, the official program was set aside to grant citizenship through individual political

42 Liv. 9.20.10; T. J. Chiusi, 'Lo straniero come compartecipe dell'esperienza giuridica. A proposito dello stato giuridico dello straniero a Roma', in *I diritti degli altri in Grecia e a Roma*, ed. L. Gagliardi and A. Maffi (Sankt Augustin 2011), 39–44; E. García Riaza, 'Sobre los mecanismos de integración de los vencidos en el Occidente romano-republicano: algunas observaciones', in Vae Victis! *Perdedores en el Mundo Antiguo*, ed. F. Marco Simón, F. Pina Polo and J. Remesal Rodríguez, (Barcelona 2012), 162.

43 S. Randazzo, 'Gli equilibri della cittadinanza romana, fra sovranità e impatto sociale', in *Integration in Rome and in the Roman World*, ed. G. De Kleijn and S. Benoist (Leiden 2014), 26–27, with related bibliography.

44 Plin. *Ep.* 10.5–7, 10.10.

45 C. González Román, 'La ciudadanía, un proceso histórico de integración en la Roma republicana', in *Ciudadanos y extranjeros en el mundo antiguo: segregación e integración*, ed. J. Mangas Manjarrés and S. Montero Herrero (Madrid 2007), 210.

actions, under the cover of ordinary legislation and the extraordinary powers granted to generals on campaign.[46]

However, the sources also indicate the existence of a series of laws that granted certain magistrates the capacity to grant Roman citizenship under a series of specific conditions. The *lex Appuleia de coloniis in Siciliam Achaiam Macedoniam deducendis* (100 BC) allowed Marius to grant citizenship to three inhabitants of each colony he founded. The *lex Iulia de civitate Latinis et sociis danda* (90 BC) granted citizenship to the free inhabitants of Latium[47] and the ability to grant citizenship to the generals of the Social War if they secured the intervention of their *consilium*.[48] The *lex Gellia Cornelia de civitate danda* (72 BC) followed the pattern of the two previous ones in granting this capacity to Pompey and Metellus. Finally, the *lex Munatia Aemilia* (42 BC) granted the same to Octavian and Mark Antony.[49] The existence of specific laws giving magistrates this power, and the fact that they all pertain to specific cases, seem to reinforce the idea of the need for a specific legal basis for granting citizenship. Therefore, it seems that this power was not part of the *imperium*, an idea that we find, for example, in Badian's treatment of Marius's concessions.[50] We can situate Cicero's speech in his defence of Archias in the same light, where he explains how Lucullus could not personally grant him citizenship, but he could have asked Metellus for it.[51]

46 L. Amela Valverde, 'Las concesiones de ciudadanía romana: Pompeyo Magno e *Hispania*', *MHA* 21–22 (2000–2001), 93.

47 I am aware of the historiographical problems that have been debated pertaining to the application of the laws *Iulia* (90 BC), *Calpurnia*, and *Plautia Papiria* (89 BC) which granted, *grosso modo*, Roman citizenship to all of Italy and transformed *Transpadani* into *Latini*. Luraschi extensively addressed the issue (1978). A review of the research on the subject can be found in S. Barbati, 'Gli studi sulla cittadinanza romana prima e dopo le ricerche di Giorgio Luraschi', *RDR* 12 (2012), 1–46. On the implementation of the *lex Iulia* in the Italic *municipia*, see L. Gagliardi, 'Droit romain et droits locaux dans les municipes italiques avant la "*lex Iulia de civitate*"', *RD* 94 (2016), 369–391.

48 It cannot be determined at this stage whether or not the *lex Iulia* known from the Bronze of Ascoli (*CIL* I$^2$, 709; *CIL* VI, 37045; EDR072269) is the same general law for Italy or another law with the same name and more specific content.

49 B. Periñán Gómez, 'Apuntes sobre la "*Lex Gellia Cornelia de civitate danda*"', in *Derecho, persona y ciudadanía. Una experiencia jurídica comparada*, ed. B. Periñán Gómez (Madrid 2010), 557–558.

50 Badian 1958, op. cit., 260–261.

51 Cic. *Arch.* 26: *Archias* was a member of Lucullus' army and had never served with Metellus. It can be assumed that Lucullus did not have a law authorizing him to create new citizens and that is why *Archias* took advantage of the *lex Plautia Papiria*. See M. Tarpin, 'Strangers in Paradise. Latins (and some other non-Romans) in Colonial Context. A Short

Moreover, the perception of Roman citizenship as an enormous privilege in the eyes of Rome is incompatible with the massive concessions by which some authors explain the large amount of Latin onomastics in *Hispania*. The presence of laws regulating the power to grant citizenship, and the information on specific cases that benefited from such, show that a part of this onomastics must be explained by grants *ob honorem*. One example would be that of *L. Cornelius Balbus* and the *lex Gellia Cornelia* of 72 BC or that of the *turma Sallvitana* and the *lex Iulia* of 90 BC. However, these same laws are evidence that massive concessions, such as the ones being proposed in relation to *clientelae*, likely could not have been made.

### 2.3 Nomina *by* imitatio

The usurpation of the *tria nomina* has often been related to the phenomenon of *clientelae*. It has been and still is one of the workhorses of historiography to explain Latin onomastics in the provinces, and has been considered a way of measuring the degree of 'Romanisation'.[52] This adoption of Roman *nomina* by natives would have been a response to their need to impress both their peers and the Roman generals of the early Republic.[53] Some historians have pointed out how other factors such as fashion, emulation, and others that are not known may have influenced the 'Romanisation' of indigenous onomastics.[54] Thus, in practice, *peregrini* would have been allowed to bear a Roman name without being legally Roman citizens.

The main problem with *imitatio* as a valid answer to the question at hand is its illegality. The importance of the legal element with respect to citizenship, and the practical impossibility of *imitatio* on a large scale, are clearly shown in some of the sources. In 95 BC, the *lex Licinia Mucia*,[55] which owes its fame to being considered by Asconius to be the main reason for the outbreak of the *bellum sociale*, obliged everyone to return to their citizenship of origin by persecuting those who had usurped Roman citizenship. The reason behind that phenomenon was that "the appropriation of a citizenship not one's own

Story of Territorial Complexity', in *Roman Republican Colonization. New Perspectives from Archaeology and Ancient History*, ed. J. Pelgrom and T. D. Stek (Rome 2014), 178.

52 For instance, Knapp 1978, op. cit., 190.

53 Badian 1958, op. cit., 256.

54 I.e. Pina Polo 2013, op. cit., 70.

55 Asc. *Corn.* 67: *Nam cum summa cupiditate civitatis Romanae Italici populi tenerentur et ob id magna pars eorum pro civibus Romanis se gereret, necessaria lex visa est ut in suae quisque civitatis ius redigeretur.*

violates the integrity of the *ius civile*".[56] The ideological basis that explains this law, and with it part of the philosophy that lies behind the fight against the *nomina* by *imitatio*, is made clear in Cicero's words: *Nam esse pro cive, qui civis non sit, rectum est non licere, quam legem tulerunt sapientissimi consules Crassus et Scaevola. Usu vero urbis prohibere peregrinos, sane inhumanum est.*[57] Thus, although the law, as handed down by Asconius, refers to Italics, it is nevertheless a clear indication of the fight against illegality. Some authors dismiss the value of this law for the Hispanic case, arguing that there are no known cases of provincials being affected by it,[58] or that it did not have much effect.[59] Even if both positions may be true (the documentation at this point prevents us from determining this), the mere existence of the law is, in itself, a sign of Rome's legal struggle against *imitatio*. Once the conflict was over, the *leges Iulia* of 90 BC and *Plautia Papiria* of 89 BC favoured access to the status of citizenship. In order to correct the excesses resulting from their application, the *lex Papia de peregrinis* was approved in 65 BC, which classified *usurpatio civitatis* as a criminal offence, and therefore such cases needed to be tried by a specific court of law presided over by a magistrate *cum imperio*. The implementation of this plebiscite, which was a reaction to the massive grants of Roman citizenship,[60] entailed the expulsion from Rome of all non-Italian *peregrini* and the review of doubtful cases.[61]

A few years later, Cicero provided a very important reflection on the relationship between onomastics and citizenship: *census non ius civitatis confirmat ac tantum modo indicat eum qui sit census ita se iam tum gessisse pro cive.*[62] This passage, to which I referred earlier, highlights that the information found in the census should not be taken at face value, as it was possible to pass oneself off as a Roman citizen using onomastics. The fact that the sources point to this eventuality proves that *usurpatio* existed, but it also is clear that Rome was fighting against this type of illegality.

---

56 Asc. *Corn.* 67–8C. Stylow 2012, op. cit., 130. It should be noted that this was not a case, as with the *lex Claudia* of 177 BC, of a physical expulsion of *Latini* from Rome at the request of their communities (Liv. 41.8.6–8), which would have harmed the ideal of hospitality of the *ius gentium*.

57 Cic. *Off.* 3.47.

58 Badian 1958, op. cit., 256.

59 Amela Valverde 2001, op. cit., 256.

60 Periñán Gómez 2010, op. cit., 550.

61 This is why it subsequently became a political weapon against Caesar, by accusing *L. Cornelius Balbus*, which we know through Cicero's *pro Balbo* and its subsequent commentary by Asconius.

62 Cic. *Arch.* 5.11.

Finally, the clearest reference, even if it is from the Imperial period, is undoubtedly the reference by Suetonius to the decree of the emperor Claudius in which he forbids *peregrini* to use Roman names and condemns any violators to be executed on the Esquiline: *pereginae condicionis homines vetuit usurpare Romana nomina dum taxtat gentilicia. Civitatem R(omanam) usurpantes in campo Esquilino securi percussit.*[63]

The existence of laws that tried to contain and solve this problem is the first indication that the *nomina* by *imitatio* existed and that, consequently, a part of the onomastics in *Hispania* can be explained by this phenomenon, even though it is impossible for us to quantify it effectively. However, these same laws prove the impossibility of it being as common a practice as has been claimed. *Imitatio* was an illegal act and, as such, was liable to be prosecuted. It is difficult to accept that all an individual had to do to benefit from the prestige and benefits of Roman citizenship was to appropriate it, without any real danger of being judged, condemned, or delegitimised for doing so.[64]

Despite the temporal distance, the request for Roman citizenship that Pliny the Younger made to Trajan for his physician is very useful in understanding the extent to which citizenship was part of a legal framework that was not open to illegal circumvention. At a time in history when the emperor's power to act was far greater than any Republican magistrate could have imagined, Pliny and Trajan would have faced disproportionate legal problems if, as some scholars argue, grants of citizenship without legal support or *imitatio* were widely permitted. Trajan's initial grant was overridden by the legal requirement that Pliny's physician, an Egyptian, must have had Alexandrian citizenship before he could have been granted Roman citizenship. Only when the physician was granted Alexandrian citizenship could Trajan legally grant him Roman citizenship.

Cases like this, because of their significance rather than their chronological placement, are a strong argument for the impossibility of usurping the legal capacity to carry *duo nomina* in an official Roman juridical act during the Republic, as has been argued for the *turma Sallvitana* in the Bronze of Ascoli.[65] This legal and very public document, sanctioned by a *consilium* formally addressed and referenced (every one of them with *duo nomina*, filiations, and *tribus*) mentions three *Ilerdenses* with Latin *duo nomina* with indigenous

63 Suet. *Cl.* 25.3.

64 Simple usurpation "would devalue the worth and prestige that Roman citizenship conferred upon an individual within his indigenous community, its value as a *praemium*, and would unnecessarily yield an instrument which was useful for Rome in dissuading and controlling provincial elites", see García Fernández 2015, op. cit., 110.

65 *CIL* I$^2$, 709; *CIL* VI, 37045; EDR072269.

filiations: [*Q?*] Otacilius Suisertarten f.; Cn. Cornelius Nesille f. and P. [F]abius Enasagin f. The fact that the only three riders bearing *duo nomina* come from the same locality, *Ilerda*, points more to the Latin colonial status of their *civitas* of origin[66] than to a case of premature *imitatio*.[67]

### 2.4 Clientelae

Cliental relations have been explored by many authors, especially in the context of the last century of the Republic. As can be deduced from Pina Polo's work, clientelism was a voluntary relationship, without legal or contractual definition, of limited duration, between unequal parties, and which was non-exclusive, not bound by *gentes*, and whose hereditary character was not automatic.[68] We are essentially dealing with an extra-legal institution sanctioned by the *mos maiorum* and supported by the power of the social class structure.[69] According to Bandelli, taking up some of Badian's ideas, *clientelae* could be the result of a conquest. A cliental bond could prosper between a victorious general and the defeated individuals who offered him the *deditio*, between the settlers and the *triumviri* who carry out the *deductio* of a colony, or between the holders of an allocation of plots of land and the promoting magistrate.[70]

At this point, the acquisition of a Roman name could have taken place in two ways, which were not necessarily exclusive. On the one hand, the client could take the name of their *patronus* as a sign of respect. On the other hand, the patron himself who would grant their client Roman citizenship by giving them a new name, or by providing a legal cover for a previously usurped *tria*

66 In favor of the Latin status of *Ilerda*: A. Degrassi, *Inscriptiones Latinae liberae rei publicae: imagines* (Berlin 1965); Galsterer 1971, op. cit., and H. Galsterer, 'La trasformazione delle antiche colonie latine e il nuovo *ius Latii*', in *Pro populo Arimenese*, ed. A. Calbi and G. Susini (Faenza 1995), 79–94; Tarpin 2014, op. cit.; García Fernández 2015, op. cit.

67 For a review of the Hispanic cases considered as *conflicto* and their evaluation with criteria similar to those followed in this paper, please see García Fernández 2011, op. cit., 49–55 and 2015 op. cit., 111–118.

68 I.e., F. Pina Polo, 'Hispania of Caesar and Pompey. A Conflict of *Clientelae*?', in *Del* imperium *de Pompeyo a la* auctoritas *de Augusto. Homenaje a Michael Grant*, ed. M. P. García-Bellido, A. Mostalac and A. Jiménez (Madrid 2008), 41–48; Pina Polo 2011, op. cit.; Pina Polo 2013, op. cit.; and Pina Polo 2015, op. cit.

69 Badian 1958, op. cit., 159.

70 Bandelli 1988, op. cit., 53.

*nomina*.[71] As an extension of this second method, many authors propose that citizenship grants were a means of attracting clients.[72]

With the first method, we would once again face a case of *imitatio*, which I have just discussed. Then again, the supposed legal capacity of the *patronus* to grant Roman citizenship to his clients, either as a reward or as a way to attract them to his cause, collides with the evidence provided by the Roman legal *corpus*. There were laws such as the *Appuleia*, the *Iulia*, the *Gellia Cornelia*, and the *Munatia Aemilia*, which, as noted above, granted certain magistrates the capacity to grant citizenship at certain times and under certain circumstances. Their existence prevents us from being able to assume that a private citizen, even if he had *imperium*, could carry out a legal act of such importance on his own initiative with the support of the law.[73] Contrary to this opinion, Amela Valverde suggests that in the provincial world the senate would have allowed patrons to grant Roman citizenship to their clients, although it would have been prevented in Rome itself.[74]

However, given that a *patronus* had no legal capacity whatsoever over his client, as *clientelae* implied no legal bond, an individual could not in any case rely on his status as *patronus* to grant Roman citizenship to a client. That a Roman general, protected by a specific law, could grant Roman citizenship to an individual who happened to be his client was casuistic. It was not their patron-client relationship that allowed this, but the patron's status as a magistrate who was allowed to do so by a law that applied to a specific historical moment in time, under certain circumstances.

This debate is closely linked to the real influence these bonds must have had in Rome.[75] The representatives of the prosopographical school of the first half of the 20th century presented Roman politics merely as a conflict among *clientelae*, *gentes*, families, and factions or "parties". In the words of Gelzer, "the most powerful man was he who by virtue of his clients and friends could mobilize the greatest number of voters".[76] In contrast, authors such as Brunt

---

71 The author who repeats this idea more often is Amela Valverde, for instance 2000–2001, op. cit., 93.

72 I.e., González Román 2007, op. cit., 210.

73 Pina Polo 2015, op. cit., 28.

74 Amela Valverde 2000–2001, op. cit., 93.

75 On how Dionysius of Halicarnassus' vision of a golden age during the Republic (Dion. Hal. 2.9), even if not based on the facts, has determined the view of much of modern historiography, especially Brunt, and the methodological problem it poses, see A. Ganter, 'Decline and Glorification: Patron-Client Relationships in the Roman Republic', in *Foreign* Clientelae *in the Roman Empire. A Reconsideration*, ed. M. Jehne and F. Pina Polo (Stuttgart 2015).

76 M. Gelzer, *The Roman Nobility* (Oxford 1969), 139.

pointed out how the mobilisation of clients only had a marginal effect on elections, which makes sense if we consider that the same client could have several patrons.[77] However, the importance of their contribution to their patron's prestige and, therefore, their social importance seems quite clear. Not so its influence on the military sphere, where the game of alliances during the civil war between Caesar and Pompey demonstrated the limited effectiveness of cliental bonds.[78] The supposed strength of *clientelae* is further diminished in relation to the provinces, as is the case being examined here. The distance that generally separated these territories from Rome meant that patron and client often met only once in a lifetime. Even if the nature of the presence of Roman magistrates in the provinces made it possible to create a bond (which could be cliental), this was not a merely theoretical relationship; there had to be at least the possibility of securing practical results.[79] On the other hand, although Cicero speaks of the ancient custom of Roman commanders becoming the patron of their defeated enemies, and that this patronage was hereditary,[80] the reality represented by the documentation indicates that the defeated became *in fidem* to the *Senatus Populusque Romanus* and not to the *imperator*.[81] All of these elements reinforce the idea that the number of *clientelae* must have been proportionally small, and could not have been the basis of Roman rule.[82]

These ideas connect with the use of provincial prosopography to determine the relative number of *clientelae* and the identity of their patrons. The greatest exponent of this trend is Badian, with his defence of the new citizen-clients who bore the *nomen* of their patron and their own name as *cognomen* in the style of the freedmen.[83] Applying this to a specific case in the Iberian Peninsula, the remark of Caesar in *Bellum civile* of how *Hispania* was bound by favours to Pompey, using the term *clientela*,[84] has led to an over-estimation of the Pompeian peninsular *clientelae*. This has also been furthered by the high concentration of *nomina* derived from *Pompeius* recorded in High Imperial epigraphic documentation. According to Badian, these would have been the

77 P. A. Brunt, *The Fall of the Roman Republic and Related Essays* (Oxford 1988), 431.
78 Bandelli 1988, op. cit., 63.
79 Pina Polo 2013, op. cit., 71.
80 Cic. *Off.* 1.35.
81 Badian 1958, op. cit., 156; García Riaza 2012, op. cit., 164; E. García Riaza, 'Foreign Cities. Institutional Aspects of the Roman Expansion in the Iberian Peninsula (218–133 B.C.)', in *Foreign* Clientelae *in the Roman Empire. A Reconsideration*, ed. M. Jehne and F. Pina Polo (Stuttgart 2015), 137.
82 Pina Polo 2013, op. cit., 78.
83 Badian 1958, op. cit., 255.
84 Caes. *Civ.* 2.18.7: *Tamen constituerat nullam partem belli in Hispaniis relinquere, quod magna esse Pompei beneficia et magnas clientelas in Citeriore provincia sciebat.*

descendants of Pompey's original clients.[85] However, other authors have developed very different theories from the same material: Amela Valverde sees the accumulation of these *nomina* as evidence of acculturation and not as an identifier of *clientelae*.[86] In opposition, Balil Illana argues that the absence of large numbers of *Pompeii* from the Republican period is due to the fact that the Pompeians wanted their *clientelae* to go unnoticed and made their clients take other, less frequent *nomina*.[87] However, nothing in the documentation leads us to determine that patrons and clients always shared the same *nomen*, nor that the new citizens took, when becoming *cives*, the *nomen* of the magistrate who processed the grant.

The main problem facing the hypothesis of *clientelae* to explain onomastics lies in the proportions. Even accepting that there were cases in which the patron could grant citizenship to his clients, or admitting that some events were illegal and passed unnoticed by the Romans, it is difficult to argue that such a large number of *clientelae* existed in the Iberian Peninsula in the Republican period. In the last few years, a new body of research has redefined the phenomenon of *clientelae* both in Rome and in the provinces. Thus, just as it is wrong to speak of massive concessions, it is also wrong to speak of massive numbers of *clientelae*.[88] About these data, we consider that in no case can we ascribe the *tria nomina* in the Iberian Peninsula to *clientelae*. If any were related to them, they should be included in the group of *ob honorem* grants or in that of the *nomina* by *imitatio*, which implies a usurpation of citizenship. Thus, the role of *clientelae* is not a viable hypothesis to the problem under discussion.

## 3 The Latin Colonies and their *iura*

Latin colonies in Italy before 89 BC had been grated four *iura*: *commercium*, *conubium*, *ius migrandi*, and *ius suffragii*. Although we do not know for certain, it appears that only the first two were granted to Hispania's colonies.[89] The

85 Badian 1958, op. cit., 278–279.

86 Amela Valverde 2001, op. cit., 259.

87 A. Balil Illana, 'Riqueza y sociedad en la España romana (ss. III–I a.C.)', *Hispania* 99 (1965), 348.

88 Jehne and Pina Polo 2015, op. cit.

89 García Fernández 2001, op. cit., 82; E. García Fernández, 'Reflexiones sobre la latinización de Hispania en época republicana', in Hispaniae. *Las provincias hispanas en el mundo romano*, ed. J. Andreu Pintado, J. Cabrero Piquero and I. Rodà de Llanza (Tarragona 2009), 384.

*conubium* sanctions a mixed marriage as *iustum* that is according to law.[90] If a Roman citizen married a local woman with *conubium*, their children would be legitimate by Roman law. Those children would have been granted the ability to inherit from their parents due to the *ius commercii*, which imparted the ability to participate in an *ius civile* act as a Roman citizen. This includes the assumption of the citizenship of their father.[91] Therefore, the situation in the Latin colonies would have allowed the coexistence of two different types of citizenships in a cohesive community. Nevertheless, all these topics are controversial.

In Hispania, the Roman administration settled on a system based on different kinds of *civitates peregrinorum*: *liberae* or free, *foederatae* or those bonded to Rome by a treaty, whether *aequum* or *iniquum*, and *stipendiariae*, who paid taxes. All of these were problematic for the settlement of the Italic immigrants who had Roman or Latin status. They would have been cut out from the community they lived in. These immigrants would have had problems conducting business with the local inhabitants of the *civitas*, but the local laws could have been used to solve these problems. Their newly born children would be illegitimate from the Roman point of view. This could be resolved by the promotion of these communities, which would be granted the necessary *iura* to avoid those problems. For this purpose, Rome established Roman and Latin colonies. The first one was like a little Rome, operating under the juridical conditions of the *Urbs*. In Hispania, these date back to the Pompey-Caesar era. The Latin colonies had only some of the *iura* of the Roman system, but enough to allow the Italic immigrants to settle down, have a family, and make their *gens* thrive: *conubium et commercium*.[92] That is, "attrarre le istituzioni locali verso i modelli civilistici romani".[93] We know for certain of the existence of these type of colonies in Hispania. They have been documented since the second century BC by literary sources (*Carteia*), monetary inscriptions (*Saguntum*), onomastics (*Carthago Nova, Ilerda*), or a combination of

90 Tit. Ulp. 5.3; Gai. *Inst.* 1.56.

91 Sherwin-White 1973, op. cit., 33–34.

92 L. Capogrossi Colognesi, '*Ius commercii, conubium, civitas sine suffragio*. Le origini del diritto internazionale privato e la romanizzazione delle comunità latino-campane', in *Le strade del potere*. Maiestas populi Romani: imperium, coercitio, commercium, ed. A. Corbino (Catania 1994), 24; S. T. Roselaar, 'The Concept of *Commercium* in the Roman Republic', *Phoenix* 66 (2012), 381–413, and S. T. Roselaar, 'The Concept of *Conubium* in the Roman Republic', in *New Frontiers: Law and Society in the Roman World*, ed. P. du Plessis (Edinburgh 2013), 102–122.

93 L. Capogrossi Colognesi, *Cittadini e territorio. Consolidamento e trasformazione della* 'ciuitas Romana' (Rome 2000), 143.

sources (*Valentia, Pollentia, Palma, Tarraco, Italica, Corduba, Gracchuris, Iesso, Gerunda, Lucentum, Ercavica, Valeria*).[94]

Only when these Italic immigrants and traders had set up in these promoted communities can we trace their history and the *iura* they brought with them. When a single immigrant settled down in a local community with a local set of laws, we are unable to ascertain if it was a temporary situation or if he had settled down and had children who carried on the business. Yet, if he settled in a Latin community, we could trace the transmission of his *nomina* through the generations. This is possible if we have a consistent sample of onomastic data over the years, as is the case for *Carthago Nova*. This data allows me to determine that *Carthago Nova* was a Latin colony. For such a record to make sense there must have been *conubium* and *commercium* in place that allowed the sons and daughters of the immigrants to inherit their father's *nomina*.[95]

## 4 Two Conclusive Case Studies: Carthago Nova and Carteia, Latin Colonies

Before the beginning of the Second Punic war, Rome had stablished commercial routes with the Hispanic Levante ports. This has been established not only by archaeological remains but also by epigraphic and literary sources. When war between the two great powers arrived in *Hispania*, Rome took advantage of its victories for a quick conquest, and an ensuing wave of settlement. This situation created new circumstances for the long-established traders who

94 Liv. 43.3.1–4 for *Carteia* dated 171 BC. de la Escosura Balbás 2021, op. cit. for *Carthago Nova* dated late second century BC. A. M. Canto, '*Colonia Patricia Corduba*: Nuevas hipótesis sobre su fundación y nombre', *Latomus* 50 (1991), 145–182 for *Italica* dated 126 BC. M. J. Pena Gimeno, 'Problemas históricos en torno a la fundación de Valencia', in *Valencia y las primeras ciudades romanas de Hispania*, ed. J. L. Jiménez Salvador and A. Ribera (Valencia 2012), 275–276 for *Valentia* dated 138 BC. see M. J. Pena Gimeno, 'La tribu *Velina* en Mallorca y los nombres de Palma y Pollentia', *Faventia* 26, no. 4 (2004), 69–90: 76 for *Palma* and *Pollentia* dated 122 BC. J. F. Rodríguez Neila, 'Introducción histórica', in *Las capitales provinciales de Hispania, Córdoba. Colonia Patricia Corduba*, ed. X. Dupré Raventós (Rome 2004) 7–20, 8 for *Corduba* dated 169/168 or 152/151 BC. D. Espinosa Espinosa, 'Reflexiones sobre la probable promoción de *Cesse/Tarraco* a colonia latina', *Klio* 98, no. 2 (2016) 570–604, 595 for *Tarraco*, dated 150/125 or 109/108 BC. The category *oppidum Latinorum veterum* in the *Historia Naturalis* of Pliny the Elder. cfr. D. Espinosa Espinosa, *Plinio y los* "oppida *de antiguo Lacio". El proceso de difusión del Latium en Hispania Citerior* (Oxford 2014) for *Gracchuris, Iesso, Gerunda, Lucentum, Ercavica* and *Valeria*. The Bronze of Ascoli (*CIL* I$^2$, 709; *CIL* VI, 37045; EDR072269) for *Ilerda*. P. P. Ripollès and J. Velaza, 'Saguntum, colonia latina', *ZPE* 141 (2002), 285–291 for *Saguntum*.

95 De la Escosura Balbás 2021, op. cit.

operated in those ports, especially those that had supported the Roman conquest: *Tarraco*, the military base, and *Carthago Nova*, the civil centre. With the creation of two *provinciae* in the Iberian Peninsula in *c.*197 BC, the *Ulterior* in the south and the *Citerior* in the Levante, *Tarraco* and *Carthago Nova* shared the status of capital of the *Citerior*. The rotating status of provincial capital depended on the residence of the governor at the time, which changed according to the period of the year.[96]

In 171 BC, the Senate agreed to the request of an embassy and granted the foundation of a Latin colony in *Carteia*, a Punic port that ran part of the "Circle of the Straits". The new colonists were a group of children of mixed unions without *conubium* between Roman soldiers and Hispanic women – and who were, therefore, illegitimate – and the Punics of the former *Carteia*.[97] The inscriptions from *Carteia* are scarce, especially those from the Republic. However, *Carteia* minted coins from 120 BC to the first century AD. The onomastics of the minting magistrates (*quaestores*, *quattuorviri*, or *censores* when the title is acknowledged) have a *duo/tria nomina* structure as dictated by Roman law. Therefore, the names in the legends must have been their official *duo nomina*, as it is highly unlikely that an illegal name would have been used in a legal document. Some of these *nomina* are understood as Semitic, while others are Italic. Hence, these immigrants (or their descendant), as result of the *iura* of the Latin colony, could have used the same privileges granted to them in Italy or inherited from their Italic parents.

*Carthago Nova* had a safe sea harbour and an exceptional position on the commerce routes connecting the Iberian Peninsula with Northern Africa. The city was a focal point for both the interior lands as well as the outlying sea. Moreover, the surrounding mountains contained large quantities of silver and lead, which were intensively mined by Iberians, Punics, and Romans, and which had attracted numerous Roman-Italics immigrants since the second century BC. Literary sources describe its unique geographical position and its flourishing economy, but do not mention its political situation or the status of its inhabitants. The city attained a level of importance that hardly seems

96 Str. 2.4.20. In favor of *Carthago Nova* as the only capital: G. Alföldy, *Tarraco* (Tarragona 1991), 24, 38, 55; E. Conde Guerri, *La ciudad de* Carthago Nova: *la documentación literaria (inicios-Julioclaudios)* (Murcia 2003), 110. In favor of *Tarraco* as the only capital: J. Ruiz De Arbulo Bayona, '*Tarraco, Carthago Nova* y el problema de la capitalidad en la *Hispania citerior* republicana', in *Miscel.lània arqueològica a Josep M. Recasens* (Tarragona 1992), 127–128.

97 Liv. 43.3.

compatible with the condition of *civitas stipendiaria*, and in the Imperial era Pliny mentions that it was a Roman colony.[98]

Conversely, onomastic data from *Carthago Nova* proves that the city must have been a Latin colony since, perhaps, the second century BC.[99] Of the 322 individuals recorded at *Carthago Nova* from 300 BC to AD 130, 319 had *duo/tria nomina*, a Roman onomastic structure, including the 123 registered during the Republic. All of them had *praenomina, nomina, filiatio/libertinitas* or *servitus*, and sometimes *cognomina*. If we had found these names at *Carteia*, we would have considered them Latins automatically; excepting, of course, the 57 individuals who are Roman (mention of *tribus*, Roman magistrates, etc.). However, Latin status has never been ascribed to the Carthaginians before. Moreover, it is possible to establish some examples of *nomina* transmission throughout all of the period studied. Without *conubium* and *commercium*, it would have been impossible to transmit these *nomina* through the generations, or even to give birth to legitimate children. Furthermore, this status would have allowed the immigrants from the Republic to flourish in *Carthago Nova*, which was one of the largest ports of the Mediterranean, one of the most thriving mining operations in the Roman world of the late second century and beginning of first century BC, and the capital of the soon-to-be largest Roman *provincia*. Only a Latin colony would be able to achieve this level of success without thwarting the ambitions of the Romans of Italy. Rome used the most uncomplicated set of laws, the Republican *ius Latii*, to create the perfect landscape to support those ambitions.

---

98 Plin. *NH*. 3.13. Abascal Palazón, placing it on 54 BC, identifying Pompey as ultimate responsible, has given the earliest dating for this legal promotion, see J. M. Abascal Palazón, 'La fecha de la promoción colonial de *Carthago Nova* y sus repercusiones edilicias', *Mastia* 1 (2002), 27.

99 De la Escosura Balbás 2021, op. cit.

CHAPTER 4

# *Quattuorviratus* and *Latium* in *Hispania*

*David Espinosa Espinosa*

## 1 Introduction

This work aims to propose a coherent interpretation for the presence of the *quattuorviratus* in the historical evidence belonging to a group of *coloniae* and *municipia* from *Hispania*, both in Republican and Imperial times. To this end, the historiographical views regarding the legal and administrative meaning of the *quattuorviratus* in the Hispanian provinces are assessed. Also, the literary, epigraphic, and numismatic references to the *quattuorviratus* coming from such *coloniae* and *municipia* are examined. Finally, as a novelty, the existence of a group of Latin colonies in *Hispania* during the Republic is considered. The result is a new proposal that explains the origin and presence of the *quattuorviratus* in the Hispanian provinces because of its establishment in some of these Latin colonies following Caesar's praetorship in *Hispania Ulterior* (61–60 BC) and the *bellum Civile* (49–45 BC).

The literary, epigraphic, and numismatic evidence belonging to certain *coloniae* and *municipia* from *Hispania* provides precious information related to the presence of the *quattuorviratus* within their political and administrative structure, both in Republican and Imperial times. This issue goes hand in hand with the granting of the Latin rights and Roman citizenship to peregrine communities, and it is part of the colonization and municipalization processes undertaken by Roman magistrates in both Italy and the Roman provinces.[1] In general, two main political and administrative structures have

1 For the specific cases of Italy, *Gallia Narbonensis*, and *Hispania*, see, for instance, A. Degrassi, '*Quattuorviri* in colonie romane e in municipi retti da *duoviri*', in *Scritti vari di antichità raccolti da amici e allievi nel 75° compleanno dell'autore I*, ed. A. Degrassi (Rome 1962a), 99–177; J. Gascou, 'Duumvirat, quattuorvirat et statut dans les cités de Gaule Narbonnaise', in *Epigrafia. Actes du colloque international d'épigraphie latine en mémoire de Attilio Degrassi pour le centenaire de sa naissance* (Rome 1991), 547–563; U. Laffi, 'Sobre la organización administrativa de Italia después de la Guerra social', in *Sociedad y política en la Roma republicana (siglos III–I a.C.)*, ed. E. Gabba and U. Laffi (Pisa 2000a), 79–94; U. Laffi, 'La Italia romana: ciudades y estructuras administrativas', in *Sociedad y política en la Roma republicana (siglos III–I a.C.)*, ed. E. Gabba and U. Laffi (Pisa 2000b), 25–40; and U. Laffi, 'La struttura costituzionale nei municipi e nelle colonie romane. Magistrati, decurioni, popolo', in *Gli statuti municipali*, ed.

 | DOI:10.1163/9789004685734_005

been identified in *coloniae Romanae*, *municipia civium Romanorum*, *coloniae Latinae*, and *municipia Latina* (the last of which were exclusive to the western Roman provinces) since the *bellum Sociale* (91–87 BC): *quattuorviratus* and *duumviratus* plus *aedilitas*. The first was the result of the election of a college of four magistrates (*quattuorviri*), who assumed in pairs judicial and aedilician functions by *sortitio* or collegiate decision. The second consisted of the election of a college of two magistrates with judicial functions (*duumviri*), to which was added the election of a second college of two magistrates with aedilician functions (*aediles*).[2]

This seemingly simple system is much more complex if the local evidence is analysed town by town over time and throughout the Roman geography, due to the presence of several variants (*quattuorviri*, *quattuorviri iure dicundo*, *quattuorviri aedilicia potestate*, *quattuorviri aediles*, *duumviri*, *duumviri iure dicundo*, *duumviri aedilicia potestate*, *duumviri aediles*, *aediles duumviri*, and *aediles*).

---

L. Capogrossi Colognesi and E. Gabba (Pavia 2006), 109–132; E. García Fernández, *El municipio latino. Origen y desarrollo constitucional* (Madrid 2001); A. D. Pérez Zurita, 'Reflexiones en torno al cuatorvirato en la *Hispania* romana', *Polis* 16 (2004), 133–168; A. D. Pérez Zurita, 'El cuatorvirato y la promoción jurídica de los municipios hispanos', *Revista General de Derecho Romano* 5 (2005); E. Bispham, *From* Asculum *to Actium. The Municipalization of Italy from the Social War to Augustus* (Oxford 2007), 247–379; E. Melchor Gil, '*Quattuorviri y aediles* en los municipios de constitución cuatorviral a fines de la República y en época altoimperial', *RSA* 43 (2013a), 133–152; S. Sisani, 'Le magistrature locali delle comunità municipali di ambito provinciale: uno studio sulla diffusione del quattuorvirato e del duovirato tra l'età tardo-repubblicana e l'età imperiale', *Gerión* 36 (1) (2018a), 41–77; S. Sisani, 'Il duovirato nei municipia italici: contributo allo studio della fase finale del processo di municipalizzazione nell'Italia centrale e meridionale', *Gerión* 39 (1) (2021), 41–93.

2 In the opinion of Sisani (2021, op. cit., 69), the difference between *quattuorviratus* and *duumviratus* went beyond the name; in other words, "la distinzione tra i due assetti magistratuali risiedeva in primo luogo nel diverso modo di creazione: se nel caso del collegio dei *quattuorviri* l'elezione avveniva congiuntamente per tutti e quattro i magistrati e la ripartizione tra la funzione giurisdicente e quella edilitaria era operata tra gli eletti tramite sorteggio o accordi interni, il duovirato si presentava già in fase di candidatura rigidamente bipartito nei due collegi *iure dicundo* e *aedilicia potestate*, ciascuno eletto separatamente". On this issue, see also Laffi 2000a, op. cit., 112; Sisani 2021, op. cit., 65. For a gradual development of the *quattuorviratus*, which was initially created without any difference of functions among its members, see Bispham 2007, op. cit., 247–379. For a comprehensive overview of these political and administrative structures, see Degrassi 1962a, op. cit.; A. Degrassi, 'Duoviri aedilicia potestate, duoviri aediles, aediles duoviri', in *Scritti vari di antichità raccolti da amici e allievi nel 75° compleanno dell'autore I*, ed. A. Degrassi (Rome 1962b), 179–184; A. Degrassi, 'Sul duovirato nei municipi italici', in *Scritti vari di antichità raccolti da amici e allievi nel 75° compleanno dell'autore I*, ed. A. Degrassi (Rome 1962c), 185–192; Laffi 2000a, op. cit.; Laffi 2000b, op. cit.; Laffi 2006, op. cit.; Bispham 2007, op. cit., 247–404; Sisani 2018a, op. cit. and Sisani 2021, op. cit.

An added factor would be the apparent coexistence of both structures in the same town (as in the case of *Aceruntia*, *Clusium*, *Marruvium*, *Nola*, *Tarentum*, *Paestum*, *Perusia*, *Pompeii*, *Sora*, *Teanum Sidicinum*, and *Verulae* in Italy; *Aeso*, *Asido*, *Edeta*, *Gades*, *Ilipula Minor*, *Munigua*, *Obulco*, and *Sabora* in *Hispania*; *Antipolis*, *Aquae Sextiae*, *Avennio Cavarum*, and *Vienna* in *Gallia Narbonensis*; and *Tingi* in *Mauretania Tingitana*, among others).[3] It also contributes to a greater complexity and the lack of consensus concerning the legal and administrative meaning of the *quattuorviratus* in both Italy and the Roman provinces, whose naming has acquired a significant flexibility depending on the historiographical approach considered. This enables, for instance, the joint identification of the two pairs of *quattuorviri* (the college of *quattuorviri* per se), but also the grouping of the colleges of *duumviri* and *aediles*.[4] This fact hinders the application of the *quattuorviratus* as a precise and solid criterion to establish the legal and administrative status of the Roman towns, which, in turn, results in a more difficult understanding of the origin and development of this political and administrative structure and leaves the researcher at the mercy of the historical evidence preserved. Finally, it also does not help that some scholars accept the presence of Roman magistrates with Latin onomastics (concretely, *praetores*, *quaestores*, and *aediles*) within some provincial communities (allegedly peregrine) during the Republican period as a transcription of native magistrates, which makes the general historical analysis even more unclear.[5]

---

3 For an overall picture of both matters, see below; Degrassi 1962a, op. cit.; Degrassi 1962c, op. cit.; L. A. Curchin, *The Local Magistrates of Roman Spain* (Toronto 1990); L. A. Curchin, *A Supplement to the Local Magistrates of Roman Spain* (Waterloo 2015); Gascou 1991, op. cit.; Pérez Zurita 2004, op. cit.; Pérez Zurita 2005, op. cit.; Bispham 2007, op. cit., 247–379; Melchor Gil 2013a, op. cit.; G. Bernard and L. Callegarin, 'La titulature des magistrats et le statut de la cité de Tanger d'après l'épigraphie monétaire', in *Le forme municipali in Italia e nelle province occidentali tra i secolo I a.C. e III d.C.*, ed. S. Evangelisti and C. Ricci (Bari 2017), 183–192; Sisani 2018a, op. cit. and Sisani 2021, op. cit.

4 On these issues, see below.

5 This approach has been suggested by scholars such as A. U. Stylow, 'El *municipium Flavium V*(---) de Azuaga (Badajoz) y la municipalización de la *Baeturia Turdulorum*', *SHHA* 9 (1991), 23; J. F. Rodríguez Neila, 'Gestión administrativa en las comunidades indígenas hispanas durante la etapa pre-municipal', in *Actas del I Coloquio de Historia Antigua de Andalucía (Córdoba 1988), vol. 1*, ed. J. F. Rodríguez Neila (Córdoba 1993), 385–387, 398, and 401–405; F. Chaves Tristán, 'El papel de los itálicos en la amonedación hispana', *Gerión* 17 (1999), 306; E. Melchor Gil, 'Instituciones de gobierno de las comunidades hispanas no privilegiadas (s. III a.C.–s. I d.C.): *senatus y magistratus*', in *Magistrados locales de* Hispania. *Aspectos históricos, jurídicos, lingüísticos*, ed. E. Ortiz de Urbina Álava (Vitoria 2013b), 127, 129–132, and 136–139; E. Ortiz de Urbina Álava, 'Sobre los procesos de (re)organización institucional cívica en *Hispania*', in *Magistrados locales de* Hispania. *Aspectos históricos, jurídicos, lingüísticos*, ed. E. Ortiz de Urbina Álava (Vitoria 2013), 282–284 and 287–289; A. D. Pérez Zurita, 'La implantación de la edilidad en *Hispania*: adopción y adaptación del modelo romano-itálico',

Besides, the above historical and methodological questions, the evidence of the *quattuorviratus* in *Hispania* is scarce, fragmentary, and difficult to date compared to the situation in Italy. In addition, based on the literary, archaeological, epigraphic, and numismatic evidence, there is an increasing awareness that the institutional history of the Hispanian towns was much deeper during Republican times and the rule of Augustus than that usually proposed because of new research approaches concerning a larger granting of the Latin rights in the western Roman provinces.[6] However, apart from the explicit references

in *De Roma a las provincias: las elites como instrumento de proyección de Roma. Juan Francisco Rodríguez Neila* in honorem, ed. A. Caballos Rufino and E. Melchor Gil (Seville 2014), 499–506, 520–521; S. Sisani, 'Latinità non latina: lo *ius Latii* come strumento di integrazione delle comunità provinciali in età repubblicana', *Gerión* 36 (2) (2018b), 341–343, among others. For example, the *praetor M. Trahius C. f.* from *Italica* (Santiponce, Seville: *HEp* 16, 2007, 535; Curchin 1990, op. cit., no. 975), the *quaestor Cn. Iulius L. f.* from *Corduba* (Córdoba, Córdoba: *CNH*, 401 and 402 no. 1–4; Curchin 1990, op. cit., no. 77), the *quaestores L. Ap. Dec.* and *Marcius* from *Urso* (Osuna, Seville: *CNH*, 367–368 no. 1–7; Curchin 1990, op. cit., no. 288 and 1054), the *quaestores C. Munius, C. Lucienus, L. Trinius L. f., T. Ahius T. f., C. Numius*, and *L. Coranius* from *Valentia* (Valencia, Valencia: *CNH*, 317 no. 1 and 4, 318 no. 8; Curchin 1990, op. cit., no. 950–955), the *aedilis L. Folcenius* from *Acinipo* (Ronda la Vieja, Málaga: *CNH*, 393 no. 12; Curchin 1990, op. cit., no. 5), the *aediles Cn. Baebius Glabrio, L. Calpurnius, L. Aemilius, M. Aemilius, M. Fabius*, and *M. Popilius Ru*[---] from *Saguntum* (Sagunto, Valencia: *CNH*, 312 no. 64, 313 no. 66, and 314 no. 75; Curchin 1990, op. cit., no. 844–845, 1172–1173, and 1186–1191), the *aedilis L. Aponius* from *Baelo* (Bolonia, Cádiz: *CNH*, 124 no. 6; Curchin 1990, op. cit., no. 28), the *aediles L. Aemilius* and *M. Iunius* from *Obulco* (Porcuna, Jaén: *CNH*, 347–349 no. 44–58; Curchin 1990, op. cit., no. 211–212), and the *aedilis M. Coranus Acrini f. Alpis* from *Sabetum* (La Rambla, Córdoba: *CIL* II$^2$/5, 521; Curchin 1990, op. cit., no. 272). Without ruling out the possibility that some of them can be explained in that way (although the legal and administrative status of these towns is unknown in most cases), the Italic provenance of these magistrates and the likely status of Latin colonies for some of these towns (as in the case of *Italica, Corduba, Valentia*, and *Saguntum*) bring a bigger complexity for the historical interpretation, so an alternative explanation is needed. See, for instance, García Fernández 2001, op. cit.; E. García Fernández, 'Movilidad, onomástica e integración en *Hispania* en época republicana: algunas observaciones metodológicas', in *Viajes y cambios de residencia en el mundo romano*, ed. J. M. Iglesias Gil and A. Ruiz Gutiérrez (Santander 2011), 47–66; E. García Fernández, '*Clientela* y difusión onomástica en *Hispania*: algunas observaciones sobre la documentación de Sagunto', in *Los espacios de la esclavitud y la dependencia desde la antigüedad. (Homenaje a Domingo Plácido. Actas del XXXV coloquio del GIREA)*, ed. A. Beltrán, I. Sastre and M. Valdés (Besançon 2015a), 589–605; P. P. Ripollès and J. Velaza Frías, '*Saguntum*, colonia latina', *ZPE* 141 (2002), 285–291; D. Espinosa Espinosa, *Plinio y los* 'oppida *de antiguo Lacio'. El proceso de difusión del* Latium *en* Hispania Citerior (Oxford 2014); D. Espinosa Espinosa, 'The Question of the *oppida veteris Latii* in Pliny the Elder's *Naturalis Historia*', *CQ* 68 (1) (2018), 232–245.

6 See, for instance, M. I. Henderson, 'Julius Caesar and *Latium* in Spain', *JRS* 32 (1942), 1–13; D. Roman, 'Aix-en-Provence et les débuts de la colonisation de droit latin en Gaule du Sud', *RAN* 20 (1987), 185–190; García Fernández 2001, op. cit.; Espinosa Espinosa 2014, op. cit.;

to *Carteia*, *Corduba*, *Saguntum*, *Palma*, *Pollentia*, and (with a higher degree of uncertainty) *Emporiae* as *coloniae*,[7] more news on the existence of *coloniae Latinae* in *Hispania* is likely lacking because those that survived the civil wars would be transformed into *coloniae Romanae*, *municipia civium Romanorum*, and *municipia Latina* by Caesar and Augustus.[8] This would have been the case of *Italica*, *Gracchuris*, *Carteia*, *Corduba*, *Valentia*, *Tarraco*, *Palma*, *Pollentia*, *Saguntum*, *Emporiae*, and *Carthago Nova*, which appear mentioned with one of these three legal and administrative statuses in Pliny the Elder's *Naturalis Historia*.[9] In this respect, the 50 pre-Flavian *municipia Latina* referred to as *oppida veteris Latii* and *oppida Latio antiquitus donata* by Pliny the Elder can be viewed as the clearer footprint of this administrative transformation process.[10] To these should be added an unknown number of *municipia Latina* created by Augustus through the granting of the Latin rights to certain *civitates*

---

Espinosa Espinosa 2018, op. cit. Even more reluctant scholars, such as P. Le Roux, 'Magistrats locaux et pouvoirs dans les cités des provinces hispaniques au Haut-Empire romain', in *Magistrados locales de* Hispania. *Aspectos históricos, jurídicos, lingüísticos*, ed. E. Ortiz de Urbina Álava (Vitoria 2013), 229–251, in the case of *Hispania*, have broadened their initial perspectives with statements such as "la mention récente, sur une monnaie, d'un édile de la colonie de Sagonte indique que les colonies latines étaient plus nombreuses qu'il n'a été dit à l'aube de la période augustéenne dans les provinces ibériques" (Le Roux, 2013, op. cit., 235; see also P. Le Roux, *L'Empire romain. Histoire et modèles. Scripta varia III* [Rennes 2022], 345).

7 For *Carteia*, see Liv. 43.3.1–4: *Latinam eam coloniam esse libertinorumque appellari*. For *Corduba*, see Strab. 3.2.1: πλεῖστον δ' ἥ τε Κόρδυβα ηὔξηται, Μαρκέλλου κτίσμα. For *Palma* and *Pollentia*, see Strab. 3.5.1 and Mela 2.7.124: *Palma et Pollentia coloniae*. For *Saguntum*, see *CNH*, 312 no. 64, 313 no. 66, and 314 no. 75, and Ripollès and Velaza Frías 2002, op. cit.: *aediles coloniae S(aguntinorum)*. For *Emporiae*, see *AE* 1984, 615 and A. Díaz Fernández, 'Notas en torno a la posible identidad de *M. Iun[ius] pro[cos]* (*AE*, 1984, 615) y el nacimiento de la ciudad romana de *Emporiae*', *Klio* 100, no. 1 (2018), 195–223: *co[l(oni) Empor(itani)]*. In addition, J. González Fernández, 'Texto legal epigráfico de una colonia latina de César o Augusto en la *Hispania Ulterior Baetica*', *SDHI* 81 (2015), 307–311, transmits news about two coins coming from *Iulia Constantia Osset* which would prove its colonial status. Also, there is a series of texts which refer to the recruitment of troops among certain colonies from *Hispania* before the founding of the first Roman colonies by Caesar and the triumvirs. On these passages, see García Fernández 2011, op. cit., 62–63; García Fernández 2015, op. cit., 595, n. 11.

8 This would be the reason by which *Palma* and *Pollentia* appear mentioned as *municipia civium Romanorum* by Pliny the Elder (*NH*. 3.5.77: *oppida habet civium Romanorum Palmam et Pollentiam*), although Mela (2.7.124) refers to them as *coloniae* shortly before.

9 For the evidence and the scholars who support the status of Latin colonies for these towns, see García Fernández 2001, op. cit.; Espinosa Espinosa 2014, op. cit.; Espinosa Espinosa 2018, op. cit.; Espinosa Espinosa 2016, op. cit., 570–604.

10 On this issue, see Plin. *NH*. 3.1.7; 3.3.18; 3.5.77; 4.22.117; García Fernández 2001, op. cit.; Espinosa Espinosa 2014, op. cit.; Espinosa Espinosa 2018, op. cit.

*stipendiariae*, *liberae*, and *foederatae* such as *Segobriga* and *Dianium*.[11] Thus, in the light of the above, it is necessary to revisit the origin and presence of the *quattuorviratus* in *Hispania*. The final goal is to establish a new general framework of historical interpretation which enables us to explain as many references to the *quattuorviratus* as possible without hindering other possible explanations for unconventional or exceptional cases.

## 2 Origin, Namings, and Legal and Administrative Meaning of the *quattuorviratus*

There is a basic consensus about the origin of the *quattuorviratus* in the *municipia civium Romanorum* from Italy after the *bellum Sociale* (91–87 BC) and its final structure at the end of the Republican period: a pair of *quattuorviri iure dicundo* and a pair of *quattuorviri aedilicia potestate* or *quattuorviri aediles*, with judicial and aedilician functions respectively.[12] But this consensus breaks down in relation to the moment at which the division of their functions might have taken place. Thus, for scholars such as E. Bispham,[13] the earliest attestations of the *quattuorviratus* in Italy would correspond to an undivided college, with no apparent divisions of rank and competence.[14] It would have only

11 For a theoretical and archaeological approach to the Augustan origin of the *municipia Latina* in *Hispania*, see García Fernández 2001, op. cit.; Espinosa Espinosa 2014, op. cit.; Espinosa Espinosa 2018, op. cit.

12 See, for instance, Degrassi 1962b, op. cit., 185; A. N. Sherwin-White, *The Roman Citizenship* (Oxford 1973), 63, 165–166; Laffi 2000, op. cit., 79–80; Laffi 2000b, op. cit., 33; Laffi 2006, op. cit., 112; Melchor Gil 2013a, op. cit., 134, 136, and 152; Bispham 2007, op. cit., 253–379; Sisani 2018a, op. cit., 64–65; and Sisani 2021, op. cit., 42–43.

13 Bispham 2007, op. cit., 333–336 and 372–374. This scholar takes as a starting point the approaches of H. Rudolph, *Stadt und Staat im römischen Italien: Untersuchungen über die Entwicklung des Munizipalwesens in der republikanischen Zeit* (Leipzig 1935) and E. Manni, *Per la storia dei municipi fino alla guerra sociale* (Rome 1947), who suggested the lack of a division of functions for this college of four magistrates until Caesar. According to E. Melchor Gil (2013a, op. cit., 136–141 and 152), the splitting of the *potestates* can only be supported by the evidence from the Caesarian period onwards.

14 Pérez Zurita 2004, op. cit., 155–158 and 165; Pérez Zurita 2005, op. cit., 12–14 and 19, came to the same conclusion regarding the internal structure of the *quattuorviratus* in *Hispania* a few years earlier. In this respect, this scholar has argued that the *quattuorviratus* and *duumviratus* would have been comparable, in his own words (Pérez Zurita 2004, op. cit., 158), "se trataba de una institución con cuatro miembros con poderes muy parecidos a los duunviros, siendo, tanto éstos como aquellos, la máxima magistratura local en *Hispania*". Also, in his view (Pérez Zurita 2004, op. cit., 158 and 161), it does not seem possible to connect the *quattuorviratus* to the aedilician functions, considering as a possible fact the coexistence of the *quattuorviratus* and *aedilitas* within a Roman town. In this same

been at the end of 70 BC that the *quattuorviratus* (with jurisdictional autonomy from the start) would have been split into two pairs of *quattuorviri* with judicial and aedilician functions. Therefore, in the opinion of this scholar, the *quattuorviri iure dicundo* and *quattuorviri aedilicia potestate* would have been the result of a gradual internal development that would have concluded with the precise delimitation of their functions.[15] By contrast, for scholars such as S. Sisani,[16] the delineation of roles would have happened at the same time as their creation, occasioning such allocation of functions by *sortitio* or collegiate decision within their own college after the election of the four magistrates.[17] In this respect, according to S. Sisani's approach concerning the origin of the local magistrates with judicial functions,[18] the *quattuorviratus* would have been created (between 90 and 82 BC) as a new political and administrative

regard, see Bispham 2007, op. cit., 226–230 and 292. For a contrary opinion, see U. Laffi, 'Osservazioni sulla *lex municipii Tarentini*', *RAL* ser. IX, 15 (4) (2004), 618–620. In the opinion of E. Melchor Gil (2013a, op. cit., 137–141 and 152; E. Melchor Gil, 'Magistrados y magistraturas en la Carmona romana', in *El gobierno municipal de Carmona a lo largo de la historia. Actas VIII Congreso de Historia de Carmona*, ed. M. González Jiménez and A. Caballos Rufino, Seville [2013c], 47–48, n. 24), the coexistence of the *quattuorviratus* and *aedilitas* could have been occasional due to the continuity of local *iura* and *instituta*. In fact, according to this scholar, from Caesar on, the legal and administrative structure of the Roman towns would have been based on the *quattuorviratus* (a pair of *quattuorviri iure dicundo* and a pair of *quattuorviri aedilicia potestate*) or the *duumviratus* plus *aedilitas*. In the first case, the apparent coexistence of *quattuorviratus* and *aedilitas* could be explained (endorsed by epigraphic and numismatic evidence) by identifying the *aediles* with the *quattuorviri aedilicia potestate* or *quattuorviri aediles* (Melchor Gil 2013a, op. cit., 137, 140–141, and 152). Similarly, see Degrassi 1962a, op. cit., 170; F. Senatore, '*Quattuorviri aediles* nella colonia romana di Pompei?', *ZPE* 1997, 287–288; Laffi 2006, op. cit., 112; Bispham 2007, op. cit., 370.

15 Bispham 2007, op. cit., 254–379. In the opinion of this scholar (Bispham 2007, op. cit., 334, 373–374), the division of responsibilities within the *quattuorviratus* could have been due to the desire to seek a more efficient administration of public affairs on the part of the local elites, as well as a clearer *cursus honorum*. These are also some of the reasons offered by U. Laffi (2000a, op. cit., 84; 2000b, op. cit., 34; 2006, op. cit., 113), A. D. Pérez Zurita (2004, op. cit., 138–139), and S. Sisani (2021, op. cit., 69) to explain the primacy of the *duumviratus* plus *aedilitas* over the *quattuorviratus* as the preferred political and administrative structure within the Roman towns. On the other hand, again according to E. Bispham (2007, op. cit., 335 and 370), the use of the titles *iure dicundo* and *aedilicia potestate* could have been optional, not compulsory.

16 Sisani 2018a, op. cit., 65; Sisani 2021, op. cit., 69.

17 On these issues, see also Degrassi 1962b, op. cit., 185; Laffi 2000a, op. cit., 79–80; Laffi 2000b, op. cit., 32–33; Laffi 2006, op. cit., 112–113.

18 Sisani 2018a, op. cit., 62–66; Sisani 2021, op. cit., 43, n. 11.

structure for the new *municipia civium Romanorum* which emerged from *coloniae Latinae* and *civitates foederatae* after the *bellum Sociale*.[19] In parallel with the setting up of the *quattuorviratus*, Rome would have created a pair of *duumviri iure dicundo* within the previous *coloniae Romanae* and *municipia civium Romanorum* that until that date were under the authority of the *praefecti iure dicundo* for the administration of justice. The latter would have been added to a preexisting pair of *duumviri* (*nude dicti*) with aedilician functions.[20]

There is also no consensus on the meaning of the simple *quattuorviratus*, that is, the references to *quattuorviri* without specification of *potestas* (informally called *nude dicti*) in the literary, epigraphic, and numismatic evidence. Overall, the references to the simple *quattuorviratus* have been understood in six different ways, depending on the municipal or colonial status of the Roman towns. First, the joint identification of the two pairs of *quattuorviri*, in other words, the college of *quattuorviri* per se (whether there is a splitting of functions or not);[21] second, the pair of *quattuorviri iure dicundo*;[22] third, the pair of *quattuorviri aedilicia potestate*,[23] fourth, would be the grouping of

19 In this same regard, see Laffi 2000a, op. cit., 79–89; Laffi 2000b, op. cit., 32–33. In the opinion of this scholar (Laffi 2000a, op. cit., 79; Laffi 2000b, op. cit., 33), the *quattuorviratus* would have been a new solution of general application, in the form of a unitary organizational structure in which organicity was combined with simplicity as a prerequisite for good functioning.

20 Similarly, see Laffi 2000a, op. cit., 83–84; Laffi 2000b, op. cit., 33–34. However, as U. Laffi has pointed out (2000a, op. cit., 83; 2000b, op. cit., 33), the magistrates of the *municipia civium Romanorum* constituted before the *bellum Sociale* and without *duumviri* (*nude dicti*) would have initially received the judicial functions from Rome. In the opinion of S. Sisani (2021, op. cit., 69), "il modello duovirale dovesse risultare la scelta più naturale nei casi in cui il conferimento della piena autonomia amministrativa si traduceva essenzialmente nell'introduzione, a fianco di preesistenti magistrati locali aventi competenze limitate all'ordinaria amministrazione, di collegi giurisdicenti eletti in loco, che andavano ad assumere le funzioni prima rivestite dai delegati del pretore".

21 See, for instance, Manni 1947, op. cit., 173, 180–181; Degrassi 1962a, op. cit., 126; Pérez Zurita 2004, op. cit., 133–134, 138, 156–157, and 165; Pérez Zurita 2005, op. cit., 12–14 and 19; Laffi 2000a, op. cit., 80; Laffi 2000b, op. cit., 33; Laffi 2006, op. cit., 112; Bispham 2007, op. cit., 291 and 293; Melchor Gil 2013a, op. cit., 136–137, 142, 146–147, and 152; Sisani 2018a, op. cit., 58–59 and 65; Sisani 2021, op. cit., 69–70.

22 In this respect, see Manni 1947, op. cit., 174–175, 179, 181, 188, and 191–193; Degrassi 1962a, op. cit., 109, 126, 166–167; Laffi 2006, op. cit. 112; Pérez Zurita 2004, op. cit., 154–155; Bispham 2007, op. cit., 375; Melchor Gil 2013a, op. cit., 142–146 and 152; Laffi 2006, op. cit., 112; Sisani 2018a, op. cit., 50, n. 62.

23 In this context, see Manni 1947, op. cit., 175, 181–182, 186, 188–190, 192, 200, 205, and 207; Degrassi 1962a, op. cit., 161–162, and 170; Senatore 1997, op. cit., 286–287; Laffi 2006, op. cit., 112; Bispham 2007, op. cit., 293 and 375. Scholars such as A. D. Pérez Zurita (2004, op. cit., 155; 2005 op. cit., 12–13) and E. Melchor Gil (2013a, op. cit., 142, 145–146, and 152) are opposed to this view. In their opinion, the references to the *quattuorviri* (*nude dicti*)

*duumviri iure dicundo* and *aediles* within Roman towns with *duumviratus* plus *aedilitas*;[24] fifth, the pair of *duumviri iure dicundo* within Roman towns with *duumviratus* plus *aedilitas*;[25] and sixth, the pair of *aediles* within Roman towns with *duumviratus* plus *aedilitas*.[26] This high variability of interpretations, partly because of *ad hoc* explanations related to singular, unusual, or regional cases, constrains the study of the *quattuorviratus* both in Italy and the Roman provinces in methodological and historical terms. In this respect, systematic application of such interpretations has a significant effect on the analysis of the evidence and the sample of cases to consider. Of all these different ways to understand the simple *quattuorviratus*,[27] that related to the alleged grouping of *duumviri iure dicundo* and *aediles* within Roman towns with *duumviratus* plus *aedilitas* has the greatest impact,[28] especially regarding the meaning and presence of the simple *quattuorviratus* in *Hispania*, where the lack of references to the *potestas* of the *quattuorviri* is the general rule.[29]

---

should correspond to the *quattuorviri iure dicundo* because, according to the epigraphic and numismatic evidence, the *aediles* are in a minority compared with the *duumviri*, and the public dedications to the local magistrates were performed in the last years of their *cursus honorum*.

24 See, for instance, Manni 1947, op. cit., 168, 175, 180–181, 204, and 207; Degrassi 1962a, op. cit., 100–101, 107–108, 111, 142, 162, and 170; Curchin 1990, op. cit., 34; Senatore 1997, op. cit., 285; Laffi 2006, op. cit., 111–112; Le Roux 2013, op. cit., 234; Le Roux 2022, op. cit., 344–345; González Fernández 2015, op. cit., 318–319; Sisani 2018a, op. cit., 42, n. 3, and 51; 2021: 71, n. 211. For a differing opinion, see Pérez Zurita 2004, op. cit., 165; Pérez Zurita 2005, op. cit., 19; Bispham 2007, op. cit., 261–263, 267–268; Melchor Gil 2013a, op. cit., 142, 149, and 152.

25 In ambiguous terms, see Curchin 1990, op. cit., 34.

26 In this respect, see Degrassi 1962a, op. cit., 106–107, 150, 154–155, 157–158, and 170; 1962b, op. cit., 180; Senatore 1997, op. cit., 285 and 288; Laffi 2006, op. cit., 112; González Fernández 2015, op. cit., 319; Sisani 2018a, op. cit., 42, n. 3, 51, and 56; Sisani 2021, op. cit., 68 and 72.

27 Some of them (such as the interpretation as the pair of *quattuorviri aedilicia potestate*) have been challenged by certain scholars; see Pérez Zurita 2004, op. cit., 155; Pérez Zurita 2005, op. cit., 12–13; Melchor Gil 2013a, op. cit., 142, 145–146, and 152.

28 This identification of the *quattuorviri* (*nude dicti*) with the *duumviri* plus *aediles* was suggested by Th. Mommsen (*CIL* X, p. 93) to explain the challenging evidence from the Roman colony of *Pompeii*. This explanation, as seen above, was widely accepted, and used mainly to justify the coexistence of *quattuorviri* and *duumviri* in certain *coloniae Romanae*, but also in several *municipia civium Romanorum* and *municipia Latina* (see, for instance, González Fernández 2015, op. cit.; Sisani 2018a, op. cit.). The use of this interpretation is certainly accommodating and discards other possible explanations based on processes of refounding of Roman towns and changes of status. On this matter, see below.

29 On this, see Table 4.1; Pérez Zurita 2004, op. cit., 157. Apart from one case coming from *Gades*, which refers to one *quattuorvir aedilicia potestate* (Table 4.1, no. 23), all the *quattuorviri* known are *nude dicti*.

In this respect, one of the main counterarguments to the soundness of this interpretation is that arising from S. Sisani's reasoning about the primacy of the *duumviratus* plus *aedilitas* over the *quattuorviratus* as the preferred political and administrative structure within the Roman towns. In the opinion of this scholar, the *duumviratus* plus *aedilitas* would have enabled the setting up of a real *cursus honorum* at a local level. In that way, "se nel caso dei *quattuorviri* le qualifiche per la candidatura dovevano essere le stesse per tutte e quattro le posizioni, indipendentemente dalle specifiche funzioni che gli eletti avrebbero rivestito una volta costituiti i due sottocollegi, il duovirato nel suo complesso si configurava propriamente come la somma di due magistature distinte e separate: una circostanza che avrebbe potuto permettere la diversificazione dei criteri di eleggibilità valevoli per le due coppie magistratuali, eventualmente riservando la possibilità di candidarsi al duovirato giurisdicente solo a quanti avessero precedentemente gerito l'edilità".[30] This is the reason by which it seems contradictory that the *duumviri*, who should have held greater *dignitas* and *existimatio* than the *aediles*, wished to be equated and mentioned as *quattuorviri* (*nude dicti*) together with them. Besides, these *duumviri* along with the *aediles* could have been mistaken for the real *quattuorviri* from other *municipia* and *coloniae*, diminishing the differentiation of status among Roman towns,[31] as well as the social and political incentives behind the *duumviratus* plus *aedilitas* that would have fostered their introduction instead of the *quattuorviratus*. Finally, the alleged use of the simple *quattuorviratus* as the equivalence of *duumviri* and *aediles* in the inscriptions and on coins contrasts with the usual presence of both colleges of magistrates (instead of the *quattuorviri nude dicti*) within the Roman statutes, such as the *lex municipii Tarentini*, the *lex municipii Irnitani*, and the *lex coloniae Genetivae Iuliae*.[32]

---

30 Sisani 2021, op. cit., 70.

31 A. Degrassi (1962a, op. cit., 100–101) had already drawn attention to this fact in relation to the use of the namings *quattuorviri* and *duumviri* to refer to the magistrates from the *coloniae* and *municipia* without distinction, because "cessarebbe ogni differenza tra il titolo dei magistrati delle colonie e quello dei magistrati dei municipi e avremmo perduto cosí ogni possibilità di determinare dal nome dei magistrati lo stato giuridico di numerose città".

32 For the *lex municipii Tarentini*, see *CIL* I$^2$, 590; Laffi 2004, op. cit. For the *lex municipii Irnitani*, see *HEp* 15, 2006, 330. For the *lex coloniae Genetivae Iuliae*, see *CIL* II$^2$/5, 1022. There is a fragment of a *lex* coming from Maguilla (Badajoz, Spain) which contains a reference to *IIIIvir co*[- - -]. J. C. Saquete Chamizo and J. Iñesta Mena, 'Un fragmento de ley municipal hallado en la *Baeturia Turdulorum* (*conventus Cordubensis*, *provincia Baetica*)', *ZPE* 168 (2009), 293–297, suggested that this *lex* would have corresponded to a *municipium Flavium* with *quattuorviratus*, and they ruled out that it could correspond to one of the nearby *coloniae Romanae*, such as *Emerita*, *Metellinum*, or *Corduba* because

## 3 *Quattuorviratus* in *coloniae* and *municipia* from *Hispania*

The analysis of the literary, epigraphic, and numismatic evidence of the *coloniae* and *municipia* from *Hispania* has made it possible to gather 57 references to the *quattuorviratus* (see table 4.1). This sample consists of 47 reliable references and 10 unclear ones,[33] which are unevenly distributed across the *provincia Baetica* and the *provincia Tarraconensis*, that is, the areas of earliest Roman presence, and probably the *provincia Lusitania* as well. In this respect, 35 references (30 considered reliable and 5 unclear) come from the *provincia Baetica*, 21 from the *provincia Tarraconensis* (17 would be reliable and 4 unclear), and 1 from the *provincia Lusitania* (unclear).[34] In all, they belong to 22 different Roman towns, 13 of which were in *Baetica* (*Asido*, *Carmo*, *Carteia*, *Ceret*, *Gades*, *Ilipula Minor*, Maguilla, Marchena, *Munigua*, *Obulco*, *Obulcula*, *Sabora*, and [- - -]*nisi-*), 8 of them in *Tarraconensis* (*Aeso*, *Clunia*, *Edeta*, *Iulia Libyca*, *Segobriga*, *Sigarra*, *Termes*, and *Valeria*), and 1 in *Lusitania* (*Metellinum*) (see Fig. 4.1).[35] According to their legal and administrative status before the *Constitutio Antoniniana* (AD 212), 2 of them were *coloniae Romanae* (*Asido* and *Clunia*), 5 *municipia civium Romanorum* (*Carmo*, *Carteia*, *Ceret*, *Gades*,

---

the *quattuorviratus* is rare within Roman towns of this type. By contrast, J. González Fernández (2015, op. cit., 307–309) proposed that it would have belonged to a *colonia Latina* from Caesar or Augustus, a view that should be explored considering the presence of *coloniae Latinae* with *quattuorviri* in *Hispania*. If J. González's Fernández proposal is accepted, this *colonia Latina* should be Caesarian or earlier, given that Augustus created the *municipium Latinum* in *Hispania* from the transformation of the preexisting *coloniae Latinae* into *municipia Latina*. On this matter, see García Fernández 2001, op. cit.; Espinosa Espinosa 2014, op. cit., and Espinosa Espinosa 2018, op. cit.

33 The size and composition of the sample vary significantly depending on the approaches used to explain the references to the *quattuorviri* (*nude dicti*). Compare, for instance, the sample of cases in Degrassi 1962a, op. cit.; Pérez Zurita 2004, op. cit.; Pérez Zurita 2005, op. cit.; Melchor Gil 2013a, op. cit., and S. Sisani 2018a, op. cit.

34 Within the reading of an opisthographic plaque coming from *Valeria* (*CIL* II²/13, 966; *HEp* 2016–2017, 353a), J. Edmondson and H. Gimeno Pascual, 'Primer testimonio de evergetismo en el foro de *Valeria* (*conventus Carthaginiensis, Hispania Citerior*): una nueva placa opistógrafa', *MDAI*(*M*) 58 (2017), 321–372, have hypothetically suggested the presence of a *quattuorvir*. This reference has not been considered in this work due to the lack of explicit epigraphic evidence.

35 The sample shaped by S. Sisani (2018, op. cit., 42 n. 3, and 51–54) is considerably reduced. This scholar dismisses a large number of cases as a result of the application of two different ways of explaining the *quattuorviri* (*nude dicti*): the grouping of *duumviri iure dicundo* and *aediles* within Roman towns with *duumviratus* plus *aedilitas* (*Iulia Libyca*, *Munigua*, *Termes*, *Obulcula*, *Sabora*, and [- - -]*nisi-*), and the pair of *aediles* within Roman towns with both colleges of magistrates (*Aeso*, *Edeta*, *Ilipula Minor*, *Sigarra*, and *Valeria*). In his opinion, the *quattuorviratus* in *Hispania* could only be traced in *Asido*, *Carmo*, *Carteia*, *Ceret*, *Clunia*, *Gades*, Maguilla (Badajoz), and *Segobriga*.

and *Obulco*), and 12 *municipia Latina* (*Aeso*, *Edeta*, *Ilipula Minor*, *Iulia Libyca*, *Munigua*, *Obulcula*, *Sabora*, *Segobriga*, *Sigarra*, *Termes*, *Valeria*, and [- - -]*nisi-*), 6 of which were *municipia Flavia* (*Aeso*, *Ilipula Minor*, *Munigua*, *Obulcula*, *Sabora*, and [- - -]*nisi-*).[36] To these should be added the evidence from Maguilla (Badajoz), which would have belonged to a *colonia Latina* or a *municipium Flavium*; Marchena (Seville), corresponding to an unidentified *municipium Latinum* or *municipium civium Romanorum*;[37] and *Metellinum*, a possible pre-Caesarian Latin colony, after that a Roman colony.[38] Finally, concerning the date of the references which comprise this sample, it is between approximately 55 BC and AD 159. Of the entire group of references, 18 are from the second half of the 1st century BC, 17 from the first half of the 1st century AD, and 13 from the second half of the 1st century AD and the 2nd century AD. However, a reliable chronology could not be established for the remaining 8 references. To these should be added again the evidence from Maguilla (Badajoz), which would be Caesarian or Flavian, depending on the interpretation accepted.

---

36 On the legal and administrative status of these Roman towns, see, for instance, Henderson 1942, op. cit.; A. Padilla Monge, '*Asido Caesarina*: consideraciones acerca de su status', *Habis* 16 (1985), 307–327; A. Padilla Monge, 'El epígrafe *CIL* II, 1305', *Habis* 20 (1989), 185–192; García Fernández 2001, op. cit.; J. Andreu Pintado, *Edictum, municipium y lex: Hispania en época flavia* (*69–96 d.C.*) (Oxford 2004); Pérez Zurita 2004 and Pérez Zurita 2005, op. cit.; J. M. Abascal Palazón, G. Alföldy and R. Cebrián Fernández, *Segobriga V. Inscripciones romanas 1986–2010* (Madrid 2011); J. González Fernández, '*Asido quae Caesarina*', in *Colonias de César y Augusto en la Andalucía romana*, ed. J. González Fernández and J. C. Saquete Chamizo (Rome 2011), 273–296; González Fernández 2015, op. cit.; Espinosa Espinosa 2014, op. cit.; Melchor Gil 2013a, op. cit.; Melchor Gil 2013c, op. cit.; I. Garcés and T. Reyes, Aeso, *d'oppidum ibèric a* municipium *romà. Isona, Pallars Jussà*, (Barcelona 2014); N. Salazar Ortiz, D. Pàmies and I. Moreno, 'De Sigarra a Prats de Segarra: noves descobertes arqueològiques al Municipium Sigarrense (els Prats de Rei, Anoia) entre l'ibèric antic i l'edat mitjana', *Tribuna d'arqueologia* (2013–2014), 115–134; Sisani 2018a, op. cit.

37 *Municipes* et *incolae* dedicated this inscription to *M. Cornelius M. f. Gal. Faustus*, *quattuorvir* and *augur* from this *municipium*. On this recent finding, see S. Ordóñez Agulla and S. García-Dils de la Vega, '786. Pedestal en homenaje a un sacerdote y magistrado local procedente del entorno de Marchena (Seville)', *Ficheiro Epigráfico* 223 (2021a), 8–16; S. Ordóñez Agulla and S. García-Dils de la Vega, 'Un municipio romano en Marchena (Seville)', in *Arqueología y numismática. Estudios en homenaje a la profesora Francisca Chaves Tristán*, ed. E. Ferrer Albelda, M. Oria Segura, E. García Vargas, F. J. García Fernández and R. Pliego Vázquez (Seville 2021b), 777–790.

38 This has been very recently proposed by J. C. Saquete Chamizo, 'Colonias en la *Hispania Ulterior* entre César y Augusto. Balance y perspectivas de estudio', in diuturna Civitas 1. Le strutture locali dell'Occidente romano, ed. E.García Fernández, E. Melchor Gil, and S. Sisani (Rome 2023), 347–376. I am grateful to Professor Saquete Chamizo for allowing me to read his manuscript before publication. For a different reading of the *quattuorvir* from *Metellinum*, see P. Mateos Cruz and Y. Picado Pérez, 'El teatro romano de *Metellinum*', *MDAI*(*M*) 52 (2011), pp. 373–410.

TABLE 4.1 Historical evidence about *Quattuorviri* in *Coloniae* and *Municipia* from *Hispania*

| No. | Bibliography | Roman town | Current city | Evidence | Date |
|---|---|---|---|---|---|
| *Provincia Baetica* | | | | | |
| 1 (r) | *CIL* II, 1315; *IRPCádiz* 4; González Fernández 2011, 273–296; Sisani 2018a, 57 | *Asido* | Medina Sidonia (Cadiz ) | Q. Fabius Cn. f. Ga[l]. Senica IIIIvir | Pre-Augustan (?) |
| 2 (r) | *CIL* II, 1379; *CILA* Se 3, 844 | *Carmo* | Carmona (Seville) | [-] Fonteius C. f. Calpurnianus IIIIvir | Late 1st *c.* BC |
| 3–4 (r) | *CIL* II, 1380; *CIL* II²/5, 457.2*; Stylow 2012, 147–148 | *Carmo* | Carmona (Seville) | L. Iunius L. f. M. n. L. pron. Gal. Rufus [I]IIIvir; quattuorvi-ral[i] potest(ate) | First half 1st *c.* AD |
| 5 (r) | *CIL* II, 5120; Melchor Gil 2011, 142; Curchin 2015: no. 177 | *Carmo* | Carmona (Seville) | L. Servilius L. f. Pol(l)io IIIIvir bis; quattuorvi-rali [potestate] | Tiberian |
| 6 (u) | *CIL* II, 128*; *HEp* 9, 1999, 504; *HEp* 13, 2003/2004, 58; Curchin 2015: no. 992 | *Carmo* | Carmona (Seville) | M. Ulpius M. f. L. n. M. pron. Quir. Strabo IIIIvir | Flavian-Antonine |
| 7 (r) | Vives 1924, IV: 24 no. 31–32; *CNH*, 419 no. 62–63; Ripollès 2010: no. 114–115; Curchin 1990: no. 65–66; Curchin 2015: no. 65–66 | *Carteia* | San Roque (Cádiz) | L. Atini(us?), C. Nucia(nus?) IIIIvir(i) | 30 BC |
| 8 (r) | Vives 1924, IV: 26 no. 56; *CNH*, 419 no. 64; Curchin 1990: no. 61; Curchin 2015: no. 61 | *Carteia* | San Roque (Cádiz) | Aufidius Rufus IIII[vir] | Second half of the 1st *c.* BC |
| 9 (r) | *IRPCádiz* 92; Curchin 1990: no. 70; González Fernández 2011: 280; Curchin 2015: no. 70 | *Carteia* | San Roque (Cádiz) | C. Curvius C. f. Ser. Rusticus IIIIvir iterum | Second half of the 1st *c.* BC |

TABLE 4.1 Historical evidence about *Quattuorviri* in *Coloniae* and *Municipia* from *Hispania* (*cont.*)

| No. | Bibliography | Roman town | Current city | Evidence | Date |
|---|---|---|---|---|---|
| 10 (r) | Vives 1924, IV: 24, no. 29; *CNH*, 419 no. 58–60; Chaves 1979: no. 23; Ripollès 2010: no. 111 and 112; Curchin 1990: no. 64; Curchin 2015: no. 64 | *Carteia* | San Roque (Cádiz) | P. Falcidius IIIIvir | 40 BC |
| 11 (r) | Vives 1924, IV: 25 no. 42; Chaves 1979: no. 30; Ripollès 2010: no. 123 | *Carteia* | San Roque (Cádiz) | Germanicus et Drusus IIIIvir(i) | AD 15 |
| 12 (u) | Vives 1924, IV: 25 no. 43; Curchin 1990: no. 62; Curchin 2015: no. 62* | *Carteia* | San Roque (Cádiz) | [-] Maecil(ius?) IIIIvir | Before 19 BC |
| 13 (r) | *CNH*, 419 no. 61; Chaves 1979: no. 24; Ripollès 2010: no. 113; Curchin 1990: no. 60; Curchin 2015: no. 60 | *Carteia* | San Roque (Cádiz) | C. Maius C. f. Pollio IIIIvir | 35 BC |
| 14 (r) | Vives 1924, IV, 25 no. 38; *CNH*, 418 no. 55–57; Chaves 1979: no. 22 | *Carteia* | San Roque (Cádiz) | C. Minius Q. f. IIIIvir ter(tium) or iter(um) | 45 BC (?) |
| 15 (r) | Vives 1924, IV: 25 no. 37; *CNH*, 418, no. 52–54; Chaves 1979: no. 20 | *Carteia* | San Roque (Cádiz) | C. Minius Q. f., C. Vibius IIIIvir IV, IIIIvir | 55 BC (?) |
| 16 (r) | Vives 1924, IV: 24–25 no. 33 and 36; *CNH*, 417–418 no. 50–51 | *Carteia* | San Roque (Cádiz) | C. Vibius, C. Minius Q. f. IIIIviri | 55 BC (?) |
| 17 (r) | Vives 1924, IV: 25, no. 34 and 35; Chaves 1979: no. 21; Curchin 1990: no. 67–68; Curchin 2015: no. 67–68 | *Carteia* | San Roque (Cádiz) | C. Vibius, C. Minius Q. f. IIIIvir, IIIIvir it(erum) | 50 BC (?) |

TABLE 4.1 Historical evidence about *Quattuorviri* in *Coloniae* and *Municipia* from *Hispania* (*cont.*)

| No. | Bibliography | Roman town | Current city | Evidence | Date |
|---|---|---|---|---|---|
| 18 (r) | Vives 1924, IV: 25 no. 39 and 40; Chaves 1979: no. 26; *CNH*, 419 and 420 no. 65 and 66; Ripollès 2010: no. 116 and 117 | *Carteia* | San Roque (Cádiz) | IIIIvir | 25 BC |
| 19 (r) | Vives 1924, IV: 26 no. 47; *CNH*, 419 and 420 no. 68; Chaves 1979: no. 27; Ripollès 2010: no. 119; Curchin 1990: no. 59; Curchin 2015: no. 59 | *Carteia* | San Roque (Cádiz) | IIIIvir | 25–15 BC |
| 20 (r) | *ILJerez* 34; Sisani 2018a: 52 and 53 | *Ceret* | Jerez de la Frontera (Cádiz) | Deci(m)us Baebius Deci(m)i filius IIIIvir | Pre-Augustan (?) |
| 21 (r) | *CIL* II, 1305; *IRPCádiz* 103; *HEp* 4, 1994, 265; *ILJerez* 29; Sisani 2018a, 52 and 53 | *Ceret* | Jerez de la Frontera (Cádiz) | L. Fabius L. f. Gal. Cordus IIIIvir | 2 BC–AD 2 (?) |
| 22 (u) | *CIL* II, 1306; *IRPCádiz* 104; *ILJerez* 30; Sisani 2018a: 53 | *Ceret* | Jerez de la Frontera (Cádiz) | L. Titius L. f. Ser. Vernus [- - - IIII]virali (?) potest(ate) | |
| 23 (r) | *CIL* II, 1727; *IRPCádiz* 123; Curchin 1990: no. 98; Curchin 2015: no. 98 | *Gades* | Cádiz (Cádiz) | L. Antonius Q. f. Gal. Antullus IIIIvir aedilicia potestate | |
| 24 (r) | Cic. *fam.* 10.32.2; Curchin 1990: no. 96; Curchin 2015: no. 96 | *Gades* | Cádiz (Cádiz) | L. Cornelius P. f. L. n. Balbus Minor *quattuorviratum sibi prorogavit* | 8 June, 43 BC |
| 25 (r) | *IRPCádiz* 361; *HEp* 18, 2009, 97; Curchin 1990: no. 102; Curchin 2015: no. 102 | *Gades* | Cádiz (Cádiz) | L. Valerius Fecula IIIIvir | 2nd *c.* AD (?) |

TABLE 4.1 Historical evidence about *Quattuorviri* in *Coloniae* and *Municipia* from *Hispania* (*cont.*)

| No. | Bibliography | Roman town | Current city | Evidence | Date |
|---|---|---|---|---|---|
| 26 (r) | *IRPCádiz* 445; Curchin 1990: no. 104 | *Gades* | Cádiz (Cádiz) | IIIIv[ir] | 2nd *c.* AD (?) |
| 27 (r) | *CIL* II$^2$/5, 897; Curchin 1990: no. 117; Curchin 2015: no. 117 | *Ilipula Minor* | Los Corrales (Seville) | L. Flavius L. f. Quir. Gallus IIIIvir; IIvir bis | 1st–2nd *c.* AD |
| 28 (r) | *AE* 2009, 582; *HEp* 18, 2009, 31 | Unknown | Maguilla (Badajoz) | IIIIvir | Caesarian or Flavian (?) |
| 29 (r) | Ordóñez and García-Dils de la Vega 2021a and 2021b | Unknown | Marchena (Seville) | M. Cornelius M. f. Gal. Faustus IIIIvir | First half of the 1st *c.* AD |
| 30 (r) | *CILA* Se 4, 1052; Curchin 1990: no. 178; Curchin 2015: no. 178 | *Munigua* | Villanueva del Río y Minas (Seville) | IIIIviri | 7 September, AD 79 |
| 31 (u) | *CILA* Se 4, 1098; Curchin 1990: no. 182 | *Munigua* | Villanueva del Río y Minas (Seville) | [- - - II?]IIIIv[ir - - -] | Early 2nd *c.* AD |
| 32 (u) | Vives 1924, III: 61 no. 52; Curchin 1990: no. 216 | *Obulco* | Porcuna (Jaén) | IIII[vir?] | 67 BC (?) |
| 33 (r) | *CIL* II$^2$/5, 1322; Curchin 1990: no. 310; Curchin 2015: no. 310 | *Obulcula* | Fuentes de Andalucía (Seville) | [II]IIviri | AD 159 |
| 34 (r) | *CIL* II$^2$/5, 871; Curchin 2015: no. 1044 | *Sabora* | Cañete la Real (Málaga) | IIIIviri; IIviri | 25–29 July, AD 77 |
| 35 (r) | *CIL* II, 1271; *CILA* Se 2, 600; | [- - -]*nisi-* | Palomares del Río (Seville) | C. Lucius [- - -] IIIIvir | |
| ***Provincia Tarraconensis*** | | | | | |
| 36 (r) | *CIL* II, 4466; Curchin 1990: no. 401 | *Aeso* | Isona (Lleida) | L. Porcius L. f. Quir. Serenus IIIIvir; IIvir | Flavian or a little later |

TABLE 4.1 Historical evidence about *Quattuorviri* in *Coloniae* and *Municipia* from *Hispania* (*cont.*)

| No. | Bibliography | Roman town | Current city | Evidence | Date |
|---|---|---|---|---|---|
| 37 (u) | *CIL* II, 2781; *ERClu* 214 | *Clunia* | Peñalba de Castro (Burgos) | [- - -]Caelius Clouti[- - -] [- - -]IIIIvir I | |
| 38 (r) | *HEp* 5, 1995, 146a; Curchin 2015: no. 1146 | *Clunia* | Peñalba de Castro (Burgos) | Fabricius IIIIvir | |
| 39 (r) | *HEp* 2, 1990, 183b; Curchin 2015: no. 1147 | *Clunia* | Peñalba de Castro (Burgos) | IIIIviri | |
| 40 (r) | Vives 1924, IV: 112 no. 3; *RPC* I 452; Curchin 1990: no. 634–637; Curchin 2015: no. 634–637 | *Clunia* | Peñalba de Castro (Burgos) | Cn. Pompeius, M. Antonius (?), T. Antonius, M. Iulius Seranus IIIIvir(i) | Tiberian |
| 41 (r) | Vives 1924, IV: 112 no. 4; *RPC* 454; Curchin 1990: no. 638–641; Curchin 2015: no. 638–641 | *Clunia* | Peñalba de Castro (Burgos) | C. Aemilius Meto, T. Cornelius Maternus (?), L. Caelius Pressus (?), C. Caelius Candidus IIIIvir(i) | Tiberian |
| 42 (r) | Vives 1924, IV: 112 no. 5 and 6; *RPC* 456–457; Curchin 1990: no. 642–645; Curchin 2015: no. 642–645 | *Clunia* | Peñalba de Castro (Burgos) | L. Iulius Rufinus, T. Calpurnius Con[- - -], T. Pompeius Longus (?), P. Iulius Avitus IIIIvir(i) | Tiberian |
| 43 (r) | *CIL* II²/14, 133; Curchin 1990: no. 783; Curchin 2015: no. 783 | *Edeta* | Llíria (Valencia) | L. Fabius Fabullus IIIIvir bis | Late 1st c. AD |
| 44 (r) | Ferrer i Jané, Velaza, and Olesti Vila 2018, 176–185 | *Iulia Libyca* | Llívia (Girona) | Bella Gaisco f., Bella Bastobles f., Adinildir Betepe[- f.], Corneli(us) Erdoild[ir f.] IIIIviratus | Augustan (?) |
| 45 (r) | *CIL* II²/13, 285; Curchin 2015: no. 1196 | *Segobriga* | Saelices (Cuenca) | [C.?] Iulius C. f. Gal. [M]ontanus IIIIvir bis | Julio-Claudian (after AD 14) |

TABLE 4.1 Historical evidence about *Quattuorviri* in *Coloniae* and *Municipia* from *Hispania* (*cont.*)

| No. | Bibliography | Roman town | Current city | Evidence | Date |
|---|---|---|---|---|---|
| 46 (r) | *CIL* II$^2$/13, 284; Curchin 2015: no. 1202 | *Segobriga* | Saelices (Cuenca) | L. Iu[l]ius Annian[i] f. Gal. Gallus IIIIvir b[is] | Flavian or a little later |
| 47 (r) | *CIL* II$^2$/13, 286; Curchin 2015: no. 1197 | *Segobriga* | Saelices (Cuenca) | T. Sempronius M. f. Pullus IIIIvir des(ignatus) | Julio-Claudian |
| 48 (r) | *CIL* II$^2$/13, 287; Curchin 1990: no. 980; Curchin 2015: no. 980 | *Segobriga* | Saelices (Cuenca) | M. Valeri[us] M. f. Gal. Reburrus IIIIvir; aedilis | 1st *c.* AD |
| 49 (r) | *CIL* II$^2$/13, 288; Curchin 2015: no. 1199 | *Segobriga* | Saelices (Cuenca) | [Ti. - - -] Ti. f. Gal. [- - -] [IIII]v[i]r II | 1st *c.* AD |
| 50 (u) | *CIL* II$^2$/13, 289; Curchin 2015: no. 1198 | *Segobriga* | Saelices (Cuenca) | [IIII?]vir | Julio-Claudian |
| 51 (r) | *CIL* II, 4479; Curchin 1990: no. 885 | *Sigarra* | Els Prats de Rei (Barcelona) | C. Vibius Lupercus IIIIvir | Second half of the 1st *c.* AD |
| 52 (r) | *AE* 1953, 267; Curchin 1990: no. 922–925; Balbín 2006: no. 56; Curchin 2015: no. 922–925 | *Termes* | Montejo de Tiermes (Soria) | L. Licinius Pilus, M. Terentius Celsus, L. Pompeius Vitulus, T. Pompeius Rarus IIIIviri | Late 1st *c.* or early 2nd *c.* AD |
| 53 (u) | *CIL* II$^2$/13, 974; Curchin 1990: no. 984; Curchin 2015: no. 984; Sisani 2018a: 52, n. 75 | *Valeria* | Las Valeras (Cuenca) | L. Ca[ecilius?] Ga[l. - - -] III[Ivir - - -] | Early Principate |
| 54 (r) | *CIL* II$^2$/13, 975; Curchin 1990: no. 960; Curchin 2015: no. 960 | *Valeria* | Las Valeras (Cuenca) | G. Gra[ttius] Nigrinus IIIIvir | 1st *c.* AD |
| 55 (u) | *CIL* II$^2$/13, 976; Curchin 1990: no. 959; Gimeno 2009: 179; Curchin 2015: no. 959; Sisani 2018a, 52, n. 75 | *Valeria* | Las Valeras (Cuenca) | [-] Vale[rius Av]itus II[IIvir] | |

TABLE 4.1 Historical evidence about *Quattuorviri* in *Coloniae* and *Municipia* from *Hispania* (*cont.*)

| No. | Bibliography | Roman town | Current city | Evidence | Date |
|---|---|---|---|---|---|
| 56 (r) | *HEp* 2016–2017, 354; Edmondson and Gimeno 2017: 341, n. 31, 357, n. 75 | *Valeria* | Las Valeras (Cuenca) | C. Grattius Nigrinus IIIIvir II | |
| ***Provincia Lusitania*** | | | | | |
| 57 (u) | *HEp* 20, 2011, 7; *AE* 2011, 482; Mateos and Picado 2011: 381–382; Saquete Chamizo (2023:355) | *Metellinum* | Medellín (Badajoz) | Cn. Pomp[eius? - - -] IIII[vir?] | First quarter of the 1st *c.* AD (?) |

(r) – reliable / (u) – unclear

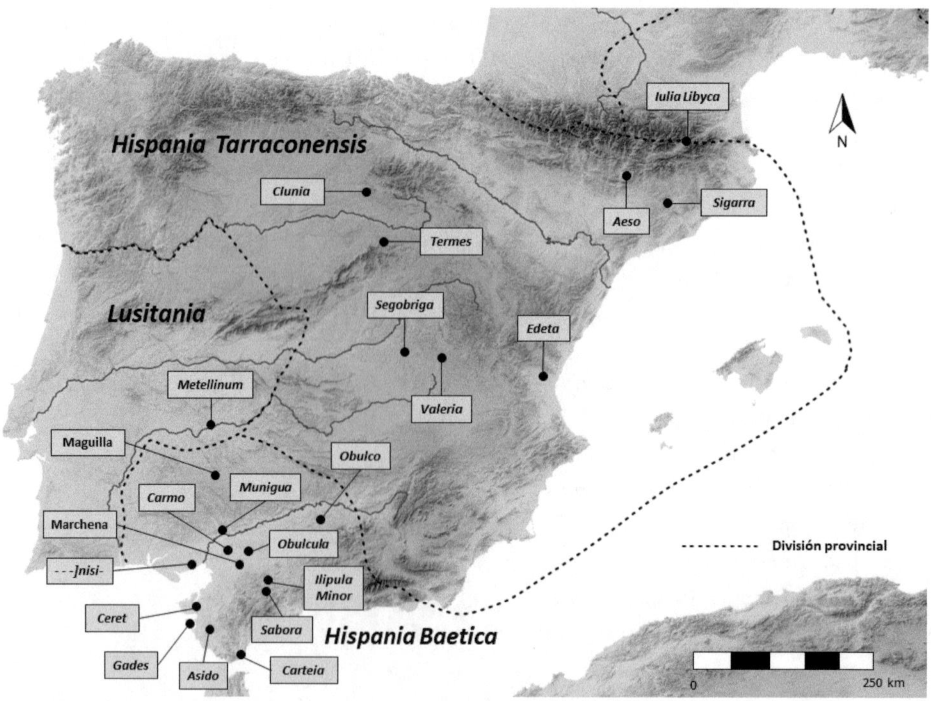


FIGURE 4.1 Location of the *Coloniae* and *Municipia* from *Hispania* with *Quattuorviratus*

Some first conclusions can be drawn from these data. On the one hand, the *quattuorviratus* is mainly present in *municipia Latina* and *municipia civium Romanorum* (with 19 towns), in comparison with the small amount of evidence coming from the *coloniae Romanae* (with 3 towns). However, there is an important question which has not hitherto been analysed, except in the case of *Carteia*. This involves the consideration of the probable status of *coloniae Latinae* of some of these towns, as in the case of *Asido, Carmo, Ceret, Edeta, Iulia Libyca,* Maguilla (Badajoz), *Obulco, Valeria,* and *Metellinum.*[39] In addition, *Asido* and *Clunia* (*coloniae Romanae*) could previously have been a *municipium civium Romanorum* and a *municipium Latinum*, respectively.[40] On the other hand, concerning the date of the references from our sample, more than half of them could be dated between the second half of the 1st century BC and the first half of the 1st century AD, that is, within the two main periods of granting of the Latin rights and Roman citizenship to the Hispanian communities by Caesar and Augustus. As to the third important period of legal and administrative assimilation of the Hispanian communities under the Flavians, the number of references is considerably more reduced, which could be related to a wider dissemination of the *duumviratus* plus *aedilitas* since Augustus.[41]

With these first conclusions in mind, two issues should be examined from the sample of cases: first, the political and administrative meaning of the simple *quattuorviratus*, and, second, the origin and presence of the *quattuorviratus* in *Hispania* considering the existence of a significant group of Republican Latin colonies. Regarding the first, the interpretation suggested by E. Melchor Gil for the *quattuorviri* (*nude dicti*) in the evidence from the Hispanian provinces seems plausible and coherent with the institutional history of the Italic and Hispanian communities (with a few exceptions, which would require particular explanations). So, taking as a starting point some of the conclusions

39 It is almost certain that *Edeta, Iulia Libyca,* and *Valeria* were *coloniae Latinae* given their consideration as *oppida veteris Latii* by Pliny the Elder (*NH.* 3.3.23; 3.3.25). On this issue, see García Fernández 2001, op. cit.; Espinosa Espinosa 2014, op. cit.; and Espinosa Espinosa 2018, op. cit. On the other hand, scholars such as Henderson (1942, op. cit.); Padilla Monge (1985, op. cit.; 1989, op. cit.); Le Roux (2013, op. cit.; 2022, op. cit.); García Fernández (2011, op. cit.; 2015, op. cit.,); González Fernández (2011, op. cit.; 2015, op. cit.); Melchor Gil (2013c, op. cit.); J. Ferrer i Jané, J. Velaza Frías, and O. Olesti Vila, 'II. Nuevas inscripciones rupestres latinas de Oceja y los IIIIviri ibéricos de *Iulia Lybica*', *DHA* 44 (1) (2018), 169–195; and Saquete Chamizo (2023, op. cit.), have suggested the Latin status for *Asido, Carmo, Ceret, Iulia Libyca,* Maguilla (Badajoz), *Obulco,* and *Metellinum.*

40 See, for instance, Pérez Zurita 2004, op. cit., 162; Pérez Zurita 2005, op. cit., 16–17; Melchor Gil 2013a, op. cit., 134–135, and 151; Espinosa Espinosa 2014, op. cit., 25–26, and 97, n. 1346; Sisani 2018a, op. cit., 57–58.

41 In this respect, see Sisani 2018a, op. cit., 51, 58, and 60.

reached by this cholar,[42] the simple *quattuorviratus* should be understood in two different ways. On the one hand, as the identification of the two pairs of *quattuorviri*, that is, the college of *quattuorviri per se*,[43] and, on the other hand, as the pair of *quattuorviri iure dicundo*,[44] the *quattuorviri aedilicia potestate* being mainly mentioned as *aediles*.[45] For example, without attempting to be exhaustive, *Clunia*, *Iulia Libyca*, *Munigua*, *Sabora*, and *Termes* seem to provide references to the college of *quattuorviri* per se,[46] *Asido*, *Carmo*, *Carteia*, *Ceret*,

42 A. D. Pérez Zurita (2004, op. cit., 157; 2005, op. cit., 14), in not accepting an institutional division of functions within the *quattuorviratus*, goes much further in his conclusions than E. Melchor Gil (2013a, op. cit., 137, 139–141, and 152; 2013c, op. cit., 45–47), who admits the division of roles from Caesar onwards. However, A. D. Pérez Zurita does not exclude that there was an informal splitting of competences as demonstrated by the epigraphic evidence.

43 In this respect, see Melchor Gil 2013a, op. cit., 142, 146–147, and 152; Melchor Gil 2013c, op. cit., 51. Similarly, see Laffi 2000a, op. cit., 80; 2000b, op. cit., 33; Laffi 2006, op. cit., 112; Pérez Zurita 2004, op. cit., 154–158; Pérez Zurita 2005, op. cit., 12–14; Bispham 2007, op. cit., 291 and 293; Sisani 2018a, op. cit., 58–59 and 65; Sisani 2021, op. cit., 69–70.

44 On this issue, see Melchor Gil 2013a, op. cit., 142–146 and 152; Melchor Gil 2013c, op. cit., 48–51. See also Degrassi 1962a, op. cit., 109, 126, 166–167; Laffi 2006, op. cit., 112; Pérez Zurita 2004, op. cit., 154–155; Bispham 2007, op. cit., 375; Laffi 2006, op. cit., 112; Sisani 2018a, op. cit. 50, n. 62.

45 On this, see Melchor Gil 2013a, op. cit., 140–147 and 152; Melchor Gil 2013c, op. cit., 47. Similarly, see Degrassi 1962a, op. cit., 170; Senatore 1997, op. cit., 287 and 288; Laffi 2006, op. cit., 112; Bispham 2007, op. cit., 370. On the *quattuorvir aedilicia potestate* from *Gades*, see Table 4.1, no. 23. On the non-coexistence of the *quattuorviratus* and *aedilitas* in the same Roman town except in rare cases of continuity of local *iura* and *instituta*, see Melchor Gil 2013a, op. cit., 137–140 and 152; Melchor Gil 2013c, op. cit., 47–48, n. 24.

46 In this respect, see Table 4.1, no. 40–42 (*Clunia*), 44 (*Iulia Libyca*), 30 (*Munigua*), 34 (*Sabora*), and 52 (*Termes*). Concerning *Iulia Libyca* (*oppidum veteris Latii* according to Pliny the Elder), M. Christol, 'Du nouveau sur les *Cerretani* et sur la Cerdagne à l'époque romaine', *Sources. Les Cahiers de l'âne rouge* 7 (2020), 54–55, seems not to accept that the four persons with Iberic names who are mentioned with the term *quattuorviratus* can be *quattuorviri* because they were not Roman citizens *per honorem* as would be expected in a Roman town with *ius Latii*. In the opinion of this scholar, based on D. Kremer, Ius Latinum. *Le concept de droit latin sous la République et l'Empire* (Paris 2006), 126–127, they should have obtained the *civitas Romana* "à l'entrée en fonction dans la magistrature". Although the literary evidence is unclear (Ascon. *in Pis.* 3 Clark; App. *BC* 2.26; Gai. *Inst.* 1.96; Str. 4.1.12; Cic. *Att.* 5.11.2), chapter 21 of the *lex Irnitana* leaves no doubt (at a legal level) that the Latin magistrates would have become Roman citizens at the end of their office (*cum eo honore abierint*). In this respect, see G. Luraschi, Foedus, ius Latii, civitas. *Aspetti costituzionali della romanizzazione in Transpadana* (Padua 1979), 165, 168, 260, 323–325, 461–462, and 484; García Fernández 2001, op. cit., 14, 23, 58–59, and 150–156; S. Barbati, 'Ancora sulle cosiddette "colonie latine fittizie" transpadane (Asc. *In Pis.* 3 Clark)', *Quaderni Lupiensi di Storia e Diritto* 3 (2013), 82–83. On the access procedure to the Roman citizenship in Roman towns with *ius Latii*, see V. Marotta, 'Doppia cittadinanza e pluralità degli ordinamenti. La *Tabula Banasitana* e le linee 7–9 del Papiro di Giessen 40

*Edeta*, *Gades*, Marchena, *Segobriga*, and *Metellinum* would offer cases of *quattuorviri iure dicundo*,[47] and *Clunia*, *Segobriga*, and *Metellinum* would prove that the coexistence of the *aedilitas* and the *quattuorviratus* should be understood as the references to the aedilician and judicial functions of the two pairs of magistrates, respectively.[48]

On the other hand, the alleged grouping of *duumviri iure dicundo* and *aediles* within the term *quattuorviratus* could be replaced with alternative reasonings to explain the apparent coexistence of *quattuorviri* and *duumviri* in some

---

col. I', *AG* 236 (3–4) (2016), 472, n. 31; E. García Fernández, '*L. Venidius Ennychus* (TH 89) y el acceso de los magistrados provinciales a la ciudadanía romana', in Gratias tibi agimus. *Homenaje al profesor C. González Román*, ed. J. Mangas Manjarrés and Á. Padilla Arroba (Granada 2021), 117–137. On the other hand, as G. Alföldy, 'Notes sur la relation entre le droit de cité et la nomenclature dans l'Empire romain', *Latomus* 25 (1966), 37–57; García Fernández 2001, op. cit., 139–150; E. García Fernández, 'Sobre la condición latina y su onomástica: los ediles de *Andelo*', *EFT*(*hist*) 25 (2012) 423–436, have proposed, the *cives Latini* could have had both peregrine names and *duo* or *tria nomina*. Therefore, there would be no problem in accepting that these four persons were the college of *quattuorviri* from *Iulia Libyca*. The fact that they had Iberic names could be explained because they were among the first *quattuorviri* chosen within this Roman town or there was not a lesser college of magistrates (such as the quaestorship) which would have enabled them to obtain the *civitas Romana* before. Alternatively, it can be considered that the supreme college of magistrates could only have provided the Roman citizenship in the case of the presence of two colleges, although the evidence from the *municipia Flavia* shows that the magistrates had the opportunity to achieve the *civitas Romana* being both *duumviri* (*CIL* II$^2$/5, 291: *Cisimbrium*, Rute) and *aediles* (*CIL* II$^2$/5, 308: *Igabrum*, Cabra). On this issue, see Luraschi 1979, op. cit., 317–329; Andreu 2004, op. cit., 135.

47 See, for instance, Table 4.1, no. 1 (*Asido*), 2–6 (*Carmo*), 7–19 (*Carteia*), 20–21 (*Ceret*), 43 (*Edeta*), 24–25 (*Gades*), 29 (Marchena), 45–49 (*Segobriga*), and 57 (*Metellinum*). As Degrassi 1962a, op. cit., 166 suggested, the cases of *iteratio* in *Asido, Carmo, Carteia, Edeta*, and *Segobriga* would correspond to *quattuorviri iure dicundo*. This seems to be confirmed by the elections chaired by *L. Cornelius Balbus Minor* in *Gades* as *quattuorvir* (*quinquennalis*) in 44–43 BC (Table 4.1, no. 24; Cic. *ad Fam.* 10.32.2; Degrassi 1962a, op. cit. 160 and 161; Melchor Gil 2013a, op. cit., 143 and 144 and the honorific *quattuorviratus* held by Germanicus and Drusus in *Carteia* under Tiberius (Table 4.1, no. 11; Degrassi 1962a, op. cit., 126; Melchor Gil 2013a, op. cit., 144). On *Carmo*, see A. U. Stylow, 'Una aproximación a la Carmo romana a través de su epigrafía. Nuevas aportaciones y revisión crítica', in *Carmona Romana, vol. 1*, ed. A. Caballos Rufino (Seville 2012), 133–148.

48 *Clunia*: for the *quattuorviri*, see Table 4.1, no. 37–42; for the *aediles*, see *RPC* I 453, 455, and 458. *Segobriga*: for the *quattuorviri*, see Table 4.1, no. 45–50; for the *aediles*, see Table 4.1, no. 48, *CIL* II, 3103–3104, *HEp* 10, 2000, 212 and 315, *HEp* 19, 2010, 138, *AE* 2010, 739, and *AE* 2014, 724. *Metellinum*: for the *quattuorviri*, see Table 4.1, no. 57; for the *aediles*, see *HEp* 2014–2015, 68; J. C. Saquete Chamizo and S. Guerra Millán, 'Una inscripción constructiva procedente de *Metellinum* (provincia Lusitania)', *ZPE* 196 (2015), 303–306; Saquete Chamizo (2023).

Hispanian towns, such as *Aeso, Asido, Edeta, Gades, Ilipula Minor, Munigua, Obulco, Sabora*, and *Metellinum*.[49] In this respect, scholars such as A. Degrassi and S. Sisani have used this traditional interpretation for cases from Italy and *Hispania*,[50] but at the same time they have suggested other feasible explanations, which they have discarded for the understanding of the *quattuorviratus* in the Hispanian provinces. These include changes in the legal and administrative status of the Roman towns and processes of refounding and reconstitution. This would explain the presence of *quattuorviri* and *duumviri* in Roman towns such as *Brixia, Mantua, Marruvium, Perusia*, and *Tarentum* in Italy and *Asido* and *Gades* in *Hispania* (among others).[51] These alternative explanations had already been suggested by scholars such as A. D. Pérez Zurita, E. Bispham, and E. Melchor Gil, who have consistently used them in their analyses of the *quattuorviratus* in Italy and *Hispania*.[52]

49 For *Aeso*, see Table 4.1, no. 36 (*quattuorvir* and *duumvir*), *CIL* II, 4458 (*duumvir*), 4464 (*duumvir*), 4468 (*duumviralis*), *IRC* II, 24 (*duumvir bis*), 27 (*duumvir*), 29 (*duumvir*), and 30 (*duumvir bis*). For *Asido*, see Table 4.1, no. 1 (*quattuorvir*) and *CIL* II, 1314 (*duumvir*). For *Edeta*, see Table 4.1, no. 43 (*quattuorvir bis*), *CIL* II, 3789 (*duumvir*), and 6014 (*duumvir bis*). For *Gades*, see Table 4.1, no. 23 (*quattuorvir aedilicia potestate*), 24 (*quattuorvir*), 25 (*quattuorvir*), 26 (*quattuorvir*), Avien., *Ora* 275–283 (*duumvir*), *CIL* II, 1313 (*duumvir*), and 1731 (*duumvir*). For *Ilipula Minor*, see Table 4.1, no. 27 (*quattuorvir* and *duumvir bis*). For *Munigua*, see Table 4.1, no. 30 (*quattuorviri*), 31 (*quattuorvir?*), *CIL* II, 1053 (*duumvir?*), *CILA* Se 4, 1072 (*duumvir bis*), 1073 (*duumvir bis*), 1074 (*duumvir*), 1075 (*duumvir bis*), and 1077 (*duumvir bis*). For *Obulco*, see Table 4.1, no. 32 (*quattuorvir?*), *CIL* II, 2126 (*duumvir*), 2129 (*duumvir*), 2131 (*duumvir designatus*), 2132 (*duumvir*), 2133 (*duumvir*), and 2149a (*duumvir III*). For *Sabora*, see Table 4.1, no. 34 (*quattuorviri* and *duumviri*). For *Metellinum*, see Table 4.1, no. 57 (*quattuorvir?*), *HEp* 5, 1995, 94 (*duumvir ter*), *CIL* II, 610 (*duumviri*), *HEp* 2016–2017, 25 (*duumvir*).

50 So, for instance, Degrassi (1962a, op. cit., 107–108, 162, and 170) and Sisani 2018a, op. cit., 42, n. 3, and 51–52; Sisani 2021, op. cit., 71, n. 211 for *Pompeii* in Italy and *Munigua* and *Sabora* in *Hispania* (among others).

51 Degrassi 1962a, op. cit., 118, 124–125, 166–167; Sisani 2018a, op. cit., 56–57, 60, and 62; Sisani 2021, op. cit., 43–48.

52 In this respect, concerning *Perusia, Pompeii*, and *Tarentum* in Italy, and *Aeso, Ilipula Minor, Munigua*, and *Sabora* in *Hispania*, see Pérez Zurita 2004, op. cit., 146 and 161; Pérez Zurita 2005, op. cit., 5 and 16), Bispham 2007, op. cit., 261–267 and 303, 357–358, 387, and 403; and Melchor Gil 2013a, op. cit., 142, n. 24, and 147–150. In the opinion of E. Melchor Gil (2018a, op. cit., 149), *Falerio Picenus* seems to be the exception to the rule since this Roman colony governed by *duumviri* and *aediles* has provided a letter from Domitian addressed to the *quattuorviri et decuriones* (*CIL* IX, 5420). In any event, the conflict that this evidence poses does not seem to invalidate alternative explanations for most cases. Finally, A. D. Pérez Zurita (2004, op. cit., 146, 160, 162–163; 2005, op. cit., 5, 15, 16–18) has added new reasonings such as the alignment of the colleges of magistrates with others which were more widely disseminated in the neighbouring towns, as in the case of the *duumviratus* plus *aedilitas*.

Second, concerning the origin and presence of the *quattuorviratus* in *Hispania*, the existence of a significant group of Republican Latin colonies (an aspect that has not been considered in previous works except for *Carteia*) may help us understand this matter in a better way. In this respect, as said above, a significant number of the Hispanian towns with *quattuorviri* were almost certainly *coloniae Latinae*: *Asido, Carmo, Carteia, Ceret, Edeta, Iulia Libyca, Obulco, Valeria,* and *Metellinum*. Some of them, as in the case of *Edeta, Iulia Libyca,* and *Valeria,* were transformed into *municipia Latina* by Augustus, to which were added, under Augustus and the Flavians, new *municipia Latina* such as *Aeso, Ilipula Minor, Munigua, Obulcula, Sabora, Segobriga, Sigarra, Termes,* and [- - -]*nisi-*. Maguilla (Badajoz), as seen before, could have been a *colonia Latina* or a *municipium Flavium*, whereas Marchena (Seville) could have been an Augustan *municipium Latinum*.[53] Therefore, in view of this, the communities with Latin rights seem to have played a significant role in the origin and dissemination of the *quattuorviratus* in the Hispanian provinces.

Considering that the *duumviratus* plus *aedilitas* are significantly present in the Hispanian evidence from *coloniae Romanae, municipia civium Romanorum,* and *municipia Latina* from Augustus onwards,[54] it is reasonable to suggest that the presence of the *quattuorviratus* during the same period could be the fingerprint of the previous political and administrative structure of certain Roman towns in Republican times. Given that Caesar and the triumvirs created the first *coloniae Romanae* and *municipia civium Romanorum* in *Hispania*,[55] those Republican Roman towns with *quattuorviratus* should necessarily be *coloniae Latinae* such as *Carteia*. With this in mind, the numismatic evidence coming from this Latin colony enables us to establish four different periods according to the Carteian magistrates responsible for the coinage: 1) *quaestores* (*c*.125–105 BC), 2) *censores* (*c*.100–95 BC), 3) *aediles* (*c*.90–65 BC), and

53 On these issues, see above.

54 So, for instance, E. Melchor Gil and A. D. Pérez Zurita, 'La concesión de honores públicos a magistrados y decuriones en las ciudades de la Bética', *FlorIlib* 14 (2003a), 173–233; Melchor Gil 2013a, op. cit., 147; Sisani 2018a, op. cit., 51, 57–60.

55 Scholars such as A. Padilla Monge, 'Algunas cuestiones en torno a la elite de Carteia', *Gerión* 29, no. 1 (2011), 260–263 and S. Sisani (2018a, op. cit., 54; 2018b, op. cit., 337–338) have suggested that *Carteia* could have been transformed into a *municipium civium Romanorum* in 90 BC as a result of the *lex Iulia de civitate*. However, scholars such as E. García Fernández (2001, op. cit., 152) have ruled out this possibility, taking into account that the *leges de civitate* should have applied only to the Italic communities within the *formula togatorum*. The *tribus Sergia* in which was included the *quattuorvir C. Curvius C. f. Rusticus* seems to suggest that *Carteia* was transformed into a *municipium civium Romanorum* by Caesar or the triumvirs.

4) *quattuorviri* (*c*.55 BC–AD 15).[56] It is not accidental that *Carteia* was governed by *quattuorviri* shortly after 61–60 BC. This was the time when Caesar carried out his praetorship in *Hispania Ulterior* and fostered some legal and administrative reforms in certain non-Roman towns such as *Gades*, where the local elite agreed to change some Phoenician-Punic *iura* and *mores*.[57]

This matter, together with the dissemination of the *quattuorviratus* among the *municipia civium Romanorum* from Italy after the *bellum Sociale*,[58] supports Caesar's alleged appeal to the *Transpadani* to elect *quattuorviri* in their *coloniae Latinae* in 51 BC,[59] and the choice of the *quattuorviratus* as the supreme college of magistrates in the *municipia civium Romanorum* from *Gallia Cisalpina* and the *coloniae Latinae* from *Gallia Narbonensis* in 49 BC,[60] provide enough evidence to suggest that Caesar could have introduced the *quattuorviratus* in the *coloniae Latinae* from *Hispania* at two different moments in time, as a result of a plan for a general political and administrative homogenisation. The latter came because of a plan for a general political and administrative homogenization: first, in 61–60 BC, during his praetorship in *Hispania Ulterior*,[61] and, second, between 49 and 45 BC, after the *bellum civile*. Up to that moment, the evidence from the probable *coloniae Latinae* from *Hispania* shows a variety

56 A. Vives Escudero, *La moneda hispánica* (Madrid 1924); On this issue, see F. Chaves Tristán, *Las monedas Hispano-Romanas de* Carteia (Barcelona 1979), 36–49; J. S. Hernández Fernández, 'Tito Livio XLIII, 3 y los *nomina* de los magistrados monetales de Carteia', *Faventia* 16, no. 2 (1994), 86–107; P. P. Ripollès, *Las acuñaciones provinciales romanas de Hispania* (Madrid 2010), 102–106; Padilla Monge 2011, op. cit., 262–263.

57 In this respect, see Cic. *Balb.* 19.43; E. García Fernández, 'Un comentario al discurso *pro Balbo* de Cicerón', in *Dialéctica histórica y compromiso social, vol. 1*, ed. C. Fornis, J. Gallego and P. López Barja (Zaragoza 2010), 152–153; Melchor Gil 2013b, op. cit., 139.

58 See, for instance, Degrassi 1962b, op. cit., 185; Sherwin-White 1973, op. cit., 63, 165–166; Laffi 2000a, op. cit., 79–80; Laffi 2000b, op. cit., 33; Laffi 2006, op. cit., 112–113; Pérez Zurita 2004, op. cit., 137–138; Bispham 2007, op. cit., 253–254; Melchor Gil 2013a, op. cit., 134; Sisani 2018a, op. cit., 60; Sisani 2021, op. cit., 42–43.

59 On this matter, see Cic. *Att.* 5.2.3. For the several interpretations of this text, see Luraschi 1979, op. cit., 389–390, 397–399, 433–434, 483–484; García Fernández 2001, op. cit., 27; Bispham 2007, op. cit., 253; Sisani 2018a, op. cit., 61.

60 On the *quattuorviratus* in the *municipia civium Romanorum* from *Gallia Cisalpina*, see Laffi 2000a, op. cit., 91; 2000b, op. cit., 35; García Fernández 2001, op. cit., 27; Bispham 2007, op. cit., 254; Sisani 2018a, op. cit., 44–45, 60–61, 67–68. On the *quattuorviratus* in the *coloniae Latinae* from *Gallia Narbonensis*, see Gascou 1991, op. cit.; García Fernández 2001, op. cit., 31–33, 37, 69–70, and 74; Melchor Gil 2013a, op. cit., 135; Sisani 2018a, op. cit., 44 and 46. Concerning the *quattuorviratus* in the *municipia civium Romanorum* from *Gallia Cisalpina*, S. Sisani (2018a, op. cit., 44–45, and 61) has proposed that this political and administrative structure was introduced in them as a result of a *lex Iulia municipalis* adopted in 45 BC.

61 See, for instance, Padilla Monge 2011, op. cit., 263.

of active magistrates, such as *praetores* (*Italica*, 90–70 BC), *censores* (*Carteia*, 100–95 BC), *quaestores* (*Carteia*, 125–105 BC; *Corduba*, 150–70 BC; *Urso*, 150–100 BC; *Valentia*, 138–75 BC), and *aediles* (*Acinipo*, 100–150 BC; *Baelo*, 100–50 BC; *Carteia*, 90–65 BC; *Obulco*, 120–100 BC; *Sabetum*, 49 BC; *Saguntum*, 2nd–1st *c.* BC). Therefore, Caesar could have standarized the political and administrative structure of the Hispanian *coloniae Latinae*, choosing the *quattuorviratus* as the main college of magistrates.[62]

As the epigraphic and numismatic evidence proves, the preference for the *quattuorviratus* would have been replaced by that of the *duumviratus* plus *aedilitas* from Augustus onwards. From that moment on, the *quattuorviratus* would have become the fingerprint of the early integration of certain Hispanian communities through the Latin rights, which were transformed by Caesar, the triumvirs, and Augustus into *coloniae Romanae*, *municipia civium Romanorum*, and *municipia Latina*, keeping that political and administrative structure as a residual college of magistrates. However, certain Augustan Roman towns (as in the case of *Segobriga* and *Sigarra*), located near those listed above (as would be the case of *Valeria* and *Iulia Libyca*, among others), could have assumed the *quattuorviratus* by emulation. The same could apply to certain *municipia Flavia* with *quattuorviratus*, such as *Aeso*, *Ilipula Minor*, *Munigua*, *Obulcula*, *Sabora*, and [- - -]*nisi-*.[63] Nevertheless, there could be an additional explanation for these, as suggested by S. Sisani for certain Roman towns with *quattuorviratus* in Italy under the Flavians.[64] In the opinion of this scholar, some *municipia civium Romanorum* and *coloniae Romanae* from Italy replaced the *duumviratus* plus *aedilitas* with *quattuorviratus* during the Flavian period for two likely reasons: first, as a result of an imperial administrative intervention,[65] and, second, as a product of the revival of the *quattuorviratus*, which represented the archetypical form of the *municipia*. This would have happened in the context of renewed legislative activity at the municipal level in both Italy and the provinces, though S. Sisani would exclude the provinces from this trend.

62 As J. González Fernández (2015, op. cit., 307–309) has suggested, the fragment of a *lex* coming from Maguilla (Badajoz) which contains a reference to *IIIIvir co*[- - -] could be assigned to this historical context. On the significant role played by Caesar in Italy in the field of local administration, see Laffi 2000a, op. cit., 91–92; 2000b, op. cit., 35.

63 In this respect, see Melchor Gil 2013a, op. cit., 150.

64 Sisani 2021, op. cit., 77–78.

65 *Gades*, like *Carsulae* in Italy, seems to have retaken the *quattuorviratus* in place of the *duumviratus* during the 2nd century AD (see Table 4.1, no. 25–26). A. D. Pérez Zurita (2004, op. cit., 163–164), in the absence of a reasonable explanation, has suggested revising the date of such references. By contrast, S. Sisani (2018a, op. cit., 56) has explained them as references to *aediles*. It is not improbable that this administrative change can be understood in relation to the antiquity and prestige of the original college of magistrates.

## 4 Conclusion

The interpretations as regards the presence of the *quattuorviratus* in a number of *coloniae* and *municipia* in *Hispania* have not taken into account the existence of a group of Latin colonies during the Republican period. Up to now, these interpretations have focused on the legal and administrative nature of the *quattuorviratus* (whose naming shows many variants in the sources), as well as the apparent coexistence of the *quattuorviratus* and *duumviratus* plus *aedilitas* in some towns. The resulting high variability of explanations, some of them *ad hoc*, is a constraint on the study of the *quattuorviratus* in *Hispania*, but also in Italy and other Roman provinces. Furthermore, this results in a more difficult understanding of the origin and development of this political and administrative structure, leaving the researcher at the mercy of the historical evidence preserved.

To overcome these challenges, a historical analysis of the literary, epigraphic, and numismatic evidence of 22 Hispanian towns has been carried out, which provides 57 references to the *quattuorviratus* (47 reliable and 10 unclear). Of these towns, 2 were *coloniae Romanae*, 5 *muninicipia civium Romanorum*, and 12 *municipia Latina* between Augustus and the Flavians, the remainder having a colonial or municipal status. This sample, dated between approximately 55 BC and AD 159, comprises several towns which would have previously been *coloniae Latinae* during the Republic, as in the case of *Carteia*, *Edeta*, *Iulia Libyca*, and *Valeria*, among others. Two issues have been examined on the basis of the sample: on the one hand, the political and administrative meaning of the *quattuorviratus*, and, on the other hand, the origin and presence of the *quattuorviratus* in *Hispania*.

In this respect, the naming of the *quattuorviratus* in *Hispania* lacks references to the *potestas*, i.e., it is not known whether the *quattuorviri* were *iure dicundo* or *aedilicia potestate*. Based on the evidence analysed, the *quattuorviratus*, informally called *nude dicti*, can be interpreted as the joint reference to the two *quattuorviri* pairs, that is, the *quattuorviri* college per se, but also as the pair of *quattuorviri iure dicundo*. Regarding the origin and presence of these magistrates in *Hispania*, its dissemination should be understood as the result of the same historical processes known in Italy after the *bellum Sociale*. Taking into account the existence of a significant group of *coloniae Latinae* during the Republican period, as well as the diversity of magistrates leading these colonies (such as *praetores*, *censores*, *quaestores*, and *aediles*), the establishment of the *quattuorviratus* in them would be the result of the homogenization of the political and administrative structure of these towns. This would be the footprint of an administrative decision taken by Caesar in *Gallia Cisalpina*, *Gallia*

*Narbonensis* and *Hispania*, which in the latter may have been implemented in two phases: in 61–60 BC, during his praetorship in *Hispania Ulterior*, and between 49 and 45 BC, after the *bellum civile*. Since the *quattuorviratus* and the *tribus Voltinia* were the distinguishing marks of the Latin rights granted by Caesar in *Gallia Narbonensis*,[66] it cannot be rejected that the establishment of the *quattuorviratus* in *Hispania* (both in the preexisting *coloniae Latinae* and in the new ones created by Caesar) had gone hand in hand with the *ius adipiscendae civitatis Romanae per magistratum* and the *tribus Sergia*.[67]

---

66 On this issue, see Gascou 1991, op. cit.; García Fernández 2001, op. cit., 31–71; Sisani 2018b, op. cit., 354.

67 The *quattuorviratus* and the *tribus Sergia* are present in *Carteia* (Table 4.1, no. 9) and probable Latin colonies such as *Carmo* (*CILA* Se 3, 890), *Ceret* (Table 4.1, no. 22; *CIL* II, 5405), and *Metellinum* (*HEp* 2, 1990, 33; *HEp* 2016–2017, 25). Given the *tribus* known in *Hispania*, it does not seem that the likely *coloniae Latinae* could have had the *ius adipiscendae civitatis Romanae per magistratum* before Caesar. See, for instance, García Fernández 2001, op. cit., 82, 102, and 153. On the granting of this right by Augustus to the Hispanian Latin colonies in relation to their transformation into *municipia Latina*, see Espinosa Espinosa 2014, op. cit., 36–37, 135–136, 218–219; Espinosa Espinosa 2018, op. cit., 243.

# PART 2

## *Acculturation*

CHAPTER 5

# Collective Organisation of Matrons in Monarchic and Republican Rome and its Visibility in Public Spaces

*Daniel León Ardoy*

## 1 Preliminary Concepts

Since the mythical dawn of Roman civilisation and the founding of the city of Rome, conventionally established in 753 BC, women formed an essential and unofficial part of the shaping of the State.[1] As can be inferred from Greco-Latin historiography, from the beginning of the *Urbs* the monopoly of legitimate violence was held by men, since we are dealing with another patriarchal, patrilineal and patrilocal society.[2] Notwithstanding, women would begin, very early on, to organise themselves collectively and to make their own decisions for the benefit of the community in the face of unsolvable situations on the part of men. This does not mean that they tried to establish a political power parallel to that of men or that they rebelled against patriarchy. Quite the opposite: from the start, Roman women accepted their totally secondary, even non-existent, role in Roman public life, fitting into the intimate and private physical and mental spaces that their fathers and husbands had assigned them.[3] Certainly, it was a passive role imposed by *mos maiorum*, which, through customary channels or private initiatives, would be legislatively endorsed. As the jurist Cnaeus Domitius Annius Ulpianus explains in his work *ad Sabinum*:

> *Feminae ab omnibus officiis civilibus, vel publicis remotae sunt; et ideo nec iudices ese possunt, nec magistratum gerere, nec postulare, nec pro alio intervenire, nec procuratores existere.*[4]

---

1 Predoctoral contract holder (FPU) attached to the Department of Ancient History at the University of Seville. Work included in the R&D&I project PID2022-138873NB-I00, funded by MCIN/AEI/10.13039/501100011033/ and 'ERDF. A way of making Europe' and in the research group "Campo y Ciudad. Estructuras sociales, económicas e ideológicas en Andalucía y el Mundo Mediterráneo durante la Antigüedad" (HUM 441)

2 E. Cantarella, *La mujer romana* (Santiago de Compostela 1991), 9.

3 R. M. Cid López, 'Mujeres y actividades políticas en la República. Las matronas rebeldes y sus antecesoras en la Roma antigua', in *Mujeres en la Antigüedad Clásica: género, poder y conflicto*, ed. A. Domínguez Arranz (Madrid 2010), 125.

4 D. 50.17.2 (Ulp. 1 *ad Sab.*).

 | DOI:10.1163/9789004685734_006

With this brief but categorical passage, Ulpian perpetuated at the beginning of the 3rd century AD those legal precepts that were fully in force in classical times concerning the capacity, or rather the incapacity, of women to act in the public-political sphere of competence, which was exclusive to men. It is abundantly clear that, at the height of the post-classical legislative tradition into which this author fits, these *officia* as a whole were a male preserve, but had this always been the case? At this point, a distinction must be made between the *officia civilia* and the *publica*. While women were always denied access to public offices such as magistracies and other technical state tasks by patriarchal customary imposition, with regard to civil offices we find a certain permissiveness that gradually disappeared between the 1st century BC and the 1st century AD.

If we follow a fragment from the sixth book of Ulpian's *ad edictum*, the prohibition for women to *postulare pro alio*, that is, to file claims for another person before the competent jurisdictional magistrate, is due to the edict issued by a praetor in the middle of the 1st century BC. This edict was enacted because of the allegedly quarrelsome actions of a woman named *Carfania*, who would act against the *pudicitia* – a specific virtue of her sex.[5] The jurist is acknowledging that, prior to the promulgation of this edict; Roman women would have had the possibility to act as plaintiffs on behalf of third parties.[6] In turn, if we now look at the content of the *senatusconsultum Velleianum*, decreed in the time of the emperor Claudius for the apparent protection of women, it prohibited them from acting as sureties for other people.[7] As P. Pavón Torrejón rightly points out, it can therefore be inferred that the female sector could have acted as guarantor until approximately the middle of the 1st century AD.[8]

5 D. 3.1.1.5 (Ulp. 6 *ad Ed.*): *Secundo loco edictum proponitur in eos, qui pro aliis ne postulent: in quo edicto excepit praetor sexum et casum, item notavit personas in turpitudine notabiles. sexum: dum feminas prohibet pro aliis postulare. et ratio quidem prohibendi, ne contra pudicitiam sexui congruentem alienis causis se immisceant, ne virilibus officiis fungantur mulieres: origo vero introducta est a Carfania improbissima femina, quae inverecunde postulans et magistratum inquietans causam dedit edicto.*

6 Special attention should be paid to the meaning of the Latin verb *postulare*, as it has been inaccurately translated as "to advocate" (E. Höbenreich, 'Andróginas y monstruos. Mujeres que hablan en la antigua Roma', *Veleia* 22 (2005), 175) when its more reliable translation would be "to sue", which does not necessarily imply that the plaintiff also takes on the role of an advocate for a third party.

7 D. 16.1.2.3 (Ulp. 29 *ad Ed.*); D. 16.1.1.2 (Paul. 30 *ad Ed*).

8 P. Pavón Torrejón, '*Infirmitas enim feminarum, non calliditas auxilium demeruit* (D. 16.1.2.3, Ulp. 29 ad ed.) o la "extrema dualidad" de la condición femenina en el senadoconsulto Veleyano', in Conditio feminae. *Imágenes de la realidad femenina en el mundo romano*, ed. P. Pavón Torrejón (Rome 2021), 131.

*Ergo*, although it was not normal and ethically expected of their sex, they were able to carry out certain *officia civilia* and that those categorical prohibitions alluded to by Ulpian and other jurists such as Paulus were not always in force with regard to the private level of women's actions.

What this whole question makes clear is the palpable contradiction between theory and praxis in which Roman society, and specifically men, would be set up in relation to the competences that women of the Roman elite would have in society. Firstly, the paternalistic tradition that perpetuated the stigma of *infirmitas* or *imbecillitas* intrinsic to the female sex would clash head-on with the determined action of matrons with a high level of cultural, rhetorical, and technical training in economic and legal matters.[9] Secondly, the contradictions would also show themselves in an even more lacerating manner in the public-political space, since the infiltration of women into this sphere of competence, which had always been an exclusively male domain, directly transgressed the *mos maiorum*. Of course, elite women never claimed access to *officia publica*, nor to vote in popular assemblies, nor to participate in the army, but is it not naive to think that, simply because they never considered equal political rights with men, they did not show interest in public-political affairs and did not want to influence them outside of laws and custom? Certainly, we note that ancient Rome was not a sociological exception: even if attempts were made to parcel it out legally, the overflowing reality continually exceeded a legal framework, which, however conservative Roman society may have been, did not escape mutability.

In any case, the acceptance of their subordination would meet success mainly due to the feeling of a certain civic inclusion and certain prerogatives that Roman women were acquiring during the first centuries of the city. It is precisely women who are presented as the fierce defenders and perpetuators of the patriarchal system through their work as educators of their children, new Roman citizens who, from their earliest childhood, will begin to assume the unequal relationship between genders as normal and correct.[10]

However, being outside the legal and customary realm of political decision-making, Roman women were able to recognise themselves, albeit unconsciously,

---

9 See E. A. Hemelrijk, Matrona docta. *Educated Women in the Roman Elite from Cornelia to Julia Domna* (London 1999); R. M. Cid López, 'La educación de la niña romana: de *puella* a *matrona docta*', in *Bien enseñada: la formación femenina en Roma y el Occidente romanizado*, ed. V. Alfaro Bech and R. Francia Somalo (Málaga 2001) 21–44; N. F. Berrino, Mulier potens. *Realtà femminili nel mondo antico* (Galatina 2006), 7–8; M. Corbier, '"Le deuxième sexe" à Rome', in *Marginación y mujer en el Imperio romano*, ed. P. Pavón Torrejón (Rome 2018), 14.

10 Cantarella 1991, op. cit., 95–97.

as individuals with their own unique characteristics. This feeling of belonging to a group was also fostered from the most archaic times in Rome through a series of exclusively female cults and rites regulated, of course, by the male authorities, which indicates that women would have, at certain times of the religious calendar, meeting places without the presence of men.[11] Obviously, these liturgical spaces, in an unpremeditated way, would serve for their collective self-affirmation in others areas, such as politics, albeit in a heterodox and very extraordinary manner.

Nevertheless, we should add that such a women's collective was never completely transversal: female Roman society was affected, as well as its male counterpart, by its historical reality, which would determine the existence for centuries of a palpable division between patrician and plebeian women. Women belonging to the early Roman aristocracy excluded Roman citizens who were not part of the small elite from their worship. It was not until the mid-4th century BC that the patrician-plebeian conflict began to subside, as a result of a protracted legislative process beneficial to the plebs and emerged a *nobilitas* of a plutocratic nature made up of the patricians and the wealthier plebeians, who were eventually able to gain access to the magistracies and thus to the Senate. Of course, women were not left out of these changes at the top of society, although still at the beginning of the 3rd century BC, patrician women vetoed plebeian women by birth or marriage from their cults, as reflected in the episode of Virginia and the plebeian *Pudicitia*.[12] However, gradually all women belonging to this new aristocracy assumed their inclusion in the same group. However, although the purely blood barrier had been solved, the economic one always remained: when circumstances required it, the wealthy women of the Middle and Late Republic, who belonged to the *nobilitas*, organised themselves as a truly privileged group, leaving the most impoverished citizens of Roman society (and, obviously, also the freedwomen) on the margins of their demands. It's true that, as we shall see, women's collective political claims were motivated as a consequence of certain legal and tax measures aimed exclusively at this wealthy sector of the population, not affecting those women who, although Roman citizens, lived in very poor conditions.

---

11 See N. Boëls–Janssen, *La vie religieuse des matrones dans la Rome archaïque* (Rome 1993); R. M. Cid López, 'El *ordo matronarum* y los espacios femeninos en la Roma antigua. Las fiestas de *Matronalia* y *Fortuna muliebris*', in *Pautas históricas de sociabilidad femenina rituales y modelos de representación: Actas del V Coloquio Internacional de la Asociación Española de Investigación Histórica de las Mujeres*, ed. M. Nash, M. J. de la Pascua and G. Espigado (Cádiz 1999), 43–49.

12 Liv. 10.23.1–10; R. A. Bauman, *Women and Politics in Ancient Rome* (London–New York 1992), 15–16.

Likewise, in the episodes we will analyse below, we observe that the classical authors place special emphasis on narrating events carried out by a specific profile of wealthy women: the *matronae*. According to Aulus Gellius, any woman who was married by *iustum matrimonium* was a matron irrespective of their economic capacity and whether or not they had children, although tradition expected them to have offspring and to behave according to the ideal established by ancestral customs.[13] However, Greek and Latin historians mostly record events related to rich matrons, which is a true reflection of what they do with men, that is to say, history of elite. For this reason, Valerius Maximus was the first author to refer to the group of the wealthy matrons led by Hortensia as *ordo matronarum*, assimilating it, presumably in a sarcastic way, with the two main ruling *ordines* of the Late Republic, the *ordo senatorius* and the *ordo equester*.[14] As defined by G. Alföldy, an *ordo* is an official, privileged and corporately organised body.[15] Since *matronae* were never recognised as such, this classical historian's use of such a concept, while illuminating the reality of the time, remains purely literary. In turn, although they did not act in a corporate manner, since they lacked such official status, the episodes we will study do respond to a premeditated feminine organisation with clear political connotations on various issues that altered the customary and legal *statu quo* of women in Roman society. Certainly, we are dealing with what the Romans called *axitiosae*, that is to say, women who took to the streets of Rome in groups, temporarily occupying those urban male landscapes of public representation, such as the *Forum* or the vicinity of the *curia*, to make political demands, usually due to lost rights or endangered prerogatives.[16] To paraphrase E. Cantarella, true political activists.[17] However, as mentioned at

---

13 Gell. 18.6.8; M. Salazar Revuelta, 'Estatus jurídico y social de la *materfamilias* en el marco de la ciudadanía romana', in Mulier. *Algunas historias e instituciones de derecho romano*, ed. R. Rodríguez and M. J. Bravo (Madrid 2013), 199–222.

14 Val. Max. 8.3.3; L. M. Webb, 'Female Interventions in Politics in the *libera res publica*: Structures and Practices', in *Leadership and Initiative in Late Republican and Early Imperial Rome*, ed. R. M. Frolov and C. Burden-Strevens (Leiden–Boston 2022) 156, 158–159. L. M. Webb is correct in stating that the *ordo matronarum* as an idea already appears in Livy's work when he describes the episodes of the plebeian *Pudicitia* (296 BC) and the abrogation of the *lex Oppia* (195 BC). Livy uses the word *ordo* to refer to other social groups which he compares to the wealthy group of married Roman women, so that he is implicitly recognizing this group as *ordo* (in 10.23.10: "*nec matronis solum sed omnis ordinis feminis*"; in 34.7.1: "*omnes alii ordines*"). However, the first to use the term *ordo matronarum* was Valerius Maximus.

15 G. Alföldy, *Nueva historia social de Roma* (Seville 2021), 152.

16 Cid López 2010, op. cit, 126.

17 E. Cantarella, *Pasado próximo. Mujeres romanas de Tácita a Sulpicia* (Madrid 1997), 119–141.

the beginning of the chapter, they did not always speak out in public for this reason: we will look at some events in which the matrons of the monarchical and republican period acted politically out of their fervent patriotism and civic responsibility, serving as true *exempla* for later generations of women.[18]

The originality of the term "*ordo matronarum*" and its practical utility led J. Gagé, historian of the last century, to retrieve it from the ancient historiography.[19]

## 2 The *Ordo Matronarum* in the Legends of the Roman Monarchy

When we follow the most widespread founding legend, whereby the Albans princes Romulus and Remus erected Rome in 753 BC, we notice that women had no part in the creation of the city. Indeed, it was an all-male enterprise controlled by the man who would become Rome's first king. Precisely because of this lack of women in archaic Rome, Romulus and the primitive senatorial institution decided to send legations to the surrounding states to establish matrimonial alliances with their women and, in this way, perpetuate themselves over time. Nevertheless, as these ambassadorships went unheeded, Romulus came up with a plan: he organised games called *Consualia* and invited neighbouring villages. The Sabine people, both men and women, turned out en masse. At one point, the king of Rome gave the order for the Romans to abduct only maidens, especially Sabine maidens, as they were the most numerous, in violation of any law of hospitality. The abducted women's parents managed to escape the ambush, declared war on Rome while Romulus justified his act to the women because their parents had refused the previous embassy, and encouraged them to give themselves affectionately to their new and attentive Roman husbands.[20] According to Livy, after the double defeat of the *Caeninenses* and the *Antemnates*, two of the outraged peoples, Romulus' wife, Hersilia, acted as representative for the daughters of the vanquished, proposing her husband that he pardon their parents and grant them Roman

---

18 S. López Moreda, M. L. Harto Trujillo and J. Villalba Álvarez, 'Introducción general: valor educativo de los *exempla*', in *Valerio Máximo, Hechos y dichos memorables: Libros I–VI* (Madrid 2003), 39–44; J. Guantes García, 'Maternidad y filiaciones en la Roma primitiva. Una revisión del rapto de las Sabinas', in *Madres y familias en la Antigüedad: Patrones femeninos en la transmisión de emociones y de patrimonio*, ed. R. M. Cid López, A. Domínguez Arranz and R. M. Marina Sáez (Gijón 2021), 100.

19 See J. Gagé, Matronalia. *Essai sur les dévotions et les organisations cultuelles des femmes dans l'ancienne Rome* (Brussels 1963).

20 Liv. 1.9.

citizenship. Romulus accepted the proposal.[21] This will not be the only time when a female crowd turned to women close to power asking them to intercede with their male relatives.

However, the Sabines, led by *Titus Tatius*, managed to enter Rome thanks to *Tarpeia's* collaboration, a woman of the Roman elite (which might partially contradict the fact that there were no proper Roman women at the time of the foundation), and entrenched themselves in the Capitoline Hill. At this point, different classical authors give different versions of what happened. According to Livy, while Romans and Sabines were fighting between the Palatine and Capitoline Hills, the site of the historic *Forum* of the *Urbs*, Sabine women, some of them pregnant, burst onto the battlefield to try to put an end to the war between their husbands and their fathers with their supplications. Romans and Sabines accepted peace and united into a single people based in Rome, establishing a diarchy.[22] Plutarch's account is quite similar: the historian of *Chaeronea* singles out *Hersilia, Hostilius*' wife, among all the Sabine women.[23] According to Dionysius of Halicarnassus and Appian of Alexandria, the Sabine wives decided to meet in assembly among themselves to discuss how they could reconcile their fathers and husbands. *Hersilia*, a member of the Sabine elite, proposed to go on an embassy to the Sabine camp, a male military space, to try to persuade their relatives to reconcile with the Romans. Once the decision was taken, the Sabine women informed the Senate. Senators ratified *Hersilia's* proposal but qualified it: those wives who did not yet have children should stay in Rome. On the other hand, those women who were mothers of several children could go to the camp with as many children as they wished. This senatorial decision makes it clear that the main reason for the abduction of the Sabine women was indeed the perpetuation of Roman civilisation. Finally, the Sabine women made their way to the Sabine camp and, after a long plea from *Hersilia*, the parents decided to make peace with their Roman

21 Liv. 1.11.2; We do not share the claim T. Stevenson ('Women of Early Rome as "Exempla" in Livy, "Ab Urbe Condita", Book 1', *Classical World* 104, no. 2 (2011), 177–178) advances concerning the rejection or distrust that Hersilia's intervention before Romulus would have caused among Roman readers. This character from the Roman legendary tradition is presented by Livy as a positive *exemplum*, a transcript of the concord that Augustan propaganda was trying to underpin as one of the fundamental pillars of the new regime. From this account, it can be inferred that neither Romulus nor the author himself is uncomfortable with *Hersilia's* interference. In fact, the king of Rome is not wary of his wife's advice, but readily accepts it (R. Brown, 'Livy's Sabine Women and the Ideal of *Concordia*', *TAPhA* 125 (1995), 302).

22 Liv. 1.13.1–5.

23 Plut. *Rom.* 14–20.

sons-in-law.[24] This will not be the only occasion on which we study the successful role of women's delegations in defending the homeland against external threats. In any case, these versions inform us about the collective political interest of matrons, on this occasion in a situation of extreme necessity for the Roman state, and their irruption into masculine spaces, such as military camps or, directly, war scenarios.

Of course, we must clarify that, as these are legendary accounts given by historians who lived centuries after the events described, we cannot grant them veracity. The Romans, as well as using legends to explain the divine origin of certain *gentes*, used them to reinforce various institutions and moral customs, such as, for example, the relationship between the legend of *Lucretia* and female *pudicitia* (and what it meant to lose it). Moreover, through legends they could establish illustrious precedents on political, legal and economic issues. In other words, the myths served as solemn and indisputable *exempla* or principles of authority for Romans, and particularly Roman women, to act according to the *mos maiorum*. In this way, they would know the consequences of transgressing them. This issue creates a dilemma: are legends a reflection of times gone by? That is to say, does the fact that legendary women of the Roman Monarchy and the Early Republic play an important role in some accounts mean that they already enjoyed an important political weight in the public sphere of these archaic times? Or are certain aspects of the current reality at the time when it was forged or written reflected in the legend? If we assume that legends are created *ad hoc* for a specific purpose, the second hypothesis would be the most plausible. In any case, a myth is not created, spread, popularised and assimilated in a short period. It's a complex sociological and psychological process.[25]

## 3 The *Ordo Matronarum* in the Early Republic

A few years after the expulsion of the Etruscan monarchy and the arrival of the Republic, and in the midst of the conflict between patricians and plebeians, the first patriotic intervention of the *ordo matronarum* took place in this new phase of Rome. We refer to the legend of *Coriolanus* and the embassy of

---

24 D. H. 2.45–47; App. *Reg.* 5; Guantes García 2021, op. cit., 109–112.

25 C. Herrmann, *Le rôle judiciaire et politique des femmes sous la République romaine* (Brussels 1964), 9; M. I. Finley, *Uso y abuso de la historia* (Barcelona 1984), 1–44; F. Rohr Vio, *Le custodi del potere. Donne e politica alla fine della repubblica romana* (Rome 2019), 13; Webb 2022, op. cit., 155.

matrons. At the beginning of the 5th century BC, at a time of famine, the patrician *Gnaeus Marcius Coriolanus*, a fervent enemy of the plebeians, proposed not to distribute wheat to the plebs unless they ceased their revolutionary practices. This opinion provoked the wrath of the tribunes of the plebs, who set a date to bring him before the people. *Coriolanus*' patrician pride prevented him from being sentenced by plebeian magistrates, so he decided not to show up to hear the verdict. Convicted in rebellion, *Coriolanus* went into exile and sought refuge with the Volscians, a people he had subdued a few years earlier by taking the city of *Corioli* (in fact, his *cognomen* comes from this military success). Seeking revenge, *Coriolanus* led the Volscian army and began to move towards Rome.[26] The Roman Senate, under pressure from the plebs, sent two delegations of parliamentarians and one of priests to the enemy camp to negotiate peace, but *Coriolanus* was adamant. It is at this point that the collective of matrons, patricians of course, enters the political scene.

In view of the failure of the previous embassies, the matrons decide to go to parley with *Coriolanus*' mother, *Veturia*, and his wife, *Volumnia*, to accompany them to the Volscian camp and try to convince their relative to end the war against Rome. Livy is not sure whether this was a female initiative or whether it was an official request to the matrons.[27] However, Dionysius of Halicarnassus, Plutarch and Appian affirm that the idea came from the women gathered in the temple of Jupiter Capitolinus, specifically from *Valeria*, *Publius Valerius Poplicola's* sister (or daughter).[28] After the senators' approval, the retinue of matrons (*mulierum agmen*) and their children presented itself to *Coriolanus*.[29] *Veturia* indignantly rebuked her son for declaring war on his homeland and not thinking of the family he had left behind. Moreover, when

26 Liv. 2.34–35.

27 Liv. 2.40.1.

28 D. H. 8.39; Plut. *Cor.* 33.1–3; App. *Ital.* 5.3.

29 Livy himself (2.40.3) uses this concept to refer to this matronly procession. J. P. Hallett, *Fathers and Daughters in Roman Society. Women and the Elite Family* (Princeton 1984), 33–34; Cid López 2010, op. cit., 131; R. M. Cid López, 'Las matronas y los *agmina mulierum* en la Roma antigua. Del matriotismo a la protesta', in *Cartografías de género en las ciudades antiguas*, ed. C. Martínez López and P. Ubric Rabaneda (Granada 2017) 209; P. D. Conesa Navarro, 'La palabra concedida. Discursos y actitudes "transgresoras" femeninas en la antigua Roma monárquica y republicana', *Arenal* 27, no. 2 (2020), 449. Although R. M. Cid López places in the episode of *Veturia* and *Coriolanus* the first occasion in which Livy uses the word *agmen* about a female group, the fact is that, shortly before, in the episode of *Cloelia* and *Porsena*, the historian used, referring to *Cloelia*, the term *dux agminis virginum* as a group of maidens' guide (2.13.6). We must also qualify the militaristic connotation that E. Valette ('Les "discours" de *Veturia, Valeria* et *Hersilia* : Les mises en scène de la parole matronale dans la tradition historiographique romaine', *Mondes Anciens* 3 (2012), 2) gives to *agmen mulierum*, situating it as "colonnes de femmes".

*Coriolanus* told his mother that he could not betray the Volscians, *Veturia* showed her great political shrewdness by proposing a temporary truce and urging him to remain in exile without holding a grudge against his fellow citizens, as *Tarquinius Collatinus* had done earlier. *Veturia's* words moved her son, who withdrew the siege of Rome.[30]

Certainly, *Veturia's* speech is a true display of political diplomacy supported by recourse to the family bond and even some emotional blackmail in warning her son that she would commit suicide if she did not succeed in her enterprise. On the other hand, we find again an episode very similar to the one Dionysius of Halicarnassus raised in the case of the embassy of matrons sent to the Sabine camp during the reign of Romulus. In all likelihood, both legends would come from a common legendary trunk. At the same time, the moral of this story is obvious: love of country must prevail even over family ties.[31] According to C. Herrmann, this success of the *ordo matronarum* shows that, although they could not officially hold political office, Roman women could, in exceptional situations, intervene in the public sphere without their honour being undermined.[32] In fact, the Senate and the people of Rome with the erection and dedication of a temple to the goddess *Fortuna Muliebris* rewarded the matrons. Her worship was to be carried out by a priestess chosen from among

The word *agmen* would refer to a group of people on the march, but it does not necessarily have to be associated with warfare.

30 Liv. 2.40.2–10. D. H. 8.44–54; Plut. *Cor.* 34–36; App. *Ital.* 5.3–5; L. Dubosson-Sbriglione, '*Veturia* : négociatrice et ambassadrice de Rome', *EuGeStA* 11 (2021), 116–124.

31 C. Martínez López, 'Las mujeres y la paz en la Historia. Aportaciones desde el mundo antiguo', in *Historia de la paz: tiempos, espacios y actores*, ed. F. A. Muñoz Muñoz and M. López Martínez (Granada 2000), 281–283; Cid López 2010, op. cit., 130–131; K. Mustakallio, 'Women Outside their Homes. The Female Voice in Early Republican Memory: Reconsidering Cloelia and Veturia', *Index* 40 (2012), 165–174; E. Redondo-Moyano, 'El encuentro de Veturia y Coriolano (D. H. *Antiquitates Romanae* 8.44–53)', *SPhV* 18 (2016), 338–342; J. Atkinson, 'Valerius Maximus on *Coriolanus*', *AClass* 60 (2017), 10–11; R. Cid López, 'Mujeres y acción política en la República tardía: las conspiradoras. Imágenes nuevas de viejas prácticas femeninas', in *Lo viejo y lo nuevo en las sociedades antiguas: homenaje a Alberto Prieto. XXXVI Coloquio del GIREA*, ed. J. Cortadella i Morral, O. Olesti Vila and C. Sierra Martín (Besançon 2018), 621; Conesa Navarro 2020, op. cit., 447–449; Webb 2022, op. cit., 167–169. This love for the country on the part of women allowed some researchers to invent and employ the admittedly controversial concept of "matriotic" (Hallett 2004, op. cit., 26; Cid López 2017, op. cit., 208). According to M. Bonjour ('Les personnages féminins et la terre natale dans l'épisode de Coriolan (Liv., 2, 40)', *REL* 53 (1975), 175), Veturia would be an *exemplum* of love for the small homeland, the *patria loci* or *patria naturae*, as opposed to the *patria iuris*.

32 Herrmann 1964, op. cit., 27–29.

all the matrons, who chose *Valeria*.[33] This indicates that, as we will see in the next section, on certain occasions, Roman women were allowed, as a diffuse reflection of the male popular assemblies, to decide on some minor issues that concerned only themselves.

A century later, between 396 and 390 BC, we again have evidence of the activity and initiative of matrons in the public life of the city. When the news reached Rome that the dictator *Marcus Furius Camillus* had ended the long war against the Etruscans of *Veii*, the Roman temples were filled with matrons thanking the gods even before the Senate had decreed it.[34] According to Herrmann, this concentration of matrons was also motivated by the imminent arrival in the *Urbs* of the goddess of *Veii*, *Iuno Regina*.[35] The Senate declared four days of thanksgiving and *Camillus* placed the temple of the new female deity on the Aventine Hill and dedicated the temple of *Mater Matuta*. These actions would cause the matrons, after meeting and discussing the matter, to hand over to the state treasury (*aerarium*) all the gold of their precious objects to the state treasury in order to solve the obstacle concerning the gift that the dictator had promised to Apollo. Once the problem was solved thanks to women's contribution, the Senate granted matrons the use of the *pilentum* and the *carpentum*.[36] In addition, in 390 BC, the Gauls, who had entered Rome causing destruction in their wake, demanded a ransom from the Romans, who were holding out on the Capitoline Hill. As state gold was scarce, the matrons gave theirs so that the sacred gold would not be used. However, *Camillus* defeated the Gauls and in 389 BC these Roman women were given back the gold they had given. Livy records that these women were given the honour of having a funeral eulogy after death (although Plutarch places this concession after the events of 395 BC).[37] Again, two very similar events: voluntary gold contribution of the matrons to solve the problems of the Roman state.[38] This led R. M. Ogilvie to believe that the episode of the gift to Apollo was, in fact, a copy

33 See L. Halkin, *La supplication d'action de grâces chez les Romains* (Paris 1953); Gagé 1963, op. cit., 106–107 and 112; Cid López 1999, op. cit., 52–55; M. Bailón García, "El papel social y religioso de la mujer romana. *Fortuna Muliebris* como forma de integración en los cultos oficiales", *Habis* 43 (2012), 108–111; Atkinson 2017, op. cit., 14–17; Webb 2022, op. cit., 155 and 159; Liv. 2.40.11–12; D. H. 8.55; Plut. *Cor.* 37.

34 Liv. 5.23.3.

35 Herrmann 1964, op. cit., 43–45.

36 Liv. 5.23.8–25.10; Val. Max. 5.6.8; Cid López 2010, op. cit., 133–134. The *pilentum* was a four-wheeled chariot and the *carpentum* was a two-wheeled chariot.

37 Liv. 5.50.7; Plut. *Cam.* 8.4; Val. Max. 5.6.8.

38 Webb 2022: 160–162.

of the other event.[39] In any case, as had happened a century earlier with the public construction of a temple to *Fortuna Muliebris* as a consequence of the decisive female role in the Volscian camp, we can see that the political initiative of these women to contribute would also have beneficial legal repercussions for the group of matrons.

Finally, although some modern scholars place the event described below in 272 BC,[40] it is possible that we should go back a few decades and place it at the end of the 4th century BC. As it could be hypothesised that the young protagonist of this story, *Papirius Praetextatus*, was one of the censors in the year 272 BC, as recorded in the *Fasti Capitolini*.[41] Aulus Gellius tells a story that had been collected by Cato the Elder: at that time, senators were allowed to bring their sons while they were still children to the *curia* when there was a session. On one occasion, having to postpone a very important senatorial question to the next day, the curious mother of one of these children, a certain *Papirius*, persistently asked her son what had been debated in the Senate. *Papirius*, knowing that he should not reveal to the women the contents of the *patres conscripti*'s meetings, lied to his mother and told her that the question was whether it was better for a man to marry two women or a woman to marry two men. She, believing the news, told the rest of the matrons and, the next day, a large number of them appeared in front of the Senate begging for the second option. The stunned senators did not understand until the young *Papirius* revealed the lie he had had to tell his mother. The Senate rewarded little *Papirius* for his loyalty and granted him to be the only child with access to the building alongside his father. He was also given the *cognomen* of *Praetextatus* for having been so prudent while still wearing the *praetexta* gown.[42]

This anecdote makes three things clear: firstly, the interest of the women of the Roman elite in knowing what was being discussed in the *curia*, that is to say, their interest in political matters. Secondly, the idea that matrons would have their own formal (such as some temples) and informal spaces for meeting and discussion is confirmed. In addition, we are faced with an *agmen mulierum* that once again breaks into public spaces of male representation and whose action entails some kind of political or legislative consequence, on this

39 R. M. Ogilvie, *A Commentary on Livy. Books 1–5* (Oxford 1965), 684; L. Peppe, *Posizione giuridica e ruolo sociale della donna romana in età repubblicana* (Milan 1984), 48.

40 For example, Herrmann 1964, op. cit., 48–49; Peppe 1984, op. cit., 81.

41 *AE* 1927, 101. His *praenomen* would be *Lucius*; T. R. S. Broughton, *The Magistrates of the Roman Republic. Volume I (509 B.C.–100 B.C.)* (New York 1951), 198.

42 Gell. 1.23; Cid López 2010, op. cit., 139–140.

occasion, the prohibition of access to the *curia* for young men.[43] In fact, this preventive measure would be aimed at nipping the curiosity of these women in the bud by preventing their young children from acting as a transmitter of information about the issues debated by the senators, many of whom were relatives of these *axitiosae*, which would manifest the evident distrust between the two sexes.

## 4 The *Ordo Matronarum* in the Middle Republic

As has been analysed by many researchers, especially since the second half of the last century, the socio-economic and legal status of Roman women, particularly among those belonging to the elite, progressively improved throughout the Roman Republic. This fact was mainly due to patrimonial and hereditary reasons, since the enactment of the *Lex duodecim tabularum* there are legal provisions that improved the status of women, although this was not their original objective. Between the 5th and 2nd centuries BC, women gradually acquired several socioeconomic rights, such as the *trinoctium*. In addition, there was an increasing use of *sine manu* marriage, the possibility of divorcing, the permission to make a will and the *testamentum per aes et libram*, the *tutoris optio* and the practical freedom that this choice entailed for women (as they were able to control their property themselves). These measures allow us to speak of "female emancipation" from men, despite the fact that, on repeated occasions, legal attempts have been made to curb it without much success, as we will see below in connection with the repeal of the *lex Oppia sumptuaria*.[44] However, these advances were not accompanied by the attainment of political rights: access to popular assemblies, magistracies and, of course, the Senate

43 Interestingly, Aulus Gellius does not use the word *agmen* to refer to this group of matrons who marched to the vicinity of the senatorial chamber to plead, but a similar term: *caterva* (1.23.10).

44 For example, see Herrmann 1964, op. cit.; S. B. Pomeroy, *Goddesses, Whores, Wives and Slaves. Women in Classical Antiquity* (New York 1975); Hallett 1984, op. cit.; Peppe 1984, op. cit.; J. F. Gardner, *Women in Roman Law and Society* (London 1986); E. Cantarella, *Pandora's Daughters. The Role and Status of Women in Greek and Roman Antiquity* (Baltimore 1987); S. Dixon, *The Roman Mother* (London 1988); Cantarella 1991, op. cit.; Cantarella 1997, op. cit.; A. Fraschetti (ed.), *Roman Women* (Chicago–London 2001); D. Gourévitch and M.-T. Raepsaet-Charlier, *La femme dans la Rome antique* (Paris 2001); J. Evans-Grubbs, *Women and the Law in the Roman Empire. A Sourcebook on Marriage, Divorce and Widowhood* (London 2002); Berrino 2006, op. cit.; F. Cenerini, *La donna romana. Modelli e realtà* (Bologna 2009); A. Valentini, *Donne e politica a Roma tra III e II secolo a.C.* (Milan 2010).

remained denied to women. Although at times women brought up this issue publicly, they never tried to subvert it because they had it perfectly assimilated. If we add to the acquisition of these freedoms the fact that, due to the beginnings of extra-Italic Roman imperialism in the 3rd century BC, a large number of fathers and husbands were killed in battle, the wealthy *sui iuris* women settled in Rome grew exponentially from this century onwards, so the emancipation was increased.

During the major war event of the 3rd century BC, the Second Punic War, we see that on several occasions rich matrons contributed financially to the defence of the Roman state through their public worships. In the winter of 218 BC, when Hannibal Barca had already managed to cross the Alps and settle with his army in Italy, due to the news of a series of alleged *prodigia* in and around Rome, the matrons dedicated a bronze statue to *Iuno Regina* on the Aventine Hill.[45] A decade later, in 207 BC, although the balance of the war was tipping in favour of the Romans, another prodigy took place. According to the interpretation of the *haruspices*, this supernatural event concerned the matrons: a lightning had struck the temple of this goddess. The matrons domiciled in the city of Rome or within ten miles of it were summoned by an edict of the curule aediles to the Capitoline Hill, and among themselves, they elected twenty-five, who would contribute small amounts of their dowries to bring *Iuno Regina* a gift.[46]

During the conflict's darkest years, specifically in 215 BC, the tribune of the plebs *Caius Oppius* proposed a law to limit female luxury, the *lex Oppia sumptuaria*, which was passed. As Livy states:

> *ne qua mulier plus semunciam auri haberet nec vestimento versicolori uteretur neu iuncto vehiculo in urbe oppidove aut propius inde mille passus nisi sacrorum publicorum causa veheretur.*[47]

Twenty years later, in 195 BC, the historical context of the Republic was very different: the Carthaginians had been defeated six years earlier and Rome had established itself as the leading political and economic power in the Mediterranean. If the situation was excellent, why was a law enacted during wartime still in force? The wealthy matrons who had been affected by it for two decades would have asked themselves this question (or even those women who had never known any other setting outside the *lex Oppia*). In fact, at the

45 Liv. 21.62.8.

46 Liv. 27.37.8–10; Webb 2022, op. cit., 161.

47 Liv. 34.1.3.

beginning of the 2nd century BC, the law was perceived by these women and by some men as a real undermining of the sumptuary prerogatives and economic freedom enjoyed by matrons. Therefore, when the tribunes of the plebs *Marcus Fundanius* and *Lucius Valerius* announced that they would present a proposal to the people to repeal the law, a new crowd of matrons, urban and rural, filled the entrances to the *Forum* to put pressure on the men and magistrates who were to debate and vote in the assembly.[48] There, the consul Marcus Porcius Cato, a paradigmatic defender of tradition and *mos maiorum*, went so far as to describe the public demonstrations of the matrons as a conspiracy. Likewise, he expressed his refusal to abrogate the *lex Oppia* by alluding to the lost ancient customs of female sobriety and obedience. Certainly, in his speech we can see a real fear of a hypothetical legal and political equality between men and women. *Lucius Valerius* then took the floor to counter-argue Cato's speech and listed all those occasions when the matrons as a collective had taken to the streets of Rome to help their homeland.

Moreover, he argued that a law that had been passed in a difficult wartime context should be repealed when peace came, that the behaviour of matrons had always been impeccable and that it would be very unfair for men to return to pre-war normality but for women not to be able to flaunt their ornamental prerogatives. The day after both interventions, the matrons continued to exert public pressure, but this time in front of the houses of the tribunes of the plebs who were against the repeal, *Marcus* and *Publius Iunius Brutus*. Women continued to demonstrate until they gave up vetoing their colleagues' proposal. Finally, after twenty years, the *lex Oppia* was repealed in the *comitia tributa*.[49] *Lucius Valerius* was right: the *ordo matronarum* had already appeared in public on other occasions as a collective capable of carrying out important actions for the state. Now was the first time that women's interest in reversing real policies that went against the few rights they had won over several centuries was so evident. Matrons were not asking for more prerogatives or access to public office and male honours. They were aware that the situation was unfair and demonstrated to demand the return of lost rights. Both Cato and *Valerius* the starting

48 Cid López 2010, op. cit., 140–143; L. M. Webb, 'Exaequatio *and* aemulatio: *Regulation of Elite Female Status Competition in Mid-Republican Rome*', in *Gender and Status Competition in Pre-Modern Societies* (Turnhout 2021), ed. M. Bayless, J. Liliequist and L. M. Webb, 43–47, 50–51, 54–58.

49 Liv. 34.1–8.3; Val. Max. 9.1.3. According to authors such as R. A. Bauman (1992, op. cit., 34) and R. M. Cid López (2010, op. cit., 142), it would not be unreasonable to assume that the pre-eminent *Aemilia Tertia*, Publius Cornelius Scipio Africanus' wife, was, from Polybius' description of her ornamental tastes (Plb. 31.26.3–5), one of the driving forces behind these street demonstrations.

point was the same: the subjugation of women to men. For the conservative Cato, such subjugation was to be achieved by a return to the most archaic customs. For the progressive *Lucius Valerius*, on the other hand, the submission of women and the maintenance of the *statu quo* between the genders would be achieved by allowing matrons to regain and enjoy the freedoms that had been in place until a few years ago. A good example of "*gattopardismo*". In this way, they would be satisfied with their situation and would not present any major problems. Certainly, this episode is paradigmatic, since the pressure exerted by that group of elite women on male public spaces resulted in the modification of the law. A few years later, in 169 BC, in a subsequent legislative counter-reform carried out by those more conservative male sectors, led by the then censor Marcus Porcius Cato, through the promulgation of the *lex Voconia de mulierum hereditatibus*.

## 5 The *Ordo Matronarum* in the Late Republic

During the end of the 2nd century BC and throughout the 1st century BC until the arrival of the Principate, the collective interventions of matrons in the public sphere appear scarcely in the works of Greco-Latin authors. However, these authors paid more attention to the individual actions of those matrons who were close to important men, such as *Sempronia, Fulvia, Porcia* and Octavia the Younger, as if they reflected the history of the Late Republic.[50] We have to highlight two episodes in which certain matrons were linked to different political events of the time.

Firstly, although it is not a collective female initiative, we must mention the singular case of *Caia Afrania* or *Carfania* for having provoked, with her recurrent proactive action in the courts of justice, another male institutional landscape, a legislative change that removed the female possibility of *postulare pro alio*. This matron, the wife of a senator named *Licinius Buccio*, is a clear example of the discomfort that men felt towards educated women who did not conform to the docile behaviour traditionally expected of them: *Afrania* was not in breach of the law, as there was no legal provision that prevented her from practising law in her own court cases. However, Valerius Maximus will

50 The same is true of authors from the late 19th century. See E. Ciccotti, *Donne e politica negli ultimi anni della Repubblica romana* (Milan 1895); F. Rohr Vio, 'La voce e il silencio: il dissenso delle matrone al tramonto della Repubblica', in *Lo spazio del non-allineamento a Roma fra Tarda Repubblica e Primo Principato. Forme e figure dell'opposizione politica*, ed. R. Cristofoli, A. Galimberti and F. Rohr Vio (Rome 2014), 102–103.

allude to her lack of modesty and go so far as to animalise her by declaring that, instead of speaking, she barked.[51]

In turn, Ulpian refers to a *Carfania* in his work *ad edictum*, addressed to the *Caia Afrania* of Valerius Maximus, raising the hypothesis that the "excessive and unseemly" actions of this matron in the judicial sphere might have annoyed a praetor. The latter decided to prohibit certain *officia civilia* for women, such as the acts of suing and defending on behalf of a third party, by means of an edict.[52] Nevertheless, there are indications that the promulgation of this edict was not related to the figure of this matron, but that Ulpian was the first to associate the prohibition with her. First, as J. Evans-Grubbs points out, neither the historian nor the jurist clearly states that *Afrania/Carfania* worked for other people.[53] Secondly, as E. Höbenreich rightly states, if this woman had motivated the praetorian decision, the news would have enough weight to have been narrated by Valerius Maximus.[54] Nevertheless, if we follow Ulpian, the notorious and recurrent presence of a woman in an institutional sphere controlled by men would have been the cause of the legislative modification, although on this occasion to the detriment of the female sector.

The last example we will analyse is diametrically different. At the beginning of 42 BC, the triumvirs decided to tax the one thousand four hundred richest matrons, many of them the wives of proscribed men, in order to continue financing their war efforts. They considered this tax measure to be a real affront to their feminine condition and decided to mobilise collectively to try to reverse it. First, following the conventional channels of female action, they tried to get women close to the triumvirs to intercede for them with their male relatives. *Julia* (mother of Mark Antony) and Octavia the Younger (sister

51 Val. Max. 8.3.2; As F. Rohr Vio points out (2014, op. cit., 95), much more acceptable for the public opinion of the time would have been to keep with traditional female virtues in front of the tribunal or popular assembly. One example would be that of *Sempronia*, the sister of Tiberius and Caius Gracchus and the widow of Scipio Emilianus, did in 102 BC. See: F. Rohr Vio, '*Matronae* nella tarda repubblica: un nuevo profilo al femminile', in Matronae in domo et in re publica agentes – *spazi e occasioni dell'azione femminile nel mondo romano tra tarda repubblica e primo impero: atti del Convegno di Venezia, 16–17 ottobre 2014*, ed. F. Cenerini and F. Rohr Vio (Trieste 2016), 5; L. González Estrada, 'La mujer como *exemplum*. Subversión, desafío y resistencia en Valerio Máximo', *Panta Rei* 12 (2018), 87.

52 See *supra* n. 5.

53 Evans-Grubbs 2002, op. cit., 60–71.

54 Höbenreich 2005, op. cit., 176; P. Pavón Torrejón, '*Feminae ab omnibus officiis civilibus vel publicis remotae sunt* (D. 50.17.2, Ulp. 1 Sab.): Ulpiano y la tradición a propósito de las mujeres', in *Marginación y mujer en el Imperio romano*, ed. P. Pavón Torrejón (Rome 2018), 41.

of Octavian) wanted to help them, but *Fulvia* (wife of Mark Antony) rejected them.[55] When matrons met Fulvia's refusal, and since no man dared to defend them, they chose *Hortensia*, the daughter of the orator *Quintus Hortensius Hortalus*, as their representative.[56] They then went to the tribunal of the triumvirs in the *Forum*, and *Hortensia* made a speech in which she argued the injustice of imposing these fiscal measures on a group that participated neither in the magistracies nor in the government of the Republic.

She also expressed the dissatisfaction of the matrons with the cruelty of financing civil wars between Romans with part of their patrimonial property. In contrast, *Hortensia* made clear the willing economic commitment of the matrons when external agents threatened the homeland by alluding to a female contribution during the Second Punic War.[57] The triumvirs, irritated by the fact that women dared to speak in the *Forum* and frightened by the popular support they had, decided to limit tax demands to the four hundred richest matrons and any man with more than a hundred thousand drachmas.[58] This was a partial success for the *ordo matronarum*'s demands. This time we do see a purely female public initiative with political objectives. According to L. González Estrada, this situation is quite analogous to the episode of the *lex Oppia*'s repeal: in both cases, wealthy matrons took to the streets to complain about the injustices committed by the political authorities, which undermined the socio-economic status of women.[59] At no point do *Hortensia* and the other women complain about not being able to access public office. Nor are they asking for equal political rights. It is not, therefore, a "feminist" discourse that fights against patriarchal dogmas.[60] All they were asking was that the institutions respect the *statu quo* that had prevailed until then, without in any way questioning whether it was oppressive towards women. However, we do see some small advances in the limited public life of Roman women when we realise that the tribune of the plebs was not in charge of defending the political

55 Therefore, the statement made by P. D. Conesa Navarro (2020, op. cit., 456) that Octavia the Younger and *Julia* did not agree, like *Fulvia*, to the request for mediation should be qualified. Appian points out that Octavian's sister and Mark Antony's mother were willing to help them (*BC* 4.32–33); Cid López 2018, op. cit., 634.

56 App. *BC*. 4.32; D.C. 47.16.1–4.

57 App. *BC*. 4.33; Val. Max. 8.3.3.

58 App. *BC*. 4.34; Höbenreich 2005, op. cit., 178–179; Cid López 2010, op. cit., 144–146; Rohr Vio 2014, op. cit., 109–111; Rohr Vio 2016, op. cit., 5; Cid López 2017, op. cit., 223–227; Cid López 2018, op. cit., 623.

59 González Estrada 2018, op. cit., 85–86.

60 In this sense, we disagree with E. Höbenreich's feminist treatment of this episode (2005, op. cit., 179), saying that *Hortensia* would be "reivindicando implícitamente la igualdad de derecho para las mujeres como grupo social".

claims of the matrons. Now it is women who dare to raise their grievances directly in the male spaces of power.

## 6 Conclusions

As we have seen, although matrons were part of a patriarchal system that displaced them from state institutions and sought to contain them in the *domus*, at certain times in monarchic and republican Rome they played a transcendental role in the political development of public life. In the more than seven hundred years of history we have studied, we have seen them meet, make important decisions in assemblies for the benefit of the community, elect representatives and spokespersons, claim rights that have been taken away and even demonstrate publicly against legal abuses affecting their collective. Of course, we have referred to that sector of married Roman women whose high social and economic status allowed them to carry out these actions: during the first centuries of the *Urbs* they were exclusively patrician matrons and, from the 3rd century BC onwards, they were matrons belonging to the patrician-plebeian *nobilitas*. Unfortunately, the classical literary sources, almost always belonging to a wealthy elite linked to the orbit of power, have not left us with the possible concerns of those Roman citizens who were married but lacked the economic resources to make their daily problems worth writing down. In any case, it seems that this assembly tradition of the matrons, which originated in the early years of Roman civilisation, did not come to a complete halt with the arrival of the Principate. Suetonius mentions a meeting of matrons (*conventu matronarum*) early in the reign of Claudius[61] and an author of the *Historia Augusta* states that Elagabalus instituted a women's senate (*mulierum senatum*) on the Quirinal Hill presided over by his mother, Julia Soaemias.[62] This hill was chosen because this is where the *conventus matronalis* were held during the republican era. Even during the so-called "Crisis of the 3rd century AD", Aurelian expressed his desire to return this female *senaculum* to the matrons, probably dissolved as a patriarchal reaction of senators and praetorians against the rule of Elagabalus upon Severus Alexander's accession to the throne.[63] However, the difference between the republican meetings and the senate of matrons of the Severan dynasty would be that the former were

61 Suet. *Galb.* 5.1.

62 Hist. Aug. *Elag.* 4.3–4; F. Cenerini, *Dive e donne. Mogli, madri, figlie e sorelle degli imperatori romani da Augusto a Commodo* (Bologna 2009), 137.

63 Hist. Aug. *Aur.* 49.6; *Elag.* 18.2–3.

unofficial gatherings and the latter an attempt to institutionalise a real legal chamber of female power.

We have also observed an evolution in the political interests of the *ordo matronarum* from the beginning of the Monarchy to the end of the Republic. At first, the legends record collective interventions in defence of Rome against external enemies (probably to instil in Roman women the importance of patriotic sentiment). However, when historians begin to write down plausibly historical events, we see that these interventions in the public sphere of the *ordo matronarum* relate to issues that concern and harm exclusively women's collective, except for a few episodes during the Second Punic War. Possibly, this evolution of matrons' interests would be a consequence of the progressive female socio-economic emancipation to which we have already alluded.

In turn, it should be noted that the historical collective organisation of matrons, these *axitiosae*, is a purely republican phenomenon, which is logical: in the Republic, a male elite exercised power collegially. It makes sense that this kind of political system induced, perhaps unconsciously, women close to power to imitate this collegiality, albeit in a unofficial way. On the other hand, with the arrival of the Principate, despite the theoretical maintenance of republican institutions, power came to be held by a single man. There was no longer so much room for these public and political demands of the *ordo matronarum* (although, as mentioned above, they will continue to meet informally). In this new regime, it was the time of female political individualism, centred almost exclusively on women who were now more closely linked to factual power, that is to say, women belonging to the imperial dynasties. A natural consequence of the transformation of the political system in ancient Rome: from Republic to Empire, from the collective to the individual.

Finally, we have been able to see how in all the previous episodes there a backbone is: the irruption of women into urban and extra-urban scenes of political-military representation linked to the male sector. At certain moments, Roman women belonging to the elite occupied these enclaves to raise their voices, to make themselves heard in a public way before their male relatives in positions of power. They observed that the private setting of the *domus*, traditionally accepted by *mos maiorum*, was not suitable for them to carry out certain patriotic or protest actions. For this reason, they decided to act collectively in a forbidden sphere to them: the public landscape – a real transgression of space, which, on certain occasions, will result in legislative changes that will benefit this group of wealthy matrons.[64]

64 Cid López 2017, op. cit., 208 and 227.

CHAPTER 6

# The Role of Women in Shaping the Funerary Landscape of Ostia and Portus

*Francisco Cidoncha-Redondo*

The necropolis of *Ostia* and *Portus* provide a wealth of information about the funerary world in Roman society.[1] Valuable data regarding the characteristics of the tombs and their owners can be obtained from the epigraphic sources. Women, both for themselves and for their relatives and loved ones often promoted the construction of tombs. Through their decisions and actions, these women contributed to the configuration of the landscapes of the necropolis located on the outskirts of the city.

Roman women, to the extent of their capacities, played an important role in the transformation of the city landscapes, both in urban and peri-urban areas. Epigraphic sources from *Ostia* and *Portus* provide numerous testimonies of the building activities promoted by women. The actions of women in the public sphere have been analysed recurrently, with particular emphasis on the placing of honorary epigraphs with an often evergetic purpose.[2] The aim of this work is, in contrast, to focus on the women who left a written record of their involvement in the construction of funerary monuments belonging to the private sphere. In addition, we shall analyse the socio-economic standing of these women within the community.

1 This research has been possible thanks to the granting of a fellowship from the Real Maestranza de Caballería of Seville at the Spanish School for History and Archaeology in Rome (CSIC). This research has been carried out within the framework of the R&D&I project within the framework of the R&D&I project PID2022-138873NB-I00, funded by MCIN/AEI/10.13039/501100011033/ and 'ERDF. A way of making Europe' and in the research group: "Campo y Ciudad. Estructuras sociales, económicas e ideológicas en Andalucía y el Mundo Mediterráneo durante la Antigüedad" (HUM 441).

2 In Augustan times, for example, *Terentia A. f. Cluvi* (*uxor*), paid for the construction of a *crypta* and a *chalcidicum* on a plot of land of her property (*AE* 2005, 301 = EDR105754 and 303 = EDR105758). Another inscription informs us about the reconstruction of the monument known as the *crypta Terentiana* several decades after its construction (*AE* 2005, 305). *Terentia* was also devoted to the *Bona Dea* and commissioned the construction of a well in the courtyard of her religious enclosure (*AE* 2005, 304 = EDR105755 and M. L. Caldelli, F. Zevi and M. Cébeillac-Gervasoni, *Epigrafia Latina.* Ostia*: Cento iscrizioni in contesto* (Rome 2010), 122).

 | DOI:10.1163/9789004685734_007

Interest in the study of the female figures of *Ostia* and *Portus* has grown in recent decades. Many works have dealt with the subject of women, addressing aspects such as evergetism. The role of women as the owners of real estate or slaves has also been touched upon, albeit without exploring the full depth of these issues. M. Cébeillac-Gervasoni, H. E. Herzig, M. L. Caldelli, C. Bruun and M. L. Hänninen are some of the researchers who have carried out the most relevant works on the subject.[3]

## 1 General Features of the Funerary Monuments Built by Women in the Necropolis of *Ostia* and *Portus*

The city of *Ostia* had several funerary areas that were organised outside its walls.[4] The largest necropolises were those of Porta Romana on the Via Ostiense and another extending along the Via Laurentina.[5] In addition, the necropolis of Piannabella should also be included. Archaeological work at these sites has documented several phases or periods. The earliest belongs to the last two centuries of the Republic, although the clearest expansion took place from the Augustan period onwards.[6] Some of the areas nearest *Ostia* were used for agricultural activities, and later changed function and became burial grounds, as is the case, for example, of the necropolis of Piannabella.[7] The necropolis of

3 M. Cébeillac-Gervasoni, '*Octavia*, épouse de *Gamala* et la *Bona Dea*', *MEFRA* 85, no. 2 (1973), 517–553; H. E. Herzig, 'Frauen in *Ostia*: Ein Beitrag zur Sozialgeschichte der Hafenstadt Roms', *Historia* 32, no. 1 (1983), 77–92; M. L. Caldelli, 'Evergetismo femminile ad *Ostia* tra tarda repubblica ed età alto-imperiale', in Matronae in domo et in re publica agentes. *Spazi e occasioni dell'azione femminile nel mondo romano tra tarda repubblica e primo impero*, ed. F. Cenerini and F. Rohr Vio (Trieste 2016), 257–275; C. Bruun, 'Le donne di *Ostia* como proprietarie di immobili e schiavi', *MEFRA* 130, no. 2 (2018), 387–393; M. L. Hänninen, 'Religious Agency and Civic Identity of Women in Ancient *Ostia*', in *Gender, Memory and Identity in the Roman World*, ed. J. Rantala (Amsterdam 2019), 63–88.

4 Roman law stipulated that burials may only be located outside of the city limits, see A. Ruiz Castellanos, *Ley de las Doce Tablas* (Madrid 1991), 90–91.

5 The work of M. Heinzelmann, *Die Nekropolen von* Ostia. *Untersuchungen zu den Gräberstraßen vor der Porta Romana und an der Via Laurentina* (Munich 2000), on these necropolises is fundamental.

6 M. Heinzelmann, 'Les nécropoles d'Ostie : topographie, développement, architecture, structure sociale', in Ostia, *port et porte de la Rome antique*, ed. J. P. Descœudres (Genoa 2001a), 375; 379.

7 P. Germoni, L. de Gregorio, C. N. Pischedda and A. d'Andrea, 'Indagini archeologiche preventive nell'area della necropoli di Pianabella (area 12): nuove acquisizioni per la ricostruzione del paesaggio extraurbano di *Ostia* Antica tra I e IV secolo d.C.', in *Ricerche su* Ostia *e il suo territorio. Atti del Terzo Seminario Ostiense (Roma, École française de Rome, 21–22 ottobre 2015)*, ed. M. Cébeillac-Gervasoni, N. Laubry and F. Zevi (Rome 2019), 227–230.

Isola Sacra was located to the north of *Ostia* towards *Portus*, along a stretch of road built in the second half of the 1st century AD. It reached the peak of its development and splendor during the following century, in consonance with the importance of the port during that period.[8]

The characteristics of the tombs varied in accord with the economic means of their owners and archaeological excavations have documented a wide range of burial types. In many cases, these structures served to communicate the economic status of their owners to the community. Likewise, the location of a plot within the necropolis area would act as another sign of the social position and wealth of the family. The price of burial land depended on location, as well as size. The tombs located on the edge of the necropolis nearest the accesses to the city would have been more visible to the passers-by. In other necropoleis throughout the Empire, there are written testimonies regarding the prices of tombs, in which the different costs are clearly reflected.[9]

Some funerary inscriptions provide information about the size of the burial plots. The funerary enclosure of Flavia Glycera and her family had an area of 78.34 m$^2$, while the tomb of Longina Diliges was approximately 8.75 m$^2$.[10] Other tombs were of an intermediate size, such as the 28.15 m$^2$ plot of the funerary monument of Ianuaria.[11] The purpose of the measurements included in the inscriptions was to prevent these spaces from being cropped by neighbouring plots or by other newly constructed tombs. The exact dimensions of these properties were recorded to limit the possibility of fraud and conflict over the boundaries.

The inscriptions sometimes include terms that can help to understand the characteristics of the funerary spaces. For instance, Terentia Ampliata and her father were the owners of a *praediolum* or small property.[12] The freedwoman Iulia Prima placed an inscription on an *aedicula* for both her and her relatives.[13] It should be noted that many of the epigraphs are not found in their

8 I. Baldassarre, 'La nécropole dell'Isola Sacra', in Ostia, *port et porte de la Rome antique*, ed. J. P. Descœudres (Genoa 2001), 386; P. Germoni, 'La nécropole de Portus à l'Isola Sacra: la fouille récente sur le côté oriental de la route antique', in Ostia, *port et porte de la Rome antique*, ed. J. P. Descœudres (Genoa 2001), 391–392.

9 R. P. Duncan-Jones, *The Economy of the Roman Empire: Quantitative Studies* (Cambridge 1982), 70.

10 *CIL* XIV, 1026–1027 = EDR152681 and 152683; *CIL* XIV, 1270 = EDR145533.

11 *CIL* XIV, 1124 = EDR155004. We also have measurements for the tombs of *Fabia Prepontis* (*EpOst* 397 = EDR175831), *Manlia Tyche* (*CIL* XIV, 1315 = EDR145273) and *Marcia Epicharis* (*CIL* XIV, 1322 = *EpOst* 679 = EDR143803).

12 *CIL* XIV, 1661 = EDR146401.

13 *EpOst* 592 = EDR177667. There is another example of the granting of an *aedicula* from one woman to another (*EpOst* 1383).

original context, and, therefore, contain essential data in order to reconstruct the original space in which they were located. On the other hand, the inscriptions belonging to the tombs are unknown. This is the case of the epitaph of Herennia Rufa: we know the tomb but have no information on the possible location of the text.[14] Finally, however, some inscriptions are found in their original context, and this circumstance provides the detail of information.

Archaeological excavations have documented many funerary plots consisting of an open-air enclosure containing one or more covered burial chambers. Some tombs with no additional ground are also known, indicating that structure was variable. At the same time, the existence of *ustrina*, essential for cremation rituals, has been attested, as well as *biclinia* or *triclinia*, intended for funerary banquets. The burial chambers were usually richly decorated both on the walls and on the floor.[15] Their inner layout depended largely on the prevalent funerary practice at the time of their construction but was often divided into small niches for cinerary urns or *arcosolia* for sarcophagi.[16] There are many well-preserved examples of the model known as "tomba a cella", a structure in the form of a house or small *cella*. The freedwoman Clodia Prepusa built a tomb of this type for herself (fig. 6.1), her husband, and her freedmen during the first half of the 2nd century AD.[17] The mausoleum had two chambers, one upper and one lower, and a large courtyard. The tomb was decorated with mosaics, as well as paintings on the walls and vaults. The chambers contained both inhumation and cremation burials, and some of the sarcophagi have been preserved. The distribution of the tombs within the mausoleum depended on

14 *NScA* 1938, 74, no. 46 = M. F. Squarciapino, I. Gismondi, G. Barbieri, H. Bloch and R. Calza, *Scavi di* Ostia *III: Le Necropoli 1. Le tombe di età repubblicana e augustea* (Rome 1958), 158 = *EpOst-P* 40 = EDR172404; *EpOst* 526 = EDR177181.

15 Baldassarre 2001, op. cit., 389.

16 These two funerary practices were simultaneous during some periods. On this subject, see A. Pellegrino, 'Le culte des morts et les rites funéraires dans le monde romain', in Ostia, *port et porte de la Rome antique*, ed. J. P. Descœudres (Genoa 2001), 367–372; F. Taglietti. 'Ancora su incinerazione e inumazione: la necropoli dell'Isola Sacra', in M. Heinzelmann, J. Ortalli, P. Fasold and M. Witteyer (eds.), *Römischer Bestattungsbrauch und Beigabensitten in Rom, Norditalien und den Nordwestprovinzen von der späten Republik bis in die Kaiserzeit — Culto dei morti e costumi funerari romani. Roma, Italia settentrionale e province nord-occidentali dalla tarda Repubblica all'età imperiale* (Wiesbaden 2001), 149–158; I. Baldassarre, 'La necropoli dell'Isola Sacra', in *Espacios y usos funerarios en el Occidente Romano*, ed. D. Vaquerizo (Cordoba 2002), 17–19; I. Baldassarre, I. Bragantini, A. M. Dolciotti, C. Morselli and F. Taglietti, 'Necropoli dell'Isola Sacra. Le ricerche 1968–89: ripercorrendo un'esperienza', in *Ricerche su* Ostia *e il suo territorio. Atti del Terzo Seminario Ostiense (Roma, École française de Rome, 21–22 ottobre 2015)*, ed. M. Cébeillac-Gervasoni, N. Laubry and F. Zevi (Rome 2019), 60.

17 *IPOstie*-A, 80 = *ISIS* 103 = EDR101460.

FIGURE 6.1 Mausoleum of Clodia Prepusa
PICTURE BY THE AUTHOR

FIGURE 6.2 Tomb of Iulia Zoe
PICTURE BY THE AUTHOR

the importance of each family member. The tomb owner, the direct descendants and other family members tended to occupy the best places, ahead of freedmen and slaves. These tombs were used for several generations and often underwent numerous modifications or repairs.

However, not all these structures were large funerary monuments. There are other examples with less notable features and smaller dimensions. The well-known "tomba a cassone" is one of the most common types and copies a small scale "tomba a cella", designed to contain the ashes or the body of the deceased.[18] The freedwoman *Epictesis* and other women such as Iulia Zoe (fig. 6.2.), Rutilia Chrysopolis and Silia Fortunata were among the owners of these tombs.[19] Many simple graves or burials contained in amphorae were also scattered throughout the necropoli and have left no written evidence as to the identity of the deceased.[20]

## 2 The Socio-Economic Status of the Female Tomb Owners

Honorific epigraphs placed in public spaces often-present matrons of the local elite who had substantial financial means. In contrast, the funerary inscriptions show a wide scope of women from different social levels who sought to ensure a space in which to bury themselves and their loved ones.

There are hardly any written funerary testimonies regarding the prominent members of the families of the local traditional elite, those who held important positions in the administration, and who appear frequently in honorific inscriptions. The absence of references in the necropolis has led some researchers to suggest that these individuals chose not to build monumental tombs and preferred other forms of burial.[21] These figures of the local society were frequently represented in the honorific monuments located in the public spaces of the city, a privilege that was not easily accessible to persons formerly enslaved.[22] It has therefore been argued that many of the owners of the

18 Baldassarre et al. 2019, op. cit., 17.

19 *ISIS* 22 = EDR101558; *IPOstie*-A, 181 = *ISIS* 80 = EDR101607; *ISIS* 60 = EDR031386; *IPOstie*-A, 230 = *ISIS* 63 = EDR101590.

20 On these types of graves, see P. Olivanti and M. Spanu, 'Necropoli dell'Isola Sacra, scavo 1988–1989: alcune riflessioni su occupazione degli spazi, cronologia delle sepolture, corredi', in *Ricerche su* Ostia *e il suo territorio. Atti del Terzo Seminario Ostiense* (*Roma, École française de Rome, 21–22 ottobre 2015*), ed. M. Cébeillac-Gervasoni, N. Laubry and F. Zevi (Rome 2019), 67–77; Baldassarre et al. 2019, op. cit., 62.

21 H. Mouritsen, 'Freedmen and Decurions: Epitaphs and Social History in Imperial Italy' *JRS* 95 (2005), 40–45.

22 Mouritsen 2005, op. cit., 55.

known tombs were freed men and women, and members of families with a servile past.

This social group was large in *Ostia* and *Portus*. Many did very well economically and were able to experience a degree of social advancement. From the Augustan period onwards, an increase is documented in the number of freedmen and freedwomen who owned monumental tombs.[23] It is possible that they felt able to express themselves in these funerary contexts, as an affirmation of their identity to the rest of the community, having overcome the need to hide their servile origins and as a symbol of the pride in their change of status. In the work of Petronius, the freedman Trimalchio described in detail what he wanted his pantheon and epitaph to look like.[24] His wishes included statues of himself and of his wife, and he provided clear directions for the pictorial decoration of the tomb, the dimensions of the funerary space, even the plant species to be planted in the grounds. The traditional aristocracy saw these freedmen as "nouveaux riches" who were characterised by their vulgarity and their desire for ostentation.[25] The freedmen were practically banned from holding public office and did not always manage to make themselves visible in the public spaces of the cities. Funerary epigraphy was therefore a powerful tool in conveying the message of their social advancement to others. A true competition would emerge between the families with a servile past to demonstrate their newly acquired economic means.

Some freedwomen managed a lot of money and were able to undertake building activities, such as the construction of large tombs for their loved ones. However, these women also displayed notable economic differences or inequalities. The funerary enclosure belonging to Baberia Fausta occupied an area of approximately 140 $m^2$, as is documented by an inscription.[26] She can therefore be considered as the owner of a large funerary enclosure. Herennia Tyche was another freedwoman who built a tomb for herself, her husband, her children and her own freedmen.[27] Sometimes, as in the cases of Nasennia Helpis or Vestoria Amanda, the women highlighted in their epitaph that they

23 Heinzelmann 2001, op. cit., 379; H. Mouritsen, 'Freedmen and Freeborn in the Necropolis of Imperial *Ostia*', *ZPE* 150 (2004), 285–287; Mouritsen 2005, op. cit., 42–43.

24 Petron. 71.

25 Petronius caricatured these enriched freedmen through the character of Trimalchio. In this sense, see A. López Fonseca, 'El viaje en la novela latina: El Satiricón de Petronio y El Asno de oro de Apuleyo', *Revista de Filología Románica* 4 (2006), 81.

26 *CIL* XIV, 4141 = M. Parca, *The Franchetti Collection in Roma. Inscriptions and Sculptural Fragments* (Rome 1995), 91–94 = EDR165881.

27 *CIL* XIV, 4957 = *EpOst* 528 = EDR108545.

paid for these constructions with their own money.[28] Other women with a servile past such as Aemilia Cypare, Antonia Pithusa, Caesia Tryphaena, Cominia Epigenia, Petronia Heliodora or Volcia Chrysan[---] also appear as owners of tombs.[29]

The use of high-quality sarcophagi and urns is indicative of the economic means of some of these women. Avienia Zosime, Claudia Olympias, Fabia Tertullina, Manlia Thymele and Pompeia Severa purchased sarcophagi to contain the bodies of their deceased relatives.[30] On other occasions, the sarcophagi were intended for their own use. Licinia Soteris, for example, expressed her wish to be buried in a sarcophagus next to her patron.[31] She also stated that her remains should remain there forever, under a penalty of 25,000 sesterces for those who did not respect her wishes. Other women, such as Fontaeia Glyca, Graecinia Callirhoe and Marcia Chrysis, commissioned cinerary urns, elegantly decorated with reliefs, to contain the cremated remains of their loved ones.[32] The rich decoration of the funerary enclosures also demonstrates the wealth of some families. The mausoleum of Roscia Selene was lavishly decorated and contained her tomb, as well as those of her son and her own freedmen.[33] Similarly, the parents of Arria Maximina commissioned a statue of the goddess Venus to be placed in the tomb of their daughter.[34] The identity of the mother of Maximina is not known, since the text mentions her only by the term parentes. Other women were responsible for the fulfilment of the testamentary wishes of their relatives. Vibia Laenilla, for example, was the beneficiary of her uncle, M. Aurelius Claudianus, an individual with a brilliant career in the Roman army.[35] After his death, she placed a statue in his honour.

Women of free birth and members of wealthy families also commissioned tombs. At the end of the 2nd century AD, Vibussia Sabina built a funerary monument in the well-known necropolis of Porta Romana for her son,

---

28 *CIL* XIV, 5179 = EDR109494; *CIL* XIV, 171 (= *ILS* 2741) = EDR143610.

29 EpOst 47 = EDR171037; IPOstie-A, 18 = *ISIS* 252 = EDR101747; *CIL* XIV, 734 = EDR151929; NScA 1938: 74, no. 48 = Floriani Squarciapino et al. 1958, op. cit., 159; A. Marinucci. Disiecta membra. Iscrizioni latine da Ostia e Porto 1981–2009 (Rome 2012), no. 82 = EDR135115; *EDCS* 290.

30 *AE* 1999, 410 = EDR031446; IPOstie-A, 59 = *ISIS* 264 = EDR101756; IPOstie-A, 205 = *ISIS* 166 = EDR101673; L. Paroli, Scavi di Ostia 12. La basilica di Pianabella 1 (Rome 1999), 58, no A70 = EDR031070; EpOst 168 = EDR175212.

31 *CIL* IX, 4822 = *CIL* XIV, 1236 = EDR165141.

32 L. Bianchi and M. Bonanno, 'Una tradizione di scultura funeraria microasiatica a Ostia', Bollettino di Archeologia 8 (1991), 11 = *AE* 1992, 225 = EpOst 463 = EDR031393; Bianchi and Bonanno 1991, op. cit., 9 = *AE* 1992, 224 = EDR144090; *CIL* XIV, 896 = EDR152183.

33 IPOstie-A, 211 = *ISIS* 28 = EDR101445.

34 *CIL* XIV, 610 (= *ILS* 8062) = EDR144112.

35 *AE* 1981, 158 = EDR078076.

T. Flavius Verus, and her husband, Cn. Ostiensis Hermes.[36] The son was a member of the *ordo equester*, although his political career was cut short by his premature death. A marble relief depicting mother and son was placed on the façade of the funerary building. The scene shows Verus riding a horse and taking part in the *transvectio equitum*, an important procession of *equites Romani*.[37] Vibussia Sabina is depicted in the scene as a witness of the political triumph of her son, as a mother proud of his achievements. The names of T. Flavius Verus and Vibussia Sabina are carved in a larger font than the rest of the text. The owner of the tomb highlighted her own name and that of her son, but not the name of her husband. The latter, Cn. Ostiensis Hermes, may have been a public freedman of the city and may have held the office of *tabellarius*.[38] However, neither the commissioner of the tomb nor her son had a servile past. Hermes may have been a second husband, after Sabina had been widowed or divorced by the father of her son. The mausoleum was divided into two spaces: the upper part, or *aedes*, was the more noble space for the tombs of Verus, Sabina and Hermes, while the lower part was left for the tombs of the family's own freedmen.

Two inscriptions, one funerary and one honorific, dedicated to P. Celerius Amandus provides information about Scantia Lanthanusa, another aristocrat of Ostia in the 2nd century AD.[39] A decree of the decurions confirmed the election of Amandus as a member of the *ordo*, a decision that may have been influenced by the social position of his father, the freedman P. Celerius Chryseros.[40] However, Amandus died at the age of eighteen and was given a public funeral, twenty pounds of incense and all of the honours befitting his status. The father of the deceased paid all of the expenses in gratitude for the honours bestowed on his son, while Scantia Lanthanusa commissioned a statue and an inscription commemorating the homage paid by the decurions. Chryseros could not take part in political life because of his servile past and had placed his hopes in Amandus. His death in youth must have been a severe blow to his parents, as their expectations were stumped by this tragic event. The parents decided that

36 *CIL* XIV, 166 = EDR144051 and *CIL* XIV, 167 = EDR144055. See Heinzelmann 2000, op. cit., 203–206. On Vibussia Sabina: A. Álvarez Melero, Prosopographie de la parentèle féminine des chevaliers romains (Seville 2021), no. 676.

37 B. E. Borg, Crisis and Ambition. Tombs and Burial Customs in Third-Century CE Rome (Oxford 2013), 27.

38 *CIL* XIV, 255 = EDR164579. Herzig 1983, op. cit., 90–91.

39 *CIL* XIV, 321 (= *ILS* 6136) = EDR143841; *AE* 1988, 196 = EDR080739.

40 G. L. Gregori, 'Loca sepulturae publice data e funera publica nel Lazio d'età romana: qualche considerazione sulla documentazione epigrafica', in Sepolti tra i vivi. Buried among the Living. Evidenza ed interpretazione di contesti funerari in abitato. Atti del Convegno Internazionale (Roma, 26–29 Aprile 2006), Scienze dell'Antichità. Storia Archeologia Antropologia 14, no. 2, ed. G. Bartolomi and M. G. Benedettini (Rome 2007–2008), 1071.

FIGURE 6.3 Mausoleum of Scribonia Attice
PICTURE BY THE AUTHOR

the epigraph on the family tomb should highlight the achievements of young Amandus, informing others of the social standing achieved by this individual who was the son of a freedman and a woman of free birth. The marble funerary stele has a relief in which different tools are depicted, possibly related to the trade of shipbuilder or carpenter. N. Tran and X. Loriot argue that these objects were linked to the source of the family wealth, possibly to the trade of *faber navalis*.[41]

Occasionally, albeit unusually, the professional activity and source of income of the female tomb owners is documented. Although there were few occupations open to women at the time, some were not satisfied with being mere housewives and found work outside the domestic sphere. Scribonia Attice (fig. 6.3), for example, commissioned the construction of a tomb for the

41 N. Tran and X. Loriot, '*Vettius Anicetus*, *quinquennalis* des charpentiers de marine', *MEFRA* 121, no. 1 (2009), 248. The name of P. Celerius Chryseros appears in a list of *fabri navales* found in *Ostia*, see H. Bloch, '*Ostia* – Iscrizioni rinvenute tra il 1930 e il 1939', *NSA* 7 (1953), 282–283. However, it has also been suggested that these tools were also used by architects, although it seems more logical that Amandus would have practised the same profession as his father, see J. H. d'Arms, 'Notes on Municipal Notables of Imperial *Ostia*', *AJPh* 97, no. 4 (1976), 398–399.

members of her family in the mid-2nd century AD.[42] This building still preserves the inscription on a marble slab at the entrance to the tomb. Two terracotta reliefs depict scenes related to the medical practice. On the one hand, a surgeon attending to a patient with all his equipment. On the other, a midwife or *obstetrix* at the moment of childbirth. Scribonia Attice and her husband M. Ulpius Amerimnus practiced the professions depicted in these reliefs.[43]

Some women came into financial resources after inheriting the property of their husband, if they were widowed. Many such women appear to have used part of the provision to build a family mausoleum. It is also possible that some were the beneficiaries of provisions made by their parents or other family members. Occasionally, they earned an income from their urban and rural properties. However, there were also poorer women for whom it was necessary to make a substantial financial effort to provide a decent place to bury their loved ones.

As the owners of funerary enclosures, women made decisions regarding the properties that were part of their personal patrimony. C. Bruun compiled evidence for the donation of funerary spaces and carried out a statistical analysis. According to her estimates, donations made exclusively by women make up 24.2% of the total number of cases. Women appear as co-owners of these spaces, alongside a male figure, in a further 11.7%.[44] Several specific examples help us to understand who these women were. Aurelia Candida provided that her mausoleum be given to Fanius Oceanus and his sons, who would become the owners of the tomb after her death and that of her husband, Aurelius Sofro.[45] References to donations of spaces within the burial chambers are numerous. For example, Atilia Fyrmina gave a place in her tomb to her dear friend Ernuleia Gaza.[46] Perella Hieronis, together with Annius Vitalis and Annia Decia, donated the floor of her tomb to L. Caecilius Victor so that he could be buried there with his family.[47] Annia Helpis, Attia Helene, Cassia Nigella, Naevia Iusta, Nobia Helpis, Octavia Zosime and Valeria Saturnina also donated space in their mausoleums to other individuals.[48] The legal and social

42 *IPOstie*-A, 222 = *ISIS* 133 = EDR101470.

43 Herzig 1983, op. cit., 88–89; M. A. Alonso, *Los médicos en las inscripciones latinas de Italia (siglos II a.C.–III d.C.). Aspectos sociales y profesionales* (Santander 2018), 120–122.

44 Bruun 2018, op. cit., 387–393.

45 *CIL* XIV, 671 = EDR151492.

46 *CIL* XIV, 966 = EDR151198.

47 IPOstie-A, 47 = *ISIS* 116 = EDR073751.

48 *CIL* XIV, 759 = EDR152100; IPOstie-A, 254 = *ISIS* 341 = EDR101537; *CIL* XIV, 197 = *CIL* VI, 2353 = EDR164469; EpOst 1417; *CIL* XIV, 821 = EDR130257; *CIL* XIV, 1702 = EDR165732; *CIL* XIV, 1051 = EDR152696.

submission that some of these women may have suffered is evidenced by the intervention of male guardians. Iulia Tyche, for example, granted a small space to M. Valerius Eutychus for cremations and celebrations of the cult of the dead.[49] Her tutor, T. Flavius Autarches, is named in the inscription referring to the donation. However, there were women who enjoyed greater autonomy and could freely dispose of their property. The *ius liberorum* allowed *ingenuae* and *libertae* to remain free of guardianship if they had a certain number of children, three for the former and four for the latter.[50] An inscription from *Portus refers* to the cession of a funerary space by Pomponia Rufina to M. Pullaenius Salvius.[51] The text indicates that the owner had the privilege of the *ius trium liberorum*, and, therefore, was no longer under the guardianship of a male relative.

The texts do not usually indicate the reasons for these donations, but there were usually ties of friendship between the donors and the beneficiaries. They could also be linked by ties of distant or cognatic kinship, without the need for them to share the same *gentilicium. Sulpicia Ampliata* donated a burial space to her daughter-in-law, Pinnia Nebris, as well as the itus ambitus or right of free access to the tomb.[52] The possibility that the donors and beneficiaries were part of a marriage must be excluded, as donations between husbands and wives were forbidden in Roman law.[53]

However, women could be the beneficiaries of donations from other individuals. The heirs of Egrilius Polytimus donated a place in the burial enclosure to serve as a tomb for Iulia Rodia and her relatives.[54] The freedwoman Trebonia Olympias also received a tomb space as a donation.[55] Perhaps Olympias did not have the financial means to afford a burial place of her own. Aemilia Nice

49 *CIL* XIV, 1701 = EDR165731.

50 Dig. 50.16.137 (Paul. 2 ad leg. Iul. et Pap.); Gai. 1.194; Gai. 3.44; Paul. Sent. 4.9.7; Paul. Sent. 4.9.9. See M. Zablocka. 'Il ius trium liberorum nel diritto romano', *BIDR* 91 (1988), 361–390. On the tutela mulierum, see J. Evans Grubbs, Women and the Law in the Roman Empire. A Sourcebook on Marriage, Divorce and Widowhood (London–New York 2002), 24–34.

51 IPOstie-A, 208 = *ISIS* 320 = EDR101515.

52 *CIL* XIV, 1650 (= *ILS* 7920) = EDR146402. On the itus ambitus, see A. Helttula, 'On itum ambitum datum: a Formula of ius sepulchri', Arctos 8 (1974), 9–17; M. De Paolis, 'Iura sepulcrorum a Ostia: consuntivi tematici ragionati', ArchClass 61 (2010), 603–609; Marinucci 2012, op. cit., no. 28 = EDR128300; IPOstie-A, 180 = *ISIS* 113 = EDR101464.

53 Dig. 24.1.1 (Ulp. 32 Sab.); Dig. 24.1.3 pr. (Ulp. 32 Sab.). See B. Biondi, Successione testamentaria, donazioni, Trattato di Diritto Romano, 9–10 (Milan 1943), 655.

54 EpOst 1409.

55 *CIL* XIV, 1682 = EDR165717.

was another beneficiary of such a donation.[56] On many occasions, a description of the donated burial space was provided. For instance, Baebia Victoria was given a place in a funerary monument described as a *porticum cum aediculis suis et cubiculum quod est supra memoriam*.[57]

The maintenance of these properties was a problem that regularly needed to be addressed by their owners. Annia Zosime and C. Canuleius Venustus proved their ownership of a tomb and repositioned an inscription to this effect.[58] The inscription may have been missing or in a poor state of preservation, thus it was important to replace it and to indicate to whom the funerary monument belonged. There are texts that mention the purchase of land within the necropolis. Longeia Sosthenis acquired a burial space for herself and her freedmen.[59] Similarly, Aelia Doris bought or was given a burial site in the *monumentum Vibianum*.[60] Also, several inscriptions refer to Valeria Trophime building a mausoleum and subsequently selling several tomb spaces to other private individuals.[61] We do not know whether this was the family tomb of Trophime or whether she built it solely for financial gain from these sales, since no epitaph to the owner or her family members has survived. H. E. Herzig has argued that some women may have taken part in speculation, buying and selling funerary spaces through which they may have obtained significant financial returns.[62]

Some documented cases present wives who participated in the construction of funerary monuments along with their husbands. The married couple Nonia Faustina and Q. Aquilius Dionysius owned a tomb to which an *adparatorium* was added, consisting of a space where banquets were held in honour of the dead.[63] Women also appear frequently in association with their husbands, particularly in the case of tombs built for their prematurely deceased sons.[64] On other occasions, they may commission funerary spaces with other

56 *CIL* XIV, 538 = EDR145838.

57 *CIL* XIV, 158–159 (= *ILS* 8091) = *IPOstie*-B, 32 = EDR147196. On Baebia Victoria, see Álvarez Melero 2021, op. cit., no. 145.

58 *CIL* XIV, 1246 = EDR165151.

59 *CIL* XIV, 5051 = EDR109323.

60 *CIL* XIV, 523 (= *ILS* 8299) = EDR145834.

61 *IPOstie*-A, 96 = *ISIS* 123 = EDR101467; *IPOstie*-A, 124 = *ISIS* 124 = EDR101468; *IPOstie*-A, 251 = *ISIS* 125 = EDR101469.

62 Herzig 1983, op. cit., 79.

63 *AE* 1988, 178 = *AE* 1996, 284 = EDR080721. The couple appears in another inscription commemorating the restoration of a statue of *Spes* in Rome (*CIL* VI, 757 = EDR186601).

64 We can mention, for example, the case of Aelia Hosia and M. Cipius Ostiensis. They ordered the construction of a burial place for their son, M. Cipius Fortunatus Iunior, and for the rest of the *Cipii* (*CIL* XIV, 808 = *CIL* XIV, 1852 = *EpOst* 224 = EDR114913).

individuals. Claudia Philete and Claudia Taposiris participated in the construction of a funerary monument in honour of Ti. Claudius Plutus, respectively their husband and father.[65] The freedwoman Cartilia Venusta, together with her freed patrons M. Antistius Epagathus and C. Cartilius Onesimus, and the daughter of the latter, Cartilia Iusta, was the owner of another tomb.[66] A decurion named P. Nonius P. f. Quir. Iustus was also buried there. The Cartilii were one of the most important families of Ostia in the last years of the Republic and the Augustan period, including C. Cartilius Poplicola, an illustrious decurion who held several magistracies.[67] It is therefore not surprising that the freedmen of these *gentes* enjoyed a privileged position in local society after their manumission.

## 3 The Wishes Expressed in the Epitaphs of the Female Tomb Owners

Some tomb owners established conditions that the heirs had to consider. The formula *h(oc) m(onumentum) h(eredes) n(on) s(equetur)* appears in some of the written records. For example, the freedwoman Manlia Irene ordered that her tomb should not become the property of her heirs.[68] The texts do not provide any information about the reasons behind this decision, and we may only hypothesize about the absence of direct descendants or a poor personal relationship. Atania Polla, Calpurnia Ptolomais, Septueia Vera and Sergia Pamphila also forbid their funerary enclosures to go to their heirs.[69] Other owners indicated a wish that persons outside the family should not inherit

Other similar cases are *CIL* XIV, 1153 = *IPOstie*-B, 88 (= *ILS* 8223) = EDR148033; *CIL* XIV, 5006 = EDR108938; *CIL* XIV, 1318 = *IPOstie*-B, 107 = EDR148189; *EpOst* 728 = EDR181388; D. Mazzoleni, *I reperti epigrafici* (Rome 1983), no. 91 = EDR076715; *IPOstie*-A, 197 = *ISIS* 132 = EDR101644; *CIL* XIV, 5089 = EDR109369.

65 Mazzoleni 1983, op. cit., no. 59 = EDR076713.

66 *AE* 1988, 183 = EDR080726. Another inscription from the city mentions the existence of a monumentum Cartilianum (N. Laubry, 'Monumentum Cartilianum. Droit des tombeaux et société locale à Ostie', *ZPE* 206 (2018), 225–233).

67 R. Meiggs, *Roman* Ostia (Oxford 1973), 39–40; 475–478; M. Cébeillac-Gervasoni and F. Zevi, 'Pouvoir local et pouvoir central à Ostie. Étude prosopographique', in *Les élites municipales de l'Italie péninsulaire de la mort de César à la mort de Domitien entre continuité et rupture. Classes sociales dirigeantes et pouvoir central*, ed. M. Cébeillac-Gervasoni (Rome 2000), 15–16. We should also add to this family another local figure named C. Cartilius Sabinus, F. Zevi, 'Brevi note ostiense', *Epigraphica* 30 (1968), 89–95; d'Arms 1976, op. cit., 390.

68 *CIL* XIV, 1311 = EDR165238.

69 *NScA* 1938, 63, no. 23 = Floriani Squarciapino et al. 1958, op. cit., 152 = *EpOst* 1350 = EDR031476; *IPOstie*-A, 57 = *ISIS* 13 = EDR101434; *IPOstie*-A, 226 = *ISIS* 324 = EDR101516; *NScA* 1938, 64, no. 24 = Floriani Squarciapino et al. 1958, op. cit., 153 = *EpOst* 1408 = EDR031477.

FIGURE 6.4 Mausoleum of Attia Psyche and C. Attius Alexander
PICTURE BY THE AUTHOR

the tombs, reflected in the epitaphs of Clodia Domitia, Septimia Successa and Verria Zosime.[70] Attia Psyche and C. Attius Alexander (fig. 6.4) specified in their funerary inscription that the *heres fiduciarius* was not allowed to access to the tomb and the sale of this property was also forbidden.[71] Occasionally, the provisions were related to the funerary ritual. The freedwoman Varia Ennuchis and her husband P. Varius Ampelus were the owners of a family mausoleum in which sarcophagi were not to be placed.[72]

Some epitaphs mention harsh economic penalties for those who did not follow the wishes of the tomb owners. Indeed, a sepulcher was a *locus religiosus*, and so it was essential to respect its conditions. Any desecration was considered a serious offense. Caesellia Macrina, for example, warned of a fine of 10,000 sesterces to be paid by anyone who was buried in her tomb against her wishes.[73] *Vibussia Sabina* also mentioned the financial penalties that

70 *CIL* XIV, 848 = *IPOstie*-B, 48 = EDR147262; *EpOst* 1406; *IPOstie-A*, 273 = *ISIS* 37 = EDR101448.

71 *IPOstie*-A, 34 = *ISIS* 57 = EDR101450. See N. Laubry, '*Iura sepulcrorum* à Ostie : un supplément', in *Ricerche su* Ostia *e il suo territorio. Atti del Terzo Seminario Ostiense* (*Roma, École française de Rome, 21–22 ottobre 2015*), ed. M. Cébeillac-Gervasoni, N. Laubry and F. Zevi (Rome 2019), 353–354.

72 *IPOstie*-A, 268–269 = *ISIS* 106–107 = EDR101461–101462.

73 *CIL* XIV, 4821 = *IPOstie*-A, 49 = *ISIS* 228 = EDR078085.

would fall upon all those who were buried in her tomb without the necessary authorisation.[74] Longinia Procla forbade both burial and access to her funerary monument to all those who had abandoned her during her lifetime.[75] The text probably referred to a number of freedmen and freedwomen with whom Longinia Procla may have had a problem and whom she banned from her tomb in revenge for some disloyalty towards her. In some cases, these women name the person or persons who are banned from burial in their tomb. Scribonia Attice (fig. 6.3), for example, named Panaratus and Prosdocia.[76]

Some families, for unknown reasons, were not buried in the same mausoleum, even when there was enough space for them all. Scantia Silvina was the owner of a tomb that she destined for herself, her son, L. Scantius Eparchicus, her granddaughter, Sulpicia Iulitta, and her own freedmen.[77] The text inscribed on a marble slab was located on the façade of this building. Another funerary inscription on a marble slab remains on the façade of another tomb that Scantia Salvina and M. Sulpicius Fortunatus built for their relatives, including a daughter named Scantia Sabina.[78] Scantia Salvina may have been the daughter of Scantia Silvina, sister of L. Scantius Eparchichus and mother of Sulpicia Iulitta; the latter would bear the same nomen as her father, M. Sulpicius Fortunatus. This family was divided between two burial places, although we do not know the reason why. It is particularly striking that Sulpicia Iulitta was buried next to her grandmother and uncle, rather than with her parents. One hypothesis is that she died before the construction of the family tomb, and so it may have been necessary to place her remains in the mausoleum that belonged to her grandmother.

The inscriptions show that family relationships were not always good. Tutilia Rufa commissioned the construction of a tomb for her family (fig. 6.5).[79] Her parents, L. Tutilius and Seia, were among those to be buried there. Likewise, the name of another individual who was initially included in the inscription later suffered the *damnatio memoriae*. His name was removed from the text, and remains unknown, but he may have been a relative. One hypothesis is that

---

74 *CIL* XIV, 166 = EDR144051 and *CIL* XIV, 167 = EDR144055.

75 *CIL* XIV, 1271 = IPOstie-A, 168 (= *ILS* 8283) = EDR101481. Vainio states that perhaps this provision of the tomb owner was a later addition to the text (*ISIS* 206). On this and similar examples, see U. Ehmig, 'Ausschlussverfahren: Eine Gruppe italischer Grabinschriften als Beispiel sozialer überassimilierung in der römischen Kaiserzeit', Epigraphica 77 (2015), 193–205.

76 IPOstie-A, 222 = *ISIS* 133 = EDR101470.

77 *CIL* XIV, 5107 = IPOstie-A, 220 = *ISIS* 14 = EDR078077.

78 IPOstie-A, 219 = *ISIS* 59 = EDR107536.

79 *CIL* XIV, 1695 = Floriani Squarciapino 1958, op. cit., 163 = EDR165728.

FIGURE 6.5 Inscription from the tomb of Tutilia Rufa
PICTURE BY THE AUTHOR

he was the husband of Tutilia Rufa. There may have been a change of plans for some reason, and he was buried elsewhere. Another possibility is that the obliterated name belonged to a brother or a different member of the family. The *damnatio memoriae* would have taken place after Tutilia Rufa had passed away, since L. Scribonius Cinna and Fabia Psyche oversaw the construction of this funerary monument in fulfillment of Tutilia Rufa's will. The tomb owner also expressed the wish that the tomb should not become the property of her heirs. The dimensions of the marble block used for the inscription indicate that the mausoleum was of notable size and that it would not have been a simple tomb. Both the burial of the deceased and their commemoration could be organised by relatives or other persons in exchange for a bequest, which was written into the will and paid after the testator's wishes had been fulfilled.[80] Furthermore, the heirs were obliged by law to pay these expenses if nothing had been provided for formally.[81]

Through the formula *libertis libertabusque posterisque eorum* we know that a high percentage of freedmen and freedwomen were granted burial rights

80 *Dig.* 11.7.4 (Ulp. 25 *ad ed.*); *Dig.*11.7.5 (Gai. 19 *Ad ed. prov.*); *Dig.* 11.7.14.2; 6–7 (Ulp. 25 *ad ed.*).

81 R. P. Saller and B. D. Shaw, 'Tombstones and Roman Family Relations in the Principate: Civilians, Soldiers and Slaves', *JRS* 74 (1984), 126. See *Dig.* 11.7.4.6 (Ulp. 25 *ad ed.*).

in tombs built by women.[82] This confirms the economic capacity of women to retain any number of freedmen who, like slaves, were also considered as members of the family. This expression was also often used to proclaim social standing as a symbol of prestige and wealth. The case of Pinnia Procula is one of many examples in which we find female patrons with servile origins who had already attained freedom.[83] Pinnia Procula married her own patron after her manumission and became the mistress of the house in which she had previously served. The freedwoman Quinctia Salvia also paid with her own money the construction of a funerary monument for several of her *colliberti* and for a freedman that she had released.[84] Many other slaves were buried without ever being freed. The study carried out by C. Bruun indicates that 23.6% of slave owners were women, exclusively, while in another 14.2% of cases they appear as co-owners with a male figure.[85] Aelia Salviane, for example, commissioned the tombstone of Sabina, her *verna* who died at the age of six.[86]

Female tomb owners sometimes expressed their concern for the maintenance of the tomb after their death and for the performance of the annual funeral rituals in their honor. The jurist Scaevola refers to the giving of clothes and money to freedmen, as provided for by a patron in his or her will, in exchange for them carrying out all of the religious ceremonies performed in honor of the deceased.[87] Trimalchio's will also included a mandate to one of his freedmen to take care of the upkeep and maintenance of the tomb.[88] The high mortality rate at the time meant that sometimes there were no direct descendants to carry out these tasks, and so it was the freedmen who were charged with fulfilling these duties. There is an interesting inscription from the 2nd century AD mentioning a woman named Iunia Libertas, who owned several estates in *Ostia*. The text describes the bequest that she made in favor

82 On this expression, see N. Laubry, 'La désignation de la postérité. Autour de la formule *libertis libertabusque posterisque eorum* dans les inscriptions funéraires romaines', in *Esclaves et maîtres dans le monde romain. Expressions épigraphiques de leurs relations*, ed. M. Dondin-Payre and N. Tran (Rome 2016), 67–79. Some examples from *Ostia* and *Portus* are *CIL* XIV, 722 = EDR143801; *CIL* XIV, 1560 = EDR165598; *CIL* XIV, 1584 = EDR165628; *CIL* XIV, 1794 = EDR144437; *CIL* XIV 1806 = EDR165798; *CIL* XIV, 4641 = 4644 = EDR080023; *EpOst* 455 = EDR176974.

83 *CIL* XIV, 4663 = EDR106887.

84 *NScA* 1953, 302–303, no. 70 = *AE* 1988, 221 = EDR080763.

85 Bruun 2018, op. cit., 387–393.

86 *IPOstie*-A, 214 = *ISIS* 89 = EDR101616.

87 *Dig.* 34.1.18.5 (Scaev. 20 *Dig.*).

88 Petron. 71.8.

of her freedmen and their descendants.[89] Her ancestors probably had servile origins, although she herself was free by birth.[90] We do not know whether she was married or whether she had children, as the epigraph does not provide any information about these aspects of her life. However, we do know that Iunia Libertas owned *horti, aedificia* and *tabernae* in the city, property that would have been part of her testamentary legacy.[91] Some researchers argue that these buildings belonged to the funerary enclosure where her tomb was located.[92] She had expressed the will to create a trust to protect the usufruct of the property, as well as to keep her own memory alive on the anniversary of her death through the celebration of the funeral cult and the care of her tomb. In addition, she had arranged for all her property to be given to the city of *Ostia* in the future, after her wishes could no longer be fulfilled because of the natural death of two generations of her freedmen and their descendants. The inscription describes a woman who enjoyed a comfortable economic position and who wanted to leave everything organised and provided for through her will. In doing so, Iunia Libertas guaranteed a livelihood for her freedmen through the income generated by her assets after her death and, at the same time, ensured the fulfillment of the funerary cults in her honour.

## 4 Conclusions

All the cases analysed in this work show us that women played an important role in the transformation of the funerary spaces outside the city walls. The epigraphic sources from *Ostia* and *Portus* have provided an important number of examples of women who were the owners of large funerary monuments that they built for their families. All these women had their names recorded in the memory of the community through the inscriptions they placed on the tombs. They had sufficient financial means to pay the expenses involved in the construction and maintenance of these properties. The different types of tombs reflect the social differences that existed within the local population.

89 *AE* 1940, 94 = *AE* 1951, 5 = *AE* 1993, 418 = *AE* 2007, 287 = *EpOst* 1384 = EDR073435. See also J. M. Blanch Nougués, 'Nuevas consideraciones acerca de la fundación funeraria de *Iunia Libertas* en *Ostia*', *RIDA* 54 (2007), 197–218.

90 S. Dixon, 'A Woman of Substance: *Iunia Libertas* of *Ostia*', *Helios* 19 (1992), 167.

91 Meiggs 1973, op. cit., 68; D. Kremer, 'Un conflit de propriété à Ostie au milieu du II$^{e}$ siècle de n.è. Nouvelles considérations sur la supposée fondation funéraire de *Iunia Libertas*', *Iura* 61 (2013), 25–45.

92 Dixon 1992, op. cit., 164–165.

Not all women built large monuments, as many of them had to make do with simple burials and even with spaces donated by other individuals.

Social relations were also mirrored in the necropolis, in which the visibility of the inscriptions bearing the names of the tomb owners was fundamental. The large funerary monuments were a reliable reflection of the economic power acquired by some families, especially by those formed by liberated slaves. Most of the women mentioned in this work belonged to wealthy families who were not part of the old local aristocracy but had a servile background. In local society, freedmen and freedwomen constituted a numerous, active, and dynamic group during the first three centuries of our era. Among the women that we have mentioned, some were free by birth and had an economic status that allowed them to create a space in which to house the bodies of their deceased loved ones. Others, on the other hand, could not afford the expenses involved in the construction of a funerary monument. The written testimonies that we have documented indicate that the role of women in Roman society was not as limited as we may have been led to believe, and through the funerary inscriptions, their names and those of their families were kept alive and remembered within the community.

CHAPTER 7

# Public and Private Employment of *Marmora* in *Italica*: a Symbol of Power and Romanness

*Daniel Becerra Fernández*

With this paper, we aim to explain the development of the use of *marmor* in the city of *Italica* from its beginning in the Augustan era until Late Antiquity.[1] The evolution of the wide-spread use of *marmora* in this Baetican city, for public as well as for private buildings, is described, showing how these highly valued stone materials were used as indicators of social status and as part of imperial propaganda, as well as to reaffirm *Italica*'s place in the Empire. The characterisation of the different stone varieties has been established by macroscopic analysis, except in specific cases in which archaeometric techniques have been required.

## 1 Introduction

In the Roman world *marmora* were employed as fundamental parts of the urban landscape, and to a lesser extent in rural contexts, occupying a highly relevant place among the prestigious materials used by the Roman elite since the late Republic period, in imitation of the large-scale Hellenistic buildings of the Middle East. *Marmora* were soon employed for decorative purposes in Roman temples and later, to display the virtues of imperial power, reflected in abundant buildings placed throughout the Empire. In other words, they became a principal feature in the assertion and exaltation of Romanity.

1 This research work was carried out within the framework of the Research Group "Antiguas ciudades de Andalucía: de la investigación arqueológica a la rentabilización social (PAI HUM882)" and the "*Proyecto Colonia Aelia Augusta Italica.* Arqueología del sector NE de la *Vetus Urbs* de *Italica* en el marco del proceso de romanización en el Guadalquivir Inferior (HAR2017-89004-P)", funded by the Ministry of Science and Innovation of the Government of Spain. The author has a Juan de la Cierva-Formación contract (FJC2019-039441-I) – funded by the State Research Agency and the University of Córdoba (Spain) – which has allowed this study to be carried out this work is incoporated into the research project 'Templum Divi Traiani. Estudio sobre la adecuación entre escultura colosal y planimetría del Traianeum de Itálica (Santiponce, Sevilla)' financed by the `plan propio de investigación, transferencia y divulgación de la universidad de Málaga' bearing in mind that Templum Divi Traiani and Traianeum go in italics.

 | DOI:10.1163/9789004685734_008

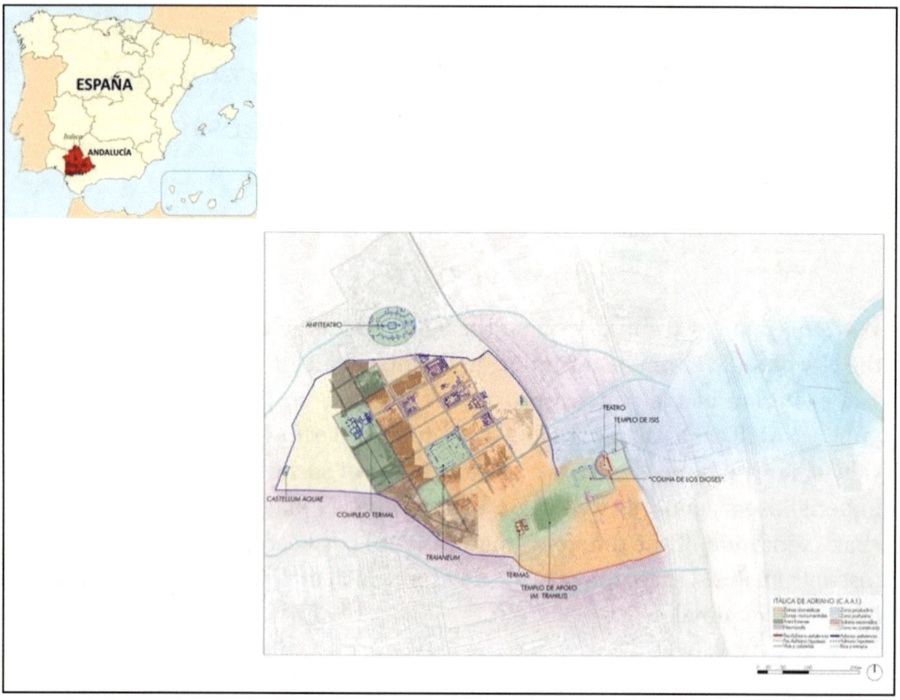


FIGURE 7.1 Location of *Italica*
COURTESY OF P. LEÓN

*Italica* (fig. 7.1) is exceptional for several reasons, among which the use of the main and most varied foreign *marmora* distributed throughout the *orbis Romanus*[2] stands out. These stone materials were employed in the construction and decoration of large public and private buildings, such as the *Traianeum*[3] or House of Demetrios de los Ríos;[4] as well as in sculptural productions, where marble from the most valued classic quarries and, to a lesser extent, those of

2 I. Rodà, 'Los mármoles de Itálica. Su comercio y origen', in *Itálica MMCC: Actas de las Jornadas del 2.200 aniversario de la fundación de Itálica (Sevilla, 8–11 noviembre 1994)*, ed. A. Caballos Rufino and P. León (Seville 1997), 155–180; J. Beltrán, 'Mármoles en la Bética durante el reinado de Adriano. El protagonismo de Itálica', in Roma, Tibur, Baetica. *Investigaciones adrianeas*, ed. R. Hidalgo and P. León (Seville 2013), 225–250; D. Becerra Fernández, '*Marmor* en Itálica. Un estado de la cuestión', *Romula* 16 (2017), 167–194.

3 P. León, *Traianeum de Italica* (Seville 1988); M. Mayer and I. Rodà, 'The Use of Marble and Decorative Stone in Roman *Baetica*', in *The Archaeology of Early Roman Baetica*, ed. S. Keay (Portsmouth 1998), 217–234; D. Becerra Fernández, *Los materiales marmóreos del* Traianeum *de* Italica (Seville 2019).

4 F. Amores and D. Becerra Fernández, '*Marmora* de la Casa Demetrio de los Ríos de Itálica (Santiponce, Sevilla)', in Tituli-Imagines-Marmora. *Materia y prestigio en mármol. Homenaje a Isabel Rodà de Llanza*, ed. A. Gutiérrez García-Moreno and D. Gorostidi Pi (Madrid 2022), 497–508.

local origin were used. The most esteemed foreign *marmora*, such as Paros marble, Luni-Carrara marble and Pentelic marble,[5] were employed as material for the sculptural program of *Italica*. The use of *marmor* for epigraphic supports has also been attested in the city, most of them made from Almadén and Sierra of Mijas marble.[6] Along with these main uses of marble are other objects of lesser entity, such as a variety of game tokens, or even, chunks of marble fragments included in the *opus caementicium* of different buildings of the *Nova Urbs*.

*Italica* is placed near to the navigable *Baetis* river, its also relatively short distance from the marble quarries of Almadén de la Plata as well as Hadrian's imperial project to undertake the monumentalisation of the family birthplace – "Patria de Emperadores"[7] (Homeland of Emperors). These locations are the main reasons why the most varied types of *marmora* are found in *Italica*, and in extraordinary amounts in comparison with other cities of the *pars Occidentalis*. The most prized *marmora* employed in the chief cities of the Empire came from imperial owned quarries. By means of a process of ownership concentration, the most valued *marmor* extraction areas came into the hands of the emperor becoming part of the *patrimonium Caesaris*. The process culminated under Tiberius' reign with acquisitions that were usually achieved by inheritance, confiscations, purchases, or new holdings. The imperial monopoly of *marmor* led to the creation of a well-organized distribution and storage network.[8] Under the Flavian dynasty, a new phase began, characterized by an extraordinary use of white marbles as building material and by a more centralized distribution system.[9] In order to fulfil this upsurge in demand for the most valued *marmora* and other aspects related to taxation, trade and the reorganisation of the system, the *ratio marmorum* was created towards the end of the 1st century AD.[10] The stone materials would be primarily used for the maintenance and construction of public buildings in Rome, as well as for the execution of imperial projects. In addition to all this, part of the marble supply was sold to private individuals, among them *negotiatores* who

5 Rodà 1997, op. cit.; Becerra Fernández 2017, op. cit.

6 D. Becerra Fernández and J. Beltrán, 'Sobre soportes epigráficos. A propósito de las inscripciones del Traianeum de Italica', *Lucentum* 39 (2020a), 269–294.

7 A. Caballos Rufino, 'Trajano, Adriano e *Italica*: de cuna de emperador a patria imperial', in *De Trajano a Adriano*. Roma matura, Roma mutans, ed. A. Caballos Rufino (Seville 2019b).

8 M. Cisneros, 'El mármol y la propaganda ideológica: El modelo del foro de Augusto', in *Religión y propaganda política en el mundo romano*, ed. F. Marco Simón, F. Pina Polo and J. Remesal Rodríguez (Barcelona 2002), 85–86.

9 P. Pensabene, 'Amministrazione dei marmi e sistema distributivo nel mondo romano', in *Marmi antichi*, ed. G. Borghini (Rome 2004), 45.

10 D. Vanhove, *Roman Marble Quarries in Southern Euboea and the Associated Road Networks* (Leiden-New York-Cologne 1996), 36.

bought stones directly at quarry sites, regional stockpiles, or the main storage yard in Rome; and then resold them, indirectly expanding the distribution of *marmor*.[11]

Imported *marmora* would have possibly reached *Italica* from their places of origin, through intermediate storage yards or from the city of Rome or Ostia itself. Most likely, *Hispalis* had a *statio marmorum*,[12] as the city was located at a point on the Guadalquivir River where the *marmor* cargo had to be unloaded from deep-draft *lapidariae* ships to smaller vessels. As described by Strabo,[13] these vessels could navigate the course of the river[14] and its tributaries in order to reach relevant cities such as *Italica*, *Corduba* or *Astigi*. However, the archaeological evidence required to support this hypothesis is still lacking. Local and regional *marmora* would have reached *Italica* by different means and from several directions; for example, Almadén de la Plata marble would have been transported by land from the source areas to *Naeva* (Cantillana) and shipped from here along the *Baetis* River.[15] In addition, Sintra limestone, for example, would have been shipped from the quarries[16] along the central-southern Atlantic coast of the Iberian Peninsula until reaching the Guadalquivir valley. Finally, other local stone material, such as Gerena granite, could have reached *Italica* either by river or land transportation.

The use of a profuse amount of valuable imported decorative stones, along with other *marmora* from southern parts of the Iberian Peninsula, is evident throughout *Italica*. Proof of this is, for example, the *opera sectilia* pavements, in which some of the pieces are made exclusively from imported *marmora*, standing out among these the "pavonazzetto" and "giallo antico" marbles.[17] Also an

11 P. Pensabene, 'Considerazioni sul trasporto di manufatti marmorei in età imperiale a Roma e in altri centri occidentali', *Dialoghi di Archeologia* 6, no. 2 (1972), 319.

12 Another possibility that should be taken into account is the existence of a *statio marmorum* in Cádiz, a well-located city that was also able to supply *marmor* pieces to southern cities of the peninsula. From Cádiz, *marmor* could be stored at another warehouse in Seville and from here be transported by boat up the *Baetis*. (Becerra Fernández 2019, op. cit., 62ff).

13 Str. 3.2.3.

14 O. Arteaga, D. Barragán, A.-M. Roos and H. D. Schulz, 'El proyecto geoarqueológico "puerto de Itálica"', *Revista Atlántica-Mediterránea* 18 (2016), 75–109.

15 Beltrán 2013, op. cit., 248.

16 Land transportation, up to 10–15 km, was needed in some of the extraction areas (I. Mañas and A. Fusco, 'Materiales lapídeos, mármoles y talleres en Lusitania', in Marmora Hispana: *explotación y uso de los materiales pétreos en la Hispania Romana*, ed. T. Nogales and J. Beltrán (Rome 2008), 497).

17 D. Becerra Fernández, '*Marmora* en los *opera sectilia* italicenses', *Itálica* 1, no. 2 (2016), 214; D. Becerra Fernández and S. Vargas Vázquez, '*Marmora* en pavimentos en *opus sectile* de

epigraphic record found on the hexagonal altar of M. Cocceius Iulianus,[18] made from Almadén marble and dated to the Severian period,[19] mentions the use of eastern imported *marmor*. The same text refers to the donation of a pair of *marmor Carystium* columns for the theater,[20] although this southern Euboea "cipollino" is easily mistaken for other marbles, such as the Spanish "anasol",[21] the Portuguese "anasol",[22] an Apuan Alps variety,[23] a Paros variety or the Almadén de la Plata banded variety.[24] In addition to the difficulty in characterizing green and white banded marbles, there is the problem with grays, with the white and gray banded, as well as with white marbles, especially the fine grain ones.

## 2 Historical Development of the Use of *Marmota* in *Italica*

*Marmor* has been employed in *Italica* since Augustan times, as attested by a large inscription located in the theater[25] made of white marble from Almadén. In the theater, and dated to the same period, *marmor Luculleum* or "africano"[26] from Teos (Asia Minor) has also been documented, as well as Italian

---

*Italica* e *Hispalis*', in Marmora Baeticae. *Uso de materiales pétreos en la Bética romana*, ed. J. Beltrán, M. L. Loza and E. Ontiveros (Seville 2018).

18 On exhibit at the Archaeological Museum of Seville, no. inv. ITA0127. *CILA* Se 2, 392 = *ERItálica* 58.

19 O. Rodríguez Gutiérrez, 'Los *marmora* en el programa arquitectónico y decorativo del teatro romano de Itálica: Antiguas hipótesis, nuevas propuestas y posibles certezas a la luz de las aportaciones de los análisis de microscopía óptica de polarización', in Marmora Hispana: *explotación y uso de los materiales pétreos en la Hispania Romana*, ed. T. Nogales and J. Beltrán (Rome 2008), 239; O. Rodríguez Gutiérrez. 'Altar hexagonal del teatro', in *Itálica, cien años, cien piezas*, ed. J. R. López Rodríguez and J. Beltrán (Seville 2014), 57.

20 Rodà 1997, op. cit., 157–158.

21 Macael marble variety.

22 Material extracted from Viana do Alentejo and Vila Viçosa – Estremoz quarries.

23 P. Morbidelli *et al.*, 'Roman Quarries of the Iberian Peninsula: "Anasol" and "Anasol"-type', *European Journal Mineralogy* 19 (2007), 125–133; P. Tucci *et al.*, '*Italica* (Seville. Spain): Use of Local Marble in Augustan Age', *Periodico di Mineralogia* 79 Special Issue (2010), 113–115; D. Becerra Fernández, E. Ontiveros-Ortega and J. Beltrán-Fortes, '*Marmora* of the *Traianeum* of *Italica* (Santiponce, Seville, Spain): New Data Provided by Archaeometric Analysis', *Geoarchaeology* (2021), 1–29.

24 Analyses based on optical microscopy polarization carried out on a series of fragments from the theater of *Italica* attested the presence of Euboean "cipollino" and Almadén banded variety. See Rodríguez Gutiérrez 2008, op. cit.

25 J. Beltrán et al., 'La explotación y el empleo de *marmora* en la *Baetica*. Un proyecto de investigación de base arqueométrica', *Itálica* 1 (2011), 71.

26 Large slabs of *marmor Luculleum* used for the *balteus* of the theater.

marble from Luni for the neo-Attic altars (fig. 7.2) that decorate this building.[27] Consequently, local and regional *marmor*, along with imported stones, began to be used in *Italica* under Augustus' rule.

During the Flavian period, the monumentalisation process, associated with the wide-spread use of *marmor*, continued in the Baetican cities. The local aristocracies began to reach important positions within the Empire,[28] being Trajan, the first Roman emperor of Hispanic origin, the most visible exemplification, while Latin and Roman citizenship was spread throughout the provinces of the Iberian Peninsula.[29]

The reign of the emperor Hadrian (AD 117–138) was of paramount importance in the widespread use of *marmora* throughout the *orbis Romanus* territories, with *Italica* standing out again in this process.[30] The city not only was awarded colonial status by the emperor but also was transformed through imperial patronage,[31] undergoing among other things, remarkable changes in its urban layout. Polychrome *marmora* would gain remarkable protagonism, highlighting the use of red and black stones for sculptural ornamentation,[32] all of which contributed to promoting the city's social status. The new colony became the destination point for a wide variety of stone materials on a scale never seen before in *Italica*. In the large Hadrianic expansion of *Italica*, named *Nova Urbs* by García y Bellido,[33] the evidence of the use of these valuable materials is abundant in the archaeological record and, most likely, were also employed at the same time in the original nucleus of the city, the *Vetus Urbs*. However, it is difficult to know the real extent of this widespread use of marble in the principal areas of the city since many buildings would be remodeled with marble elements in later historical times. Under Hadrian, sculptural programs were made with this prized material, also complex building projects[34] as

27 Rodà 1997, op. cit., 166.

28 A. Caballos Rufino, 'Adriano, la *Colonia Aelia Augusta Italicensium* y una nueva inscripción del "*Traianeum*" de Itálica', in *Pluralidad e integración en el mundo romano*, ed. F.J. Navarro (Pamplona 2010a), 271–272.

29 A. Caballos Rufino, *Itálica y los italicenses: aproximación a su historia* (Seville 1994), 81.

30 P. León, '*Italica*. Génesis y desarrollo del proyecto adrianeo', in Adventus Hadriani. *Investigaciones sobre arquitectura adrianea*, ed. G. E. Cinque, R. Hidalgo, A. Pizzo and A. Viscogliosi (Rome 2020a), 279–295.

31 A. Caballos Rufino, J. Marín and J. M. Rodríguez Hidalgo (eds.), *Itálica arqueológica* (Seville 1999).

32 R. Gnoli, 'Introduzione', in *Marmi antichi*, ed. G. Borghini (Rome 2004), 14.

33 A. García y Bellido, *Colonia Aelia Augusta Italica* (Madrid 1960).

34 P. León, '*Italica* de la madurez trajanea a la mutación adrianea', in *De Trajano a Adriano.* Roma matura, Roma mutans, ed. A. Caballos Rufino (Seville 2019), 729–750.

FIGURE 7.2 Neo-Attic altar from *marmor Lunense*
Note: On exhibit at the Archaeological Museum of Seville, no. inv. ITA0126

well as the epigraphic supports associated to them.[35] All these elements indicate that during Hadrian's reign, *Italica* developed into an urban and artistic reference in the Roman province *Baetica*, way ahead of *Corduba*, the provincial capital, as well as all other capitals of the *conventus*.[36]

The temple of the imperial cult known as the *Traianeum* is an architectural complex built during Hadrian's reign, which coincides with other architectural projects commissioned by the emperor, the most direct parallel – layout and time – is undoubtedly Hadrian's Library in Athens.[37] Hadrian's *Traianeum* temple is a clear exponent of the relevance *marmor* had in the new colony. On the one hand, imperial evergetism supplied *marmora* from the most important quarries, along with a limited number of decorative stones from southern parts of the Iberian Peninsula for the ornamental and propagandistic program on a par with the greatest cities of the Empire. On the other hand, *Italica*'s aristocracy also made itself present in the sanctuary through numerous silver figure offerings and epigraphic monuments, the latter made with materials from southern Spain, such as Almadén de la Plata and the Sierra of Mijas marbles.[38] The assemblage of *marmora* varieties found in this temple complex of *Italica* consists of Almadén de la Plata marble, "africano"[39] (*marmor Luculleum*) from Teos, "cipollino" (*marmor Carystium*) from Euboea, "cipollino rosso" (*Marmor Iasense* or *Marmor Carium*) from Iassos,[40] Estremoz marble from *Lusitania*, "giallo antico" (*marmor Numidicum*) from North Africa, "greco scritto" (possibly from North Africa, although Asia Minor cannot be ruled out), "lumachella carnina" from Sintra, Luni-Carrara marble (*marmor Lunense* or *lapis Lunensis*) from North Italy, Mijas marble, white marble from Paros in Greece (*marmor Parium*), "pavonazzetto" (*marmor Phrygium, Synnadicum* or *Docimium*) from the ancient Phrygian area, "Piedra de Mina" (Mine Stone) from Córdoba, "porfido rosso" (*lapis porphyrites*) from the eastern desert area of Egypt, "portasanta" (*marmor Chium*) from Chios, "proconnesio" (*marmor Proconnesium*) from the Sea of Marmara, "rosso antico" (*marmor Taenarium*) from Cape Tenaro, "breccia di Sciro" or breccia di settebas (*marmor Scyrium*), "serpentino" (*marmor Lacedaemonicum* or *lapis Lacedaemonius*) from Lacedaemon,

35 Becerra-Fernández and Beltrán 2020, op. cit.

36 J. Beltrán, 'Itálica en época adrianea', in *Adriano. Emperador de Roma*, ed. J. González Fernández and P. Pavón (Rome 2009), 27–47.

37 León 2019, op. cit.

38 Becerra-Fernández and Beltrán 2020, op. cit.

39 Both varieties are known as "verde africanato" and "bigio africanato".

40 The only object made from this material appears banded, although it is not large enough to rule out that it could possibly be "rosso brecciato" (*marmor Iasense* or *marmor Carium*).

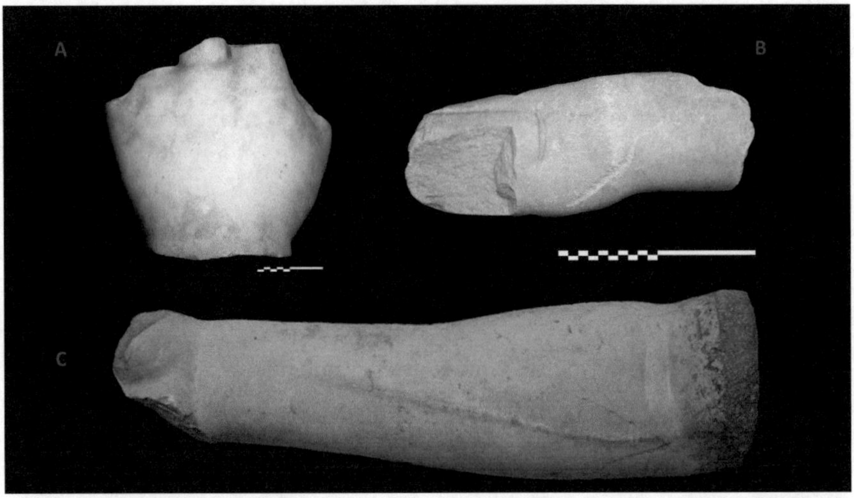


FIGURE 7.3 Marble fragments belonging to colossal statues from the *Traianeum*. A) Statue hand fragment made from Luni marble. B) Finger fragment made from Paros marble and C) forearm made from Thasos marble

marble from the island of Thasos,[41] and "antico green" (*marmor Thessalicum* or *marmor Atracium*) from Larissa. It should be noted that Thasos and Pharos marbles were reserved exclusively for statuary, as in the sculptural program of the imperial cult temple, and likewise, *marmor Lunense*[42] (fig. 7.3). Hence, the variety of *marmor* used in the *Traianeum* is an outstanding indicator of the city's new status, an ostentatious display element for the social elite and another component of imperial propaganda to be considered.

---

41 Thasos marble is present only in the dolomitic variety, mostly from Cape Vathy, see M. Price. *Decorative Stone: The Complete Sourcebook* (London 2007), 63 or from Saliara, see M. P. Lapuente, B. Turi and Ch. Blanc, 'Marbles and Coloured Stones from the Theatre of *Caesaraugusta* (Hispania): Preliminary Study', in *ASMOSIA VII Actes du VII*^e^ *colloque international de l'ASMOSIA Thasos 15–20 septembre 2003*, ed. Y. Maniatis (Athens 2013), 509–522.

42 Becerra Fernández 2017, op. cit.; Becerra Fernández 2019, op. cit.; P. León, 'Restos de acrolitos del *Traianeum* de *Italica*', in *Escultura romana en Hispania IX: Actas de la Reunión Internacional celebrada en Yecla del 27 al 29 de marzo de 2019*, ed. J. M. Noguera and L. Ruiz Molina (Murcia 2020b), 369–378; P. León, 'Nuevas consideraciones sobre el *Traianeum* de *Italica*', in Adventus Hadriani. *Investigaciones sobre arquitectura adrianea*, ed. G. E. Cinque, R. Hidalgo, A. Pizzo and A. Viscogliosi (Rome 2020c), 297–308; P. León, 'La contribución del mármol al prestigio de la arquitectura y de la escultura en la Italica adrianea', in *Tituli-Imagines-Marmora. Materia y prestigio en mármol. Homenaje a Isabel Rodà de Llanza*, ed. A. Gutiérrez García-Moreno and D. Gorostidi Pi (Madrid 2022), 229–236.

At the same time as huge quantities of *marmora* were being imported from the main quarries of the Empire, the production at local outcrops also increased, in many cases exploited by the people living nearby. Presumably, regional *marmora* were worked on in local workshops, while imported marbles could arrive as un-worked blocks, semi-manufactured or already finished.[43]

An inscription from the Severian period[44] mentions the existence of a *statio serrariorum Augustorum*, where *marmora* blocks would arrive to be worked on or given a final finish. This inscription refers to the donation of a *tabula marmorea* to the marble craftsmen and is currently on display in the Archaeological Museum of Seville. It was found near the monastery of San Isidoro del Campo, along with another inscription, now lost and incomplete,[45] that would have contained similar information. Thus, in our opinion, the *statio* would have been located outside *Italica*'s walls, south of the city and near the river,[46] a large area that is unfortunately occupied by houses and buildings of the current town of Santiponce, limiting all research. The inscription probably stood in the *schola* of the *collegium serrariorum*, near the *statio*. Most likely, it would be the same *statio* founded under Hadrian's rule and linked to the *portus* of *Italica*.[47] In J. Beltrán's opinion, the marble yard, *statio marmorum*, would have been located close to the statio *serrariorum*. Its origin would date back to at least Hadrian's time[48] and, according to this author, it was the only *statio marmorum* in the province *Baetica* that was linked to a river port.[49]

Prof. J. Beltrán has further pointed out that large granite elements, imported from the main imperial quarries, are lacking in the architectural decoration of *Italica*'s public buildings, contrary to what is usual in other Baetican cities such as Hispalis, Corduba and Astigi. This may be due to a specific interest in which *Italica* should stand out among all other *civitates* of *Baetica* by using eye-catching materials such as "cipollino" and "portasanta". Although this was not the rule in private areas, as seen in the House of the Birds, where three

43 A.J. Parker, Ancient *Shipwrecks of the Mediterranean and Roman Provinces* (Oxford 1992), 19.

44 *CIL* II, 1131 = *CILA* Se, 2, 390 (= *ILS* 7285) = *ERAItálica* 44.

45 *CIL* II, 1132 = *CILA* Se, 2, 391 = *ERAItálica* 45 + 46.

46 M. Cisneros, *Mármoles hispanos: su empleo en la España romana* (Zaragoza 1988), 50.

47 Rodà 1997, op. cit., 173–174; A. Padilla Monge, '*Pagus Marmorariensis, mons Mariorum, statio serrariorum Augustorum* y canteras de Almadén de la Plata. Algunas precisiones', *BMAN* 3 (2018), 119–129.

48 Beltrán 2013, op. cit., 244–245.

49 J. Beltrán, 'Explotación y rutas de comercialización de los *marmora* béticos', in *Rome,* Portus *and the Mediterranean*, ed. S. Keay (London 2012), 281.

shafts of “granito della troade” stand next to local granite columns.[50] From the 3rd century onwards, the network that supplied large blocks of imported *marmor* ended and a gradual process to reuse semi-abandoned public spaces began. Along with the recycling of marble elements, large amounts of imported *marmora* remained piled in the stockyards of the Empire, like in the *stationes marmorum* of Rome. Local stones began to be used to mitigate the marble shortage, along with the plunder and recycling. Quarries in *Baetica*, like the imperial quarries in the East, reduced their production considerably during the 4th century, forcing imperial policies to concentrate on making the quarries profitable again, as the earnings went to the *Aerarium Sacrum*. Measures carried out for this purpose included: legislation aimed at preventing the reuse of *marmor* from prior structures, the opening of imperial quarries to private initiative,[51] increased demands on private quarry operators and finally, the banning of all activity in private quarries.[52] A fundamental work for economic studies of *marmor* is the *Edictum de pretiis*, issued under the government of Diocletian and, in which over eighteen different marble varieties are mentioned, as registered in the Aphrodisias fragment.[53]

Although, it must be considered that most of the large *opus sectile* pavements (fig. 7.4) documented in *Italica*[54] date to the 3rd and 4th centuries; hence the taste for *marmor* is an aspect that should not be overlooked. The fact is that the amount of important foreign *marmora* in *Italica* during Late Antiquity is outstanding, whether it is by the presence of reused elements or by the number of pieces manufactured in the Italian Peninsula from *marmora* deposited in the vast storage yards of Rome and its surrounding stockpiles. In this period, a variety of local or regional stones with a very limited distribution[55] began to be extracted and exported, for example, *marmor Celticum*, also documented in *opus sectile* at *Italica*. When compared to previous centuries, in Late Antiquity

50 O. Williams-Thorpe and P. J. Potts, ‘Geochemical and Magnetic Provenancing of Roman Granite Columns from Andalucía and Extremadura, Spain’, *OJA* 21 (2002), 167–194; Becerra-Fernández 2017, op. cit. 186.

51 *CTh.* 10.19.1 (dated 320, to the *rationalis Africae*) y *CTh.* 10.19.2 (dated 363, to the *comes Orientis*).

52 *CTh.* 10.19.10 (dated 382, to the *praefectus praetorio de Oriente*) and *CTh.* 10.19.11 (dated 384, to the new *praefectus praetorio de Oriente*).

53 K. T. Erim *et al.*, ‘The Copy of Diocletian Edict on Maximum Prices from Aphrodisias in Caria’, *JRS* 60 (1970), 120–141.

54 Becerra-Fernández 2016, op. cit.; Becerra Fernández and Vargas 2018, op. cit.

55 R. Gnoli, *Marmora Romana* (Rome 1971), 13.

FIGURE 7.4 *Opus sectile* from the House of the Exedra in *Italica* on display in the Archaeological Museum of Seville

*marmor* was employed chiefly in private surroundings, a circumstance that can be related to the declining of evergetism among the elite.[56]

## 3 The Site of Cerro San Antonio

We have recently carried out an in-depth study on a collection of marble pieces recovered at Cerro de San Antonio, Santiponce. Specifically, on material found in 2008 during an archaeological intervention on a plot owned by the Junta de Andalucía in this municipality,[57] and supported by the Archaeological Site of Italica. The urban plot, number 19 of la Feria Street, is situated on the northern side of Cerro de San Antonio. This small hillock has attracted many researchers'

56 A. Padilla Monge, 'Algunos comentarios sobre las canteras de la Bética durante los siglos III–V', *HAnt* 23 (1999), 321–330.

57 M. L. Loza *et al.*, Marmora de Italica: elementos arquitectónicos en la calle La Feria 19 (Santiponce), in Italica. *Investigaciones arqueológicas en la* Vetus Urbs, J. Beltrán and J. L. Escacena (Seville 2021), 171–196.

interests over a long time mainly due to the significant sculptures and monumental buildings discovered here. The theater is set on the northeastern slope of this elevation,[58] while the remains of various large edifications stand on the top of the hill, where several statues of deities have also been found.[59]

The *marmor* pieces recovered during the excavation at nº 19 La Feria St. consisted exclusively of decorative architectural elements used as building material. The marble pieces were found in secondary contexts, more specifically, as part of fills that date mostly to late Roman period, and apparently without relation to the structures or buildings documented at the excavation. The fragments recovered correspond mostly to coatings, wall veneers and pavements; among them, are small slabs that possibly belong to *opus sectile* geometric pavements, made mostly from imported *marmora*. In addition, there are three molding fragments made from Luni and Almadén de la Plata marbles. Also among the group of revetment pieces are various fragments of *opera sectilia* wall facings and a piece of wall molding all made from "portasanta" marble. A few other pieces belong to an opus sectilie, or more than one, made with "serpentino" rock. Several complete pieces are very similar to the geometric *sectilia* plaques and slabs dated to Hadrian's time (triangles, circles, crescents, etc.) and preserved in different pavements of Villa Adriana in Tivoli.[60] During preceding periods and after Hadrian, *sectilia* geometric patterns were manufactured with smaller pieces, like large marble *tesserae*, allowing an approximate date for the fragments described.

## 4 Conclusions

In the current state of knowledge, we can note that the use of *marmora* – local, regional and imported varieties – in *Italica* began under the reign of Augustus, being the theater area, including Cerro de San Antonio, the best exponent of

58 A. Jiménez Sancho, 'Nuevas aportaciones sobre la construcción y evolución del graderío del teatro de Itálica: los resultados de las campañas de excavación de 2009 y 2011', *Italica* 2 (2012), 99–126; A. Jiménez Sancho, 'La porticus del teatro de *Italica* y su transformación en santuario de Isis', in *La* porticus post scaenam *en la arquitectura teatral romana*, ed. S. F. Ramallo and E. Ruiz Valderas (Murcia 2020), 83–100.

59 J. M. Rodríguez Hidalgo and A. Jiménez Sancho, 'Itálica, la Colina de los Dioses. De Augusto a Adriano', in Navigare necesse est. *Estudios en homenaje a José María Luzón Nogué*, ed. J. García, I. Mañas and F. Salcedo (Madrid 2015), 231–242; León 2019, op. cit.; P. León, *Italica. La ciudad de Trajano y Adriano* (Seville 2021).

60 P. Cinque, 'Policromia marmorea nei rivestimenti pavimentali e parietali della Villa Adriana di Tivoli: Nuove scoperte e verifiche', *Romula* 11 (2012), 161–204.

this commencement. The import and use of *marmora* continued up to Late Antiquity, Hadrian's era being the moment of greatest splendor, as attested by the public and private monumental buildings in the *Nova Urbs*. However, it should be noted that recent studies have evidenced a widespread use of marble also in Hadrian's time on the public buildings of the pre-Hadrianic or *Vetus Urbs* area. The use of *marmora* is still valued in Late Antiquity as seen by the presence of *opus sectile* coatings, some of a great quality and showing complex patterns.

*Marmora* played a fundamental role among the local elite as an indicator of prestige and an example of Romanity, being also a political propaganda element throughout the Empire. While in *Italica*, especially during the early Empire, the use of marble was intended mostly as material for public areas; in Late Antiquity, it was employed mostly for the luxurious ornamentation of private spaces, being *opera sectilia* a clear example.

CHAPTER 8

# *Damnosa hereditas*? *Italica* and the Imperial Evergetism: an Approach to the Urban Vitality of the Colony in the Post-Hadrian Period (AD 138–211)

*Diego Romero Vera*

## 1 Introduction[1]

The 2nd century was a period of singular importance for urban Hispanic communities. Most cities followed a constant rhythm of monumental growth, spurred, first, by the legal processes promoted by Caesar and Augustus and, later, by the extension of the *ius Latii* during the Flavian dynasty.[2] Thus, in addition to being fully integrated into the Roman legal system, the Hispanic provinces underwent a process of urban and monumental growth that probably reached its peak in the first third of the 2nd century AD.[3] However, this process of constant growth did not last beyond the second century. In that century, we find signs of exhaustion, which seemingly heralded a cyclical change. In fact, without entering into historiographical discussions, it is evident that in the period under study structural changes took place that affected, to a greater or lesser degree, the whole Iberian Peninsula, such as an economic slowdown, the contraction of evergetism and a lack of internal dynamism in the cities,

1 This research has been carried out within the framework of the R&D&I project "Italica Adrianea: la Nova Urbs. Análisis arqueológico del paradigma urbano y su evolución, y contrastación del modelo" (Ref. PID2020-114528GB-I00), funded by Ministry of Science and Innovation and the State Research Agency of the Government of Spain.

2 Plin. *NH.* 3.30. B. Goffaux, 'Promotions juridiques et monumentalisation des cités hispano-romaines', *Saldvie* 3 (2003), 143–161 [= B. Goffaux, *La vie publique des cités dans l'Occident romain* (Rennes 2016) 71–85]; Andreu 2004, op. cit.

3 E. Ortiz de Urbina, *Las comunidades hispanas y el derecho latino: Observaciones sobre los procesos de integración local en la práctica político-administrativa al modo romano* (Vitoria 2000); E. Ortiz de Urbina (ed.) *Ciudad y comunidad cívica en Hispania* (*siglos II y III d.C.*) (Madrid 1993); G. Alföldy, 'Hispania bajo los Flavios y los Antoninos: consideraciones históricas sobre una época', in *De les estructures indígenas a l'organització provincial romana de la Hispania Citerior*, ed. M. Mayer, J. M. Nolla, and J. Pardo (Girona 1998), 11–32; D. Romero Vera, 'Continuidad y transformación en las ciudades hispanorromanas del siglo II d. C.: la fase trajano-adrianea (98–138 d. C.)', *Arqueología Iberoamericana* 47 (2021a), 31–40.

 | DOI:10.1163/9789004685734_009

which preluded the so-called 'crisis of the 3rd century'.[4] From the material point of view, from the reign of Antoninus Pius onwards, there was, broadly speaking, a significant decrease in public buildings and epigraphy related to self-representation.[5] Likewise, archaeology reveals that certain cities, which until that time had been thriving, abandoned the maintenance of their urban and monumental apparatuses in the late Antonine period. The process of urban crisis, although it did not affect all the Hispanic cities of the Antonine period, seems to have begun at that time and increased with the passage of time.[6] Thus, in the 2nd century we can find the first steps in a regressive process that would change not only the physiognomy of the cities, but also the ancient behaviours of their citizens and leaders and ultimately lead to the disappearance of the classical urban way of life.

In relation to the above discussion, *Italica* (Santiponce, Seville) is probably the best-known Hispano-Roman city in terms of the phase corresponding to the 2nd century AD. Several circumstances explain this situation: the fact that it was in a depopulated area, that some of its main buildings have been so well preserved and the fact that it was the place of origin of Trajan and Hadrian, all of which have provided an incentive for research. This attraction dates to the Renaissance, but it was not until the 19th century that the site was investigated

4 J. Arce, 'Inestabilidad política en Hispania durante el siglo II d.C.', *AEA* 54 (1981), 101–116; G. Chic, 'Marco Aurelio y Cómodo: el hundimiento de un sistema económico', in *La Hispania de los Antoninos (98–180)*, ed. L. Hernández Guerra (Valladolid 2005), 567–586; G. Alföldy, 'El Imperio romano durante los siglos II y III: continuidad y transformaciones', in *Tarraco christiana civitas*, ed. J. M. Macias, A. Muñoz Melgar (Tarragona 2013), 25–28; G. Bravo, 'La otra cara de la crisis: el cambio social', in *Ciudad y comunidad cívica en Hispania (siglos II y III d.C.)*, ed. E. Ortiz de Urbina (Madrid 1993), 156; G. Bravo, '¿Otro mito historiográfico? La crisis del siglo III y sus teóricos en el nuevo debate', *Studia Historica. Historia Antigua* 30 (2012), 121; P. Le Roux, 'Peut-on parler de la cité hispano-romaine aux IIe–IIIe s. ? Questions de forme et questions de fond pour une absence de synthèse', in *Ciudad y comunidad cívica en Hispania (siglos II y III d.C.)*, ed. E. Ortiz de Urbina (Madrid 1993), 187–195.

5 F. López Sánchez, 'La crisis de las ciudades hispanas comenzó con Adriano: ¿decadencia interna o falta de estímulos externos?', in Oppida labentia. *Transformaciones, cambios y alteración en las ciudades hispanas entre el siglo II y la tardoantigüedad*, ed. J. Andreu (Uncastillo 2017), 157–176; D. Romero Vera, 'Conjeturas en torno a la ruptura del modelo urbanístico altoimperial en Hispania: la fase tardoantonina y primoseveriana (138–211 d. C.)', *Arqueología Iberoamericana* 47 (2021b), 41–52.

6 S. Ramallo and A. Quevedo, ed., *Las ciudades de la Tarraconense oriental entre los s. II–IV d.C. Evolución urbanística y contextos materiales* (Murcia 2014); L. Brassous and A. Quevedo, ed., *Urbanisme civique en temps de crise. Les espaces publics d'Hispanie et de l'Occident romain entre le IIe et le IVe siècle* (Madrid 2015b); Andreu 2017, op. cit.; J. Andreu Pintado and A. Blanco, eds., *Signs of Weakness and Crisis in the Western Cities of the Roman Empire (c. II–III AD)* (Stuttgart 2019).

using scientific methodology.[7] In fact, almost all the information available on the city is limited to the so-called *Nova Urbs* and Hadrianic period. Therefore, we do not think it appropriate to describe in detail this important phase of the city, which is already well known.[8] Rather, we find it more interesting to delve into the evolution and transformations that took place in the post-Hadrianic phase of *Italica*,[9] that is, the time span from the death of Hadrian to the end of the reign of Septimius Severus (AD 138–211).

According to Appianus,[10] *Italica* was the first site founded by Rome in *Hispania*. The Romans chose to establish a field hospital there during the Second Punic War (specifically, in 206 BC). Its proximity to a branch of the river *Baetis* and to a rich mining area, as well as to the fierce fighting on the battlefields, must have played an important role in this choice.[11] The founding of *Italica* seemingly occurred in similar fashion as with any indigenous city under the Romans, meaning a nucleus of Turdetan roots, inhabited by a few families

7 J. M. Rodríguez Hidalgo, 'Historia de la investigación', in *Itálica*-Santiponce. Municipium *y* Colonia Aelia Augusta Italicensium, ed. A. Caballos Rufino (Rome 2010), 17–34; J. Beltrán Fortes and J. M. Rodríguez Hidalgo, 'Las primeras excavaciones oficiales en Itálica: Los trabajos de Ivo de la Cortina en el año 1839', *Itálica* 2 (2012), 31–52.

8 See, e.g. García y Bellido 1960, op. cit.; J. M. Luzón, *La Itálica de Adriano* (Seville 1975); A. Blanco, 'La Itálica de Trajano y Adriano', in *Itálica* (*Santiponce, Seville*), ed. P. León (Madrid 1982), 291–298; R. Corzo, '*Colonia Aelia Augusta* Itálica' in Hispania. *El legado de Roma* (Zaragoza 1998), 405–410; J. M. Rodríguez Hidalgo, 'Reflexiones en torno a la Itálica de Adriano', *Habis* 17–18 (1987–1988), 583–589; J. M. Rodríguez Hidalgo, 'La nueva imagen de la Itálica de Adriano', in *Italica MMCC*, ed. A. Caballos Rufino and P. León (Seville 1997), 87–114; M. T. Boatwright, 'Italica and Hadrian's Urban Benefactions', in *Italica MMCC*, ed. A. Caballos Rufino and P. León (Seville 1997), 115–136; A. Caballos Rufino and J. M. Rodríguez Hidalgo, 'Hadrien et sa patrie d'Italica', in *Hadrien. Trésors d'une villa imperiale*, ed. J. Charles-Gaffiot and H. Lavagne (Milan 1999a), 16–25; P. León, 'La Itálica adrianea', in *Adriano Augusto*, ed. J. M. Cortés and E. Muñiz (Seville 2004), 125–138; Beltrán 2009, op. cit., 27–47; J. Beltrán, 'La arqueología de Itálica de época de Trajano y Adriano', in *El legado de los emperadores hispanos*, ed. M. Romero Recio (Seville 2018), 153–176; León 2019, op. cit., 729–750.

9 Caballos Rufino 1994, op. cit., 129–146; A. Caballos Rufino, A. Marín and J. M. Rodríguez Hidalgo 1999, op. cit., 33–34; R. Hidalgo, 'En torno a la imagen urbana de Italica', *Romula* 2 (2003), 121–123; A. Caballos Rufino, 'Hitos de la historia de Itálica', in *Itálica*-Santiponce. Municipium *y* Colonia Aelia Augusta Italicensium, ed. A. Caballos Rufino (Rome 2010b), 10–13; J. Román, 'Transformaciones postadrianeas del ámbito doméstico en la *Nova Urbs* de Itálica: una aproximación a partir de la Terra Sigillata africana', *Romula* 9 (2010), 289–314.

10 *Iber.* 38.

11 P. Garrido, F. Guisado and M. E. Costa, 'Itálica y las minas: de la hegemonía ilipense al *municipium* augusteo (ss. III-I a.C.)', *Itálica* 2 (2012), 147–164.

of Italic origin.[12] The true transformation of *Italica* into a city with a Roman stamp only occurred, though, in the time of Augustus, when it underwent the first phase of monumentalisation that must be related to its legal promotion to the rank of *municipium*.[13] Unfortunately, little evidence exists for analysing the urban development of the Augustan city because the hamlet of the present-day Santiponce is located just above the site of pre-Augustan *Italica*.[14]

It was not until Hadrian occupied the imperial throne that *Italica* completely changed its urban image. As Aulus Gellius states,[15] the italicenses themselves asked the emperor to promote the colonial development of their city. Thanks to imperial patronage, this provincial city expanded enormously and acquired an appearance similar to that of a great Hellenistic city, reaching an extraordinary degree of monumentalisation.[16]

Among the many splendid gifts with which, in the words of Cassius Dio,[17] Hadrian beautified his homeland, we must highlight the great thermal baths with adjoining palestra (known as the Major Baths), a majestic amphitheatre, the magnificent imperial sanctuary (the so-called *Traianeum*) as well as an aqueduct.[18] All these buildings were erected in a new quarter of town that practically doubled the size of the old urban centre. This extension, approximately 51 ha in size and known in the scientific literature as *Nova Urbs*, had a regular urban layout organised around wide streets with porticoes, fountains, and a sewage system.[19]

---

12 J. M. Luzón, *Excavaciones en Itálica. Estratigrafía en el Pajar de Artillo* (Madrid 1973); S. J. Keay, 'Early Roman *Italica* and the Romanisation of Western *Baetica*', in *Italica MMCC*, ed. A. Caballos Rufino and P. León (Seville 1997), 21–48; Hidalgo 2003, op. cit., 91–96.

13 Caballos Rufino *et al.* 2002, 21–27.

14 P. León, 'Itálica: problemática de la superposición de Santiponce al yacimiento', in *Arqueología de las ciudades modernas superpuestas a las antiguas* (Madrid 1985), 213–230; A. M. Canto, '*La Vetus Urbs* de Itálica, quince años después. La planta hipodámica de D. Demetrio de los Ríos, y otras novedades', *CPAM* 25 (1999), 145–191.

15 Gell. 16.13.4.

16 See note 8.

17 D.C. 69.10.1. The direct action of the emperor is also evidenced by the inscriptions on a *fistula aquarium* (*CILA* Se 2, 366) and on two milestones found around the city (*CILA* Se 2, 367; *HEp* 5, 708).

18 A. M. Canto, 'El acueducto romano de Itálica', *MDAI(M)* 20 (1979), 282–337; P. León, Traianeum *de Itálica* (Seville 1988); J. R. Corzo Sánchez, 'El anfiteatro de *Italica*', in *El anfiteatro en la Hispania romana*, ed. J. M. Álvarez Martínez and J. J. Enríquez (Badajoz 1994), 187–212; L. Gómez Araujo, 'Las termas de Itálica y la arquitectura termal adrianea', in Roma, Tibur, Baetica. *Investigaciones adrianeas*, ed. R. Hidalgo and P. León (Seville 2013), 293–318; A. Jiménez Hernández, 'Errores de replanteo en el anfiteatro de Itálica', *Arqueología de la arquitectura* 15 (2018) 5–18.

19 García y Bellido 1960, op. cit.

FIGURE 8.1 Portrait of Hadrian from *Italica*, Archaeological Museum of Seville

However, the splendour of the colony turned out to be rather ephemeral. As is well known, the expansion and monumentalisation of *Italica* was not the result of developments achieved by its citizens, but instead a consequence of Hadrian's will. Therefore, the change was not motivated by its demographic growth or its economic flourishing, but by the emperor's eagerness; as was to be expected, it was short-lived, fading away soon after his death. The idea that *Italica* suffered an early crisis is not a recent one. In the 1980s, J. M. Luzón proposed that the buildings of the Hadrianic extension had to be abandoned in the 3rd century AD due to the unsound nature of the land on which the city stood, which was subject to the influence of expansive clay soil.[20] This theory was quickly challenged, first by A. M. Canto and then by J. M. Rodríguez Hidalgo, who argued that the premature decline of the city was more for political and economic reasons and not due to the physical characteristics of the terrain.[21] The maintenance of such a monumental facility must also have consumed considerable resources, not a trivial matter at a time when the first signs of a general economic slowdown were beginning to be detected.[22]

Thus, although it may seem shocking, in the medium- and long-term imperial munificence may have caused the Italicenses considerable hardship.[23] This raises an important question: Might the building programme planned and paid for by Hadrian to ennoble his small homeland have been detrimental to the stability of the city in the medium and long term? Or, asked differently, could it have constituted a case of *damnosa hereditas*? The building programme constituted a counterproductive inheritance whose debts exceeded its benefits according to Roman law. To properly assess the vitality of the colony in the post-Hadrian period, we analyse the most important changes to the urban topography during this period (constructions, alterations, possible abandonment, and so forth), as well as the main official or public epigraphic documents dating between AD 138 and 211.

---

20 J. M. Luzón, 'Consideraciones sobre la urbanística de la ciudad nueva de Itálica', in *Itálica (Santiponce, Sevilla)*, ed. P. León (Madrid 1982a), 88.

21 A. M. Canto, 'Excavaciones en "El Pradillo" (Itálica): un barrio tardío', in *Itálica (Santiponce, Sevilla)*, ed. P. León (Madrid 1982), 236; Rodríguez Hidalgo 1987–1988, op. cit., 588–589.

22 See, e.g. R. Duncan-Jones, 'Economic Change and the Transition to Late Antiquity', in *Approaching Late Antiquity. The Transformation from Early to Late Empire*, ed. S. Swain and M. Edwards (Oxford 2004), 20–52; G. Chic, 'Marco Aurelio y Cómodo: el hundimiento de un sistema económico', in *La Hispania de los Antoninos (98–180)*, ed. L. Hernández Guerra (Valladolid 2005), 567–586; W. Jongman, 'Gibbon was Right: the Decline and Fall of the Roman Economy', in *Crises and the Roman Empire*, ed. O. Hekster et al. (Leiden 2007), 183–200; L. Arias, *Hispania en el siglo II d.C. Circulación y perduración de la moneda* (Oxford 2012), 203–212; G. Chic, 'Aspectos fiscales y de tributación a partir de Marco Aurelio: indicios de cambio', in Oppida labentia: *transformaciones, cambios y alteración en las ciudades hispanas entre el siglo II y la tardoantigüedad*, ed. J. Andreu (Uncastillo 2017), 117–156.

23 E. Melchor Gil, 'La construcción pública en la Hispania romana: iniciativa imperial, municipal y privada', *MHA* 13–14 (1992–1993), 133; E. Melchor Gil, 'La regulación jurídica del evergetismo edilicio durante el alto Imperio', *Butlletì Arqueològic* 31 (2009b), 150–152.

## 2 Development

### 2.1 *Forum and Similar Public Spaces*

It has not been possible to analyse any interventions after Hadrian in the primitive forum, as it is buried under the hamlet of Santiponce.[24] Some of the main sources of information we have to trace the development of the colony, epigraphs and sculptures, do not provide a certain context of discovery: most of them come from ancient excavations or chance discoveries or else there are no references as to where they were found. However, we must consider the fact that they were originally located in the public spaces (either the forum or other similar places) that existed in the colony and were the preferred settings for the self-representation of the *Italicenses*.

A large group of epigraphs belong to the late Antonine period,[25] foremost of them being the *oratio de pretiis gladiatorum minuendis* (also known as *tabula gladiatoria*), a bronze that records the provision, dated AD 177, by which Marcus Aurelius and Commodus intended to limit the magistrates' expenditure on amphitheatre spectacles.[26] A fragmented honorary pedestal commemorates the homage paid to M. Rutilius Cosinius Calvus,[27] procurator of the imperial patrimony for the province of *Baetica*.[28] Likewise, another honorary piece paid homage to the procurator of the provinces of Macedonia, Lusitania and Mauretania, C. Vallius Maximianus,[29] by the *res publica Italicensium*, being *duumviri Licinius Victor* and *Fabius Aelianus*. The inscription, beyond its ornamental or honorific function, is a document of enormous importance because

---

24 León 1985, op. cit. There is only one sketch of the SE sector of the forum, the result of excavations carried out by Ivo de la Cortina (1839–1840). Some of the sculptured pieces preserved today have been correctly contextualised thanks to the meticulousness of the excavation drawing; see P. León, *Esculturas de Itálica* (Seville 1995), n. 1 and 15.

25 The main reference work on the epigraphy of *Italica* continues to be A. M. Canto, 'Epigrafía romana de Itálica', (Ph.D. diss., Complutense University of Madrid, 1985). At this time, there is evidence of the cult of the *Lares Augusti*, as testified by the epitaph of *C. Marcius Apilus, magister larum Augustorum et genii Caesaris Augusti* (*CIL* II, 1133 = *CILA* Se 2, 385 = *ILS* 3623 = *ERItalica* 21). Similarly, an ex-voto dedicated to *Domina Regia*, probably an epithet for Isis by *Fortunatus, sacerdos*, proves the existence of minor priesthoods in *Italica* at the end of the 2nd century (*AE* 1984, 504 = *CILA* Se 2, 351 = *ERItalica* 10).

26 *CIL* II, 6278 = *ILS* 5163 = *CILA* Se 2, 339 = *EAOR* VII, 3 = *ERItalica* 168; A. Ceballos Hornero, 'El coste de los espectáculos gladiatorios en las ciudades del Occidente romano', *AEA* 80 (2007), 107–118; M. Carter, 'Gladiatorial Ranking and the "*SC de Pretiis Gladiatorum Minuendis*" (*CIL* II 6278 = *ILS* 5163)', *Phoenix* 57, no. 1 (2003), 83–114.

27 *PIR*² R 246.

28 A. Caballos Rufino, 'Un nuevo *procurator Augusti* de la Bética', in *II Congresso Peninsular de Historia Antiga* (Coimbra 1993), 715–740 = *AE* 1993, 1005 = *HEp* 5 (1995): 718.

29 *PIR*² V 251.

it served to confirm that *Baetica* (and probably *Italica* itself) was affected by the raids of the *Mauri*, which *Maximianus* confronted, restoring peace to the province.[30]

On the other hand, we know that at the end of the 2nd century, *Italica* was under the patronage of C. Iulius Pacatianus,[31] a personage belonging to the equestrian order who have had an extraordinary military career and reached the government of several provinces. The colony dedicated a *tabula* to his *patronus merentissimus* in his birthplace, *Vienna*, in *Gallia Narbonensis*.[32] As far as sculptures are concerned, the last imperial representation found in *Italica* is a portrait of Marcus Aurelius as crown prince.[33]

Unfortunately, there are no records of interventions (whether architectural or decorative) at the *Traianeum* in the period between its dedication and its final abandonment.[34] The intense looting of the sculpture since its abandonment has led to a lack of archaeological information about it.[35] However,

---

30 *CIL* II, 1120 = *ILS* 1354 = *CILA* Se 2, 378 = *ERItalica* 74; G. Alföldy, 'Bellum mauricum', *Chiron* 15 (1985), 8–105; Caballos Rufino 1994, op. cit., 135–138; G. Bernard, 'Las incursiones mauritanas en la Bética bajo el reinado de Marco Aurelio', in Fretum Hispanicum. *Nuevas perspectivas sobre el Estrecho de Gibraltar durante la Antigüedad*, ed. A. Álvarez Melero, A. Álvarez-Ossorio Rivas, G. Bernard and V. A. Torres González (Seville 2018), 205–224.

31 *PIR*[2] I 444.

32 *CIL* XII, 1856 = *ILS* 1353 = *ILN* V/1, 65; C. Cortés Bárcena and M. A. Alonso, 'Reflexiones en torno a la epigrafía de los patroni civitatis en Hispania y el Norte de Africa: los ejemplos de Baetica y Mauretania', in *L'Africa Romana. Trasformazione dei paesaggi del potere nell'Africa settentrionale fino alla fine del mondo antico* (Sassari 2012), 2073–2092; Melchor Gil 2018, op. cit., 193ff.

33 P. León, *Retratos romanos de la Bética* (Seville 2001), 316–319. From the topographical context of the Alcantarilla necropolis comes a female torso with *chiton*, dated to the mid-second century. It is not known whether, in accordance with its provenance, it had a funerary function or whether it was a sculpture of an ideal character transferred to this site in a later period; see León 1985, 134–135; J. Beltrán, 'La escultura', in *Itálica-Santiponce.* Municipium *y* Colonia Aelia Augusta Italicensium, ed. A. Caballos Rufino (Rome 2010), 124.

34 I. Rodà ascribed to the *Traianeum* a set of *marmora* present in a workshop located in a *taberna* in the house of the Cañada Honda that dates to the end of the 2nd century or the beginning of the 3rd century. Thus, he suggested that the sanctuary would have been abandoned at that time. However, *Vibia Modesta* made a great donation that same year, and in principle, this evergetic act would not then coincide with the abandonment of the temple; see Rodà 1997, op. cit., 171.

On the plundering of the marbles of the *Traianeum*, see D. Becerra, 'Expolio y reutilización de materiales marmóreos del Traianeum italicense. Balance historiográfico y nuevas líneas interpretativas', in Exemplum et Spolia: *la reutilización arquitectónica en la transformación del paisaje urbano de las ciudades históricas*, vol. 2, ed. P. Mateos and C. Morán (Mérida 2020b), 603–611.

35 S. Vargas, 'La techumbre marmórea del *Traianeum* de *Italica*', in Marmora Baeticae. *Usos de materiales pétreos en la Bética romana. Estudios arqueológicos y análisis arqueométricos*, ed. J. Beltrán, M. L. Loza and E. Ontiveros (Seville 2018), 215.

scholars have determined based on an analysis of its architectural decoration that certain pieces were not carved with the appropriate care or that they were left unfinished. This has been linked to the desire to finish the temple quickly, and it is even thought that this haste was related to a hypothetical cessation of funding after Hadrian's death.[36]

Another place where public epigraphy is concentrated is the great imperial cult complex dedicated to Trajan.[37] Several pedestals with votive dedications were found during its excavation, which had the dual purpose of embellishing the enclosure and serving as a means of self-representation for the Italic elites. Of these pedestals, two are confined to the period of our study. On the one hand, *M. Sentius* Maurianus, *aedilis, duumvir and augur perpetuus* of the colony, dedicated a statue consisting of 100 pounds of silver to Apollo Augustus.[38]

Marcus Antistius dedicated to Jupiter and to the Genius of the colony another inscription, very fragmentary.[39] On the other hand, there are fragmentary remains of a pedestal dedicated to Q. Vibius[40] and another well-known pedestal that Vibia Modesta dedicated to Victoria Augusta.[41] This Italican lady, although probably of Mauritanian origin, held the offices of *flaminica* and priestess in the colony, with many making large donations to her,[42] specifically a silver statue weighing 132 pounds, two and a half ounces and a large

36 León 1988, 81; S. Rodero, 'Algunos aspectos de la decoración arquitectónica del Traianeum de Itálica', *Romula* 1 (2002), 106.

37 A. Blanco, 'Hallazgos epigráficos', in *Traianeum de Itálica*, ed. P. León (Seville 1988), 103–117; D. Becerra and J. Beltrán 2020a, op. cit., 269–294.

38 *AE* 1983, 520 = *CILA* Se 2, 342.

39 *AE* 1988, 708 = *CILA* Se 2, 344.

40 *AE* 2010, 682; Caballos Rufino 2010[a], op. cit., 265–277.

41 *AE* 1982, 521 = *CILA* Se 2, 358 = *ERItalica* 22b: *Vict(oriae) · Aug(ustae) · Vib(ia) Modesta · G(aii) · Vib(ii) Libonis · fil(ia) · ori[g(ine)] / Mauretania · iterato · honore bis flaminica sacerdo[s] / statuam · argenteam ex arg(enti) · p(ondo) · CXXXII (librarum) ((unciarum duarum semunciae)) cum · inauribus · trib(acis) [mar?]/garitis n(umero) X · et · ge(m)mis · n(umero) XXXX · et berull(is) n(umero) VIII · et corona aur[ea] / cum · gem(m)is · n(umero) XXV · et gem(---) · areis (!) ((sextantis)) · Accept(o) · loc(o) · ab · splendid(issimo) o[r]/dine · in templ(o) · suo · corona(m) · aurea(m) · flaminal(em) · capitul(a) · aure[a / tr?]ia Isidis · alter(um) · Cerer(is) · cum m{a}anib(us) · arg(enteis) · item · Iunoni(s) po[s(uit)]*. On *Vibia Modesta*, see, e.g. S. Lefebvre, 'Les migrations des *Africani* en Péninsule Ibérique : Quelle verité?', in Migrare. *La formation des élites dans l'Hispanie romaine*, ed. A. Caballos Rufino and S. Demougin (Bordeaux 2006), 146; P. Le Roux, '*Oriunda Mauretania*', in Ubique amici. *Mélanges offerts à Jean-Marie Lassère*, ed. C. Hamdoune (Montpellier 2001), 239–248 [= P. Le Roux, *Espagnes romaines. L'Empire dans ses provinces. Scripta varia II* (Rennes 2014), 569–576]; M. D. Mirón, 'Las sacerdotisas béticas del culto imperial: ciudadanía, movilidad y control territorial', in *El mundo religioso hispano bajo el Imperio romano: pervivencias y cambios*, ed. L. Hernández Guerra (Valladolid 2007), 167–169.

42 J. Beltrán and J. M. Rodríguez Hidalgo, *Itálica. Espacios de culto en el anfiteatro* (Seville 2004), 142–147.

FIGURE 8.2 Pedestal dedicated to *Victoria Augusta* by *Vibia Modesta*, Archaeological Museum of Seville

collection of jewellery, which was probably attached to the divine image. This epigraph, the latest one from the *Traianeum*, testifies to the cultural vitality of the sanctuary in the Severan period.

### 2.2 *Urban Infrastructure*

According to the information provided by the archaeological discoveries, it seems that the 38 ha of surface area from the Hadrianic extension were not completely occupied by buildings, a fact that emerged because of the geophysical surveys carried out to extend the *Nova Urbs*.[43] The space between the northwestern part of the walls and the Major Baths was divided into four

43 J. M. Rodríguez Hidalgo, *et al.*, 'La Itálica de Adriano: resultados de las prospecciones arqueológicas de 1991 y 1993', *AEA* 72 (1999) 73–98.

*insulae*. The surveys carried out in this area only documented traces of the sewers along the urban road, but they did not reveal any evidence of buildings. This circumstance could also be due to the destruction or dismantling of the buildings, but in this case, the looting trenches or the traces of the foundations themselves should also have been detected.[44]

Likewise, the archaeological surveys and partial soundings carried out between the *castellum aquae* and the Major Baths did not reveal any evidence of the presence of buildings in this part of the city: only a pipeline that began at the *castellum aquae* and supplied water to the thermal building.[45] What is more, this tongue of land remained a barren space devoid even of the division into plots, which has been detected to the north of the Major Baths.[46] Moreover, no anomaly has been detected in the maintenance of the sewage network during the second half of the 2nd century AD.[47]

### 2.3 *Entertainment Buildings*

#### 2.3.1 Theatre[48]

The theatre was the site of the last documented renovation of a public space in the city, dating from the end of the 2nd century and the beginning of the 3rd century AD. Erected in the Augustan period, the theatre underwent a major decorative reform that essentially affected the *scaneae frons*.[49] Specifically, the *columnatio* was replaced by an order composed of shafts of Carystian marble

44 Rodríguez Hidalgo et al. 1999, op. cit., 91–92; Rodríguez Hidalgo 1987–1988, op. cit., 120.

45 Rodríguez Hidalgo 1997, op. cit., 109; Rodríguez Hidalgo et al. 1999, op. cit., 91–92. All this would confirm the lack of constructions already proposed by M. Pellicer following the negative results of an excavation in this same area at the end of the 1970s; see M. Pellicer, 'Excavaciones en Itálica (1978–1979): muralla, cloaca y cisterna', in *Itálica (Santiponce, Sevilla)*, ed. P. León (Madrid 1982), 211.

46 Rodríguez Hidalgo et al. 1999, op. cit., 92.

47 A. Jiménez Sancho, '*Italica*. La red de alcantarillado', in *La gestión de los residuos urbanos en Hispania*, ed. J. A. Remolà and J. Acero (Mérida 2011), 145–156.

48 The *porticus postscaenam* contained a place of worship dedicated to Isis. Four votive plaques were found there, broadly dating to between the 2nd and 3rd century AD, confirming that this sanctuary was still in use at the time of our study (*HEp* 5, 714–717); see J. Alvar, 'La sociedad y el culto a Isis en la Bética', in *La sociedad de la Bética. Contribuciones para su estudio*, ed. C. González Román (Granada 1994), 11; Á. Jiménez Sancho, O. Rodríguez Gutiérrez and R. Izquierdo, 'Novedades arqueológicas adrianeas en el teatro de Itálica y su entorno', in Roma, Tibur, Baetica. *Investigaciones adrianeas*, ed. R. Hidalgo and P. León (Seville 2013), 286–291.

49 J. M. Luzón, 'El teatro romano de Itálica', in *Actas del Simposio El Teatro en la Hispania Romana* (Badajoz 1982b), 183–201; R. Corzo and M. Toscano, *Excavaciones en el teatro de Itálica* (Seville 2003); O. Rodríguez Gutiérrez, *El teatro romano de Itálica: estudio arqueo-arquitectónico* (Madrid 2004a).

and capitals, cornices and bases of white marble from Almadén de la Plata. The pictorial decoration of the *murus pulpiti* was also renewed, with a cornice of cypollinated marble being added to it.[50] The *murus pulpiti* was also decorated with new mural paintings, the pavement inscription of *litterae aureae* was restored and two fountain sculptures of sleeping maenads were placed on both sides of the *proscaenium*.[51] Curiously, two statues wearing a toga were reused for the execution of both pieces.[52] Part of this intervention was a hexagonal altar commemorating the participation of M. Cocceius Iulianus, his wife, Iulia Africana, and their son, Quirinus, in the renovation of the theatre.[53] The *ara*, decorated with representations of the benefactor and his family, mentions the donation of two marble columns from *Carystus*, an architrave and bronze grilles, as well as the altar itself.

### 2.3.2 Amphitheatre

The dimensions and complex architectural articulation of this superb spectacle building contrasted with the austerity of its decoration.[54] It seems that decoration of the western façade of the amphitheatre was never completed, as evidenced by some bases that were only sketched out.[55] On the other hand, it should not be forgotten that an important place of worship dedicated to *Nemesis-Caelestis* was located in a room at the eastern entrance of the building. This *sacellum* was in a former service area of the building.[56] A series of marble plaques with the name of this divinity, as well as *vestigia*, footprints or footwear, have been found both in this space and in the eastern corridor. The chronology provided by the votive offerings shows that the *Nemeseion* remained in use throughout the 2nd century and well into the 3rd century.[57]

---

50 O. Rodríguez Gutiérrez, 'Programas decorativos de época severiana en Itálica', in *La decoración arquitectónica en las ciudades romanas de Occidente*, ed. S. F. Ramallo (Murcia 2004b), 355–377.

51 Rodríguez Gutiérrez 2004, op. cit., 357 and 373; Caballos Rufino et al. 2002, 97.

52 M. L. Loza, 'El agua en los teatros hispanorromanos. Elementos escultóricos', *Habis* 25 (1994), 270–273; León 1995, op. cit., 166–169.

53 *CILA* Se 2, 392 = *ERItalica* 58. See also, M. Navarro Caballero, Perfectissima femina. *Femmes de l'élite dans l'Hispanie romaine*, Bordeaux, 2017, pp. 448–449, nº 127.

54 P. Gros, *L'architecture romaine : du début du III^e siècle av. J.-C. à la fin du Haut-Empire. 1, Les monuments publics* (Paris 2002), 334; R. Hidalgo, 'Anfiteatros', in *Arte romano de la Bética. Arquitectura y urbanismo*, ed. P. León (Seville 2008), 222–226; Jiménez Hernández 2018, op. cit., 5–18.

55 R. Corzo, 'El anfiteatro de Itálica', in *El anfiteatro en la Hispania romana*, ed. J. M. Álvarez Martínez and J. J. Enríquez (Badajoz 1994), 203.

56 Beltrán and Rodríguez Hidalgo 2004, op. cit., 71–79.

57 Beltrán and Rodríguez Hidalgo 2004, op. cit., 141–149.

### 2.4 *Domestic Architecture*

The lack of a stratigraphic record, according to which the excavations of most of the dwellings documented in *Italica* were carried out, makes it necessary to take into consideration other types of information.[58] In this sense, study of the mosaic pavements has made it possible for scholars to trace the general evolution of domestic architecture in *Italica*. Thus, of the eighty-two mosaics and *opera sectilia* that the site has yielded, most of them have been dated to the second half of the 2nd century AD.[59] This chronology is also consistent with coins found in the construction strata belonging to the House of the Planetarium and the House of the Mosaic of Neptune (in the latter case, numismatic documentation puts its construction in the mid-second century).[60] This dating, which is certainly late, illustrates the process of urbanisation of the *Nova Urbs*. The planning and construction of the road layout, sewers and aqueduct was first carried out, followed by the erection of the public buildings and monumental spaces (*Traianeum*, Major Baths, amphitheatre, and so forth). Finally, during the reign of Antoninus Pius, most of the dwellings were built and decorated.[61] This sequence makes it clear that there was a certain time lag between the architecture of the imperial or public initiative and private building.

On the other hand, the only house whose abandonment is recorded in the 2nd century is the House of the Columns, which was abandoned at the end of that century (although it was reoccupied again at the end of the 3rd century).[62] However, decorative interventions in the domestic sphere are not limited to the late Antonine period, as certain specific actions have been detected dating back to the Severan period.[63] In fact, four pavements from the House of the Birth of Venus and the *opus sectile* from the House of the Exedra (the result of the resurfacing of a room) belong to this phase.[64]

58 I. Mañas, 'Arquitectura doméstica', in *Itálica-Santiponce. Municipium* y *Colonia Aelia Augusta Italicensium*, ed. A. Caballos Rufino (Rome 2010), 82.

59 I. Mañas, *Mosaicos romanos de Itálica (II): mosaicos contextualizados y apéndice* (Madrid 2011), 91.

60 F. Chaves Tristán, 'Las monedas de la Casa del Planetario (Itálica)', *Habis* 5 (1974a), 206; A. Blanco and J. M. Luzón, *El Mosaico de Neptuno de Itálica* (Seville 1974), 9.

61 I. Mañas, 'Pavimentos decorativos de Itálica. Una fuente para el estudio de la ampliación adrianea', *Romula* 8 (2009), 197.

62 L. Abad, 'Estratigrafía de la Casa de las Columnas', in *Itálica (Santiponce, Sevilla)*, ed. P. León (Madrid 1982), 146–148

63 Mañas 2009, op. cit., 194–196.

64 A. M. Canto, 'El mosaico del Nacimiento de Venus de Itálica', *Habis* 7 (1976), 293–318; L. Roldán, 'La casa de la Exedra de Itálica (Santiponce, Sevilla). Un intento de valoración espacial a través de las técnicas constructivas', in *La casa urbana hispanorromana: ponencias y comunicaciones* (Zaragoza 1991), 303–311.

## 2.5 *Necropolis*

In contrast to the amount of knowledge that exists about most of the public spaces, the necropolis is one of the least known aspects of *Italica*, even though several burial areas have been identified. Thus, the information available for the period of our study is basically restricted to funerary epigraphy evidence.[65] Most *tituli* consist of small marble plaques that were originally embedded in simple tombs, such as cyphos or *cupae*.[66] In this regard, a *cupa structilis*, built in brick with the exterior surface rendered and painted red, from the northern part of the city stands out. This tomb, dated to the end of the 2nd century or the beginning of the 3rd century AD, was equipped with a *mensa libatoria* and preserved the epitaph of the deceased, Aurelius Ugaiddillus.[67]

It is striking that no large funerary monuments date back to the period of our study, a dynamic that can be attributed to despoilment, to the lack of methodological rigour in the excavations or to the Italicenses' obvious choice of funerary structures of low monumentality.[68] Nor can we rule out the fact that the local elites would have preferred to install their tombs in private necropolises located in *villae* and also in remote, but highly visible, places. The tendency described above, which is not only recorded in *Italica* on the peninsular level, is related to the rejection of the ostentation of funerary monuments in the early imperial period, at a time when a predisposition towards intimacy and introspection developed in every matter related to the funerary world.[69]

---

65 Canto 1985, op. cit., 346–524.

66 D. Vaquerizo, *Necrópolis urbanas en Baetica* (Tarragona–Seville 2010), 261–262.

67 *AE* 1994, 904 = *HEp* 1995, 711; Vaquerizo 2010, op. cit., 256.

68 Vaquerizo 2010, op. cit., 261.

69 H. von Hesberg, Monumenta. *I sepolcri romani e la loro architettura* (Milan 1994), 65–69; D. Romero Vera, 'Notas sobre topografía y costumbres funerarias en las necrópolis urbanas de Hispania del siglo II d.C.', *Ágora. Estudos Clássicos em Debate* 23 (2021c), 175–177. This same dynamic can be detected in the *Urbs*, in *Astigi* (precisely during the phase of greatest monumental and economic boom in the colony) and also, although less clearly, in *Augusta Emerita*; see M. Heinzelmann, 'La situazione di Roma', in *Römischer Bestattungsbrauch und Beigabensitten in Rom, Norditalien und den Nordwestprovinzen von der späten Republik bis in die Kaiserzeit*, ed. M. Heinzelmann, J. Ortalli, P. Fasold, and M. Witteyer (Wiesbaden, 2001b), 23–34; A. B. Ruiz Osuna, 'Arquitectura funeraria en la Bética: el ejemplo de las capitales conventuales', *AAC* 17 (2006), 176; J. M. Murciano, Monumenta. *Tipología monumental funeraria en Augusta Emerita. Origen y desarrollo entre los siglos I a.C. y IV d.C.* (Mérida 2019), 143–232 and 382–384.

## 3 Discussion. Reflections on *Italica* in the Late Antonine and Early Severan Phase

The city of *Italica* is an important landmark in our line of study.[70] This is one of the Hispanic cities, which is better chronologically dated to the 2nd century (essentially the Hadrianic period). It is also part of a group of cities that apparently suffered a certain urban regression by the end of the High Empire, a process that began a few decades after the great Hadrianic intervention. These circumstances, together with the cross-referencing of epigraphic and archaeological data, lead us to engage in numerous points of reflection.

To begin with, it is already well known that the enlargement and monumentalisation of *Italica* was not the result of the development achieved by its citizens, but a consequence of Hadrian's will. The emperor wished to honour his city of origin in two different ways: from a political-institutional standpoint, by granting it colonial status, and from the urbanistic standpoint, by giving the city the urban physiognomy of a Hellenistic *polis*.[71] The expansion of the urban centre was not motivated, therefore, by demographic growth or economic prosperity, but by the emperor's eagerness to honour his legacy; as was to be expected, it was a short-lived endeavour, fading away soon after his death. The austerity and lack of completion of certain elements of architectural decoration belonging to the amphitheatre and the *Traianeum* could be linked to an absence of interest or economic resources, possibly generated after Hadrian's death.

From an urban standpoint, the so-called *Nova Urbs* was never fully occupied. Only one public building was erected at the north-western end of the Hadrianic extension, which was surrounded to the north and west by unoccupied spaces. Therefore, we are dealing with a large area of intra-urban land that was never built on. The explanation for this phenomenon is probably to be found in the ephemeral nature of the Hadrianic project. Thus, it seems that the enlargement did not have enough inhabitants to occupy the entire urban space. Perhaps these empty spaces were nothing more than reserve areas for the growth of the colony. Once again, the driving cause of this urban phenomenon, which not only affected *Italica*, created a mismatch between the

70 Our research on this line of work has its origin in the following doctoral thesis: D. Romero Vera, *La ciudad hispanorromana en el siglo II d.C. Consolidación y transformación de un modelo urbano* (Ph.D diss., University of Cordoba 2016a).

71 R. Syme, 'Hadrian and Italica', *JRS* 54 (1964), 142–149 [= R. Syme, *Roman Papers* II (Oxford 1979), 617–628]; Boatwright 1997, op. cit.

expectations of population growth and the actual situation that the city eventually experienced.[72]

It should not be forgotten that the building expenses did not usually include the costs generated by the operation of the buildings. Thus, the community itself had to take charge of maintaining the monumental framework bequeathed by Hadrian, which clearly exceeded the real needs of the Italicenses.[73] It has been proposed that the costly maintenance of these public spaces may have destabilised local finances and triggered a regressive process that ultimately precipitated the abandonment of the city.[74]

In our opinion, maintaining the monumental apparatus created between the Augustan period and the beginning of the 2nd century AD would have been considerably difficult for many cities of the late Antonine period.[75] The communities, animated by economic prosperity and civic patronage, then competed to prove their Romanness via architectural achievement.[76] This great effort had its consequences once communities experienced economic difficulties. As we have indicated, such a monumental display required not only a large financial outlay of resources for its creation, but also significant sums of money for its maintenance, and would, over time, constitute an enormous burden that troubled communities were unable to sustain.[77]

---

72 D. Romero Vera, 'Espacios no construidos en la ciudad romana: problemas y perspectivas de estudio a partir de varios casos hispanos', *MDAI(M)* 57 (2016b), 393–408.

73 E. Melchor Gil, 'Aportaciones pecuniarias de los notables locales a las finanzas municipales de las ciudades hispanas', in *Sociedad y economía en el occidente romano*, ed. J. F. Rodríguez Neila, C. Castillo, and F. J. Navarro (Pamplona 2003b), 199–230.

74 Melchor Gil 1992–1993, op. cit., 132–134; Melchor Gil 2009, op. cit., 150–152.

75 There is an evident parallelism between the evergetism developed by Septimius Severus in his native city, *Lepcis Magna*, and our case study, Ibid. This monumental display, which included the new Severan forum as well as the tetrapylon arch, a *nymphaeum*, a large porticoed road and the port, seems to have exceeded the needs of the Leptitans, and its maintenance consumed enormous resources. In fact, the new port built by the emperor was practically abandoned after its construction due to the difficulties and cost of dredging it. The rapid decline of the city, beginning already in the 3rd century, seems to be related to imperial evergetism; see J. B. Ward-Perkins, 'Severan Art and Architecture at *Lepcis Magna*', *JRS* 38 (1948), 60; I. M. Barton, 'The Effects of Imperial Favour. Septimius Severus and *Lepcis Magna*', *Museum Africum* 6 (1977–1978), 60–63.

76 M. Martín-Bueno, 'La ciudad Julio-Claudia, ¿una estrella fugaz?', in *II Congreso de Arqueología Peninsular*, vol. IV, ed. R. de Balbín and P. Bueno (Zamora 1997), 117–122; C. Witschel, 'Hispania en el siglo III', in Hispaniae. *Las provincias hispanas en el mundo romano*, ed. J. Andreu et al. (Tarragona 2009), 494; Alföldy 1998, op. cit., 19.

77 M. Martín-Bueno, 'La ciudad hispanorromana: deseo y realidad', in Oppida labentia. *Transformaciones, cambios y alteración en las ciudades hispanas entre el siglo II y la tardoantigüedad*, ed. J. Andreu (Uncastillo 2017), 3–35; J. Andreu Pintado, 'From *Splendidissima Ciuitas* to *Oppidum Labens*: on the Causes of the Financial Problems and Material Ruin of

Of course, maintaining the *Italica* conceived by Hadrian could have caused many headaches and consumed an enormous number of resources. However, we should not lose sight of the fact that in the decades following Hadrian's death, no abandonment of a public building or urban sector has been detected. Nor has any domestic abandonment been recorded during this period, apart from the amortisation of the House of the Columns. Moreover, the decorative apparatus of the dwellings (as demonstrated by the study of the mosaic pavements) began during the reign of Antoninus Pius and continued throughout the second half of the 2nd century AD. Therefore, the archaeological documentation does not point to drastic urban regression in the late Antonine period.

On another note, *Italica* stands out as one of the cities most affected by the *Mauri* raids. In 172 and 177 AD, troops of Berber origin crossed the Mediterranean to sack the cities of *Baetica*. The literary and epigraphic sources describing this event note that the attacks were quite violent.[78] To the existence of documents discussing the presence of troops of the *legio VII Gemina*, we must add the epigraph that the Italicenses dedicated to C. Vallius Maximianus, procurator of *Mauretania Tingitana*, who *provinciam Baeticam caesis hostibus paci pristinae restituerit*.[79] These raids may have caused episodes of distress in the colony, but the archaeological record has not yielded any evidence of destruction or violence.

In the Severan period, *Italica* seemingly underwent a period of expansion. To this phase belongs the important decorative reform of the theatre, accompanied by other improvements, as illustrated by the donation of M. Cocceius Iulianus. It is also significant that this refurbishment took place at a later period when some Hispanic theatres had already been abandoned.[80]

---

Roman Provincial Cities at the End of the High-Empire', in *From* Splendidissima Ciuitas *to* Oppidum Labens: *Financial Problems and Material Ruin in Roman Provincial Cities at the End of the High-Empire. The Hispanic Provinces. Archaeology and Economy in the Ancient World. Proceedings of the 19th International Congress of Classical Archaeology*, ed. J. Andreu (Heidelberg 2020), 7–16.

78 Hist. Aug. *Vita Marci* 21.1: *Cum Mauri Hispanias prope omnes vastarent, res per legatos bene gestae sunt.* Hist. Aug. *Vita Severi* 2.3–6: *Sed dum in Africa est, pro Baetica Sardinia ei attributa est, quod Baeticam Mauri populabantur*. Epigraphic information is mainly provided by two inscriptions from *Italica* and *Singilia Barba* (*CIL* II, 1120 = *ILS* 1354 = *CILA* Se 2, 378 = *ERItalica* 74 and *CIL* II$^2$/5, 783 = *ILS* 1354a). For the rest of the sources related to this event, see G. Bernard, 'Les prétendues invasions maures en Hispanie sous le règne de Marc Aurèle : Essai de synthèse', *Pallas* 79 (2009), 357–370.

79 Caballos Rufino 1994, op. cit., 135–138.

80 P. Diarte, 'Redefining the Urban Landscape in Hispania: Entertainment Buildings and their Transformations in Late Antiquity', *Hortus Artium Medievalium* 20, no. 1 (2014a), 26; L. Brassous, 'Les édifices de spectacles d'Hispanie entre les IIe et IVe siècles', in *Urbanisme civique en temps de crise*, ed. L. Brassous and A. Quevedo (Madrid 2015a), 282;

In the section on domestic buildings, certain mosaic pavements belong to this period. Likewise, the spectacular donation of Vibia Modesta was made in the Severan period. However, the finances of the colony must have been in a crisis at that time; this is the only way to understand the intervention of M. Lucretius Iulianus as *curator reipublicae* between AD 209 and 211.[81]

It is curious that the city, despite being economically distressed, chose to dedicate two pedestals with their corresponding sculptures to the figure indicated previously. It is precisely in this context of cost containment in the face of an increasingly difficult economic situation (not only for *Italica* but also for many other civic communities) that we must place the *tabula gladiatoria* found in the amphitheatre.

Considering the documentation that we have presented and commented on throughout this work, it does not seem feasible to affirm that *Italica* suffered an early urban crisis, nor that the effects of imperial evergetism provoked an immediate regression. It seems clear that the Hadrianic urban project can be described as excessive and that, as was eventually demonstrated, it suffered from a lack of real planning, since it did not account for the enormous resources necessary for its maintenance, costs that would fall directly on the local population. Nevertheless, the colony maintained the monumental display sponsored by Hadrian at least until the Severan period.

During the Trajanic-Hadrianic phase, not only *Italica*, but practically all the Hispano-Roman populations, showed signs of great dynamism.[82] However, from the time of Antoninus Pius onwards, the situation described above changed, and in most of the cities, the building boom ended. The dedication of epigraphs in a public context diminished considerably and, although some decorative and constructive interventions have been discovered, their volume declined sharply in comparison with the previous period.[83] It should be added that at this time, some cities experienced a material decline that led to urban collapse within a short period.[84] This process had a particular impact on civic centres, which suffered from neglect and pillage, triggering a dynamic of ruin

D. Romero Vera, 'Edificios de espectáculos en la Hispania del siglo II d.C.: un análisis sincrónico', *Lucentum* 39 (2020a), 250–252.

81 *CILA* Se 2, 379.

82 J. M. Abascal Palazón, 'El hábito epigráfico en Hispania entre Trajano y Adriano', in *De Trajano a Adriano*. Roma matura, Roma mutans, ed. A. Caballos Rufino (Seville 2019), 275–296; Romero Vera 2021, op. cit.

83 López Sánchez 2017, op. cit.; Romero Vera 2021, op. cit.

84 According to our criteria, and taking into consideration the archaeological information, *Bilbilis, Carthago Nova, Emporiae, Labitolosa, Lucentum, Iulia Lybica, Dertosa, Cartima, Arucci/Turobriga, Lesera*, Torreparedones, Tiermes and Los Bañales, among other cities, would fit the dynamics we are describing.

and functional readjustment. The sewage system was no longer maintained, nor was the street cleaning system, and dumps appeared inside the city walls.[85] As can be seen, *Italica* did not follow the pattern of other cities that suffered the rigours of the urban crisis in the late Antonine period.

Nevertheless, the bulk of the Hispanic civic communities discussed within the framework of our study exhibited signs of maintenance and continuity. The *colonia Aelia Augusta Italicensium* belonged to this group of cities. The cities essentially thrived based on the monumental framework developed until the Trajan-Hadrian period. From a material standpoint, once the previous 'golden' age had passed and the urban apparatus had been completed, only certain reforms and ornamental works were recorded, except in isolated cases. The monumental landscape underwent few changes in comparison to the previous period.[86] However, roads and sewers were regularly maintained and both leisure and entertainment buildings and *fora* remained in use and in some cases economic investment did focus on domestic architecture.[87]

As we can see, the city in question follows the general continuity we are describing. However, some changes can be detected in relation to the epigraphic documentation. It is an established fact that the volume of civic inscriptions naming the local elites decreased as the 2nd century progressed, and only isolated examples have been found after the Severan period.[88] According to the epigraphic record, the institutional life of the colony continued with a certain

85 E. Boube, 'La mort lente du forum dans les villes des provinces hispaniques à la fin de l'Antiquité ou le symbole d'une société en cours de profonde mutation', in *Le forum en Gaule et dans les régions voisines*, ed. A. Bouet (Bordeaux 2012), 356–363; P. Diarte, *La configuración urbana de la Hispania tardoantigua. Transformaciones y pervivencias de los espacios públicos romanos, ss. III–VI d.C.* (Oxford 2012), 247–251; M. D. Ruiz Bueno, *Dinámicas topográficas urbanas en Hispania: el espacio intramuros entre los siglos II y VII d. C.* (Bari 2018), 76–93.

86 D. Romero Vera, '138–192 d.C.: el punto de inflexión. Una aproximación a las transformaciones de las áreas forenses hispanas entre los reinados de Antonino Pío y Cómodo', in Exemplum et Spolia: *la reutilización arquitectónica en la transformación del paisaje urbano de las ciudades históricas*, vol. 2, ed. P. Mateos and C. Morán (Mérida 2020b), 707–714.

87 D. Romero Vera, 'Caracterizando a la ciudad hispanorromana de época antonina: muralla, viario y red de saneamiento', *Conimbriga* 58 (2019), 233–254; D. Romero Vera, 'Consideraciones sobre la arquitectura doméstica urbana de Hispania en el siglo II d.C.', *Spal* 29, no. 1 (2020c), 243–270; D. Romero Vera, 'Termas públicas en la Hispania de época antonina: una aproximación a su secuencia evolutiva', *Pyrenae* 51 (2020d), 69–98; Romero Vera 2020a, op. cit.; D. Romero Vera, 'Los foros de Hispania en el siglo II d.C.: intervenciones arquitectónicas, escultóricas y epigráficas', *Latomus* 80 (2021d), 82–112.

88 J. Arce, 'Epigrafía de la Hispania tardorromana de Diocleciano a Teodosio: problemas de historia y de cultura', in *La terza età dell'epigrafia*, ed. A. Donati (Faenza 1988), 211–227; M. Kulikowski, *Late Roman Spain and its Cities* (Baltimore 2004), 28–38.

degree of normality between the late Antoine and early Severan periods. Signs can also be found of civic munificence and economic boasting, one of the best examples being the donation of lavish silver sculptures placed in the sanctuary of the imperial cult chapel. All this indicates that local elites still aspired to participate in public life at this time.[89]

On the other hand, in line with the general trend of building stagnation that we have been describing, fewer actions were taken in the field of leisure and spectacle buildings as the second century progressed. In fact, in the chronological framework of our study, the first cases of abandonment of spectacle buildings, especially theatres, occurred during this period.[90] As we have seen, the *Italica* theatre not only did not fall into disuse, but also underwent a major refurbishment in the Severan period, which was at least partly financed by private initiative.

In short, *Italica* shows a line of vitality that was not abruptly interrupted after Hadrian's reign. Inevitably, the colony had to deal with the same problems that generally affected the Hispanic provinces in the late Antonine period. It is even possible to identify some of the difficulties that were present in the post-Hadrian city: the invasion of the *Mauri*, the cost of maintaining an excessive monumental infrastructure, a municipal finance crisis, and so forth. Nevertheless, these obstacles did not destroy the city (as was the case with many other urban centres at that time). On the contrary, the civic community maintained the disproportionate monumental landscape bequeathed by Hadrian for at least seven decades. Therefore, the *res publica Italicensium* existed within the parameters of monumental urbanism and the Roman municipal model throughout the 2nd century and well into the 3rd century. More insurmountable problems would only emerge after the Severan period, when the process of disarticulating the high imperial urban model proved unstoppable.[91]

89 E. Melchor Gil, 'François Jacques tenía razón: sobre el no declinar de las élites locales y de la vida municipal durante el siglo II y el primer tercio del siglo III d.C.', in Oppida labentia. *Transformaciones, cambios y alteración en las ciudades hispanas entre el siglo II y la tardoantigüedad*, ed. J. Andreu (Uncastillo 2017), 217–244.

90 See note 80.

91 A. Cepas, *Crisis y continuidad en la Hispania del siglo III* (Madrid 1997), 109–254; P. Diarte, 'Un camino sin retorno: la desarticulación de la ciudad clásica en la Antigüedad Tardía (ss. IV–V d. C.)', in *Modelos edilicios y prototipos en la monumentalización de las ciudades de Hispania*, ed. M. Martín-Bueno and J. C. Sáenz (Zaragoza 2014b), 97–106.

CHAPTER 9

# Home, Honour, *Hispania*: the Case of L. Minicius Natalis Quadronius Verus

*Anna-Maria Wilskman*

> Consider what city this is, what is it you seek, who you are. Every day or so, as you go down to the Forum, you must repeat to yourself: "I am 'new'; I seek the consulship; this is Rome".[1,2] (Q. Cic. *pet.* 2. Translation by D. R. Shackleton Bailey)

•••

> Surely, I think that he and all natives of Italian towns have two fatherlands, one by nature and the other by citizenship. Cato, for example, though born in Tusculum, received citizenship in Rome, and so, as he was a Tusculan by birth and a Roman by citizenship, had one fatherland, which was the place of his birth, and another by law.[3] (Cic. *leg.* 2. 5. Translation by Clinton W. Keyes)

∴

This chapter discusses the self–presentation of Roman magistrates in relation to places. As the above citations illustrate, *origo* and personal awareness of the spatial context receive special attention. Observations based on the case study suggest that state magistrates enjoyed commemoration in their *patria* mostly in the beginning of their career and that the presence in the home

1 This work is part of the project "Law, Governance and Space: Questioning the Foundations of the Republican Tradition". This research has received funding from the European Research Council (ERC) under the European Union's Horizon 2020 research and innovation programme (grant agreement No. 771874).

2 *Civitas quae sit cogita, quid petas, qui sis. prope cottidie tibi hoc ad forum descendenti meditandum est: 'novus sum, consulatum peto, Roma est'.*

3 *Ego mehercule et illi et omnibus municipibus duas esse censeo patrias, unam naturae, alteram civitatis, ut ille Cato, cum esset Tusculi natus, in populi Romani civitatem susceptus est; ita, cum ortu Tusculanus esset, civitate Romanus, habuit alteram loci patriam, alteram iuris.*

 | DOI:10.1163/9789004685734_010

city weakened within a couple of generations.[4] In addition to this notion, the material illustrates how the intended audience, place, and motives affect representations, for example regarding the language and offices mentioned.

The study concentrates on the 2nd century AD Roman state magistrates with a cultural background on the Iberian Peninsula and their epigraphic evidence. To identify the magistrates at the threshold of different local identities, the focus is on the minor Roman magistrates, namely the *IIIviri monetales a(uro) a(rgento) a(ere) f(lando) f(eriundo)*. L. Minicius Natalis Quadronius Verus[5] offers the main material for the research as a case study.

First, I present my general approach and the challenges that the material recognises. Second, I discuss the case study. In the last part of the paper, I review the observations briefly in relation to other Hispanic magistrates of similar background.

To start with, I would like to name some scholars who have been influential in this current work, and whom a student interested in these matters might want to be acquainted with. Werner Eck has published a great deal about the relationship between inscriptions and self-presentation.[6] He also mentions *L. Minicius* as an example of some themes that are also dealt with in this paper, such as the authorship and multiple inscriptions.[7] The work of Géza Alföldy is likewise important, especially concerning magistrates in Hispania and their representations.[8] Antonio Caballos Rufino and his *Los senadores hispanorromanos y la romanización de Hispania*[9] is essential when working with questions regarding the *origo* of these magistrates. I mention further fundamental scholars and works in the notes.

Although Roman state magistrates and their careers and monuments have been researched from many perspectives, this article aims to bring together

---

4 A. Krieckhaus, *Senatorische Familien und ihre* patriae (*1./2. Jahrhundert n. Chr.*) (Hamburg 2006), 167.

5 PIR[2] M 620; A. Caballos Rufino, *Los senadores hispanorromanos y la romanización de Hispania* (*siglos I–III*) (Écija 1990), no. 128; F. des Boscs-Plateaux, *Un parti hispanique à Rome? Ascension des élites hispaniques et pouvoir politique d'Auguste à Hadrien* (*27 av. J.-C.–138 ap. J.-C.*) (Madrid 2005), no. 124.

6 See, for example, the papers in W. Eck, *Monument und Inschrift. Gesammelte Aufsätze zur senatorischen Repräsentation in der Kaiserzeit* (Berlin 2010b), especially 'Statuendedikanten und Selbstdarstellung in römischen Städten' and '"*Tituli honoraria*", *curriculum vitae* und Selbstdarstellung in der Hohen Kaiserzeit'.

7 Eck 2010c, op. cit. 154, 157–158.

8 For example, Alföldy 1969, op. cit., and G. Alföldy, 'Bildprogramme in den römischen Städten des *Conventus Tarraconensis* – Das Zeugnis der Statuenpostamente', *Revista de la Universidad Complutense de Madrid* (1972), 177–276.

9 A. Caballos Rufino 1990, op. cit.

in novel manner notions about the places of residence, the career, and the motives of individual magistrates in relation to different places.

## 1 *Origo*, Inscriptions, Identity

The *origo* – the place of origin – of a Roman magistrate is often ambiguous or difficult to determine, especially if the sources do not mention it directly.[10] Such a direct indication would include words such as *natus*, *origo*, and *ortus* in the Latin sources. However, since these are largely missing in the epigraphic sources of Roman magistrates, scholars have sought to answer questions concerning place of origin by careful examination of the onomastics and *tribus* of the individual. For example, a frequent occurrence of a specific *nomen* in a region can indicate that the name holders found elsewhere perhaps originated or had property there.[11]

Inscriptions are a very important material for the study of the Roman world. In addition to giving information about the possible *origo* of the individual or his family, they can record his career and give other personal information. As a primary material, they offer us a direct glimpse into a world almost 2,000 years away. Inscribed stones and other materials recorded official degrees and other administrative information, honoured individuals publicly and conserved the memory and deeds of the deceased, as well as ownerships of areas or properties.[12] The term *epigraphic habit*, introduced by Ramsay MacMullen in 1982, describes the attempt to answer the question why the Romans wrote in

10 From a legal point of view, see Y. Thomas, *« Origine » et « commune patrie ». Étude de droit public romain (89 av. J.-C.–212 ap. J.-C.)* (Rome 1996.)

11 M. Díaz de Cerio Erasun discusses these matters in the context of Lusitanian senators. M. Díaz de Cerio Erasun, 'Los senadores originarios de Lusitania (1982–2012)', *EFT(hist)* 25 (2012), 327–354. Benet Salway offers a good general overview on Roman onomastics: B. Salway, 'What's in a Name? A Survey of Roman Onomastic Practice from c. 700 B.C. to A.D. 700', *JRS* 84 (1994), 124–145. I would also like to mention the *Repertorium* of Latin *gentilicia* and *cognomina*, which is a very useful tool for research concerning onomastics and epigraphy: H. Solin and O. Salomies, *Repertorium nominum gentilium et cognominum Latinorum*, editio nova (Olms 1994). Regarding the study of Roman names, especially those we see in the inscriptions of magistrates, I. Kajanto, *The Latin Cognomina* (Helsinki 1965) and O. Salomies, *Die römischen Vornamen: Studien zur römischen Namengebung* (Helsinki 1987), and O. Salomies, *Adoptive and Polyonymous Nomenclature in the Roman Empire* (Helsinki 1992) are essential.

12 The list of possible references concerning Latin epigraphy is endless. As a relatively recent, comprehensive presentation about Latin epigraphy, see, for example, C. Bruun and J. Edmondson (ed.), *The Oxford Handbook of Roman Epigraphy* (Oxford 2014).

stone throughout the empire.[13] Because most of the material in this study falls either into the categories of "honorific", "funerary" and "dedication", the simplified answer would be that the erectors wanted to honour and remember the individuals presented in the inscriptions.

Unsurprisingly, the reality is not that simple. The epigraphic habit is often explained as a way of preserving memory. Inscriptions leave a mark about one's existence for future generations, not only for contemporaries.[14] However, I follow MacMullen's idea of the "sense of audience", but instead of putting the emphasis on *remembrance*, I approach the inscriptions as a way of communication; that is, they were erected for contemporaries, not only for posterity. By this, I mean that both the subject and the erector(s) used (especially the honorific) monuments for their own contemporary means. Of course, the idea of remembrance and lasting memory is also a part of this. Instead of concentrating only on the honoured, we should expand our focus and pay attention to the erectors and especially the intended audience of the inscription, as well as the spatial context.

This brings us now to the spatial framework of this paper. Landscapes and environment "are meaningful, socially constructed places involving bodily and cognitive experience" that "exist in relation to human actors who engage with them and imbue them with meaning".[15] The "audience" of the inscription differs whether the stone stands on the central forum of a big city or a small municipality, a cultic area, or a private estate or house. Geographically speaking, this paper concentrates on the Iberian Peninsula and Italy, but also touches upon other parts of the Empire. Different regions naturally have different cultural histories and commemorative practices. The nature of Roman inscriptions in the region also depends on the nature of the Roman presence.

The Iberian Peninsula is this paper's point of departure. Strabo, the 1st century BC geographer, and historian tells in his *Geography* 3.2.15 how the Turdetanians adopted the Roman lifestyle: most of them have Latin rights, they wear togas, and they have forgotten their native language. He also mentions the jointly settled cities of locals and Roman colonists, namely *Pax Augusta, Augusta Emerita* and *Caesaraugusta*. People of this class are even called

13 R. MacMullen, 'The Epigraphic Habit in the Roman Empire', *AJPh* 103 (1982), 233–246. See also especially Woolf 1996, op. cit., 22–39; E.A. Meyer, 'Explaining Epigraphic Habit in the Roman Empire: The Evidence of Epitaphs', *JRS* 80 (1990), 74–96 and F. Beltrán Lloris 2015, op. cit., 131–148.

14 For a slightly more detailed analysis, see Beltrán Lloris 2015, op. cit., 132ff. and references.

15 B. David and M. Wilson, *Inscribed Landscapes: Marking and Making Place* (Honolulu 2002), 6.

"*Togati*".[16] Another example from an ancient writer is Plutarch (*Sertorius* 14), where the author tells how young locals became practically the general's hostages. Sertorius then trained them so that they would make good magistrates for the local (Roman style) administration. This happened during the Spanish revolt (80–72 BC). R. Haeussler uses these as examples of "forced assimilation" and how by adopting Roman lifestyles and language, a community becomes 'Roman'.[17]

Nevertheless, how does one become a Roman senator? As mentioned earlier, this research concentrates on the magistrates *IIIviri monetales*, who issued and oversaw coinage, first under the Senate and then under the Princeps. This office was a part of a board known as *viginti(sex)viri*.[18] According to Cassius Dio, Augustus reformed the board and stated that equestrians could enter the *vigintiviri* offices, and that in practice holding such an office became a prerequisite for entering the Senate.[19] In other words, these officeholders could be young men with no previous experience in Roman administration, and who (at least in theory) could enter the Roman senate from outside the traditional power families. While preparing this paper, I also included the office of *decemviri stlitibus iudicandis* in my study, and I briefly refer to them at the end of the paper. The reason for choosing these offices is that they are the oldest and most distinguished offices amongst the *viginti(sex)viri* and appear most often in inscriptions.

Instead of focusing on the Hispanic local magistrates and non-elite, who recently and rightly received more attention from the scholarship, I choose to focus on the state magistrates.[20] Especially the notion by Plutarch highlights the importance of Roman administration as a strategy and tool for assimilation.

---

16 The manuscript tradition, however, gives reasons to doubt this, see Strabo, *Geography, Volume II: Books 3–5*. Translated by Horace Leonard Jones. Loeb Classical Library 50. Cambridge, MA 1917, 3.2.15 note.

17 Of course, as Haeussler shows in his work, it is not so simple. Haeussler discusses *humanitas*' part as a key concept and its role in the process of becoming 'Roman' – at least in the eyes of the Romans. R. Haeussler, *Becoming Roman? Diverging Identities and Experiences in Ancient Northwest Italy* (London 2013), 52–53.

18 In addition to *decemviri stlitibus iudicandis* and *tresviri monetales*, the board included the offices of *quattuorviri viarum curandarum, triumviri capitales, quattuorviri praefecti Capuam Cumas*, and *duoviri viis extra urbem purgandis*. The two last-mentioned offices were disbanded in the Augustan era, resulting in a total number of twenty men on the whole board.

19 D.C. 54.26.5–6.

20 See, for example, Curchin 1990, op. cit., with the new edition *A Supplement to the Local Magistrates of Roman Spain* (Waterloo 2015). For the Roman West, L. Revell, *Ways of Being Roman: Discourses of Identity in the Roman West* (Havertown 2016).

As Clifford Ando remarks, "(…) the expansion of Roman law, on the one hand, and the intellectual and ideological superstructures of Roman urbanism on the other – must be addressed together by any serious historian of the empire, for two reasons". The first is that the cities in the empire were to be looked at as instantiations of Rome, and the second reason is that it enables us to understand how Romans included "alien individuals and populations within the structures of their state".[21]

However, this paper is not about the early days of the Roman presence in the Iberian Peninsula, and we should keep in mind that people's perceptions changed over time. Looking at the ways people expressed "identity" in the 2nd century inscriptions is completely different compared to the source material of similar media from the early days of the Roman expansion into West. It is possible that a "cosmopolitan élite identity that incorporated the leading people across the Empire" existed.[22] This in turn creates a larger gap between the élite and the non-élite.[23]

Instead of only looking at the material from the point of view of "cosmopolitan élite identity" or "local identity", we should remember that social identity fluctuates and depends on the *context*. Ralph Haeussler has as an example of the way that a person could privately use his indigenous name instead of his *tria nomina*, for example in graffiti.[24] Based on this, we can surmise that high state magistrates could also portray their heritage when they saw fit, for example in inscriptions.

Latin inscriptions to Roman magistrates can then illustrate the locality, administration, and the individual and the community. By looking at where and why the inscriptions existed, we can study the interplay between the individual and local communities. Nevertheless, challenges are always present when dealing with primary sources. The dating of the inscriptions might be quite imprecise, especially if the stone is fragmentary and does not possess any clues about the date. The fragmentary state of the stone hinders the possibility of determining the precise reason, the erector, and the target of the commemoration. People re-used and moved around the inscriptions already in antiquity, and therefore even if we know the exact find location, it might

21 C. Ando, 'Law and the Landscape of Empire', in S. Benoist, A. Daguet–Gagey and C. Hoët–van Cauwenberghe (eds.), *Figures d'empire, fragments de mémoire. Pouvoirs et identités dans le monde romain impérial (IIe s. av. n. è.–VIe s. de n. è.)* (Villeneuve d'Ascq 2011).

22 T. G. Parkin and A. J. Pomeroy, *Roman Social History: A Sourcebook* (London 2007), citation from Haeussler 2013, op. cit.

23 Haeussler 2013, op. cit., 53; cf. C. Ando, *Imperial Ideology and Provincial Loyalty in the Roman Empire* (Berkeley–Los Angeles 2000).

24 Haeussler 2013, op. cit., 57 and 67 with references.

not present the original spatio–temporal situation. Another thing to consider is that many of the inscriptions were statue bases, and that the text and image were originally inseparable, but now we only have the text. These problems are important to acknowledge, but because this is a qualitative rather than a quantitative study, we can still make some remarks based on the information that has survived on the stones.

## 2 The Inscriptions of L. Minicius Natalis Quadronius Verus

When preparing this chapter, I collected all the inscriptions that mention the offices of *IIIvir auro argento aere flando feriundo/monetalis* and *Xvir stlitibus iudicandis* published thus far (June 2021). I then consulted A. Caballos Rufino and his *Los senadores hispanorromanos y la romanización de Hispania* (1990) in order to recognise the magistrates with Hispanic origin.[25] Rather than writing about all of them and risking presenting only a list, I decided to concentrate on L. Minicius Natalis Quadronius Verus, consul of AD 139, because of his versatile epigraphic evidence.[26] On the following pages, I approach *Minicius*' inscriptions through the key questions of *when* and *where* these inscriptions were erected, *what* they were, *who* erected them, and *why*.

## 3 Linking Oneself to a City

Some cities are more important for different individuals than others, and the *patria* is perhaps the most significant. As the quote by Cicero states in the beginning of this paper, a Roman magistrate could have two *patriae*: Rome, and the place of his birth.

L. Minicius Natalis Quadronius Verus was born in *Barcino* (Barcelona), and even after his rise to the Roman Senate and eminent offices, he continued

25 In addition, I collected the non-Hispanic magistrates that served in Hispania based on the mentions in the inscriptions, and those mentioned in Alföldy 1969, op. cit. For them and about the administration of Hispania Citerior, see also P. Ozcáriz Gil, *La administración de la provincia Hispania Citerior durante el Alto Imperio Romano: organización territorial, cargos administrativos y fiscalidad* (Barcelona 2013). See also F. des Boscs-Plateaux 2005, op. cit. for the rise of Hispanian elites in the Roman Empire.

26 For a fuller discussion about Minicius, see E. Groag, in *RE* XV, 2, 1932, s. v. 'Minicius', no. 19, col. 1836–1842.

to be visible in his home city.[27] Both dedications by him (*CIL* II, 4509 = 6145 (= *ILS* 1029) = *IRC* IV, 30 and *CIL* II, 4511 = *IRC* IV, 33) and honorific inscriptions to him serve as evidence of this. The dedications in *Barcino* clearly illustrate how Minicius wanted to make his presence and importance known and remembered. The first inscription commemorates how he and his father L. Minicius Natalis (cos. suff. AD 106)[28] built a *balineum cum porticibus* in *Barcino*. It dates to the mid career of the younger Minicius, here mentioned as *tribunus plebis designatus*. The name of the father and his consular offices are in larger letters on the first row, and the reason for the inscription appears on the last row in large text. Our young Minicius, however, is easily missed. His name and offices are on a same letter height as his father's offices, thus disappearing into the *cursus* of the father. The find location of this inscription is unknown, as fragments of it appeared from different parts of the town.[29] According to Eck and Navarro, it is very possible that the original location was at the baths of today's San Miguel square, which also included the inscription by Carthage, discussed below.[30]

While the building inscription dated to the mid-career of Minicius, the other dedication by him (*CIL* II, 4511 = *IRC* IV, 33) dates to the later career and highlights Minicius' will to be commemorated actively in *Barcino* also in the future. He orders a donation to his fellow citizens annually on his birthday so that the Augustales and the *decuriones* of the city can celebrate his birthday every year. The primary source editions supplement Minicius' name and the majority of *cursus*, and they are widely accepted. Unfortunately, the original location of this stone is unknown. In any case, this stone illustrates the personal link of Minicius to his original home city, and it is therefore an important example of a phenomenon that was not particularly common for senatorial families,

27 There is a probable kinship with L. Minicius Apronianus, local magistrate and *flamen divi Traiani Parthici* in *Tarraco* (*CIL* II$^2$/14-4, 2293; *CIL* II, 4488 = *IRC* IV, 34); E. Groag, in *RE* XV, 2, 1932, s. v. 'Minicius', no. 18, col. 1835 and L. Petersen, in *PIR*$^2$, 292 ad M 619. For Minicius in *Barcino*, see also Krieckhaus 2006, op. cit., 94–114.

28 For a fuller discussion, see E. Groag, in *RE* XV, 2, 1932, s. v. 'Minicius', no. 18, col. 1828–1836 and *PIR*$^2$ M 619.

29 W. Eck and F. J. Navarro, 'Das Ehrenmonument der *Colonia Carthago* für *L. Minicius Natalis Quadronius Verus* in seiner Heimatstadt *Barcino*', *ZPE* 123 (1998), 237.

30 Eck and Navarro 1998, op. cit., 248. The site was excavated and published by F. Pallarés, 'Las excavaciones de la plaza de San Miguel y la topografía romana de Barcino', *Cuadernos de Arqueología e Historia de la Ciudad* 13 (1969), 5–42. See also A. Krieckhaus 2006, op. cit., 101–102.

especially from *Hispania*.[31] However, it is possible that Minicius returned to spend his final years in his patria.[32]

These two inscriptions of Minicius present a straight relation between the city and the individual through *actions* (building and celebrating), but Minicius was also visible in Barcino (in a slightly less active way) through honorific inscriptions by *colonia Iulia Carthago* and L. Sempronius Carpio.[33] The dedication by Carthage is – like the other inscriptions – very fragmentary. Re–used, it covered the steps of a bathhouse on the square of San Miguel already during Antiquity. According to Eck's and Navarro's reconstruction, the inscription was originally very large. The type of the monument remains uncertain, but according to parallels, it is possible that it was a statue base for a group or a *biga, quadriga*, or an *aedicula* construction.[34] The dedication by Carpio seems to be a statue base, but its original location is unknown. However, because the location is given on a degree of the *decurio*, we can safely assume that it was outside Minicius' property, and therefore public. Carpio was Minicius' *cliens*.

The inscriptions by Carthage and Sempronius Carpio demonstrate associations or motives that are less straightforward when it comes to the choice of the monuments' city than the earlier discussed two dedications. Eck and Navarro conclude that the colony decided to erect the monument to Barcino because Minicius chose to do so. By having a grand monument by an important provincial colony, Minicius' prestige in his home city increased.[35] Minicius wanted to be remembered in *Barcino*, as is evident from the inscription stating his will to be celebrated on his birthday. As mentioned by Eck and Navarro, other (perhaps more natural) choices for these honorific inscriptions would be Rome or *Tibur*, which is discussed below.

However, both Carthage and Sempronius Carpio chose *Barcino*. Was Carpio's motive the same as Carthage's, i.e. he followed Minicius' wishes? Did he perhaps have a personal agenda? This is the only epigraphic evidence we have about Sempronius Carpio. He does not appear as a local magistrate in Curchin (1990 and 2015), and he does not give any other attributes for himself save the fact that he is the client of Minicius. It is common that an individual mentions

31 Eck and Navarro 1998, op. cit., 247.

32 Krieckhaus 2006, op. cit. 110.

33 *IRC* IV, 34; *CIL* II, 4510 = *IRC* IV, 32.

34 Eck and Navarro 1998, op. cit., 245; D. Erkelenz, 'Ubique gentium quadriuges et seiuges currus: Gespannmonumente für Angehörige der hohen *ordines* im römischen Reich', *JRA* 16, 2003a, 211.

35 Eck and Navarro 1998, op. cit., 247; Krieckhaus 2006, op. cit. 108–109; D. Erkelenz, Optimo praesidi. Untersuchungen zu den Ehrenmonumenten für Amsträger der römischen Provinzen in Republik und Kaiserzeit (Bonn 2003b), 224.

his office or profession in the honorific inscription he dedicates, but this is not the case with Carpio.[36] Therefore, the whole focus turns to Minicius. Would the reason for this be that he is a local man of *Barcino*, already well known, and who was also able to negotiate a suitable place for the monument with the *decurio*? From this point of view, this is the only example of how *Barcino* honoured Minicius, who had invested so much in the city.

If we did not have Minicius' dedications and especially the inscription that states that *Barcino* is his birthplace, we would not perhaps be able to form such a strong connection between this individual and the city based only on the honorific inscriptions. Sometimes, the text indicates a city where the monument was to be located (in the inscription by Carthage, the mention of *Barcino* is added to the edition), but this is not always the case, as is apparent, for example, in the honorific monument by Carpio. The bond between Minicius and *place* was less emphasised and somewhat overlooked textually, while the link between Minicius as Carpio's personal *patronus* was more visible.

Individuals could also serve as the *patronus* of a city.[37] *Barcino* did not link itself to Minicius directly and verbally, whereas *Tibur* as a city honoured him publicly. The honorific inscriptions seem to record his offices in full. The statue base found during excavations[38] records Minicius' various offices carefully and reveal his connection to *Tibur* as the *patronus* and *curator fani Herculis*, as well as his connection to Hadrian – the most important inhabitant of the city – as his former *quaestor candidatus*.[39] The fact that the inscription was set up by the *decuriones Tiburt(ini) / ex aere collato q(uin)q(uennali) maximi exempli* highlights the respect *Minicius* enjoyed in the city. Another text from *Tibur* is first recorded as re–used in a building at the sanctuary of *Hercules Victor* (*CIL* XIV, 3600 = *InscrIt* IV/1, 114), so it is possible or even probable that it was also originally there or nearby. The inscription is very fragmentary, but it is probable that it is for Minicius, because it has some diagnostic offices or formulas, such as [*pat*]*ris sui* and *IIIvir monetalis auro argento aere flando feriundo*.

36 See, for example, W. Eck, 'Statuendedikanten und Selbstdarstellung in römischen Städten', in Eck 2010c, op. cit., 127–141.

37 For civic patronage, see especially Nicols 2014, op. cit. with a chapter concentrating on epigraphic evidence of different regions, ranks of patrons and benefactions in 'Chapter 7: Civic Patronage in the Epigraphical Record', 239–277. See also 'Chapter 6: Civic Patronage in Roman Law', 207–237.

38 *CIL* XIV, 3599 = *ILS* 1061 = *InscrIt* IV/1, 113 = EDR092740: *Tivoli* (Roma), nella piazza dinanzi la chiesa di S. Andrea, nel corso di scavi.

39 Minicius served also as the *duumvir* in Tibur. On this topic, see A. Caballos Rufino, 'De *Hispania* a *Tibur*: elites imperiales en el entorno de Villa Adriana', in Roma, Tibur, Baetica. *Investigaciones adrianeas* (Seville 2013), ed. R. Hidalgo and P. León, 21–76.

The honorific inscriptions of *Tibur* aim to link Minicius directly to the city itself, both by mentioning the city as the erector and because of the local offices of Minicius. Furthermore, evidence of Minicius' own dedications survive. By dedicating *ex voto* for specifically Tiburtian *Hercules Victor* and *praetorian* gods, Minicius links himself to the region and its important divinities, as well as to praetorian rank.[40] The first record of this inscription was at the church of S. Vincenzo. For the Savior Asklepios (Ἀσκληπιὸς θεὸς Σωτήρ), he dedicated a temple (ναός) and an altar (βωμός). The inscription was first read near the so–called Acropolis, and it is an important testimony that a temple for Asklepios existed in *Tibur*.[41]

These two honorific inscriptions make clear that Minicius acted and most probably lived in *Tibur*, which had a notable Spanish community.[42] However, this Iberian identity is not visible in the inscriptions.

## 4 Brief Visits

Both *Barcino* and *Tibur* seem to be places *where Minicius* lived. Another certain place is Rome, but that city remains under–represented in Minicius' material.[43] It is highly possible that he had inscriptions in the *Urbs*, but those stones have not survived to our day. The only exception to this is the dedication, which might be by either him or his father.[44] The places served as somewhat stable or permanent places for Minicius, and his personal connection to the place is often somehow explained in the stones, or it is otherwise obtainable, for example thanks to other, more detailed stones in the area. Minicius did have, however, inscriptions also in places where his stay seems to be briefer or only passing.[45]

---

40 *IGR* I, 376 = *IG* XIV, 1125 = *InscrIt* IV/1, 33; *CIL* XIV, 3554a (= *ILS* 3415) = *InscrIt* IV/1, 56 = EDR129896, dated 138–161.

41 C. F. Giuliani, *Forma Italiae. Regio I – volumen septimum. Tibur, pars prima* (Rome 1970) 31. For discussion about the temples on the acropolis, see ibid. 119–143.

42 See especially R. Syme, 'Spaniards at Tivoli', *AncSoc* 13–14 (1982–1983), 241–263 [= R. Syme, *Roman Papers* IV (Oxford 1988), 94–114]. Eck and Navarro also discuss *Tibur* as Minicius' place of residence.

43 But note the monument of the father in Rome: *CIL* VI 31739 = *CIL* VI 41109 = EDR093383. For this and other monuments of the elder Minicius, see D. Erkelenz, 'Ehrenmonumente des *L. Minicius Natalis* in Rom und Africa', *ZPE* 123, 1998, 257–269.

44 *CIL* VI, 31112: [- - -] / *L(ucius) Minicius / Natalis / v(otum) s(olvit)*.

45 For senatorial possessions and estates in Italy, see A. M. Andermahr, Totus in praediis. *Senatorischer Grundbesitz in Italien in der Frühen und Hohen Kaiserzeit* (Bonn 1998).

One such example is the Greek inscription from *Megara* that mentions parts of Minicius' name and *cursus*, starting from the office of *IIIvir auro argento aere flando feriundo*.[46] The name and offices of Minicius are in the accusative, suggesting that this is an honorific inscription. Unfortunately, the first row of the inscription is not preserved, so the discussion remains cursory. A very fragmentary, bilingual inscription (dated 153–170) was found inside an aqueduct in the area near Viterbo.[47] Based on this, we can assume that the inscription was re-used, perhaps from somewhere nearby. The stone is attributed to Minicius due to the well–preserved parallels. It records a dedication to the gods in Greek, and the *cursus* of the dedicator in Latin, seemingly in detail. R. Zucca suggests a supplementation [Διὶ Ἡλίῳ Σα]ράπ[ιδι καὶ Εἴσιδι μυ]ριω[νύ]μῳ καὶ [τοῖς συννάοι]ς θεοῖς.[48] This is based on another inscription by *Minicius*, found in Minturno (*IGR* I, 1391 = EDR072014, dated 154–165).[49] The area from which this latter inscription was found was originally a site of the goddess *Marica*, but in the first and second centuries AD it was a site of Egyptian cults. Another dedication by L. Minicius Natalis is the Latin dedication for Apollo from Vulci, from the area of Musignano.[50]

The inscription from *Olympia* is highly interesting (*I.Olympia* 236). The *cognomen Natalis* survives, stating how he won the Olympic Games in AD 129 as *vir praetorius* (στρατηγικός) and how he dedicated a *quadriga*. The text also mentions his offices as consul and proconsul of *Africa* (ὕπατος, ἀνθύπατος Λιβύης). This means that he dedicated the monument more than a decade after his victory – or indeed almost three decades later – which is completely

46 *IG* IV²/2, 1119 = *IG* VII, 89. P. J. Smith, *The Archaeology and Epigraphy of Hellenistic and Roman Megaris, Greece* (Oxford 2008) has *IG* VII, 89 and is dated to 138. However, the inscription does not seem to mention the office of *cos. suff.*, and the date 121/2 given in *IG* IV²/2 is at least as possible.

47 *CIL* XI, 3002 = *IG* XIV, 2260 = EDR092743. *CIL* mentions the find context of the inscription only as "antico acquedotto", without further specifications. A recent online addition to the EDR record says "Viterbo, reimpiegata all'interno di un acquedotto nelle vicinanze della città (area del Bullicame?)".

48 R. Zucca, 'Fruizioni idroterapiche e culti idrici nel Viterbese', in Usus veneratioque fontium. *Atti del Convegno Internazionale di Studio su « Fruizione e Culto delle Acque Salutari in Italia »*, ed. L. Gasperini (Rome 2006), 146–160. Unfortunately, I was unable to consult the article, and I have to rely on the information given in EDR. The page numbers for the article given there are 390–391, 397–400.

49 EDR record states: "Minturno (Latina), riva destra del Garigliano, presso la foce, nelle vicinanze dei resti del tempio di *Marica* (a. 1904)".

50 Here withouth the *cognomina Quadronius Verus*. Dated to 153–170 CE. *CIL* XI, 2925 (= *ILS* 3221) = EDR092744.

possible.[51] He wanted to show the audience how he rose from praetorian status to that of consul. It has been suggested that this monument is the same one that Pausanias mentions (5.20.8) when he talks about a contemporary Roman consul who "[W]ishing to leave behind, as a memorial of his victory, a bronze statue with an inscription, he proceeded to dig, so as to make a foundation".[52] Pausanias mentions this when he talks about "the pillar of Oenomaüs, which is in the direction of the sanctuary of Zeus as you go from the great altar".[53] If indeed the senator is our Minicius – as is widely accepted –, the location of his statue was very central.[54] Even if the senator is someone else, we can safely assume that Minicius' choice of location for his monument was probably in a very public place.

There are still a couple of inscriptions mentioning Minicius. A text from *Callatis* of *Moesia Inferior* is missing the name of the person honoured, but the *cursus* corresponds to that of Minicius.[55] Another inscription from *Moesia*, from *Troesmis*, mentions Minicius only in his office of *legatus Aug. pr. praetore*.[56] Finally, we have an inscription dated to AD 149–150 from *Lepcis Magna* for L. Minicius Natalis Quadronius Verus, who is celebrated by the Lepcitanians as their patron.[57] Unfortunately, the find location is unrecorded. Here Minicius appears as the *proconsul Africae* and nothing else in addition to the patronage is given.

---

51 Discussed in W. Dittenberger and K. Purgold, *Die Inschriften von Olympia* (Berlin 1896), no. 236, col. 347–348.

52 Pausanias. *Description of Greece, Volume II: Books 3–5 (Laconia, Messenia, Elis 1)*. Translated by W. H. S. Jones and H. A. Ormerod. Loeb Classical Library 188. Cambridge, MA: Harvard University Press, 1926; Dittenberger and Purgold 1896, op. cit., col. 347–348.

53 Paus. 5.20.8.

54 W. Gurlitt, *Über Pausanias* (Graz 1890), 421 n. 846; Pausanias, *Guida della Grecia. 5, Libro v: L'Elide e Olimpia*. Testo e traduzione a cura di G. Maddoli. Commento a cura di G. Maddoli e V. Saladino (Milan 1995), 308. It is also possible that the dedication and monument that Pausanias mentions are two separate monuments. Pausanias, *Description de la Grèce. T. 5, Livre V: l'Élide (I)*. Texte établi par M. Casevitz, traduit par J. Pouilloux, commenté par A. Jacquemin (Paris 1999), 228.

55 *IGR* I, 653 = *IScM* III, 114.

56 *AE* 1972, 547 = *IScM* V, 141. The military diploma *CIL* XVI, 177 mentions him in a consular dating.

57 *IRT* 536.

## 5 The Influence of Place in Presentations

In many instances, Minicius' offices explain the inscriptions in certain places, such as in *Moesia Inferior* and in *Africa*.[58] In the stones of *Troesmis* and *Lepcis Magna*, his whole *cursus* is unmentioned, and the focus draws especially towards the magistracy.

*Minicius* does not include his whole *cursus* in all his inscriptions. In dedications, he often concentrates only on his most prestigious offices, such as consul, *proconsul Africae*, *augur*, and *legatus Augusti pro praetore Moesiae inferioris* (in *Tibur* and Vulci). In Minturno, he adds the office *curator operum publicorum et aedium sacrarum* to the list. Although the first line of the inscription in Viterbo is reconstructed with the help of the stone in Minturno, it lacks the mention of this office.

While the dedications concentrate on his high offices, the honorific inscriptions record his whole *cursus* (expect the inscription in *Lepcis Magna*). The local curia agreed on the location of the honorific inscriptions, suggesting that they should be in public places. These honorific stones tend to come from the places where Minicius lived or had lived and had invested in the cities through public buildings. Perhaps because of this "more permanent" presence, Minicius also wanted to make his life and career more comprehensive in these cities.

Excluding the inscriptions which only mention Minicius as a way of dating (a military diploma and the inscription of *Troesmis*), Minicius presumably had some kind of agency and power to decide the location and the content of the stone.[59] Furthermore, the stones illustrate code switching. This is evident especially with the dedications. In *Tibur*, he served as the *curator fani Herculis Victoris*. He also made a dedication to Tiburtian Hercules, thus rooting himself directly to the area and receiving prestige in the eyes of the locals. Minicius illustrates how he changes languages and acknowledges the audience. The case of the Olympian dedication is a clear example. In the famous Greek site, Minicius uses only Greek, but still includes his Roman offices. While mentioning his highest offices, he simultaneously highlights that he won the Olympic race as *vir praetorius*, but later became a consul and proconsul.

Particularly interesting is the Greek dedication to Asklepios. Why did *Minicius* decide to use Greek in his dedication to Asklepios in *Tibur*? The

58 For provincial administration and governor's seats, see R. Haensch, Capita provinciarum. *Statthaltersitze und Provinzialverwaltung in der römischen Kaiserzeit* (Mainz 1997). For honorific monuments of Roman magistrates, see D. Erkelenz 2003b, op. cit.

59 For discussion about *Minicius*' agency, see Eck and Navarro 1998, op. cit.; Eck 2010c, op. cit., "Statuendedikanten und Selbstdarstellung in römischen Städten" and "'*Tituli honorarii*', *curriculum vitae* und Selbstdarstellung in der Hohen Kaiserzeit".

language does not seem to be very common in the inscriptions of the area.[60] One possibility is that he wanted to acknowledge the Greek origin of Asklepios when addressing him. Another possibility is perhaps that he wanted to show off his learning.[61] At this point, the famous philhellene and Minicius' acquaintance Hadrian had already acquired his luxurious villa in *Tibur*, and it is possible that Minicius wanted to appear 'fashionable' in his Greek dedication. These possibilities do not rule each other out. We can only speculate.

In Minturno and Vulci, Minicius perhaps chose to dedicate bilingual monuments to 'Zeus Helios the Great Sarapis and the Thousand–faced Isis' because the gods were linked to the Imperial family and illustrate a link to the Ptolemaic–Greek tradition.[62] Minturno was also an important trading centre, so perhaps Minicius wanted to acknowledge both the gods and the visitors of the sanctuary.[63] A search in *EDCS* resulted in only a couple of inscriptions in the region of Viterbo that are either bilingual or in Greek. For Minturno's, the result was only one.[64] Like in *Tibur,* Minicius chose to use a language that was not mainstream in the area, but this time he also used Latin to present himself and his career. Perhaps he did this to reach the viewers who did not understand Greek. If we follow this thought further, this will mean that he presumed that the audience in *Tibur* would understand Greek better than the people of Viterbo and Minturno would.

## 6 Uses and Abuses of Onomastics

Minicius was not the first senator in his family, and it is highly probable that the past generations affected his future. Thanks to the inscriptions in *Barcino*, we can trace the career of the elder L. Minicius.[65] His first office was *quattuorvir*

60 *IG* records only four Greek inscriptions in *Tibur*: *CIL* XIV, 3533 = *IG* XIV, 1123 = *InscrIt* IV/1, 31 = EDR 127312 and *IG* XIV 1124–1126 (= *InscrIt* IV/1, 32–33 and 38). These seem like private dedications directly to the god and do not seem as public as the grand dedication of *Minicius*.

61 If this is the case, it is interesting that the inscription states Μυσία rather than Μοισία. At this point of linguistic development, this spelling is possible, but an educated writer would avoid it. So did Minicius himself decide the spelling, or was it the stone cutter? We cannot say. I thank Urpo Kantola for bringing this curiosity to my attention.

62 J. Quack and S. Takacs, 'Serapis', in *Brill's New Pauly*, consulted online on 2 June 2021 http://dx.doi.org.libproxy.helsinki.fi/10.1163/1574-9347_bnp_e1109510.

63 G. Uggeri, '*Minturnae*', in *Brill's New Pauly*, consulted online on 2 June 2021 http://dx.doi.org.libproxy.helsinki.fi/10.1163/1574-9347_bnp_e805900.

64 H. Solin, *Studi storico–epigrafici sul Lazio antico* (Rome 1996), 226–227, no. 63, with photo.

65 *PIR*[2] M 619.

*viarum curandarum*, which belongs to the vigintivirate, but is under *IIIvir monetalis* in the hierarchy.[66] As the son would do later, the father first served as *legatus* and then as proconsul in *Africa*. Minicius the elder served in military offices and distinguished himself in war, whereas the young *Minicius* leaned towards civilian offices. The father's success most probably helped the son, who also worked directly under him in *Africa*, as mentioned in inscriptions. Furthermore, the young *Minicius* was close to the Emperor from early on. Through the office of *monetalis*, the younger *Minicius* worked with the Emperor, who authorised the coinage of the Empire. Soon after, he became the *quaestor* of the Emperor. Inscriptions with his full *cursus* always mention the close connection with the Principate.[67] It is noteworthy that the son became *augur* quite early, already before his plebeian tribunate.[68]

The surviving epigraphic evidence of *Minicius* father and son differ. The only dedication by the father is the *balneum* to *Barcino*. Honorific inscriptions in *Africa Proconsularis* by communities also exist.[69] Otherwise, he appears mainly in dating formulas. The younger *Minicius* was certainly more vocal and had more agency in his representations.

L. Minicius Natalis Quadronius Verus and his many survived inscriptions offer an interesting glimpse into how a Roman senator wanted to appear in certain places. His career posts explain some inscriptions, such as those by the people of *Lepcis Magna* and the inscription by Carthage in *Barcino*, and the stones in *Moesia*, whereas some places, namely *Megara*, Vulci, and Minturno,

66 E. Groag, 'Patricier und *IIIviri monetales*', *Archäologisch-epigraphische Mitteilungen aus Österreich-Ungarn* 19 (1896), 145–146; S. Brassloff, 'Die Grundsätze bei der Commendation der Plebejer', *JÖAI* 8 (1905), 60–70; E. Birley, 'Senators in the Emperors' Service', *PBA* 39 (1953), 197–214; G. Alföldy, *Konsulat und Senatorenstand unter den Antoninen. Prosopographische Untersuchungen zur Senatorischen Führungsschicht* (Bonn 1977); A. P. Steiner, '*The Vigintivirate during the Empire. A Study of the Epigraphical Evidence*' (Ph. D. diss., University of Ohio, 1974), 73–74. Discussed more in detail in S. Hillebrand, '*Der Vigintivirat: Prosopographische Untersuchungen für die Zeit von Augustus bis Domitian*' (Ph. D. diss., University of Heidelberg, 2006), 24–28.

67 See also J. Crook, Consilium Principis. *Imperial Councils and Counsellors from Augustus to Diocletian* (Cambridge 1955), 231, nr. 174 for friendship with Hadrian.

68 For the important religious offices, see L. Schumacher, 'Die vier hohen römischen Priesterkollegien unter den Flaviern, den Antoninen aund den Severern (69–235 n. Chr.)', in W. Haase (eds.), *Aufstieg und Niedergang der römischen Welt. Geschichte und Kultur Roms im Spiegel der neueren Forschung*. II. *Principat.* Volume 16, no. 1, *Teilband Religion (Heidentum: Römische Religion, Allgemeines)* (Berlin–New York 1978), 777–780.

69 *CIL* VIII, 7069 = *ILAlg* II/1, 659 and *CIL* VIII, 22785 = *ILTun* 65 = *ILPBardo* 19. Unfortunately, the name of *Minicius* has not survived in the stones, so there remains a possibility of other identifications, even though the interpretation seems highly probable.

are not so easy to explain straightforwardly. With his many dedications to different gods, *Minicius* paints a picture of himself as a pious man in the cult areas of *Latium* and *Campania*. Nevertheless, he always includes at least some of his offices in the dedication, thus dedicating it to the gods but also representing himself to the mortal audience. The only exception to this is the dedication in Rome (*CIL* VI, 31112), which might be either by him or his father.[70] Another place where we know *Minicius* served as *legatus Augusti* is *Britannia*, but he is invisible in inscriptions found from the island so far. Another "missed possibility" in the light of the current sources is the office of *curator viae Flaminiae* because no attestations of him appear on its route.

## 7 Other Hispanic Magistrates

In addition to L. Minicius, the only examples of Hispanic *IIlviri monetales* or *Xviri stlitibus iudicandis* are Q. Licinius Q. f. Silvanus Granianus Proculus,[71] P. Mummius P. f. Sisenna Rutilianus,[72] P. Alfius P. f. Maximus Numerius Licinianus,[73] M. Messius M. f. Rusticus Aemilius Afer Cutius Romulus Priscianus Arrius Proculus,[74] M. Messius M. f. Rusticianus Aemilius Lepidus Iulius Celsus Balbinus Arrius Proculus,[75] and Hadrian.[76] These individuals are also attested

70 [- - -] / *L(ucius) Minicius / Natalis / v(otum) s(olvit)*.

71 *PIR*[2] L 249; A. Caballos Rufino 1990, op. cit. no. 102.

72 *PIR*[2] M 711, Tomares, Sevilla (Baetica): *CILA* Se 2, 589; A. Caballos Rufino 1990, op. cit., no. 132; F. des Boscs-Plateaux 2005, op. cit., no. 126.

73 *PIR*[2] A 535, Tarraco (Hispania citerior): *CIL* II[2]/14-2, 971; A. Caballos Rufino 1990, op. cit., no. 535; F. des Boscs-Plateaux 2005, op. cit., 131.

74 *PIR*[2] M 523, Hispalis (Baetica): *CILA* Se 1, 18; A. Caballos Rufino 1990, op. cit. no. 122; F. des Boscs-Plateaux 2005, op. cit., 121.

75 *PIR*[2] M 520b, *CILA* Se 3, 961 and possibly *CILA* Se 3, 962; A. Caballos Rufino 1990, op. cit., no. 120; F. des Boscs-Plateaux 2005, op. cit., 129.

P. Mummius' inscription is too fragmentary to say who dedicated it, but P. Alfius' was dedicated by his son and M. Messius Afer by the community of *Siarum*. The office of *Xvir* is mentioned in the stone as his only office. His other inscriptions are a funerary inscription from Castel Madama by his parents. It seems that he did not serve as a Roman magistrate after his decemvirate. The other Messius is also attested in *Baetica* a couple of times, and is also once connected to *Siarum*, and in nearby regions with the other Messius inscriptions. This Messius served as *tribunus plebis designatus* when his father erected the honorific statue for him with his own money (*CILA* Se 3, 961).

76 *PIR*[2] A 184; A. Caballos Rufino 1990, op. cit., no. 7; F. des Boscs-Plateaux 2005, op. cit., 84. See note 86.

in other regions and served as *Xviri stlitibus iudicandis*.[77] The only exception is Q. Licinius, who is attested only in *Baetulo* and served as *IIIvir monetalis*.

In fact, Q. Licinius had a lot in common with L. Minicius. They originated from the same region, were probably related through the maternal line, and their fathers served as consuls together at AD 106.[78] Licinius' grandfather had served in important non-senatorial offices in *Hispania* and had inscriptions in *Tarraco*.[79] Licinius' father made a hospitality agreement with the city of *Baetulo* in 98 CE, thus creating a link between the family and the city (*IRC* I, 139).[80] The bronze tablet is dated to June 8th and extends the agreement to *Q. Licinius* and his posterity. The only inscription of the son Q. Licinius Q. f. Silvanus Granianus Proculus[81] is a statue base dated to AD 110–138 and erected for his honour by the decree of the local *ordo* (*CIL* II, 4609 = *IRC* I, 138). The well–preserved inscription records Q. Licinius as *IIIvir ad monetam*, which can be understood as *IIIvir auro argento aere flando feriundo*, and *tribunus militum legionis VI Victricis Piae Fidelis*. Since the stone does not record other offices, we can assume that he received the honour while still a rather young man in his twenties and before he became a *quaestor*. Another possibility is that his career as a state magistrate did not continue.

A look[82] into the inscriptions found from Badalona reveal that honorific inscriptions and inscriptions relating to official cults were almost all re-used in the church of S. María, where also this statue base was also found. They

---

77 P. Mummius in *Tibur* (XXvirate), consular dating in *Ostia* and *Velletri*; P. Alfius in possible other inscriptions in *Ancyra* and in *Carnuntum* (if he is the same person); and *M. Messius* in Castel Madama (*Latium et Campania / Regio I*) (XXvirate).

78 R. Syme, 'Rival Cities, Notably Tarraco and Barcino', *Ktèma* 6 (1981), 282 [= Syme 1988, op. cit., 89]; R. Syme, 'Spaniards at Tivoli', *AncSoc* 13–14 (1982–1983), 247–248 [= Syme 1988, op. cit., 100]; R. Syme, 'Clues to Testamentary Adoption', in *Epigrafia e ordine senatorio* 1 (Rome 1982), 403 [= Syme 1988, op. cit., 165]. Salomies 1992, op. cit., 141–142; Caballos Rufino 1990, op. cit., 183 and 229. Caballos Rufino's remarks that the kinship with T. Iulius Maximus Manlianus Brocchus Servilianus A. Quadronius Verus L. Servilius Vatia Cassius Camars, who was honored in *Nemausus* as the *patronus* by *Calagurritani ex Hispania Citeriore*, is more difficult to attest, Caballos Rufino 1990, op. cit., 228; see also P. Le Roux, 'Les sénateurs originaires de la province d'*Hispania Citerior* au Haut-Empire romain', in *Epigrafia e ordine senatorio* 2 (Rome 1982), 446 [= P. Le Roux, *Espagnes romaines. L'Empire dans ses provinces. Scripta varia* II (Rennes 2014), 358–359].

79 *CIL* II$^2$/14–2, 1147–1148 and 1178. See also Alföldy 1972, op. cit.; G. Alföldy, *Die römischen Inschriften von Tarraco* (Berlin 1975).

80 Museu de Badalona, inv. MB inv. 3277.

81 *PIR*$^2$ L 249.

82 Searched from *EDCS* (http://db.edcs.eu/epigr/epi_ergebnis.php) and *Hispania Epigraphica* for the localization of Badalona.

correspond to the area of forum, temples and public baths.[83] In any case, the location of the inscriptions was of high prestige. Another remark is that the honorific inscriptions are almost all to the emperor or other members of the imperial family – at least those that are extant enough and we can say little about them. The exceptions are the honorific inscription of Q. Licinius, and that of M. Fabius Nepos of *Iesso*, who was a local magistrate (Curchin 1990, 182) and who is commemorated for his administration and integrity (*CIL* II, 4610 = *IRC* I, 141). These two inscriptions are roughly from the same period, whereas some of the imperial inscriptions are from the 3rd century AD.

The inscription for Q. Licinius illustrates how a *municipium* continued to link itself to the family after a couple of generations. We do not know if the young Licinius was active in the region anymore, or if he ever was. Nor do we know how Licinius executed his patronage towards *Baetulo*. His inscription lacks any mention of *ob merita* or other indications. It is possible that he still had properties in the region because he had agreed to have an honorific statue in the *municipium* instead of somewhere else – in other words, he perhaps benefitted from the statue especially in this region. The *municipium* surely had some kind of reason for erecting the monument; otherwise, it would not have spent any money on it, especially when this kind of honorific inscription seems to be quite rare in the city.

## 8 Conclusions

As Cicero remarks at the beginning of this chapter, it is important to remember who you are, what you want, and where you are. Being a rare example, L. Minicius declared publicly that he is from *Barcino*, but he did this only locally in the city. He did not bring his Hispanic origin forward in any other place, at least not in the textual evidence. No statues or other visual presentations have survived, so we cannot say if they included some hints towards his origin. He always included his Roman offices in the attestations but varied the number of the offices. However, his important posts as consul, *legatus Augusti pro praetore* in *Moesia*, and especially his proconsulship in *Africa* were always included. His lesser offices, such as *IIIvir monetalis*, are mentioned mostly in places where he probably had property, such as *Barcino* and *Tibur*. These are also commemorations of him as a *patronus*.[84] He clearly wanted to be remembered throughout

83 *IRC* 1, p. 176.

84 The inscription in *Megara* mentions the office, but it is difficult to say who dedicated it.

the Empire as a versatile and educated person, and he varied the language of his attestations according to the places and deities.

While preparing this chapter, I studied the epigraphic evidence of all the magistrates who mentioned that they had served as *IIIvir monetalis* and whose origin was in the Iberian Peninsula. As a comparison, I also studied those who had served as *Xviri stlitibus iudicandis*, which was a vigintivirate office just under the *monetalis*. The number of *stlitibus iudicandis* and *IIIviri monetales*, who rose to the Senate and whose Hispanic *origo* is certain or probable, is 13.[85] The total number of *Xviri stlitibus iudicandis* and *IIIviri monetales* is currently 426 individuals, resulting in a Hispanic percentage of ~4% of known officeholders.[86] In many of the cases, we can define the *origo* of the magistrate only as close as "*Baetica*", and perhaps give a possible name of the city with a question mark.[87] The inscriptions themselves do not mention directly the *origo*. In fact, the amount of epigraphic evidence regarding these Hispanic magistrates in Hispania is very small.

The inscriptions mentioning either *Xviri stlitibus iudicandis* or *IIIviri monetales* are mostly either from the eastern coast or from the area of Seville. Outside the Iberian Peninsula, the largest amount of epigraphic evidence of

85 Collected from Caballos Rufino 1990, op. cit. This number excludes the men whose origin have been disputed, namely the *Roscii* and *Pompeii* (*PIR*[2] P 602, *PIR*[2] P 651, *PIR*[2] P 656, *PIR*[2] R 89). See discussion e.g. in Caballos Rufino 1990, op. cit.; Salomies 1992, op. cit.; de Cerio Erasun 2012, op. cit. These individuals are also excluded from the analysis. One famous *Xvir stlitibus iudicandis* with Hispanic origin is left out from the extensive survey, namely the Emperor Hadrian. This is done because of the sheer number of stones mentioning him. Therefore, I only briefly mention the sole inscription that mentions the office of *Xvir stlit. iud.* It is at Athens, and it was erected to honour Hadrian as the archon (ἡ ἐξ Ἀρείου πάγου βουλὴ καὶ ἡ τῶν ἑξακοσίων καὶ ὁ / δῆμος ὁ Ἀθηναίων τὸν ἄρχοντα ἑαυτῶν / Ἁδριανόν): *CIL* III, 550.

86 It is noteworthy that 9/13 served as *Xviri stlitibus iudicandis*. The office of *IIIviri auro argento aere flando feriundo* has traditionally been seen as higher in the hierarchy of *vigintiviri*. The officeholders were mostly patrician, or they had ancestors in high–office or connections to the ruler, whereas *Xviri stlitibus iudicandis* could be *homines novi*. Addressing this question here risks going too far from the article's focus and must remain to be discussed elsewhere later.

87 For *origo*, see esp. Caballos Rufino 1990, op. cit.; C. Castillo García, 'Los senadores béticos. Relaciones familiares y sociales', in *Epigrafia e ordine senatorio*: 2. (*Tituli* 5) (Rome 1982), 465–519 [= C. Castillo García, Vestigia antiquitatis. *Escritos de epigrafía y literaturas romanas. Scripta a sodalibus collecta in honorem Carmen Castillo* (Pamplona 1997), 375–391] and Le Roux 1982, op. cit., 439–464 [= Le Roux 2014, op. cit., 355–379]. See also P. Le Roux, 'Les sénateurs originaires d'Espagne citérieure (2) : un bilan 1982–2006', in *Epigrafia 2006. Atti della XIV*[e] *rencontre sur l'épigraphie in onore di Silvio Panciera con altri contributi di colleghi, allievi e collaboratori*, III, ed. M. L. Caldelli, G. L. Gregori and S. Orlandi (Rome 2008), 1003–1027 [= Le Roux 2014, op. cit., 381–401].

the Hispanic magistrates is on the western coast of Italy, and especially on the *Regio I Latium* and *Campania*. The single most popular cities are Rome and *Tibur*. Rome's popularity is understandable due to its special role as the capital. *Tibur*, in turn, is a place where many Spaniards moved. Otherwise, the inscriptions are scattered around. The career of an individual explains some clusters.[88] However, inscriptions in the Iberian Peninsula are surprisingly low in number. Even the individuals who held office there do not have a particularly large number of attestations. It seems that *Hispania* was an office post for several magistrates, but at least in the light of this data set, it did not produce high numbers of public honorific monuments for senatorial magistrates originating outside the Iberian Peninsula. In addition, the number of dedications by Hispanic communities outside the peninsula is very small.[89]

According to this material, these magistrates are visible in the inscriptions by Hispanic communities at quite an early stage, or later as high magistrates in monuments erected by them or their clients. The magistrates themselves wanted to make their influence known in the city by investing in it, and the person or community that honoured them might have wanted to commemorate them or gain influence to secure their benevolence. Outside *Hispania*, the places for inscriptions relate mostly to their offices. *Tibur* is a city where the magistrates also serve in local offices, especially as the curator of the sanctuary of Hercules.

My material suggests that the connection of Roman senators to their home region could remain strong at least for a couple of generations. The person could be honoured as an upcoming member of the Senate (when the inscriptions mostly mention the vigintivirate), but after the family branch had secured their position, the stronger connections to the home region seem to have weakened. Unlike in the inscriptions of freedmen and local magistrates, the *origo* of Roman senators does not appear verbally. Nonetheless, the origin of a Roman state person interested people, as is evident from the biographies, such as Hadrian's in the *Historia Augusta*.[90] It seems that once a person entered the Senate, this "native fatherland" is invisible in the textual monuments. The origin and the connections through shared heritage could affect relationships, as

88 Such is the case with the milestones of L. Fabius M. f. Cilo Septiminus Catinius Acilianus Lepidus Fulcinianus (PIR² F 27), for example.

89 This comment is based only on a preliminary survey. The community of *Calagurritani* dedicated a couple of inscriptions to their patrons: *CIL* V, 6987 = EDR113312 in Torino (unknown person) and the *CIL* XII, 3167 (= *ILS* 1016) in *Nemausus*. Note also the famous golden statue by *Hispania Baetica* for Augustus in the Augustan Forum in Rome (*CIL* VI, 31267 (= *ILS* 103) = EDR100525).

90 Hist. Aug., *Hadr.* 1,1.

the case of the shared *cognomen* of the younger Minicius and Licinius suggests. *Tibur* became the home of many Spaniards, and even if they did not necessarily have a direct contact to their home peninsula anymore, they could choose to stay in the area with people from a similar cultural background. Without visual representations of these magistrates, we cannot say if they illustrated their heritage in a non-verbal way.

# PART 3

## *Interconnectedness*

CHAPTER 10

# Between *Mauretania* and *Numidia*

## *Provincial Boundaries, Land Connections and Imperial Administration in North Africa (1st–4th Centuries* AD*)*

*Sergio España-Chamorro*

## 1 Introduction[1]

Like other provinces in the area, the name *Mauretania* derives from the *Mauri*, the main population of the region, or apparently from the Roman understanding of the ethnic African inhabitants in the region. The origin of this concept dates much earlier than its provincial configuration, and *Mauretania*, as the land of the *Mauri*, is identified with tribal groups originating from the north African mountains.[2] Such peoples are not mentioned in Herodotus' compendium of populations, although they are mentioned in the *Bellum Africum* and in Sallust.[3]

This type of process is typical of the Roman ethno-geographical conception of the world, where space and inhabitants are intrinsically interlinked and interdependent. We see similar cases with, for instance, *Lusitania*, which takes its name from the *Lusitani*, in *Gallia*, so named by the *Galli*, or *Dacia*, as land of the *Daci*, where an ethnic simplification was made and the name of the main group was applied to a broad region placed under provincial administration, a process not incompatible with incorporating diverse ethnic groups within the same space. In the African case, the process of conquering a new space and incorporating it as a province within the Roman Empire rendered an area geographically diffuse and without defined boundaries, since it became a part

1 This research was funded by Marie Skłodowska-Curie Individual Fellowship (*IMPACTVM*. Mapping the impact of the Augustan colonies on the Early Roman Empire Grant Agreement nº 101025799) and the I +D Project "Identidades norteafricanas en transformación" (MINECO Ref. PID2019-107176GB-I00). I am grateful to Hernán González Bordas and Fabiola Salcedo Garcés, and the editors for comments on earlier drafts of this paper, and to Hernán (again) for letting me see a copy of his chapter on imperial properties in Africa in advance of publication.

2 D. J. Mattingly, *Tripolitania* (London 1995), 19.

3 E. A. Benito Lázaro, 'Los pueblos líbicos en el imaginario grecorromano: percepción y representación de realidades autóctonas norteafricanas entre los siglos VIII a.C. y III d.C.', (Ph.D. diss., Complutense University of Madrid, 2018), 85.

 | DOI:10.1163/9789004685734_011

of the Roman ecumene, which was constantly developing and expanding through other campaigns of conquest. The Mauretanian region became part the Roman sphere of influence with the formal conquest of Africa,[4] thus giving rise to a clash with republican provincial reality. At that time, the republican administration of provincial areas was not a perfectly delimited system of administration, but a system of shifting jurisdictions over a geographical space subject to ongoing conquest and colonisation efforts.[5] This system changed with Augustus, when the so-called "Augustan revolution"[6] brought about many changes in politics and culture. One such multiple change was the reterritorialisation of the Empire, replacing the republican model of colonial management with a more modern model of territorial administration entailing a different model of management that promoted clear geographical divisions and a massive expansion of the way in which geographical space was measured and apportioned.

It was not until the time of Claudius[7] that *Mauretania Caesariensis* was created as a province, and thus, conceived as a clearly defined geographical unit. Until then, the boundaries of the region of *Mauretania* had been designed according to the hodological conception of space, which was typical of ancient geography and in line with the provincial model of the Republic. In the pre-Claudian Roman conception of the region, *Mauretania* included the lands beyond the *Ampsaga* River (today's Rhumel River) populated by the *Mauri*, which extended as far as the ocean. Thus, according to hodological conceptions *Mauretania* was a space beyond the area of direct Roman

4 M. Coltelloni-Trannoy, *Le royaume de Maurétanie sous Juba II et Ptolémée (25 av. J.-C.–40 ap. J.-C.)* (Paris 1997).

5 G. Wesenberg, in *RE* XXIII, 1, 1957, s. v. 'provincia', col. 997; A. Caballos Rufino, 'Significación político-administrativa de la provincia en el alto imperio romano: la mistificación de un concepto', in Lavdes provinciarvm: *retórica y política en la representación del imperio romano*, ed. J. Santos Yanguas and E. Torregaray Pagola (Vitoria 2007), 79; F. Martín, 'Sobre el significado de provincia', in Vrbs aeterna. *Actas y colaboraciones del coloquio internacional, Roma entre la literatura y la historia: homenaje a la profesora Carmen Castillo*, ed. C. Alonso del Real, P. García Ruiz, A. Sánchez-Ortiz and J. B. Torres Guerra (Pamplona 2003), 177–186; J.-M. Bertrand, 'À propos du mot *provincia* : étude sur les modes d'élaboration du langage politique', *JS* (1989), 191–215; J. Richardson, 'Fines provinciae', in *Frontiers in the Roman World: Proceedings of the Ninth Workshop of the International Network Impact of Empire (Durham, 16–19 April 2009)*, ed. O. Hekster and T. Kaizer (Leiden 2011), 3; A. Díaz Fernández, 'When did a *Provincia* become a Province? On the Institutional Development of a Roman Republican Concept', in *Provinces and Provincial Command in Republican Rome: Genesis, Development and Governance*, ed. A. Díaz Fernández (Zaragoza 2021), 41–69.

6 About landscapes, see in S. España-Chamorro and M. C. Moreno Escobar (eds.), *Landscapes and the Augustan Revolution in the Western Provinces* (London 2024).

7 Coltelloni-Trannoy 1997, op. cit., 123.

control, in this case a land bordering *Numidia*. The geographical features of the Mediterranean bound the area that roughly forms the Mediterranean strip of present-day Morocco and Algeria to the north, the Sahara to the south, the *Ampsaga* River to the east and the Atlantic Ocean to the west. Although it was named after the *Mauri*, other Berber tribes also inhabited the territory.[8] It is impossible to grasp the social complexity of the numerous groups and sub-groups in the region, as they are known only from Roman sources that describe them from a colonial perspective.

However, the process of provincialisation occurred much differently in *Africa* than in western Roman Europe, which can be understood through the process of conquest. Famed French historian René Cagnat more than a hundred years ago summarised this process (and hence, the process of provincial expansion and the southward movement of the boundary of the Roman Empire) as having occurred in three stages corresponding to three specific periods, divisions that are nowadays accepted without question:

1. The first stage of conquest took place approximately in AD 42 in an area corresponding to the coastal strip[9] where the first colonies were located.
2. The second stage lasted until the time of Trajan[10] and Hadrian, and it corresponded to the area extending up to the high plains.[11]
3. The third and final stage corresponds to the incursions and campaigns of conquest of the Severi, and it extended to the northernmost area,[12] where the military *castella* of the well known *limes Mauretanus* are located, taking the *castellum Dimmidi* as the most extreme point.[13]

While the Romans conquered the areas of north of proconsular Africa and *Numidia* early on and subjected them to provincial administration, *Mauretania*

8 On the ethnic complexity, see J. Desanges, *Catalogue des tribus africaines de l'antiquité classique à l'ouest du Nil* (Dakar 1962); and more recently, Benito Lázaro 2018, op. cit.

9 R. Cagnat, *L'armée romaine d'Afrique et l'occupation militaire de l'Afrique sous les empereurs* (Paris 1913), 610; N. Benseddik, 'Limes, Mauretania Caesariensis', in *Dizionario epigrafico* IV, 43.2, ed. E. De Ruggiero (Rome 1984–1985), 1376/54–64; Y. Le Bohec, *Frontières et limites militaires de la Maurétanie Césarienne sous le Haut-Empire* (Algiers 1982).

10 R. Bloch, 'Une campagne de fouilles dans la vallée du Chéliff. Les *Tigava castra*', *MEFRA* 58 (1941–1946), 9–11, who modified Cagnat's idea about the earlier colonisation in Hadrian's time.

11 Cagnat 1913, op. cit., 612; P. Romanelli, *Storia delle province romane dell'Africa* (Rome 1959), 406–407; Ch. A. Julien, *Histoire de l'Afrique du Nord* I (Paris 1968), 135; P.-A. Février, *Approches du Maghreb romain* I (Aix-en-Provence 1989), 119–120; Le Bohec 1982, op. cit.

12 Cagnat 1913, op. cit.; Le Bohec 1982, op. cit.

13 As can be seen in G. Ch. Picard's, *Castellum Dimmidi* (Paris 1947), 50, this author even speculated about possible southern Roman forts at Ksar el Fedje or in the modern Langhouat as uncertain points of Roman occupation. However, archaeological proof is still lacking.

was a later construction. It emerged as part of an evolving Roman process of adapting to the different groups it conquered and the different geographical areas it incorporated and regulating its administrative borders.

This difference undoubtedly affected provincial boundaries, making their configuration an even more complex matter, since the most important early imperial sources that explained the administration of the Empire, such as those by Strabo or Pliny, refer only to the earliest phase of their provincial configuration and do not provide additional information. On the other hand, Late Antique sources are, in some cases, much more explicit than elsewhere, which helps in the configuration of at least the last provincial stage. While other publications have addressed the subject of Roman provincial boundary making and administration in North Africa,[14] they have not delved into the complexity of the construction process or its implications.

One of the most crucial sources on the administrative reconstruction process and the limits of the magistrates' jurisdiction (provincial boundaries) is that of Pliny, who focused on the first stage of provincialisation. Nonetheless, he provided much less administrative description of the African provinces than of *Hispania*, *Gallia* or Italy, where he offered a detailed description of numerous *oppida*. He subdivided his descriptions based on provinces, *conventus* and *regiones*. Pliny's descriptions of the two *Mauretaniae*, *Numidia* and Africa (*NH.* 5) are limited to indications he must have taken from the periplographic sources, since he only mentions coastal or nearby villas, even though he was aware of the civic complexity of the whole of North Africa and its high

14 Cagnat 1913, op. cit.; P. Salama, *Les voies romaines de l'Afrique du Nord* (Algiers 1951a), 143 and image on XII; N. Benseddik, *Les troupes auxiliaires de l'armée romaine en Maurétanie Césarienne sous le Haut-Empire* (Algiers 1982); Benseddik 1984–1985, op. cit., have always understood boundaries in relation to other aspects, such as the army or the road network. The monographic work by Y. Le Bohec, 'Frontières et limites militaires de la Maurétanie Césarienne sous le Haut-Empire', in *Frontières et limites géographiques de l'Afrique du Nord antique*. Hommage à Pierre Salama, *ed. C. Lepelley and X. Dupuis* (*Paris 1999*), focuses on the early provincial stage and explores it only in the southern part of the province from a military point of view; J-P. Laporte, 'La limite entre les Maurétanies Césarienne et Sitifienne', in *Frontières et limites géographiques de l'Afrique* du Nord antique, and R. Rebuffat, 'La frontière de la Tingitane', in *Frontières et limites géographiques de l'Afrique du Nord antique. Hommage à Pierre Salama*, ed. C. Lepelley and X. Dupuis (Paris 1999) both focus on the subdivision within Mauretania; G. Camps, 'Essais de cartographie culturelle : À propos de la frontière de Numidie et de Maurétanie', in *Frontières et limites géographiques de l'Afrique du Nord antique. Hommage à Pierre Salama*, ed. C. Lepelley and X. Dupuis (Paris 1999), centred his research on the pre-Roman cultural differences.

density of populations and civic communities.[15] This lack of attention in his writing was since Roman control was limited only to the coastal strip.

Thus, it is interesting to question the role of provincial boundaries in the organisation of the ecumenical order and how this was embodied in the African provinces in a practical and pragmatic manner. This can be done looking at the interactions between Romans and indigenous populations as well as the historical developments that led to the shaping of these administrative entities. The weight of nomadic populations and the natural composition of North Africa (from a Mediterranean coastline to a semi-desert area and finally a desert area, but with oases), meant that the ancestral corridors of mobility were decisive in its development. These also influenced the creation of new routes that modified the models of indigenous movement to adapt them to a more central administration.

## 2 A Subdivided Region: Some Brief Notes on the Boundary between *Mauretania Tingitana*, *Mauretania Caesariensis* and *Mauretania Sitifiensis*

The provincial configuration of Africa was a challenge due to the pre-Roman political structures, which had hierarchised the territory in complex ways and included the existence of numerous civic communities and the presence of indigenous populations (some of them nomadic). All these factors made it more difficult to implement the administrative Augustan territorial model. The complexity of the region can clearly be seen in the changing system by which the Romans made sense of the pre-existing structures and peoples. It was not until Claudius that *Mauretania* became part of the Empire from a legal and administrative standpoint. At that time, the provincial territories were reorganised in a way that provided stability until the time of Diocletian's reforms.

*Mauretania* as a geographical region comprised the entire coastal strip of the Mediterranean between the *Ampsaga* River and the Atlantic Ocean. The Atlas Mountains generally demarcated the region's southern boundary.[16] The port city of *Siga* marked the coastal boundary between *Mauretania Tingitana*

---

15 Specially for *Numidia* and *Africa Proconsularis* (Plin. *NH*. 5.4: Between the *Ampsaga* River and this boundary in Africa lived 516 peoples who accepted allegiance to Rome).

16 A. dalla Rosa, 'Mauretania', in *Roma e le sue province. Dalla prima guerra punica a Diocleziano*, ed. C. Letta and S. Segenni (Rome 2015), 269.

and *Mauretania Caesariensis*,[17] being the westernmost point in *Mauretania Caesariensis*, next to the River *Malva*.[18] There are notable differences between the two provinces: while *Tingitana* was more compact and better protected,[19] *Caesariensis* was more heterogeneous and its river valleys shaped the travel and trade routes of the nomadic populations. The nomads represented a conflicting factor for the conquest, colonisation, and establishment of the Roman urban system.[20] Modéran[21] has already pointed out that this diversity between the two parts of the region probably corresponded to a much older difference pertaining to climatic differences as well as cultural differences due to the diversity of trade circuits (*Tingitana* was linked to the Strait of Gibraltar and *Hispania*, while *Caesariensis* was centred on Italy). Therefore, the region could not be controlled as a single entity, and this is why the initial subdivision of *Mauretania* gave rise to different forms of administration in the two provinces.[22]

In the Severan Period (more exactly, in the year AD 201[23]), the *Nova Praetentura*,[24] a military demarcation, determined the intersecting spaces of provincial administration: this entity was a political-military protection unit created by Septimius Severus in the south of the province of *Mauretania Caesariensis* to encourage the colonisation of this area and to prevent further

17 *Siga oppidum ex adverso Malacae in Hispania situm, Syphacis regia, alterius iam Mauretaniae*; it seems to correspond with the archaeological site at the mouth of the river Tafna, approximately 135 km. from Melilla.

18 Itin. Anton. 12.1–2: *Flumen Malva dirimit Mauretanias duas, incipit Caesariensis*; Ptol. 5.1.4.

19 S. El Bouzidi and A. Ouahidi, 'La frontière méridionale de la Maurétanie Tingitane : contribution à la carte archéologique de la région de Volubilis', *DHA* 40, no. 1 (2014), 97–108.

20 R. Rebuffat, 'Mobilité des personnes dans l'Afrique romaine', in *Mobilité des personnes en Méditerranée de l'époque antique à l'époque moderne, procédures de contrôle et documents d'identification*, ed. C. Moatti (Rome 2004), 155–203; R. Rebuffat, 'Nomadisme et archéologie', *L'Afrique dans l'Occident romain, Ier siècle av. J.-C.–IVe siècle apr. J.-C.* (Rome 1990), 231–247.

21 Y. Modéran, in *Encyclopédie berbère* 31, s. v. 'Maurétanies (Provinces)', 4737–4751 (online): [https://journals.openedition.org/encyclopedieberbere/523].

22 R. Rebuffat, 'Notes sur les confins de la Maurétanie Tingitane et de Maurétanie Césarienne', *Studi Magrebini* 4 (1971), 33–64; Rebuffat 1999, op. cit., 265–286.

23 E. Albertini, 'La route frontière de Maurétanie Césarienne entre Boghar et Lalla-Maghnia', *Bulletin de la société de géographie et d'archéologie d'Oran* (1928), 33–48.

24 Its name appeared on milestones: L. Demaeght, 'Inscriptions inédites de la Maurétanie Césarienne', *Bulletin de la société de géographie et d'archéologie de la province d'Oran* 12 (1892), 276–277, no. 1166, 1170–1171; *CIL* VIII, 22611; *CIL* VIII, 22602–22604; R. Cagnat, '15 Juin 1919. Séance de la Commission de l'Afrique du Nord', *BCTH* 1919, CCXV. See also Z. Kasdi, '*P. Aelius Peregrinus Rogatus* et le gouvernement de la province de Maurétanie césarienne', *CGG* 27 (2016), 325–360.

attacks by Mauretanian populations. Mommsen defined it as a middle region between the pacified and conquered area and the "barbarian" territory.[25] The *praetentura* was located exclusively in *Caesariensis*, although it was relatively close to the provincial boundary, which in fact served as a protective element of the main road axis leading to the heart of *Tingitana* and connecting directly with the cities of *Tocolosida*, *Taza* and, above all, *Volubilis*. *Lucu* was one of the main garrison centres for the Ist Pannonian Cohort, and we know the place name and its significance by quotes found on milestones. Road management must have been an important and exclusive aspect of this administrative unit, and we know this from the road epigraphy, erected by the administration centred in *Lucu*, where the proconsuls of Augustus carried out certain tasks (at least in the period of the joint reign of Septimius Severus, Caracalla and Geta). Nevertheless, urban settlement in the hinterland of the area bordering the Mauretanian populations was less dense, meaning there was less interaction and mobility than on the border with *Numidia*.

The process of connecting the *Nova Praetentura* began with the merging of the 2 provinces between approximately AD 202 and 211, at which time Cn. Haius Diadumenianus and Q. Sallustius Macrinianus[26] governed all of *Mauretania* (*procuratores utriusque Mauretaniae*[27]) and attempted to unify the two administrations,[28] but to no avail. Later, between 290 and AD 293, the eastern part of *Mauretania Caesariensis* was separated and made into a new province with its capital at *Setif*. The name *Mauretania Sitifiensis* again followed the system of provincial nomination by taking the *cognomen* of the provincial capital. Only the episcopal list of AD 484 gives information about its territorial extension, as it mentions the provincial location of the seats of the various bishops. This list, already studied by Gsell, Salama and Laporte,[29] identified the cities of *Saldae*, *Tubusuctu*, *Equizetum*, *Lemellef*, *Thamalulla*, *Flumen*

25 *Praetenturae vocabulo Momsennus putat designari regionem mediam inter territorium pacatum et agrum barbaricum*, comment in *CIL* VIII, 22611, p. 2167.

26 Cn. Haius Diadumenianus *PIR*² H 8; Q. Sallustius Macrinianus *PIR*² S 93.

27 For this title, see B. E. Thomasson, *Praesides provinciarum Africae* (Lund 1969), 193–196. (documented in *AE* 1941, 79; *AE* 1969/70, 747; *CIL* IX, 4194 = *ILS* 8969); M. Christol and A. Magioncalda, *Studi sui procuratori delle due Mauretaniae* (Sassari 1989), 45, 47, 63–64.

28 M. P. Speidel, 'A Thousand Thracian Recruits for *Mauretania Tingitana*', *AntAfr* 11 (1977), 167–173.

29 S. Gsell, 'Observations géographiques sur la révolte de Firmus', *Recueil de la société archéologique de Constantine* 36 (1902), 43; P. Salama, *Carte du réseau routier de l'Afrique romaine* (Algiers 1949); Laporte 1999, op. cit.

*Piscense* and *Zabi*,[30] all of which corresponded to the division of a narrow eastern strip from north to south.

## 3 The Northern Boundary between *Mauretania* and *Numidia*

### 3.1 *The First Stage: The Coastal Strip*

Returning to Pliny's description of *Mauretania*, he provided the names of towns belonging to *Caesariensis* along the coast (*Portus Magnus, Mulucha*,[31] *Quiza Xenitana, Arsennaria*) some not strictly speaking along the coast (*Cartenna, Gunugu*,[32] *Caesarea Iol, Tipasa, Icosium, Rusguniae, Rusazus, Saldas, Igilgili* and *Tucca*[33]), and a few farther inland (*Succhabar, Tubusuptu, Timici, Tigvae* and other villages and rivers). Again, he then clarified that the *Ampsaga* River separated *Mauretania* from *Numidia* (*NH*. 5.3). The sources insist that the river formed the boundary between the two provinces, reiterated by Pomponius Mela (1.6.30, speaking of the Numidian boundary and understanding to as referring to the *Mulucha* River: *ab eo Numidia ad ripas exposita fluminis Ampsaci*) as well as Ptolemy (4.2.1 and 4.2.11) and Late Antique geographical compilations.[34] This provincial boundary is a historical boundary, as indicated in several of the sources. The only author who seemingly contradicted this geographical delimitation was Strabo (6.4.2; 17.3.12).[35]

---

30 These places are provided by Laporte 1999, op. cit.: *Saldae* (S. Gsell, *Atlas archéologique de l'Algérie* (Alger 1911) = *AAA* f. 8, no. 12), *Tubusuctu* (*AAA* f. 8, no. 27), *Equizetum* (*AAA* f. 15, no. 91), *Lemellef* (*AAA* f. 26, no. 19), *Thamalulla* (*AAA* f. 26, no. 19), *Flumen Piscense* (*AAA* f. 25, no. 70) and *Zabi* (*AAA* f. 25, no. 85).

31 In the list, Pliny names a place that is not a town, but rather two *populi* that define the boundary: the *Bocchi* and the *Maesyli* (*Bocchi Maesylorumque finis*).

32 After this name, Pliny quotes another place called *promontorium Apollinis*, identified with Cape Mestegan.

33 See *Pliny. Natural History, Volume II: Books 3–7*, translated by H. Rackham. Loeb Classical Library 352 (Cambridge, MA, 1942), corregir *Portus Magnus, Mulucha, Quiza Xenitana, Arsennaria* (Arzen), *Cartenna* (Tenez), *Gunugu, Caesarea Iol, Tipasa, Icosium, Rusguniae, Rusazus, Saldae, Igilgili* and *Tucca*.

34 Dimens. provinc. 25 *Gaetulia et Mauritania finiuntur <ab> oriente flumine Ampsaga, ab occidente oceano <Atlantico>* (…) and 26 *Africa Carthag<inensis>, Numidia finiuntur ab oriente Syrti minore, ab Occidente flu<mine> Ampsaga* (…); Divisio orb. 25 *Africa Carthaginensis et Numidia finiuntur ab oriente Syrti minore, ab occidente flumine Ampsaga* (…) and 26 *Gaetulia et Mauretania finiuntur ab oriente flumine Ampsaga, ab occidente oceano Atlantico* (…). Edit. P. Schnabel, 'Die Weltkarte des Agrippa als wissenschaftliches Mittelglied zwischen Hipparchen und Ptolemaeus', *Philologus* 90 (1935), 405–440, esp. 430–431 and 439.

35 See Coltelloni-Trannoy 1997, op. cit., 69–70.

There is only one problem with such a formulation, and that is the location of the town of *Tucca*.[36] Pliny included *Tucca* on his list of Caesarian cities, placing it exactly at the mouth of the *Ampsaga* River along the coastline (*inpositum mari et flumini Ampsagae*), and it can therefore be considered key to fixing the coastal limit between *Mauretania* and *Numidia*. Its precise location can be fixed at present-day Sidi Abdelaziz, in Algeria, but the *Tabula Peutingeriana* shows a coastal road running through this area and connecting *Igilgili* with *Chullu*, with an intermediate *mansio* called *Paccanis Matidiae*, without naming *Tucca*. Similarly, the text of the Anonymous Cosmographer of Ravenna indicates the same *mansio*, *Paceanis/Paciani*, along the route. However, it also mentions an intermediate *mansio* on the interior road connecting *Cuicul* with *Igilgili*, giving it the name *Tucca fines Affrice et Mauretanie*. The text of the Ravenna Cosmography likewise describes a *civitas Tuca, quae iuxta mare magnum dividitur inter provinciam Numidiam et ipsam Mauretaniam Sitifensem*.[37] Ptolemy mentioned a Τοῦκκα in *Numidia* (4.3.7[38]) and another in *Mauretania Caesariensis* (4.2.6), although they do not coincide in terms of place and have been related to the *Notitia Dignitatum* (Occ. 25.13; 34), which seems to speak of another *Tucca* in the *limes* of *Tangensis/Taugensis*. Neither can we discard a certain confusion due to the liminal character of the town.

The Late Antique sources mention *Tucca* in the verbal edicts of the religious conferences of AD 411 as *civitas Tuccensis*, which was part of the Donatist diocese of *Mileu* (currently Mila), despite having a Catholic bishop,[39] prompting Gsell[40] to suppose that it would not have been far from that town. Another interesting fact is that an *episcopus Thuccensis* is mentioned in a notice of AD 484, as is a Τύκκη near Στιτίφη cited in a Byzantine list of bishops,[41] indicating that in the 5th and 6th centuries AD the provincial boundary remained the same as in the Plinian account, unchanged for more than 500 years. However, none of this resolves the question of its location.

Epigraphy does not make much progress in this respect either. Two inscriptions have been found that could refer to this town. The first is *CIL* VIII,

---

36 It should be noted that the toponym *Tuca/Tucca/Tucca/Thucca/Thugga* is present among at least three homonymous populations, this one being in *Mauretania*, with two others in *Numidia* (one in Henchir-El-Abiodh, Algeria, which seems to be *Thugga Terebentina*, and the other in Dougga, Tunisia). The intercalated h, double c or the change of velar c/g are perfectly compatible as markers of the same toponym with a different spelling.

37 Ravenn. 3.6.16.

38 This must be Thugga; see *AAA* f. 8, no. 5.

39 Conc. Carth. a. 411, I, 65 and 130–131.

40 *AAA* f. 17, no. 59.

41 R. Pococke, *A Description of the East and Some Other Countries*, vol. I (London 1743), 279–280.

8270 = *ILAlg* II/3, 7557[42] which mentions a *decurio coloniae Tutcensium* from Tadjenanet (in French colonial times called Saint-Donat), while the second is a fragmentary epigraph that names a female as *colon(a?) Tu(tcensis?)* found at Aïn-Melouk,[43] both within the vicinity of the site proposed at Henchir-el-Abiod. Gsell[44] already commented on all these problems in the sources and therefore thought that *Tucca* could have been located close to Merdja, on the right bank of the oued el-Kebir, the end of the Rhumel (the present name of the *Ampsaga* River), which flows into the Mediterranean. Earlier authors such as Reboud and Goyt, who explored the area at the end of the 19th century, indicated that this was the most likely place for such a town. They also reported a controversial inscription, which has been interpreted as a dedication to a *G(enio) m(unicipii) T(uccensis)*, although the initials do not go far enough to really reveal the truth, meaning this inscription must be taken with caution.[45]

In sum, no conclusive evidence has thus far been provided for the location of this border town, the most important coastal point between the two provinces. The historical information is contradictory, since the *Tabula Peutingeriana* does not seemingly place it on the coast, while both Pliny and the Anonymous Cosmographer of Ravenna insisted on its location by the sea. The most logical solution is to propose the existence of an urban centre probably not physically located on the coast with the toponym of *Paccanis Matidiae*,[46] which appeared in the *Tabula Matidiae* as a kind of *vicus* that functioned as a port of *Tucca* itself. It also seems to have been the case with the Hispanic city of *Baesipo*, which in the itinerary sources appears as *Baesipo civitas* and *Baesipo portus*.

---

42 A. Poulle, 'Inscriptions de la Numidie et de la Maurétanie sétifienne', *Recueil des notices et mémoires de la société archéologique du département de Constantine* 17 (1875), 417–422, no. 33 provided the first edition of this inscription, and he indicated the place name *Tuycensium*. Héron de Villefosse indicated that the Y could be a T with a short and round shaft, and this suggestion was accepted and corrected in the *CIL* edition.

43 R. Cagnat, 'Chronique d'épigraphie africaine', *BCTH* (1895), 310 (= *ILAlg* II/3, 8471).

44 *AAA*, f. 8, no. 5.

45 The commentaries of *CIL* VIII, 20207 and on *EE* V, 909 and VII, 794 already mentioned this fact, noting that this inscription could also be a *tria nomina* of the offeror. See *AAA*, v. 8, 71–72.

46 Itin. Anton. 18.4 and on the *Tabula Peutingeriana*. This place name would have indicated it as the property of *Matidia Maior*, with whom it is traditionally associated. *Matidia* owned large plots of land in *Mauretania Caesariensis* and *Numidia*, as can be seen in this and other place names, such as *Rusibricari Matidiae* or *castellum Medianum Matidianum* (see M.-O. Charles-Laforge, 'Patrimoines et héritages des femmes à Rome : l'exemple des princesses antonines', in Arcana Imperii. *Mélanges d'histoire économique, sociale et politique offerts au Professeur Yves Roman*, ed. C. Chillet, C. Courrier and L. Passet (Paris 2015), 244–245).

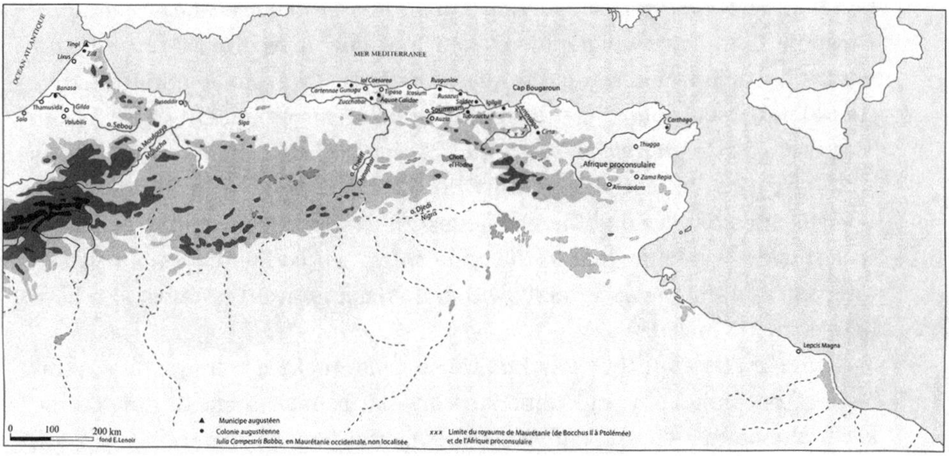


FIGURE 10.1 Mauritania at Juba II and Ptolemy times (Coltelloni-Trannoy 2010)

The strip of land running along the Mediterranean coast would have formed the original core of the early imperial province. We only know of certain specific sites in areas identified by the territorial administration as cities of importance, but we do not know much about the exact limits of Roman authority south of this strip in other parts of the province.[47] This limit seems to coincide with the limits of the ancient kingdom of *Mauretania* (at least from Bocchus II to Ptolemy) with respect to proconsular Africa,[48] which would reflect the fact that the social and mobility dynamics favoured Roman administrative efforts at this early stage and that Rome adapted its political strategy to fit the existing urban and social network.

The city of *Cuicul* is another border town. The present-day village of Djemila in Algeria provides much epigraphic evidence of its former status as a Roman town. Its colonial role is still a controversial issue, but the city must have been founded during the reign of Nerva.[49] It also shared historical parallels with the town of Sétif, the use of members of the *Papiria* tribe as builders (work evident in the colonial foundations of Nerva and Trajan) and historical sources

47 Y. Modéran, in *Encyclopédie berbère* 31, s. v. 'Maurétanies (Provinces)', 4737–4751 (online): [https://journals.openedition.org/encyclopedieberbere/523].

48 Salama 1951, op. cit.; M. Coltelloni-Trannoy, in *Encyclopédie berbère* 31, s. v. 'Maurétanie (Royaumes)', 4717–4737 (online): [https://journals.openedition.org/encyclopedieberbere/521].

49 Several inscriptions mention the status of colony (*CIL* VIII, 8318–8319 = *ILAlg* II/3, 7793–7794; 8326 = *ILAlg* II/3, 7908; 8329 = *ILAlg* II/3, 7899; 20144 = *ILAlg* II/3, 7653), but all of them are from the 2nd century AD.

mentioning it as a colony and dating it to the middle or end of the 1st century.[50] However, there is no epigraphic evidence of how it received its name (*cognomina*), which would settle this question decisively. From an administrative standpoint, Gsell, following the interpretation of an epitaph for a soldier from Tigzirt cited as *milita(vit) moratus Cuiclo*, argued that it could have served as a military post during the 1st century AD, although the text of this inscription is vague and complex and therefore constitutes very circumstantial evidence. Nevertheless, we know that in the 2nd century AD certain imperial legates[51] intervened in the town, certainly with imperial approval,[52] as must also have happened in Timgad.[53]

Source material of the early Empire does not make much progress in this respect, but epigraphy and Christian conciliar sources seem to provide the key to the matter. The *Tabula Peutingeriana* mentions the *mansiones* of Sétif, *Mons*, *Culchul colonia* (i.e. *Cuicul*) and *Tucca fines Affrice et Mauretanie*. Since it clearly mentions the towns of Sétif and *Tucca*, one might think that this section of the road ran through *Caesariensis*/*Sitifiensis*. However, epigraphic documentation from the 3rd and 4th centuries AD reveals that this town was under the legates of Augustus, in fact the governors of *Numidia*,[54] and the episcopal notices of 484 indicate its location also in the province of *Numidia*. This once again raises important questions about *Cuicul*. As we have seen, its location midway between Sétif and *Cirta*, two important political and administrative poles, caused it to oscillate between the two. It belonged to *Numidia* for good historical reason, since, despite its proximity to Sétif, its historical link would have been with *Cirta*. Therefore, as noted previously, the historical frontier of the kingdom of *Mauretania* was maintained, preserving the structures and

---

50 *AAA* f. 16, no. 233 and J. Gascou, *La politique municipale de l'Empire romain en Afrique proconsulaire de Trajan à Septime Sévère* (Rome 1972), 108–110 proposed a Trajanic promotion, while Cagnat 1913, op. cit.; J.-M. Lassère, Ubique populus. *Peuplement et mouvements de population dans l'Afrique romaine de la chute de Carthage à la fin de la dynastie des Sévères (146 a.C.–235 p.C.)* (Paris 1977), 250–261 and X. Dupuis, 'Les origines de la colonie de Cuicul', *BSAF* 2001 (2006), 158–159 supported the idea of a Nervan promotion, taking the case of Sétif as the best example of one of his colony's in the area.

51 *CIL* VIII, 8326 = *ILAlg* II/3, 7908; 8309 = 20135 (= *ILS* 3957) = *ILAlg* II/3, 7751; 20144 = *ILAlg* II/3, 7653.

52 F. Jacques, '*Ampliatio* et *mora* : Evergètes récalcitrants d'Afrique romaine', *AntAfr* 9 (1975), 169–171.

53 *CIL* VIII, 2353.

54 The post of *consularis sexfascalis provinciae Numidiae* is mentioned in the inscriptions from the 4th century AD: *CIL* VIII, 8324 (= *ILS* 5535) = *ILAlg* II/3, 7881; *CIL* VIII, 10896–10897 = 20157–20158 = *ILAlg* II/3, 7882; *CIL* VIII, 20156 (= *ILS* 5536) = *ILAlg* II/3, 7878; *ILAlg* II/3, 7876–7877; 7879; 7885.

dependencies of local power prior to Rome, but now newly converted to serve the imperial administration. This ties in with another great debate, which is whether it belonged to the *Cirta* confederation or not. Many questions remain about this town, but until now evidence does not support including it within the confederation,[55] instead indicating that *Cirta* was on the fringes.[56]

The milestones for Sétif are abundant, which is logical since it was the capital of the Diocletian subdivision of *Mauretania Sitifiensis*. They have been found along numerous roads. If we pay attention to the road discussed in the Antonine Itinerary, the milestones[57] also identify Sétif as *caput*, and they continue until the well-known site of *Mons*/*Mopth*.[58] Between *Mons* and *Cuicul* lies the so-called *pagus Thigillavensium*, which is known from epigraphic evidence,[59] and which, unsurprisingly, would have been associated with an urban entity. Gsell has already indicated that it must surely have been *Cuicul* since the *Carthago* Conference of AD 411 indicated that Bishop *Donatus* was unwell and interrupted his journey to return to his see of *Thigillava* in *Numidia*. More proof exists at the archaeological site of *Novar* in the form of inscriptions indicating the Mauretanian era,[60] giving us one more reason to consider it as having been located within that province. This gives us the key to understand that the colonial territory of *Cuicul* must have included the *pagus Thigillavensium* and the provincial boundary must have always been fixed along the course of the *Ampsaga* River and continued to its headwaters.

It is interesting to note that the area of *Cuicul*, which is less than 100 km from the coast, nevertheless belongs to the second phase of the consolidation of the

---

55 *AAA* f. 16, no. 233 and f. 17.

56 "H.-G. Pflaum a suivi fidèlement ce programme, alors même qu'à la suite de S. Gsell il réaffirmait que la colonie de *Cuicul* n'avait jamais fait partie de la Confédération ; en bonne logique, les inscriptions de cette cité auraient donc dû être intégrées au volume consacrée à la Numidie militaire": X. Dupuis, 'Cuicul, la Confédération Cirtéenne et les Suburbures : Des limites ambiguës', in *Frontières et limites géographiques de l'Afrique du Nord antique. Hommage à Pierre Salama*, ed. C. Lepelley and X. Dupuis (Paris 1999) (quoting H.-G. Pflaum, in *ILAlg* II/1, p. 40).

57 The inscription *AE* 1969/70, 718 was found at both archaeological sites, while the inscription *CIL* VIII, 22407 appeared also in *Mons*. This serves only as fragmentary evidence, and Sétif is not mentioned as the *caput*, but the reconstruction of the text matches that of *CIL* VIII, 10351–10352 = 22402 (= *ILS* 761) and *CIL* VIII, 10364.

58 Several inscriptions mentioning the *annus provinciae* were found in *Mons*: *AE* 1972, 764; *AE* 2007, 1753; P.-A. Février, 'Remarques sur les inscriptions funéraires datées de Maurétanie Césarienne orientale (IIe–Ve siècle)', *MEFRA* 76 (1964), 150, nº 299; *CIL* VIII, 8667. This can be considered good evidence that they belonged to *Mauretania*.

59 Another inscription mentions the *magister* of the *pagus Thigillavensium*, *ILAlg* II/3, 7612.

60 *Novar*: *CIL* VIII, 20430; one also in *Mons*: *CIL* VIII, 8667, and in Sétif: *CIL* VIII, 20278; see S. Guédon, *La frontière romaine de l'Africa sous le Haut-Empire* (Madrid 2018).

conquest and colonisation of North Africa. Février has already pointed out that from the period of Caligula's consolidation from around AD 40 to the end of the century, no documents mentioning urban foundations have been found for this area,[61] which corresponds to the eastern part of the ancient kingdom of Juba. This suggests that this area was a marginal space of no real interest in the early phase of territorial administration. Once Nerva's colonising policy began in Sétif and in *Mons*[62] and once *Cuicul* had been promoted at the same time to the rank of colony, it is discernible that this area took on greater importance and the two towns greatly expanded in size. The road marking the interprovincial boundary must have already been in operation, as can be seen from the concatenation of urban centres. However, milestones prior to AD 124[63] have not been found. It was also during Hadrian's time that the *pagus Thigillavensium*[64] was seemingly established. This reveals that, after the foundational phase of the colonial centres involving the settlement of Roman veterans, the process of urban development, greater interconnection and agrarian colonisation took place in the following decades.

### 3.2 *The Second Stage: The Nerva–Antonine Dynasty*

Further to the south of the urban centre of *Cuicul* and the road to it, we can still perceive the administrative differences between *Mauretania* and *Numidia*, as reflected in the road's epigraphy. The milestones for *Cuicul*[65] and the *Suburbures*[66] from Caracalla to Emilianus have similar expressions relating to a renewal of the road system in the area. Such similarities between the two Numidian entities differ from the Sétif milestones,[67] which do not indicate any similar restructuring along the lines of a collective strategy. Furthermore, the

61 Only two pieces of evidence exist of new foundations in the rest of *Mauretania*: the port of *Rusucurru* (Tigzirt), mentioned by Pliny (*NH*. 5.2 also in *CIL* VIII, 8995 = 20710 (= *ILS* 6874)), and *Oppidum Novum* in the Chélif Valley (Aïn-Defla), also mentioned by Pliny (*NH*. 5.2, also in *CIL* VIII, 9643 (= *ILS* 6880); *AE* 1926, 23; *AE* 1973, 654).

62 P.-A. Février, 'Aux origines de l'occupation romaine dans les hautes plaines de Sétif', in *La Méditerranée de Paul-Albert Février* (Rome 1996), 54–58, who bases his claim on a reinterpretation of *CIL* VIII, 8655 and historical context.

63 Mile III, *CIL* VIII, 10355; mile IV *CIL* VIII, 22404 and another milestone without a number: *CIL* VIII, 22406.

64 R. Cagnat, 'Chronique d'épigraphie africaine', *BCTH* (1894), 344.

65 *CIL* VIII, 22397 (= *ILS* 5871); *CIL* VIII, 22399; *AE* 1911, 101; *AE* 1911, 104 (= *ILS* 9498); *AE* 1912, 155, with the expression *vias exhaustas restituit ac novis munitionibus dilatavit*.

66 *CIL* VIII, 10335 (= *ILS* 5862); *AE* 1942/43, 68, with the expression *vias torrentibus exhaustas restituit*.

67 P. Salama, 'Les bornes milliaires de Djemila-Cuicul et leur intérêt pour l'histoire de la ville', *Revue africaine* 95 (1951b), 216–219; Dupuis 1999, op. cit.

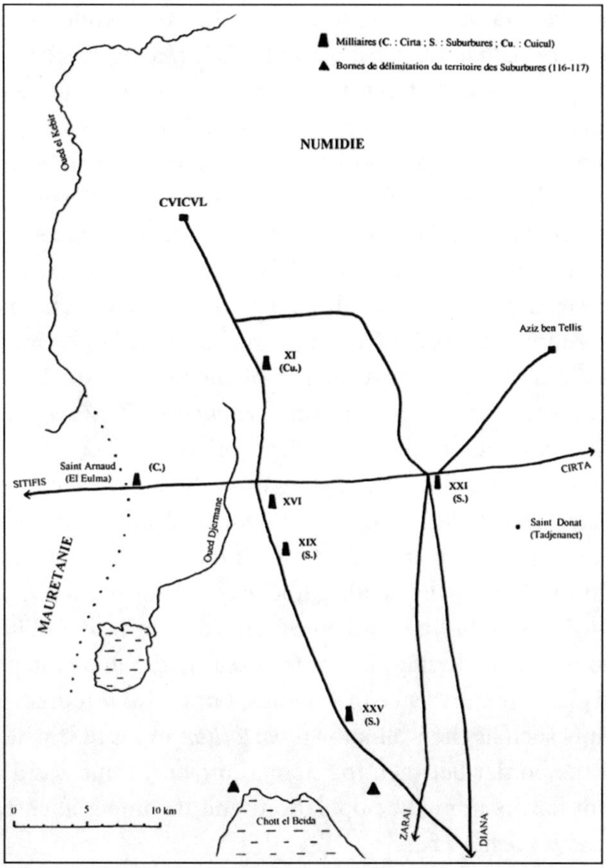


FIGURE 10.2 *Cuicul* and *Suburbures* region (Dupuis, 1999)

*caput viae* for the three cities was different. Regarding the southern boundary of *Cuicul*, Gsell determined that its territory could not have extended much further than 11 miles south based on a milestone erected by the *res publica Cuiculitanorum* at a place called Aïn Djira,[68] which would probably have marked the route from *Cuicul* southwards.

The jurisdiction seems to have been cut off close to the *Cuicul-Lambaesis* road, where Salama indicated an unpublished milestone that would have always

68 *AAA* f. 16, no. 295, who indicates that he does not know whether this milestone corresponded exactly to this point or to another one. Gsell pointed out that at the time he published the atlas, it was unpublished and was subsequently published by P. Alquier, 'Épigraphie latine & libyque du département de Constantine (1926–1930)', *Recueil des notices et mémoires de la société archéologique, historique et géographique du département de Constantine* 59 (1928–1929), 398–400, no. 113–114.

showed that *Cirta* maintained authority over this road, while the roads to the south would have been in the territory of the *Suburbures*, which we know from the milestones. We know that they belonged to *Numidia*,[69] and their territorial reorganisation seems to have taken place under Trajan (AD 116–7) because of the *termini* found in the area.[70] Both the mention of the *caput viae* of *Cirta* on milestones and the epigraph alluding to the *Genius Subtabarti* (see note 68) allow us to place the boundary point between the two provinces at Eulma.

The founding process and the rural implementation of these Nerva–Antonine settlements was not restricted to the interprovincial area. The parallel road to the coast running from Sétif to the west began to be fortified with military camps dating from the first quarter of the 2nd century AD, with place names such as *Rapidum*,[71] *Auzia* and *Thanaramusa Castra*,[72] which joined the *Oppidum Novum*, dating from the Flavian period. *Albulae*, *Tiguava Castra*[73] and other more westerly hill forts dating from the 2nd and 3rd centuries AD were added to protect this corridor. This fortified line made it possible to extend the provincial domain and administration to the south, while maintaining the River *Malva* as the dividing line between the two *Mauretaniae*. This frontier of the Empire clashed head on with the dynamics of mobility that prevailed in the region, including the routes used by the nomadic populations. The latter explains the presence of veterans, but it also favoured commercial meeting points such as the well-known *portorium* of *Zarai*,[74] which not only represented the border between the Roman provinces but was a mandatory crossing point for the nomadic populations and the imperial customs linked to the *quattuor publica Africae*.[75]

---

69 Dupuis 1999, op. cit. Its territory probably reached the surroundings of El Eulma, where an inscription mentioning the *Genius Subtabarti* was found (*ILAlg* II/3, 7543a). Gsell indicated that *Subtabarti* could be an indeclinable place name (*AAA* f. 16, no. 422).

70 *ILS* 9380 = *ILAlg* II/3, 7529; *ILS* 9381 = *ILAlg* II/3, 7534; *AE* 1969/70, 696 = *ILAlg* II/2, 4343; Février 1996, op. cit., 59; Cortés Bárcena 2013, op.cit., 173–177.

71 J.-P. Laporte, Rapidum, *Le camp de la cohorte des Sardes en Maurétanie Césarienne* (Sassari 1989), 305; Le Bohec 1999, op. cit., provides a list of inscriptions that are related to the *Cohors II Sardorum*: *CIL* VIII, 5364 = 17357 = *ILAlg* I, 474; *CIL* VIII, 9198 = 20829; 9200; 9202 = 20830; 9207; 9209 = 20830; 9831 (= *ILS* 3257); *CIL* VIII, 9833; 10949 = 21721; 21523; 21667; 21704; 21720 (= *ILS* 2607); *AE* 1920, 27; *AE* 1929, 133; *AE* 1932, 31; *AE* 1951, 145; *AE* 1956, 159; *AE* 1975, 953; *AE* 1991, 1738–1739; *AE* 2003, 2027; *ILAlg* II/3, 7947 (doubtful).

72 Benseddik 1984–1985, op. cit., 1376/57.

73 Bloch 1941–1946, op. cit., 9–42; Benseddik 1982, op. cit., 171.

74 J. France, 'Normes douanières et réglementation des échanges. Trois questions simples sur le tarif de Zaraï (Numidie)', *AntAfr* 50 (2014).

75 P. Ørsted, '*Quattuor publica Africae*: Custom Duties or Landtax?', in *L'Africa romana. Atti del IX convegno di studio su « L'Africa romana ». Nuoro, 13–15 dicembre 1991*, vol. II, ed. A. Mastino (Sassari 1992), 812–829; France 2014, op. cit., 101.

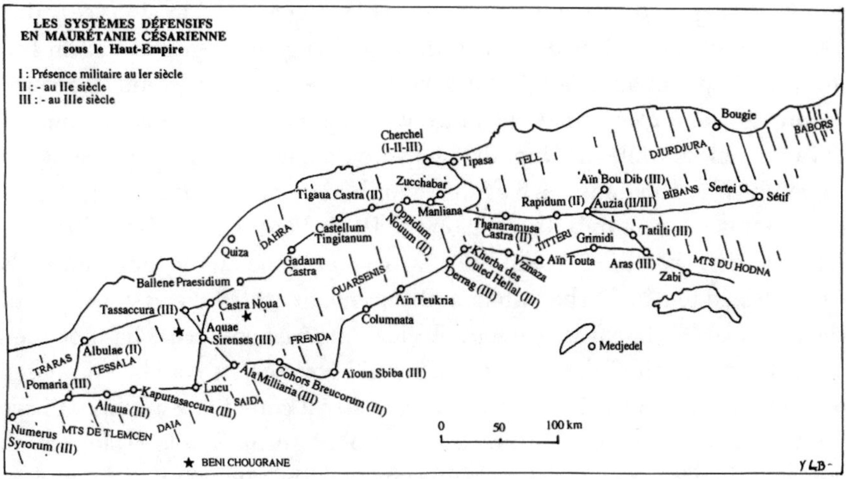


FIGURE 10.3 The defensive systems of *Mauretania Caesariensis* (Le Bohec 1999)

### 3.3 *The Third Stage I: The Hauts Plateaux*

The southern boundary between the two provinces has long fascinated several scholars. Several key works have addressed this question,[76] promoting a wealth of possibilities for study, such as the conquest by and implications of the army being involved in the provincial constitution of the area. Other issues targeted were the advance of Roman colonisation or the cultural clash between the Romans and the nomadic populations, although nowadays this question has been revisited from a fresher and renewed point of view that delves into perspectives that are more open.[77]

Février's epigraphic explorations determined the existence of large areas that were imperial domains in the south of the Sétif plateau.[78] The agrarian colonisation of the region has been studied through the *centuriationes*. However, epigraphy is again a very important source for understanding the colonisation of this area. This allowed Février to consider the area of Aïn Oulmene and the

76 Cagnat 1913, op. cit.; Salama 1951, op. cit., 143; Benseddik 1982, op. cit., 285; Benseddik 1984–1985, op. cit., 1376/47–67; Le Bohec 1982, op. cit.

77 Guédon 2018a, op. cit.; S. Guédon, 'La frontière de l'Afrique romaine à l'époque tardive : Le cas emblématique de Tobna et du *limes Tubuniensis* (Notitia Dignitatum, Occ., 25.25)', *Historia* 67, no. 3 (2018b); S. Guédon, 'Road Network and Roman Frontier in Numidia: The Region of Tobna', in *Roman Roads: New Evidence – New Perspectives*, ed. A. Kolb (Berlin and Boston 2019).

78 Concerning the imperial properties in this area and in the African provinces, see H. González Bordas, 'Africa', in *The Emperor and his Properties in the Roman World (44 BC–284 AD). Geography, Economy, History*, ed. A. dalla Rosa and M. Maiuro (Bordeaux, forthcoming).

southern ridge separating it from Chott el Hodna as a colonial process that developed at the end of the 2nd century AD. Février suggested that in this area, the imperial boundary would have been perceived differently since the Mauretanian part would have included vast imperial domains dating from the Severan period, while the Numidian part would have included lands assigned to nomadic populations, such as the Suburbures or the *Nicibenses*. However, these domains seem to be centred on the Hauts Plateaux and did not extend further south than the Saharan Atlas, with *Lemellef* being the most southerly case attested to date.[79] They would only have demarcated the eastern limit of the province,[80] while management of these imperial properties has not been documented south of the mountains. Several possibilities could be proposed for why this was not the case: such as the natural conditions would not have been suitable for this form of rural exploitation. Also, the Severan colonisation changed the model of agrarian colonisation; or the opening up of the plain towards the salt pans of Chott el Hodna, not far from Tobna and an area of apparent instability, may have meant that this system could not be implemented south of the mountain range.

There is also a visible chronological difference between the two parts. While the Mauretanian colonisation ended in Sétif during the time of Nerva, the colonisation carried out by Trajan continued southwards into *Numidia*. Two major Numidian centres in the area were Timgad and *Diana Veteranorum*. Timgad was known and promoted as the colony *Ulpia Thamugadi*, or also as the colony *Marciana Traiana Thamugadi*,[81] which gives us a clear Trajanic chronology. Its ascription to *Numidia* is unquestionable, as several sources indicate.[82] *Diana*

79 This is the case of the *coloni* (*CIL* VIII, 8808) placed in the imperial properties. Following the *lex Hadriana* (see H. González Bordas and J. France, 'A New Edition of the Imperial Regulation from the Lella Drebblia Site near Dougga (*AE* 2001, 2083)', *JRA* 20 (2017), 407–428), this kind of settlement was organised in a particular way, much like a castellum. These *coloni* made dedications to the emperors; see K.-P. Johne, J. Koehn and V. Weber, *Die Kolonen in Italien und den westlichen Provinzen des römischen Reiches* (Berlin 1983), 372–410; E. Smadja, 'Culte impérial et religion en Afrique du Nord sous le Haut Empire romain', *Dialogues d'histoire ancienne. Supplément 1. Hommage à Pierre Lévêque* (Besançon 2005), 234–235.

80 It should not be understood that there were only imperial properties in *Mauretania*, but those in *Numidia* seem to have been located somewhat further away from the provincial boundary; see F. Jacques, 'Propriétés impériales et cités en Numidie Méridionale', *CGG* 3 (1992), 123–139; A. Chérif, 'Le *Fundus Tapp*(*hugabensis*) – Henchir Chaïeb : Un domaine agricole de la région de Bou Arada (Tunisie)', *AntAfr* 55 (2019), 97–126.

81 *CIL* VIII, 2355 = 17842 (= *ILS* 6148); *CIL* VIII, 17843.

82 See *AAA*, f. 27, no. 255. Regarding the evidence, epigraphy is very explicit in this respect, with epitaphs of the legates of Augustus in *Numidia* having been found in the colony itself, as well as the tombstone of *L. Aelius Perpetuus* (*CIL* VI, 1803 = EDR179980), found

*Veteranorum*, which received municipal status under Trajan (although it has been suggested that it might also have received such status during the time of Flavian) is also Numidian in origin. In Hadrian's time, the *municipium* of *Lambaesis* (it later became a colony under Septimius Severus) was included in the year AD 128.

The southern border is the most disputed section of the province. General scholarly opinion tends to maintain the line drawn by Camps, who proposed following the division between the two provinces through Djebel Braou,[83] which is logical since it is a perfect territorial landmark located in the great plain between Sétif and land to the south of El Eulma. However, it should be noted that the suggestive toponym *Ad Portum* (a *mansio* indicated in the *Tabula Peutingeriana*,[84] linking two distinct roads from Sétif to the southeast) could be concealing a liminal toponym (next to the gates of *Mauretania* or *Numidia*). Although this theory is purely speculative, it would not be unreasonable to think that such a toponym was in the proximity of this territorial landmark and that such a mountain would have been known as the provincial "gates". In any case, Camps' proposal[85] to the south consists of tracing a straight line that then turns westwards to reach the Hodna, leaving the *castella* of *Perdices* and *Macri* on the Mauretanian side and including *Zarai*, *Cellas* and *Capsum Iuliani* in *Numidia*. Camps' proposal should be reconsidered, at least in part, as it is not so clear whether *Zarai* or *Cellas* were Numidian.

### 3.4 *The Third Stage II: The Southern Boundary*

To the south of the peripheral Trajan-Hadrian colonisation of the Hauts Plateaux in the Mauretanian part of the province and the Numidian points of *Diana Veteranorum*, *Thamugadi* and *Lambaesis* lies the outpost of *Zarai*, a strategic point for the roads running southwards. The ancient town of *Zarai*, known from epigraphy[86] and with an obvious phonetic continuity with the current Zraia, reveals the first phase under Hadrian through its epigraphic record, although it was not subject to a true colonisation process but more to the advance of a cohort to the south. The situation remained stable until the ineffective management of the Trajan-Hadrian *limes* in *Mauretania*. The

in Rome, which indicates a particular *origo*: *patriae suae coloniae Ulpiae Thamugadis ex Numidia*.

83 Camps 1999, op. cit.

84 It is difficult to guess where the place it, see *AAA* f. 17, no. 335. Gsell made no proposal, but he indicated that this road was directly connected with *Sigus* at a total distance of 115 miles.

85 Camps 1999, op. cit.

86 *CIL* VIII, 4511.

colonisation efforts of these emperors did not include the Tell massifs, which became evident at the end of the 2nd century AD and inspired Septimius Severus to begin the advance southwards in AD 198, starting with the area of *Auzia* and leading to the creation of a direct *Auzia*-Sétif route.[87] A few years later, Hadrian's advance on *Zarai* represented an important point in the process, which we know about thanks to his famous law of AD 202 regulating the *portorium* and the customs tariff.[88] Although the episcopal notice of AD 484 included his bishop in *Numidia*, Ptolemy (4.2.7) included it in *Mauretania Caesariensis*, a certain contradiction in the sources that must have been due to the fact that it was the provincial meeting point. In truth, what seems to have happened is that the provincial boundary would have followed a road running from north to south, meeting at the crossroads in *Zarai*, which formed the perfect junction between the points of military interest in the area and was an ideal location for the well-known *portorium*, the meeting place between the two provinces.[89] Furthermore, *Zarai* was the point where two road systems met, perhaps corresponding to the different provincial administrations: one linking the town with *Cellas* and *Thubuna* and the other linking it with *Nicibes*. The importance of *Zarai*'s law perhaps causes us to overvalue the uniqueness of this place, but maybe there were other similar meeting points in this area as well.

The ancient site of *Cellas* or *castellum Cellense* was located at Kherbet Zerga. An inscription[90] indicates the year and province of *Mauretania*, which is strong evidence for placing it in *Mauretania* and not in *Numidia*. In addition, the episcopal notice of AD 484 placed it also in *Mauretania Sitifensis*.[91] This town was connected to *Zarai* by a direct road, which, through the *mansio ad Capsum Iuliani*,[92] was supposed to avoid the massif to the northeast of Gosbat.

Further south lay *Thubuna*, an important crossing point for nomadic pastoralists.[93] There is much controversy among the sources regarding the *municipium* of *Thubuna*/*Thubunas*/*Tubonis*, currently Tobna (Biskra). Ptolemy (4.2.7) listed it among the cities of *Mauretania Caesariensis*, while the episcopal

87 Benseddik 1982, op. cit., 184.

88 *CIL* VIII, 4508 = 18643.

89 A. Hilali, 'Recherche sur les frontières de l'Afrique romaine: espaces mobiles et représentations', in *Frontiers in the Roman World: Proceedings of the Ninth Workshop of the International Network Impact of Empire (Durham, 16–19 April 2009)*, ed. T. Kaizer and O. Hekster (Leiden 2011), 104.

90 *CIL* VIII, 8777 (= *ILS* 6888). See *AAA* f. 26, 135.

91 Salama 1951, op. cit. included this place in *Numidia*, though.

92 *AAA* f. 26, no. 69.

93 Picard 1947, op. cit., 49–66.

notices cited one Tobna in *Numidia* and another in *Mauretania*. The episcopal notices thus might indicate the existence of two cities, although there is only epigraphic evidence of one site with such a place name. An inscription by a legate of Augustus[94] was found at Tobna, which would link its administration to *Numidia*. It is therefore difficult to find a plausible solution for the discrepancy between the sources. It could be thought that the town initially belonged to *Mauretania* (the mention of a *curia* named *Victoria Antonini* prompted Gsell to link it to Geta[95] in origin and its inhabitants as belonging to the *Papiria* tribe), which would perhaps explain why Ptolemy placed it in *Mauretania*. The town was supposedly promoted to a *municipium* during the Severan dynasty,[96] which would coincide with the Severan reorganisation of the area and the implementation of the southern network of military *castella*. The latter is the reason that could have motivated this jurisdictional change and the cession of this part of the province to *Numidia* with a view to promoting a corridor of protection. The mention of Tobna in the episcopal lists of AD 484 is more difficult to justify, although perhaps it has to do with the liminal character of the town. Nevertheless, it seems that from the time of the Severan dynasty there is no doubt that it was considered Numidian.

The *Tabula Peutingeriana* mentions both *Tubonis* and the *Nubonenese* salt mines. This somewhat strange name of *Nubonense* can be corrected to *Tubonenses*, reflecting Tobna's administrative dependence on this resource as well as the nearby mines. This leads us to think that the salt mines of Chott el Hodna would also have belonged to *Numidia*, reflecting its administrative dependence on the resource, and would likewise have shifted the provincial boundary, forming a spit of land that would have extended across the southern part of *Mauretania Caesariensis*. The salt mines themselves would also have acted as an interprovincial boundary since the cities to the north of them are Mauretanian (see below). The *Notitia Dignitatum* reaffirms once again that in the Late Antique period, the administrative dependence of this area was Numidian: the citation of the office of the *praepositus limitis Tubuniensis* (Not. Dig. 25) corresponds with the *comes* of Africa and not with the *dux et praeses provinciae Mauritaniae*. This ascription is also linked to another

94 S. Gsell, 'Notes d'archéologie algérienne', *BCTH* (1901), 315, no. 16: +++[---] / *III*, *co*(*n*)*s*(*uli*) [---], / [*leg*(*atus*) *Aug*(*usti*) *pr*(*o*)] *pr*(*aetore*) *le*[*g*(*ionis*) *III Aug*(*ustae*)].

95 *AE* 1901, 2; see *AAA*, El Kantara f. 37, no. 10.

96 For inscriptions such as *CIL* VIII, 4482 = 18634 or the above-mentioned inscription of the *curia* (in previous note), see first publication and commentary by R. Cagnat, '13 Novembre 1900. Séance de la Commission de l'Afrique du Nord', *BCTH* (1900), CLXXIV–CLXXV.

epigraphic reference found in the fort of *Centenarium Aqua Viva* (Moloukal)[97] and dated to AD 303,[98] which cites the same office, although it links it to this specific fort. The office of *praepositus limitis* is linked to maintaining order and managing the behaviour of the tribes beyond the imperial frontier and always associated with North Africa.[99]

The transformation of the African provinces in the time of Diocletian led to the subdivision of *Numidia*, the southern part of which became known as the province of *Numidia Militaris*.[100] This military character of the province is evident from the *cognomen* added to the ephemeral provincial division and, although it was later reunified as a single *Numidia*, the incorporated part would have remained Numidian. The region between the Zab Mountains and Chott el Hodna would have been, according to Modéran's hypothesis,[101] one of the most hostile areas in the region, as it was an obligatory crossing point for nomadic populations and one of the best protected southern borders in the whole Africa. We know that based on the network of *castella* placed in the region in conjunction with the so-called linear structures, which may have served as separation walls to ensure provincial stability. Several hypotheses addressed how they would have functioned: to redirect nomadic flows into controlled and guarded corridors, to separate areas of Roman and non-Roman jurisdiction, to separate cultivable areas from non-cultivable areas, to mark the limit of Roman civilian settlement, even perhaps offering some protection to aquifers,[102] with the subsequent problems that these structures also entail.[103] Further south, still in *Numidia*, lies a *castellum* known as *Ausum*[104] (probably constructed before AD 248, although with doubtful chronological evidence,[105] which does not allow us to clarify the question) and the so-called *castellum Dimmidi*,[106] a fort built in AD 198 and evacuated in AD 235–8,[107] when

97 *AAA* f. 37, no. 10.
98 *AE* 1942/43, 81.
99 Guédon 2018a, op. cit.; Guédon 2018b, op. cit., 368–369. She claims that the charge is quoted in both Africa and *Mauretania* and can be found in scattered epigraphic evidence in those provinces and in Tripolitania.
100 G. Goyau, 'La *Numidia Militiana* de la liste de Vérone', *MEFRA* 13 (1893), 251–279.
101 Y. Modéran, *Les Maures et l'Afrique romaine* (*IV*$^{e}$*–VII*$^{e}$ *siècle*) (Rome 2003), 395.
102 P. Salama, 'Un point d'eau du *limes* maurétanien', in *Maghreb et Sahara, Mélanges*, ed. J. Despois (Paris 1973), 342.
103 See the discussion about its function and chronology in Guédon 2018a, op. cit.; Guédon 2018b, op. cit., 374–376.
104 M. Lenoir, *Le camp romain. Proche-Orient et Afrique du Nord* (Rome 2011), 217–219.
105 See Guédon 2018a, op. cit.; Guédon 2018b, op. cit., 376–377.
106 Picard 1947, op. cit., 84; Lenoir 2011, op. cit., 223–228.
107 Guédon 2018b, op. cit., 376.

the frontier was moved back. This area was built up from a hodological perspective: the route of conquest, which followed the orogeny of the area, determined the provincial advance. Both the route and mountains run parallel to the south. This hodological system of conquest can be seen in other valleys in which the conquest continued parallel to the network of small towns and *castella*: for example, in the El Kantara Valley, the Mesarfelta area (probably El Outaya) and the successive *villae* placed next to oases to the south. Still running parallel, but this time on the western side and in Mauretania, the area of Djebel Amoiud seems to have followed the same system of conquest, although in that area the remains have been less explored.[108] This gives rise to the idea that the effective limits of a province and the routes through it was determined by the controlled hodological space, with the province, the empire and the *limes* extending as far as Roman control could accommodate.

After this long excursus, it is necessary to return to the north and to the interprovincial meeting point near Tobna. In the neighbouring region of Aïn Touta, some interesting milestones have been discovered that reveal the complex network of roads running through the valleys. The road between Tobna and Seba Mgata contains milestones[109] that show that the *territorium* of the *municipium* of Tobna extended approximately 12 miles to the east and another 12 miles to *Ad Calceum*.[110] However, milestones[111] placed to the north of *Ad Calceum* mention the *caput viae* at *Lambaesis*, indicating that its jurisdiction would have led to this valley. For that reason, Baradez[112] proposed a direct connection between Tobna and *Lambaesis* to the north of *Ad Calceum*. The interest of this area lies in the fact that an inscription[113] found in Aïn Touta bears the *annus provinciae* of *Mauretania*, which creates a geographical problem. The appearance of this date lies within the provincial boundaries, but, as we have seen, the valley is at a crossroads between Tobna, *Lambaesis* and the

108 P. Morizot, 'La présence romaine dans le Djebel Amour (Algérie) : Apport des images Spot et de la photographie aérienne', in *Frontières et limites géographiques de l'Afrique du Nord antique. Hommage à Pierre Salama*, ed. C. Lepelley and X. Dupuis (Paris 1999).

109 E. Albertini, 'Le réseau routier de la Numidie méridionale', *CRAI* 75, no. 4 (1931a), 363–370; E. Albertini, 'Inscriptions d'El Kantara et de la région', *Revue africaine* 72 (1931b), 193–261; Guédon 2019, op. cit., 326–327.

110 Guédon 2019, op. cit., 326–327.

111 *AE* 1954, 133a.

112 J. Baradez, 'Inscriptions de la région du *limes* de Biskra à Tobna', *Libyca* 1 (1953), 162–165; see also Guédon 2019, op. cit., 327–328.

113 P. Salama, 'Un chapiteau inscrit d'époque chrétienne à Aïn Touta (Algérie)', in *Mélanges d'antiquité tardive*. Studiola in honorem Natalis Duval, ed. C. Balmelle, P. Chevalier and G. Ripoll (Turnhout 2004), 37–45.

southern part of *Numidia* (Mesarfelta and the southern oases), physically separated from *Mauretania* by the cities of *Nicibies* and Tobna. The year indicated is on the inscription is AD 461–2, a time when Vandals occupied *Mauretania* and part of *Numidia*, which could have led to the occupation of this border area and, at a time of political-administrative instability, to the ephemeral adoption of this system of time measurement. We have also considered that this road was mainly used for military purposes.[114]

To recapitulate, the interprovincial crossing at *Zarai* seems to be the last clear point where the interprovincial boundary was drawn. The road to the east of *Zarai* already allowed for communication with Numidian cities, such as the town of Henchir Merouana,[115] called *Lamasba* on the milestones. It was probably founded during the time of Caracalla because the epigraphic repertoire has not revealed any evidence of its existence before AD 214. The other town mentioned is *Nicivibus*, which would have been the capital of the *Nicibenses* peoples (Plin. *NH*. 5.4.30; Ptol. 4.3.6). A Byzantine epitaph mentioning an *episcopus Nicibensis*[116] confirms its location in N'Gaous. Gsell[117] proposed its location in *Numidia* based on an inscription revealing the words *p(raeses) p(rovinciae) N(umidiae)*.[118] Also, the episcopal notice of AD 484 indicated that this bishopric belonged to the province of *Numidia*. Considering the controversial ascription explained above, the southern town of Tobna was Numidian, which makes it inevitable that the provincial boundary was necessarily located to the north and east of its territory and must have run parallel to the road leading to *Cellas*.

The presence of indigenous populations, such as the *Nicibi*, along the provincial boundary confirms Février's hypothesis for the area between Sétif and the *Suburbures*. We continue to find populations of an indigenous character settled along the Numidian border, although we no longer find imperial properties in this area.

There are no such problems of provincial ascription north of Chott el Hodna. From *Cellas* (see above, note 89), the settlements belonged to *Mauretania*. Among them, the important town of *Zabi Iustiniana*, located to the north of the salt mines and in a region with numerous rural and military[119] structures,

114 Guédon 2019, op. cit., 330–334.

115 *AAA*, f. 27, no. 86.

116 S. Gsell, 'Chapelle chrétienne d'Henchir Akhrib (Algérie)', *MEFRA* 23 (1903), 12.

117 *AAA*, f. 27, no. 161.

118 *CIL* VIII, 4469.

119 S. Slimani and H. Kherbouche, 'Les formes d'occupation antique dans le Hodna : état des lieux', in *La frontière méridionale du Maghreb : approches croisées (Antiquité-Moyen Âge)*, ed. S. Guédon (Bordeaux 2018), 193–206.

is mentioned in the sources as Mauretanian. This great southern road between *Zarai* and *Numerus Syrorum*[120] acted as a protective element crossing the entire province. The road as well as the perpendicular roads penetrating the different massifs[121] provided good north-south connectivity. However, the roads ended not only at the boundaries of the province, but in fact, they constituted the *limes*.

## 4 Conclusions

African border studies have always placed great emphasis on the imperial frontier and *limes* as a space of shifting otherness[122] that allows us to understand the colonial clashes of opposing realities. However, indistinct internal boundaries are less obvious and more difficult to trace, hence they are less often studied. The establishment of certain provincial boundaries corresponded to political-administrative purposes as well as economic purposes. In some other cases, areas with a common historical background were divided into different units. How these boundaries were defined influenced and changed the administrative, juridical and mobility processes of the regions and determined a new social change in terms of new forms of identity.

African history during Roman times differed from the European history of Hispanic, Gallic, Germanic, or Dalmatian realities, which had developed certain models of communication and interaction prior to the conquest and whose urban settlement model was not so different from Latin realities. Similarly, Roman administration in the East became diverse, having previously passed through a Hellenistic process of change. The African case presented the challenge of incorporating nomadic realities and changing spaces in a natural environment that was certainly hostile to Mediterranean standards. This meant that the process of provincial development was slower and more gradual. While on the coast, as we have already seen, the Julio-Claudian territorial administration was like the models in the Mediterranean basin; the transition to the other social and natural realities of the south meant that its development had to be postponed until the time of Nerva, Trajan and Hadrian. The

120 In Lalla Maghnia, between Oujda and Tlemcen. Its position is known by the milestones, which mentioned this place as the *caput CIL* VIII, 10468–10470, but slight differences in the name are evident: *numerus Severianus Alexandrinus Syrorum*. See P. Salama, 'La voie romaine de la vallée de la Tafna', *Bulletin d'archéologie algérienne* 2 (1966–1967), 183–217.

121 Benseddik 1982, op. cit., 183.

122 F. Salcedo Garcés, 'Indigenismo y aculturación en la frontera de la Tripolitana romana', *RdA* 44 (2020).

finalisation of the socio-urban network of the north and in-depth knowledge of the indigenous populations thanks to recent explorations made possible the agricultural colonisation of this area. Even so, it is striking that in the great plateau of Sétif, the process of creating and consolidating rural settlements took so long. Only the creation of large and important urban centres made the conquest of the region possible, with the subsequent shaping and division of provincial spaces. This meant integrating more and more populations, many of which were still maintained nomadic cycles of mobility, undoubtedly determined the way provincial administration took shape. Thus, as Février had already noted, the large imperial properties remained on the Mauretanian side of the border, even though they did not form part of the province, leaving in *Numidia* a zone of protection with colonies of veterans interspersed with areas of nomadic mobility. The *portorium* of *Zarai* reflects the threshold existing between all these realities and the difficulties in fiscally regulating so many heterogeneous realities found along these corridors of north-south mobility.

Roman roads played a decisive role in colonisation, as their purpose was to alter the cyclical dynamics of the indigenous populations and to control these nomadic flows. Thus, we can see how even as the conquest advanced southwards, the great corridors of mobility ran parallel to the coast (east west). They were fortified with camps and veteran settlements. This military interconnection with the existing road systems was certainly not a synthetic model of mobility, but it did mean the province could promote social and mercantile traffic in a different manner. This is the reason why there were more military camps and posts than cities[123] on the two great military routes of *Mauretania Caesariensis*, both the central and southern routes. This reality clashed with the two documented military camps on the coast (*Castra Germanorum* and *Castra Puerorum*).

In sum, this brief analysis of the boundaries between *Mauretania* and *Numidia* reveals a far from casual constitution of their jurisdictions, even though at certain points we lack enough data to understand the choice of their layout. It does not mean that their organisation was random, but rather that their study allows for a historical understanding of their territorial and administrative development. The way in which the spaces were laid out was not exclusively the result of strategic considerations of a political nature. They were also of a social nature, with the aim of maintaining order and peace, including relations with nomadic tribal societies. The clear implications for interregional mobility were the result of their agro-pastoral economy.[124]

123 Benseddik 1982, op. cit., 168–169.

124 Hilali 2011, op. cit., 100.

FIGURE 10.4 Map of the traditional frontier between *Mauretania* and *Numidia* (Camps 1999)

The provincial boundary between *Mauretania* and *Numidia* provides a chronological timeline of the history of the two regions. This palimpsest allows us to see the different phases and strategies of colonisation from the pre-Roman period to Late Antiquity, providing a thread running through their history. The strategy of territorial administration, but also the organising of society, can be observed along these boundaries. Both went from being a unitary system on the coast to diverging in the south, with functioning structures between one provincial unit and the other. The southern militarisation of *Numidia* and the integration of indigenous populations on the provincial margins highlights the process of agrarian colonisation carried out in *Mauretania*, which aimed at a form of economic production different from the areas of encounter and confrontation on the southern frontier of the empire.

CHAPTER 11

# Blurred Boundaries and Terrestrial Connections between *Baetica* and *Tarraconensis*

## *The* Territorium *of Acci and the Influence of the Landscape*

*Antonio López García*

## 1 Introduction[1]

Before becoming the dominant city in the southeastern part of the Iberian Peninsula, *Acci* was under the influence of *Basti*, a significant city that controlled the northern area of the current province of Granada.

In the 3rd century BC, several military incursions through the *Via Heraklea* resulted in a reorganisation of the road system in the territory of *Bastetania*. Roman interest in this area was due to a need to control the extraction of metals from around the city of *Castulo*, which was not easy to access from other parts of the peninsula. In 214 BC, the Romans tried to penetrate *Bastetania* through the *Via Heraklea* and conquer the *Bastetani*, but before arriving they encountered a strong military offensive that forced them to deviate northward through the *Baetis* Valley (along the Guadalquivir River). At that time, the mining area of *Castulo*, in the high *Baetis* Valley, was conquered. In 209 BC, P. Cornelius Scipio managed to seize *Bastetania* by first conquering *Carthago Nova*.[2] The Iberian Peninsula was divided into two provinces in 197 BC: *Hispania Citerior* and *Hispania Ulterior*.[3] *Hispania Citerior* occupied the entire eastern part of the peninsula and extended inland towards its center. *Hispania Ulterior* occupied the southwestern third to the Duero River.

1 This work is part of the project "Law, Governance and Space: Questioning the Foundations of the Republican Tradition". This research has received funding from the European Research Council (ERC) under the European Union's Horizon 2020 research and innovation programme (grant agreement No. 771874). This research has also received funding from the Next Generation framework of the European Commission through the programme "María Zambrano" for the attraction of international talent that I have at the University of Granada.

2 Liv. 26.44.

3 App. *Ib.* 99–100; F. Pina Polo, 'Las comisiones senatoriales para la reorganización de Hispania', *DHA* 23, no. 2 (1997), 83–104; F.J. Navarro, 'La organización provincial de Hispania durante el Imperio Romano (Siglos I–III)', in Hispaniae. *Las provincias hispanas en el mundo romano*, ed. J. Andreu Pintado, J. Cabrero Piquero and I. Rodà de Llanza (2009), 346.

 | DOI:10.1163/9789004685734_012

With the progressive conquest of the peninsula, several important colonies were set up in the south of *Hispania*. The establishing of colonies allowed for greater administrative control over the conquered territory. During the next century, in the context of the civil wars between Pompey the Great and Julius Caesar, some new colonies were founded in *Hispaniae*. Between 49 and 45 BC, the south of *Hispania* was the site of several battles between supporters of Caesar and Pompey. In 48 BC, Q. Cassius Longinus provoked the anger of several cities by extorting money from them and ended up being killed in *Corduba*.[4] In 45 BC, clashes occurred between the sons of Pompey and the army of Caesar. According to Strabo and Orosius, Caesar crossed from the peninsular east to *Castulo* and *Obulco* and faced the Pompeians at the battle of *Munda*.[5] It is quite possible that in this context, a military contingent was established at the Iberian settlement of *Acci*. The strategic position of this enclave made it possible to control the passage between the east Mediterranean coast, the northern part of *Hispania Citerior*, the southern coast, and the *Baetis* Valley. Strabo mentioned the existence of a coastline link with *Castulo*, which undoubtedly served as a passage for the transportation of silver from the Sierra Morena Mountains through the largest port in the southeast, located in *Carthago Nova*. Therefore, control of *Bastetania* should have helped protect the mineral resources from *Castulo*.

## 2 Control of Resources and Territorial Administration

Several studies have revealed the importance of mineral resources in the southern part of *Bastetania* before the arrival of the Romans. From the 3rd century to the 1st century BC, mining became the main productive activity in the foothills of the Sierra Nevada Mountains.[6] A series of fortified indigenous settlements in the hills of El Cardal (Ferreira),[7] La Calera (Dólar),[8] Peñón de Arruta (Jérez

4 A. López García and A. Reyes Martínez, 'Apuntes para una historiografía de la Arqueología en la ciudad de Guadix (Granada). Entre los mitos y la realidad', in *Colecciones, arqueólogos, instituciones y yacimientos en la España de los siglos XVIII al XX*, ed. S. España Chamorro, R. Arranz Santos and A. Romero Molero (Oxford 2018), 68.

5 R. Corzo Sánchez and M. Toscano San Gil, *Las vías romanas de Andalucía* (Seville 1992), 34.

6 A. Caballero Cobos *et al.*, 'Bastetania antes de Roma. El poblado fortificado íbero de La Calera (Dólar, Granada)', *Cuadernos de Prehistoria y Arqueología de la Universidad de Granada* 30 (2020), 408.

7 C. González Román, 'Ciudad y poblamiento romano en la provincia de Granada durante el Alto Imperio', *Habis* 32 (2001), 271–296.

8 A. M. Adroher Auroux, A. López Marcos and J. A. Pachón, *Granada arqueológica. La cultura ibérica* (Granada 2002).

del Marquesado),[9] and also perhaps around the castle of Alquife controlled the eastern corridor of Fiñana, making it possible for local people to mine iron, lead, and silver ore. After the Roman conquest, a redistribution of the settlements took place. Mining activities were transferred to Sierra de Gor and Sierra de Baza,[10] and agricultural development expanded throughout the plains.[11] The core area around the *oppidum* of *Basti* succumbed to Roman control between the 2nd and the 1st century BC.[12] *Basti* and *Tutugi*, two of the main *oppida*, lost their control over the territory when the fortified settlements were abandoned in the late republican period.[13] In the early imperial era, these *oppida* experimented with a notable form of urban transformation. *Basti* became a *municipium* and *Tutugi* a *civitas*. Both cities had some juridical privileges, but the lower-ranked *oppidum* of *Acci* replaced *Basti* as the main urban center of the region. Ptolemy was the first to record the name and location of *Acci* when he mentions it last on a list of fifteen cities dominated by the indigenous *Bastetani*.[14]

How did this area become integrated into Roman administration? After the battle of *Philippi*, Augustus effectively controlled the Hispanic provinces,[15] but in 27 BC he received from the Roman Senate the *imperium* over the provinces of *Hispania*, *Syria*, and *Gallia* for ten years. Augustus was transferred to *Hispania* for a period of two years to fight the Cantabrians. He maintained the control over *Hispania Citerior* and the western fringe of *Hispania Ulterior* – the Lusitanian territory – while the southern part of *Hispania Ulterior* – later

---

9 C. González Román, A. M. Adroher Auroux and A. López Marcos, 'El Peñón de Arruta (Jerez del Marquesado, Granada): una explotación minera romana', *FlorIlib* 8 (1997), 183–213.

10 A. Caballero Cobos, *et al.*, 'Evolución del paisaje minero en las Sierras Andaluzas Orientales que orlan los altiplanos de Baza y Guadix. Desde los orígenes hasta inicios de la Edad Moderna', in *Presente y futuro de los paisajes mineros del pasado. Estudios sobre minería, metalurgia y poblamiento*, ed. L. J. García, L. Arboledas, E. Alarcón and F. Contreras (Granada 2017), 327–339.

11 N. Marín Díaz and J. C. Gorlat, 'Los orígenes de *Acci* y su configuración como importante centro urbano en la Antigüedad', in *Tres estudios sobre Guadix y su tierra*, ed. M. Espinar Moreno (Guadix 1990), 1–34.

12 J. A. Salvador Oyonate, 'La Bastitania romana y visigoda: Arqueología e historia de un territorio' (Ph.D. diss., University of Granada, 2011), 704; A. Caballero Cobos, 'Vías de comunicación en las comarcas de Baza y Huéscar. Una aproximación histórico-arqueológica desde la Prehistoria Reciente a la Edad Media' (Ph.D. diss., University of Granada, 2014), 244.

13 A. M. Adroher Auroux, 'Fortificaciones republicanas entre la Citerior y la Ulterior: en las tierras de Bastetania', in *Las Guerras Civiles romanas en Hispania. Una revisión histórica desde la Contestania*, ed. F. Sala and J. Moratalla (Alicante 2014), 169–182.

14 Ptol. *Geogr.* 2.6.60: Ὑπὸ δὲ τούτους καὶ παρὰ τοὺς Ὠρητανοὺς Βαστιτανοί, ἐν οἷς πόλεις μεσόγειοι.

15 App. *Civ.* 5.10; Cass. Dio. 48.1.

known as *Baetica* – remained under the direct control of the Senate.[16] After Augustus was victorious in the Cantabrian Wars in 19 BC, the peninsula was completely subjugated, and administration of the territory was reorganized. In 13 BC, *Hispania Ulterior* was divided into two provinces: *Baetica* and *Lusitania*.[17] *Lusitania* remained under the authority of a praetorian *legatus*. Nonetheless, the administration of *Hispania Baetica* was different. The province was governed by a *proconsul* of praetorian rank, as was his proconsular *legatus*, and by a *quaestor*. At the same time, *Hispania Citerior* was under the command of a *legatus* of consular rank, a praetorian *iuridicus*, three (then one) legions under the command of a praetorian legatus, and several *procuratores*. This asymmetrical scheme shows different levels of cultural assimilation and pacification of the provinces of *Hispania* in the early imperial era. *Hispania Citerior* was divided into seven *conventus iuridici* to improve the management of the various regions. In this historical context, the southeastern part of *Hispania Citerior* formed the *conventus Carthaginiensis*, an area that became one of the most developed parts of the province.

Did the city and *territorium* of *Acci* always belong to *Hispania Citerior*? Traditionally, historians have interpreted the north face of the Sierra Nevada Mountains and the western side of them as part of the same historical ensemble.[18] This historical amalgamation has usually led to a certain amount of confusion regarding two completely different geological landscapes that nowadays – and for more than a millennium – are closely bound together: the areas of contemporary Granada and Guadix. The Sierra Nevada Mountains and Sierra Harana create a natural frontier that in ancient times constituted the administrative border between *Hispania Citerior/Tarraconensis* and *Hispania Ulterior/Baetica*.

The transition from one type of landscape to another is clearly visible (fig. 11.1). The one side contains the rich and blooming countryside of central Andalucía, starting from *Illiberris* (Granada) to the west. The other side

16 Strab. 3.4.20.

17 Alföldy 1969, op. cit., 224; P. Ozcáriz Gil, 'Organización administrativa y territorial de las provincias hispanas durante el Alto Imperio', in Hispaniae. *Las provincias hispanas en el mundo romano*, ed. J. Andreu Pintado, J. Cabrero Piquero and I. Rodà de Llanza (2009), 324.

18 E. Albertini, *Les divisions administratives de l'Espagne romaine* (Paris, 1932), 34–35; J. M. Santero, 'Colonia Iulia Gemella Acci', *Habis* 3 (1972), 216; C. Asenjo Sedano, *De Acci a Guadix: aproximación a la protohistoria de una ciudad del sudeste peninsular hispánico, inserta en un fenómeno de mutación de topónimo: una hipótesis de reconstrucción urbana* (Granada 2002), 57–58; M. Pastor Muñoz, 'Epigrafía y sociedad en la *colonia Iulia Gemella Acci*', in *Actas del I Congreso Internacional de Historia Antigua "La Península Ibérica hace 2000 años", Valladolid, 23–25 de noviembre 2000*, ed. L. Hernández Guerra, L. Sagredo San Eustaquio and J. M. Solana Sáinz (2002), 425–439.

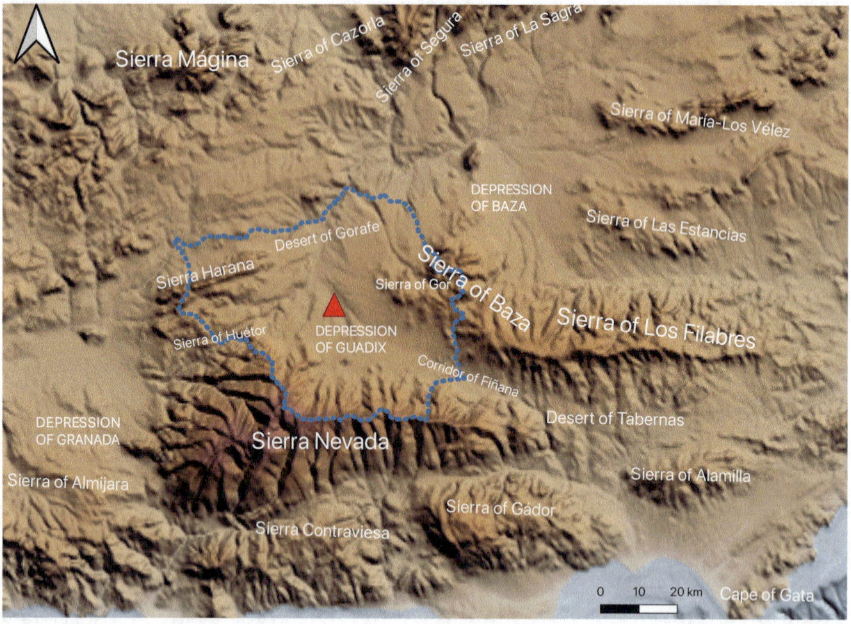


FIGURE 11.1 The mountainous geography around Guadix

contains a semi-desertic landscape with some dispersed fertile areas surrounded by dry mountains, a common landscape of the southeast peninsula and the Spanish Levante, starting from the land of ancient *Acci* on the northern side of the Sierra Nevada. This natural transition in the environment may have provided Romans with the motivation to integrate *Accitania* with *Hispania Citerior*. But two finds have prompted scholars to suggest that this area was part of *Hispania Ulterior/Baetica*. First, some of the oldest coins minted in *Acci* show some common features with the coins minted in the cities of *Hispania Baetica*. This factor may show a strong connection between *Acci* and the eastern cities of the *Baetica*.

Second, the existence of an inscription found in Guadix may provide a further clue that *Acci* had been part of *Hispania Baetica* for some time:

> *P(ublio) Octavio / Flavo / flamini / divor(um) Aug(ustorum) / provinc(iae) Baet(icae) / P(ublius) Octavius / Priscus / patri testamento / poni iussit.*[19]

The inscription found in Guadix contains a dedication to the *flamen* of *Hispania Baetica*, P. Octavius Flavus (fig. 11.2). This epigraph has been dated to

19 *CIL* II, 3395 = *ILPGranada* 72 = *CILA* Gr 4 127.

FIGURE 11.2 Epigraph of P. Octavius Flavus, *Flamen* of *Baetica*

the Flavian period, arousing the interest of some scholars since in this period the city was already fully integrated into *Hispania Citerior/Tarraconensis*.

It is possible that even during the Flavian era; Acci had strong religious links with *Hispania Baetica*. The links probably had to do with the fact that *Acci* had previously belonged to *Hispania Ulterior/Baetica*. Fluent contacts between individuals on both sides of the Sierra Nevada may well have supported the preservation of religious links. Nevertheless, the contacts between the communities of *Hispania Baetica* and *Hispania Tarraconensis* in religious matters may differ completely from the reality of commercial contacts or the transportation of goods between the provinces. The city of *Castulo* provides a similar example of such a relationship,[20] so we should not exclude that possibility that both cities preserved their religious ties with *Hispania Baetica* even after they had fully integrated into *Hispania Tarraconensis*.[21]

With the new administrative reform of Augustus between 7 and 2 BC, the colony became definitively integrated into the province of *Hispania Citerior/Tarraconensis*. Pliny mentions the *colonia Accitana Gemellensis* with *ius Italicum*, saying that it belonged to the *conventus Carthaginiensis* within *Hispania Tarraconensis*.[22] This area of *Bastetania* was probably transferred to *Hispania Citerior* as the *saltus Castulonensis*.[23]

The provincial changes have been verified in the oldest coins produced in *Acci*, which have the same features as the coins minted in the closest cities of *Ulterior/Baetica*.[24] However, the coins become like those of *Tarraconensis* during the reigns of Tiberius and Caligula. This has been interpreted as an administrative change resembling the customs for other colonies given the new provincial circumstances. One of the reasons for the administrative changes in *Bastetania* could have stemmed from the need for the emperor to control the mining areas of the southeastern part of the peninsula, which represented

20 *CIL* II, 3271 = *CILA* Ja 3, 92; Navarro 2009, op. cit., 352; M. Pastor Muñoz, 'Epigrafía y culto imperial en la Granada romana', *FlorIlib* 26 (2015), 112; D. Faoro, 'Praefectus fisci Germaniae', *ZPE* 205 (2018), 250–252.

21 Another example of this kind of religious connection between two provinces is the case of the *flaminica provinciae Baeticae* in the Lusitan city of *Norba*. See J. L. Gómez-Pantoja and J. V. Madruga, 'Flaminica Provinciae Baeticae et Norbensium', in *De Roma a las provincias: Las élites como instrumento de proyección de Roma, Juan Francisco Rodríguez Neila in honorem* (Seville 2014), ed. A. Caballos Rufino and E. Melchor Gil.

22 Plin. *NH*. 3.3; see Albertini 1932, op. cit., 34–35; R. Thouvenot, *Essai sur la province romaine de Bétique* (Paris 1940), 164.

23 Ozcáriz Gil 2009, op. cit., 324; C. González Román, '*Colonia Iulia Gemella Acci* (Guadix, Granada)', in *Colonias de César y Augusto en la Andalucía romana*, ed. J. González Fernández and J. C. Saquete Chamizo (Rome 2011), 297.

24 F. Chaves Tristán, 'Las monedas de *Acci*', *Numisma* 138–143 (1974b), 141–148.

FIGURE 11.3 The *territorium* of *Acci* in the *conventus Carthaginiensis* of *Hispania Tarraconensis*

a remarkable source of wealth.[25] The presence of a military contingent was required to protect such resources, and *Baetica*, which had already been pacified and fully integrated into the empire, could not guarantee the safety of the mining areas. Thus, the imperial province and its legions ensured the protection of the valuable commodities.[26]

*Acci* was the only city with *ius Italicum* status in the southern part of the peninsula. According to Paul's *Digesta*, in all *Hispaniae* only *Pax Iulia* and *Augusta Emerita* in *Hispania Lusitania*, and *Ilici*, *Valentia*, and *Acci* in *Hispania Tarraconensis* had this status.[27] The final provincial reorganisation of *Hispaniae* took place at the end of the third century, when Emperor Diocletian reformed the internal administration and included a new subdivision: the *diocesis*. The *diocesis Hispaniarum* was further subdivided into six provinces. The former *conventus Carthaginiensis* was transformed into *provincia Carthaginiensis*, which included the *territorium* of *Acci* (fig. 11.3). The inclusion of the *territorium* of *Acci* in the province of *Carthago Nova* required no significant changes to the administration because *Acci* had been tied to the capital already for two centuries.

## 3 The Colony

The context of the military *deductio* and the social stratigraphy of the colony has been extensively studied, but there is no consensus about the foundation of *Acci*,[28] which meant creating a garrison in an indigenous settlement.[29] The coins minted in *Acci* show some elements that have been interpreted as a record of the *deductio* of the city. Legionary eagles and double military insignias appear, along with abbreviations of the name of the colony.[30] Though much has been written about the foundation of the colony in the last forty years, the answer to the question of its founding is still unclear due to the lack of written sources.[31]

---

25 P. Corrales Aguilar, 'La provincia romana de la *Baetica*: Notas para el establecimiento de su límite oriental y su compartimentación conventual', *Baetica* 19, no. 1 (1997), 416–417.

26 Thouvenot 1940, op. cit., 164.

27 *Dig.* 50.15.8 pr.

28 F. Vittinghoff, *Römische Kolonisation und Bürgerrechtspolitik unter Caesar und Augustus* (Wiesbaden 1952), 88; A. Degrassi, 'L'amministrazione delle città', in *Scritti vari di antichità raccolti da amici e allievi nel 75° compleanno dell'autore IV* (Trieste 1971), 89; Chaves Tristán 1974, op. cit., 143–144; González Román 2011, op. cit., 310.

29 Cic. *Phil.* 2.25.62.

30 Chaves Tristán 1974, op. cit., 141–148.

31 An excellent summary on this topic can be found in C. González Román, 'La colonia *Iulia Gemella Acci* y la evolución de la Bastetania', *Dialoghi di Archeologia* 10, no. 1–2 (1992), 161–163.

The settlement, located on a hill, was an easily defensible area, making it possible to control the entire *Acci* River valley. Near San Miguel Street, archaeologists have documented remains of houses dating back to the ninth century BC, including several cabins carved into the circular rock.[32] An Iberian *oppidum* would have occupied the historical center of the city in the sixth century BC. In the old Cine Acci, the plans for a series of rectangular domestic structures with internal subdivisions and adobe walls with stone baseboards were discovered in 1996.[33] In 1997, domestic structures from the same period were discovered on Palacio Street.[34] Some large walls and domestic structures were discovered at that time as well. The most remarkable discovery was perhaps a possible *cryptoporticus* from the era of the Roman Republic.

The discovery of a Roman theater in 2008 further highlighted the importance of the Roman colony (fig. 11.4). The appearance of a series of Roman-era stalls during the construction of a parking lot led to the discovery of a very interesting theater, since, unlike most of Hispania's theaters, it contains a *porticus post scaenam*,[35] which puts the building in relationship with the theater at *Carthago Nova*, the capital of the *conventus*. The influence of *Carthago Nova* and *Acci* is clearly visible in some architectural features of the Roman theaters in both cities, which were likely designed following quite similar patterns.

The urban fabric of *Acci* is still not well understood, which makes it difficult to accurately interpret the cityscape. Dozens of isolated archaeological remains from the Roman era have been discovered throughout the center of the city in the last few decades.[36] Nonetheless, the lack of connection between these remains and the mixt of remains from Islamic, early modern and recent buildings makes it impossible to reconstruct the urban fabric of *Acci* during

32 A. M. Adroher Auroux and A. López Marcos, 'El vertedero de un metalurgo del bronce final (excavación arqueológica de urgencia en el solar de la calle San Miguel, 39 de Guadix, Granada)', *Anuario Arqueológico de Andalucía 1997*, vol. 3 (2001a), 293–298.

33 C. Pérez Bareas, R. Lizcano Prestel, P. J. Casado Millán and A. Burgos Juárez, 'Actuación arqueológica de urgencia realizada en el Cine Acci de Guadix, Granada', *Anuario arqueológico de Andalucía 1998*, vol. 3 (2001), 351–358.

34 A. M. Adroher Auroux, A. Caballero Cobos and A. López Marcos, 'Excavación arqueológica de urgencia en la calle Palacio s/n (Guadix, Granada)', *Anuario Arqueológico de Andalucía 1997*, vol. 3 (2001b), 285–292.

35 A. López Marcos, 'La "porticus post scaenam" del teatro de Guadix', in *La* "porticus post scaenam" *en la arquitectura teatral romana*, ed. S. F. Ramallo Asensio and E. Ruíz Valderas (Murcia 2018a), 101–117; A. López Marcos, F. J. García Tortosa, A. Díaz Herrero and A. Arribas, 'Inundaciones históricas en el teatro romano de Acci (Guadix, Granada) a través del registro sedimentológico', in *Geomorfología del Antropoceno. Efectos del Cambio Global sobre los procesos geomorfológicos*, ed. C. García, L. Gómez Pujol, E. Morán Tejeda and R. J. Batalla (Palma de Mallorca 2018b).

36 A. López García and A. Reyes Martínez 2018, op. cit.

FIGURE 11.4 The excavations of the Roman theatre of *Acci* in August 2021

the Roman era.[37] We have no evidence of the forum or the main street axis of the city. Some local intellectuals have tried to rebuild the Roman street network of the city based on the plan for the current city, but later archaeological excavations have always contradicted such assumptions.[38] Only an extensive campaign of geophysical surveys around the city center could offer some information about the urban development of the ancient city.

## 4 The Hinterland of *Acci*

Concerning the territory surrounding the city, the *ager*, it is very difficult to know exactly its full extent. The absence of even one of the most common elements in the organisation of the territory, such as the Roman *centuriationes*, complicates the task of knowing the full extent of the *ager Accitanus*. So far, no remains of those *centuriationes* have been located, though numerous archaeological sites are closely related to the agricultural holdings of the imperial era. Several archaeological surveys have unearthed the remains of

37 A. López García, 'La ciudad andalusí: El caso de Guadix', *Péndulo: Papeles de Bastitania* 8 (2007), 21–50.

38 Asenjo Sedano 2002, op. cit., 57–58.

settlements and small *villae* in the surrounding territory.[39] Undoubtedly, one of the elements that limited the territory of *Acci* was the *Solorius Mons* – the current Sierra Nevada mountains. Strabo described the mountainous region of the southeast as follows: "Commencing our particular description from *Calpe* [Gibraltar], there is [first] the mountain chain of *Bastetania* and the *Oretani*. This is covered with thick woods and gigantic trees and separates the seacoast from the interior. In many places it also contains gold and other mines".[40] Strabo never visited the Iberian Peninsula, but the description shows that the mountain chains of the southeast were considered a geographical continuum.

Other description of the southeastern region of *Hispania* by Strabo mentions that "at the commencement it consists of bare hills, but after traversing the Plain of *Spartarium*, falls in with the forest lying above Carthage [Cartagena], and the regions round *Malaca* [Málaga]. It is named Orospeda".[41] Though Strabo tries to convey the difficult landscape of the region, his efforts also illustrate the difficulty of describing a landscape that he never visited. The later descriptions by Pliny in *Historia Naturalis* clarify the orography of the region. Pliny the Elder described the *Solorius Mons* as the boundary between *Baetica* and *Citerior*:[42] "Tarraconensian Spain lies on one side, contiguous to the Pyrenees, running downwards along the sides of that chain, and, stretching across from the Iberian Sea to the Gallic Sea, is separated from *Baetica* and *Lusitania* by Mount *Solorius* [Sierra Nevada], the chains of the Oretani [Sierra de Cazorla and Sierra de Segura] and the *Carpetani* [Montes de Toledo and Sistema Central], and that of the Astures". Nevertheless, the description by Pliny also demonstrates a certain degree of geographical confusion. In any case, the presence of these cordilleras marked the subdivision of *Hispaniae* and limited the interaction nodes to certain points that allowed for the transportation

39 Most of the settlements discovered in the *ager* of *Acci* are from the High Empire. C. González Román lists the following sites: Cortijo del Torcuato, Cortijo de S. Roque, El Puntal, Cerro Margarito, Cortijo Álamos Negros, Cortijo del Ceque, Los Villares, Cortijo de Peñas Blancas, Cortijo de Almida, El Palomar, El Palomar II, Venta del Amparo, Cortijo del Carmen, Cortijo del Carmen II, and Cortijo de las Mesillas. See González Román 2011, op. cit. Remains of several *villae* have been discovered in the Fardes Valley. See A. F. Buendía Moreno and F. E. Villada Paredes, 'Prospección arqueológica de superficie realizada en las cuencas de los ríos Fardes y Aguas Blancas (Granada)', *Anuario Arqueológico de Andalucía 1987*, vol. 2 (1990), 118–129; C. González Román, A. M. Adroher Auroux, and A. López Marcos, 'Prospecciones en la zona norte del Río Fardes y Río Guadahortuna, (Granada)', *Anuario Arqueológico de Andalucía* 2 1992 (1995), 145–152.

40 Strab. *Geogr.* 3.4.2 (translation by H. C. Hamilton and W. Falconer).

41 Strab. *Geogr.* 3.4.10 (translation by H. C. Hamilton and W. Falconer).

42 Plin. *NH*. 3.2 (translation by J. Bostock and H. T. Riley).

of goods and made safe commercial and extractive activities. This is the case with *ager Accitanus*, a *territorium* shaped by a less rugged landscape, which made feasible the transportation of goods and settlement of populations in an area surrounded by rich mineral resources.

The following paragraphs explain the complex boundaries of *ager Accitanus*. One of the biggest difficulties has to do with defining the northwestern boundary of *ager Accitanus*. In a place called Cortijo de Periate, 45 km west of *Acci* (fig. 11.5), an epigraph was discovered dating back to the 2nd century AD:

> *L(ucio) Aemi[lio] / Propinq[uo] / Accitano vete[ri] / ex d(ecreto) ord[in(is)] / Accit(anorum) vet[er(um)] / L(ucius) Aemilius A[- - -]/nus pater / h(onore) a(ccepto) i(mpensa) r(emissa) p(onendum?) [c(uravit?)].*[43]

The epigraph honors L. Aemilius Propinquus, considered *Accitanus Vetus*, while the decurions who decreed the erection of such a monument are considered part of an *Ordo Accitanorum Veterum*. A. Stylow[44] has proposed the existence of another *municipium* called *Acci Vetus* in the area surrounding the current town of Iznalloz. It is difficult to recognize the existence of a previous settlement also called *Acci* existing only approximately 40 kilometers from the colony of *Acci*. No further evidence of such a toponym – *Acci Vetus* – exists in the written sources. Some archaeological remains from the Roman era have been found in Cortijo de Periate, but they are far from being considered an urban settlement. So, it is possible they are from a *mansio* or agricultural *villa* belonging to some important character from the colony of *Acci* who settled in that part of the *ager* after exercising his magistracy in the city. Considering that point, we could delimit the northwestern boundary of the *territorium* of *Acci* along the natural corridor of the Montes Orientales following the "wall" of Sierra Harana until the Cubillas River.[45]

---

43 *CILA* Gr 4 107 = *AE* 2000, 782 = *HEp* 10, 2000, 321.

44 A. U. Stylow, 'Die *Accitani veteres* und die Kolonie *Iulia Gemella Acci*. Zum Problem von *veteres*, Alt-Stadt und Kolonie in der *Hispania Ulterior*', *Chiron* 30, 775–806; M. Pastor Muñoz, 'Nueva inscripción latina de Piñar (Granada)', *HAnt* 24 (2000), 155–164; C. González Román, '*Acci*, la *colonia* y sus *cives*', in *Andalucía romana y visigoda. Ordenación y vertebración del territorio*, ed. J. González Fernández and P. Pavón Torrejón (Rome 2009), 229–252; C. González Román, 'Homogeneidad y diversidad en las colonias romanas: reflexiones desde Acci', in Debita verba. *Estudios en homenaje al profesor Julio Mangas Manjarrés*, ed. R. M. Cid and E. B. Fernández (Madrid 2013), 31–51; González Román 2011, op. cit., 297.

45 M. Orfila Pons, M. A. Castillo Rueda and P. J. Casado Millán, 'Estudio preliminar de los elementos constructivos hidráulicos de época romana del río Cubillas (Tramo Deifontes-Albolote, Granada)', *AAC* 7 (1996), 83–114.

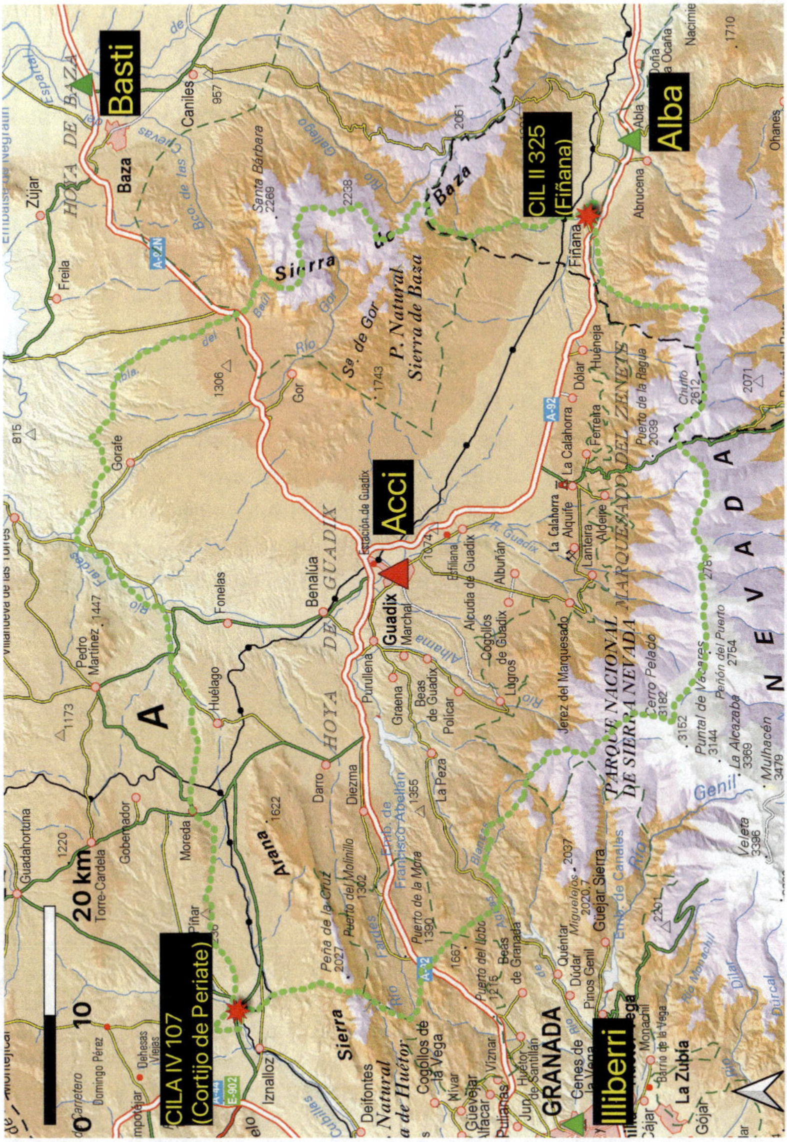


FIGURE 11.5 The natural borders of the *territorium* of *Acci*, the main Roman centres of the region (in green), and the location of the farthest epigraphic elements that mention the colony (in red)

The northern boundary of this immense *territorium* may have extended from the area of Cortijo de Periate in the northwest to the northeast following the mountains south of Piñar or the Piñar River through the current towns of Moreda and Laborcillas. Then, it followed the gorge of Huélago until encountering the Fardes River in the surroundings of Fonelas. The margin of the Fardes River was followed until encountering the gorge at Gorafe near the baths of Alicún de las Torres. The desert of Gorafe constituted the firmest and longest boundary to the north of *Acci*. The difficulty of the landscape and aridity made cultivation impossible in this area. Perhaps the gorge at Baúl delimited the boundary between the *territoria* of *Acci* and *Basti*. A major road that was part of the southern branch of the *Via Augusta* and traversed the current municipality of Gor following the mountainsides of Sierra de Gor and Sierra de Baza connected the two cities.[46] The sierras constituted the natural boundary to the southeast. The only pass between Sierra de Baza and the Sierra Nevada mountains was the wide corridor of Fiñana,[47] which connected the colony of *Acci* and the *municipium* of *Alba*.[48] Perhaps the spring of El Cortal on the mountainside of the Sierra de Baza and the River Izfalada/Huéneja established the limit between the *municipia*. Thirty-seven kilometers away from *Acci* to the southeast, archaeologists have discovered remains that suggest that the *ager Accitanus* extended to the natural corridor of Fiñana (fig. 11.5). Some scholars[49] have suggested that a lost inscription found in Fiñana – between *Acci* and

46 L. Sánchez Quirante and L. Fernández Sanjuan, 'Prospección arqueológica superficial de la Sierra de Baza y Altiplano de Baza-Caniles', *Anuario Arqueológico de Andalucía 1987*, vol. 2 (1990), 48–50; L. Sánchez Quirante, 'Prospección arqueológica superficial del sector occidental de la Sierra de Baza, Campaña de 1990', *Anuario arqueológico de Andalucía 1990*, vol. 2 (1992a), 124–127; L. Sánchez Quirante, 'Investigación Arqueológica en la Sierra de Baza-Gor', in *Investigaciones arqueológicas en Andalucía: 1985–1992. Proyectos*, ed. J. M. Campos Carrasco and F. Nocete Calvo (1992b), 329–340.

47 F. Buzón Calderón *et al.*, 'Informe de las prospecciones arqueológicas superficiales en el pasillo de Fiñana (Almería). Campaña de 1988', *Anuario Arqueológico de Andalucía 1988*, vol. 2 (1990), 9–13; N. López Godoy, A. Escobar Sánchez, B. Risueño Olarte and C. Ruiz González, 'Prospección en el pasillo de Fiñana (Almería)', *Anuario Arqueológico de Andalucía 1987*, vol. 2 (1990), 73–76; A. López Marcos and A. M. Adroher Auroux, 'Un asentamiento rural romano en las estribaciones septentrionales de Sierra Nevada. Cortijo Cecilio (Fiñana, Almería)', in *1ª Conferencia Internacional de Sierra Nevada. Conservación y desarrollo sostenible*, ed. J. Chacón and J. L. Rosúa (Granada 1996), 11–28.

48 A. M. Adroher Auroux, 'Arqueología en torno al territorio romano de Abla (Almería)', in *El municipio romano de* Alba *(Abla, Almería). Administración, sociedad y economía*, ed. A. J. Ortíz Ocaña (Almería 2016), 39–78.

49 Santero 1972, op. cit., 215; M. H. Gallego Franco, 'La mujer hispanorromana y la actividad económica: las profesiones', *Minerva* 7 (1993), Apéndice epigráfico, 123, n. 1.

*Alba* – by J. Gruter and others[50] could give a clue about the foundation of the colony and the extent of its hinterland to the east:

> *C(aiae) · Planciae · Ro(manae?) · ingen/ti praedio donatae / in agro Accitano ob / oper(am) · bene in rem · p(ublicam) / navatam C(aius) · Longin(us) · con(sularis) · of(fert) · sol(us).*[51]

The inscription mentions the donation of a *praedium* in the *territorium* of *Acci* to C. Plancia during the consulate of a certain C. Longin(us). Various scholars have questioned the originality of this text.[52] The fact that the inscription is so faded in parts makes it impossible to know exactly the content of the original text and verify its originality. The possible mention of the title of consulate (*CON*) for C. Longinus does not make it any easier to interpret. We know few members of the *gens Cassia* who were appointed to the consulate in the 1st century BC. One of them was C. Cassius Longinus, who served as consul in 73 BC. However, no references exist about the presence of this consul in *Hispania*. A L. Cassius Longinus was suffect consul[53] in AD 11, and his son, also named L. Cassius Longinus,[54] was suffect consul in AD 30. The son married Drusilla, the sister of Caligula. None of them served directly in *Hispania*. Another suffect consul in AD 30 named C. Cassius Longinus also served as a proconsul of *Asia*[55] in AD 40–41 and as a governor of Syria from AD 41 to 49; he is mentioned in several sources. We only have further news, though, of his forced exile to *Sardinia* in AD 65 by Nero, and his return to Rome at the time of Vespasian.[56] No evidence exists of his presence in *Hispania*.

---

50 J. Gruter, *Inscriptiones antiquae totius orbis romani* (Amsterdam 1602), 452, n. 4; J. Strada, *In tabulis xilographicis adiectis ad ... praeterea addidimus omnes antiquitates quae passim in tota Hispania* (Frankfurt 1575), 162, n. 13; P. Suárez, *Historia del Obispado de Guadix y Baza* (Guadix 1696), 9.

51 *CIL* II, 325.

52 R. Lázaro Pérez, 'Epigrafía del Municipio Romano de *Alba Bastetanorum* (Abla-Almería)', in *El municipio romano de* Alba *(Alba, Almería), administración, sociedad y economía*, ed. A. J. Ortíz Ocaña (Almería 2016), 149. One of the most questionable elements of the text is the mention of the cognomen *Ro(manae)*, if that is meant as a continuation. *Romanus* only appears in Late Antique Christian inscriptions. España Chamorro mentions that the epigraph is not counterfeit, but perhaps it was incorrectly transcribed. See S. España Chamorro, Unde incipit Baetica. *Los límites de la Baetica y su integración territorial* (*s. I–III*) (Rome 2021), 225.

53 *Fasti Capitolini*: *InscrIt* XIII/1, 1ab.

54 *PIR*[2] C 501.

55 Suet. *Cal.* 57; Dio, 59.29.3.

56 V. Rudich, *Political Dissidence under Nero: The Price of Dissimulation* (London 2014), 139.

The inscription may then refer to Q. Cassius Longinus, the brother or cousin of the C. Cassius Longinus who conspired against Julius Caesar in 44 BC. This Quintus was a quaestor of Pompey in *Hispania Ulterior*[57] in 52 BC, and afterwards governor of the same province in 48 BC and supporter of Caesar during the civil war.[58] His cruelty towards the indigenous population in *Hispania* ended with a revolt against him.[59] Traditionally, the inscription at this spot has been interpreted as evidence of the route taken by Q. Cassius Longinus through the landscape of *Acci* on his way to *Corduba* with two legions. Some scholars[60] have suggested that perhaps this trip occurred at the time of the military *deductio* for the colony of *Acci*. But this is not the only member of the *gens Cassia* with a similar name who could be associated with the person mentioned in the inscription. Another candidate may be the *Longinus* mentioned in the inscription of Fiñana is Q. Cassius, legate of Q. Cassius Longinus in *Hispania* in 48 BC and praetor in 44 BC.[61] In any case, scholars have generally interpreted this inscription as a sign of the impact of the Romans on the territory of *Acci* before the death of Caesar.

There are several reasons for questioning the interpretation of this inscription as indicating a high level of Romanisation for the *ager Accitanus* in the mid-1st century BC, especially in the context of a military conflict. Some elements of the text could indicate that the epigraph should not be attributed to the late Republican period at all, but rather to an advanced stage of the imperial era. However, the imprecision of the early modern scholars who copied the text makes an accurate dating and interpretation of the text impossible. Longinus is a name that appears in several parts of the Roman dominions from the late Republican period to that of the late empire. Not all the Longinus/Longinius referred to in the literature and epigraphy belong to the *gens Cassia*. One good example is Cn. Pompeius Longinus, a suffect consul in AD 90. The presence of this Longinus is attested to in Judaea, *Moesia*, and *Pannonia*, but E. Dąbrowa[62] has proposed that his place of origin could have been *Hispania*. Other known cases are M. Longinius Longus, *praefectus cohortis* in AD 131;[63] C. Longius Priscus, a Roman soldier in Egypt during the reign of

57 Cic. *Att.* 6.6.4; *Fam.* 2.15.4; *Bell. Alex.* 48.1, 50.1; D.C. 41.24.2.

58 L. Amela Valverde, 'Q. Casio Longino, Cuestor de la Ulterior', *Minerva* 16 (2002–2003), 123–130.

59 D.C. 41.15.24, 42.15.16, 43.29; Liv., *Epit.* 111; App. *Civ.* 2.33.43; *Bell. Alex.*, 48–64.

60 Santero 1972, op. cit., 215.

61 *Bell. Alex.* 52.3, 57.1–4; Cic. *Phil.* 3.26.

62 E. Dąbrowa, Legio X Fretensis. *A Prosopographical Study of its Officers (I–III C. A.D.)* (Stuttgart 1993), 33.

63 *P. Berol.* 7124. *CIL* XVI, 104. See *PME* L 28.

Trajan;[64] C. Longinus Aquila and C. Longinus Apollinarius, both veterans in AD 189;[65] and C. Longinus Castor, a veteran of the fleet of *Misenum* in AD 176.[66] In conclusion, the name Longinus was a common name during the Roman imperial era, meaning that the C. Longin(us) mentioned in the lost inscription may even have been an unknown consular official of *Hispania Citerior* who donated a *praedium* to C. Plancia in the *ager Accitanus*. My hypothesis is that the *territorium* of *Acci* ended at the ancient *municipium* of *Alba* in the current area of Fiñana. There is no reason to doubt the originality of that inscription found in a minor settlement in the early modern era.

The natural frontier of the *ager Accitanus* to the south, and equally, the borderline between the Roman provinces of *Hispania Baetica* and *Hispania Tarraconensis*, was the Sierra Nevada Mountains – the *Solorius Mons* mentioned by Pliny the Elder. The land of *Acci* progressed to the southwest through the current Marquesado del Cenete in Andalusia, encountering a secondary passageway that connected *Acci* with the *municipium* of *Illiberris* – contemporary Granada – in the area surrounding the Aguas Blancas River near Quéntar. In that location, some archaeological remains from Roman times have been discovered.[67] The boundary then crossed the Sierra de Huétor and continued until the source of the River Fardes. Perhaps the boundary crossed Sierra Harana at some point between Peña de la Cruz and Cerro de Orduña and progressed through the northern side of the Sierra Nevada mountains before encountering the gorge at Periate and the Piñar River.

## 5 A Node of Roads

During Roman times, land routes were much more abundant in *Hispania Baetica* than in the other provinces of *Hispania*. A major road known as the *Via Augusta* connected *Hispania Tarraconensis* and *Hispania Baetica*, running along the Mediterranean coast from the capital *Tarraco* to the main cities of *Baetica*: *Corduba*, *Gades*, *Hispalis* and *Astigi* (fig. 11.6). The *Via Augusta* had its origin in the oldest road from the Iberian era, known as *Via Heraklea*, which linked the Greek colonies of the northeast with *Turdetania* in the southwest. We

64 *P.Oxy.* VII, 1022. See also *CIL* X, 8131 = *CLE* 428 from *Stabia* (EDR 122237) and *AE* 1980, 486 = EDR 077896 from *Classe* (possible Egyptian origins); see also *FIRA* III, 25 = *AE* 1919, 23 = *AE* 1921, 35 and *CIL* VI, 21503: are *Longinii/ae*, whilst the soldier mentioned in *P.Oxy.* VII, 1022 is *C. Longius Priscus*.

65 R. Alston, *Soldier and Society in Roman Egypt. A Social History* (London 1998), 125.

66 J. G. Keegan, 'The Will of *Caius Longinus Castor*', *BASP* 31, No. 3/4 (1994), 101–107.

67 Buendía Moreno and Villada Paredes 1990, op. cit., 118–129.

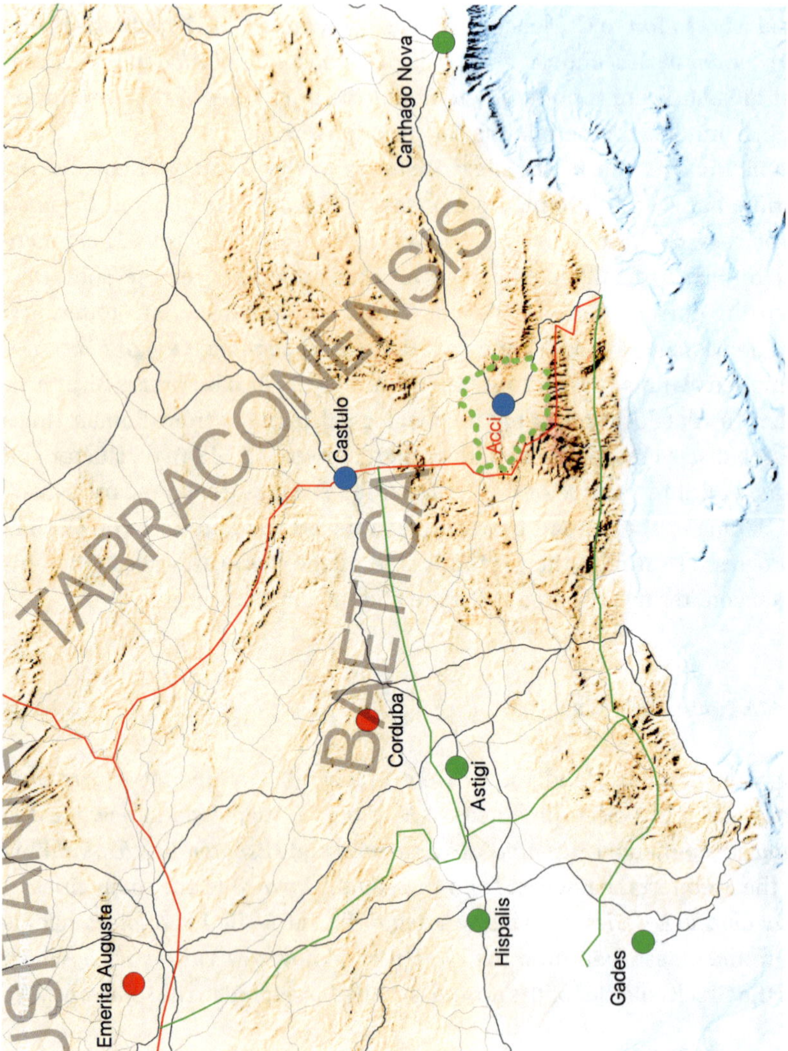


FIGURE 11.6 The road network of the region (in black), the border between the provinces (in red), and the *conventus* (in green)

know of the existence of the *Via Heraklea* thanks to the writer Polybius.[68] He visited the Iberian Peninsula around 133 BC and described the layout of a road that led to the Strait of Gibraltar, known as the Columns of Hercules. However, the description is not completely clear as to whether the route ran throughout southeastern *Hispania*.[69] Written sources like the Itinerary of Antonine mention a branch of the road[70] that ran through the southeastern part of *Hispania* and connected the main centre of the *conventus Carthaginiensis* with *Acci* before continuing to the mines of *Castulo*.

The cities of *Basti* (Baza), *Eliocroca* (Lorca), and finally *Carthago Nova* – or *Carthago Spartaria*, depending on the historical period – existed to the east of *Acci*. Most of the route has been identified thanks to the discovery of several milestones between *Carthago Nova* and *Basti*.[71] Nevertheless, the section between *Basti* and *Acci* was completely unknown until recently because of a lack of archaeological and epigraphical sources. Likewise, recently some sectors of this road have been located between Guadix and the town of Gor, halfway to Baza.[72] Several land and aerial surveys have made it possible to reconstruct the track between these two points along the *Via Augusta*. The complex infrastructures required of a paved road (fig. 11.7) and supporting constructions were discovered around Peñas Negras (Hernán Valle, Guadix) and Cuesta de Guadix (Gor). This road followed the foothills of Sierra de Gor and then entered Sierra de Baza at the *territorium* of *Basti* before passing through the municipality of El Baúl. Perhaps, this point formed the northeastern boundary of the *ager Accitanus*.

The Itinerary of Antonine mentions two routes between the cities of *Acci* and *Castulo* (fig. 11.8). The western route overlapped with a road going to *Illiberris*. It reached the area of the Montes Orientales after traversing the slopes of Sierra Harana, but at a certain point, the road turned north. This route connected with *Hispania Baetica* by way of *Castulo* via a road that passed through

68 Pol. 3.39.6.

69 R. C. Knapp, '*La "Via Heraclea"* en Occidente: Mito, arqueología, propaganda, historia', *Emerita* 54 (1986), 103–122.

70 *Itin. Anton.* 402.1, 404.6.

71 Milestones have been discovered in Mazarrón (*CIL* II, 4944 = *CIL* XVII/1, 68), Totana (*CIL* II, 4936 = *CIL* XVII/1, 70), La Tova (*CIL* XVII/1, 75), El Hinojar and La Hoya (*CIL* XVII/1, 72), Lorca (*CIL* II, 4937 = *CIL* XVII/1, 74), La Fuensanta and El Hornillo (*CIL* XVII/1, 73), Los Alamicos (*CIL* II, 4939 = *CIL* XVII/1, 77), Vélez Rubio, Chirivel (*CIL* II, 4938 = *CIL* XVII/1, 78; *CIL* II, 4940 = *CIL* XVII/1, 81; *CIL* II, 4942 = *CIL* XVII/1, 80), Cullar (*CIL* II, 4941 = *CIL* XVII/1, 83), and Guadix (*CIL* II, 4943 = *CIL* XVII/1, 85).

72 Caballero Cobos 2014, op. cit., 244; A. López García, 'The Discovery of a Roman Road between *Carthago Nova* (Cartagena) and *Iulia Gemella Acci* (Guadix), Spain', in *The Archaeologies of Roads*, ed. T. Kalayci (Grand Forks 2023), 146–168.

FIGURE 11.7 Remains of the Roman road of Peñas Negras (Hernán Valle, Guadix)

the current towns of La Guardia, La Cerradura, Cerro Maquiz, Mengíbar, Magdalena de Castro, and finally, the mining area of *Castulo*. This road was the final stretch of a track that began in Narbonne and extended along the entire Hispanic coast of the Levant. Despite the historiographic problems that the Antonine Itinerary poses for the enclaves of *Acatucci* and *Viniolis*, the cities of *Castulo*, *Mentesa Bastia* (La Guardia), and *Acci* have been well documented from an archeological standpoint. Ten milestones have been preserved along this road between *Acci* and *Castulo*. However, none of the section between *Acci* and La Cerradura remains, which makes it impossible to know the exact route.

The eastern itinerary between *Acci* and *Castulo* possibly shared the initial part of the route with a road that led to *Illiberris*. The exact route along this road is not very clear due to a lack of archaeological remains. We know that it had to have passed through several *mansiones*, such as *Fraxinum* or *Salaria*, mentioned in the Itinerary of Antonine, but the hypotheses proposed for the toponyms are not to this point satisfactory.[73] Likely, this route followed the rivers to the northeast of *Acci*, running along the Fardes River and linking up with the Guadiana Menor River. Then, the path would have run through the *Baetis* valley and reached *Castulo* via a southeastern route. An alternative hypothesis is that the path shared a route through the foothills of Sierra Harana before

73 P. Sillières, *Les voies de communication de l'Hispanie méridionale* (Paris 1990), 391–393; España Chamorro 2021, op. cit., 229.

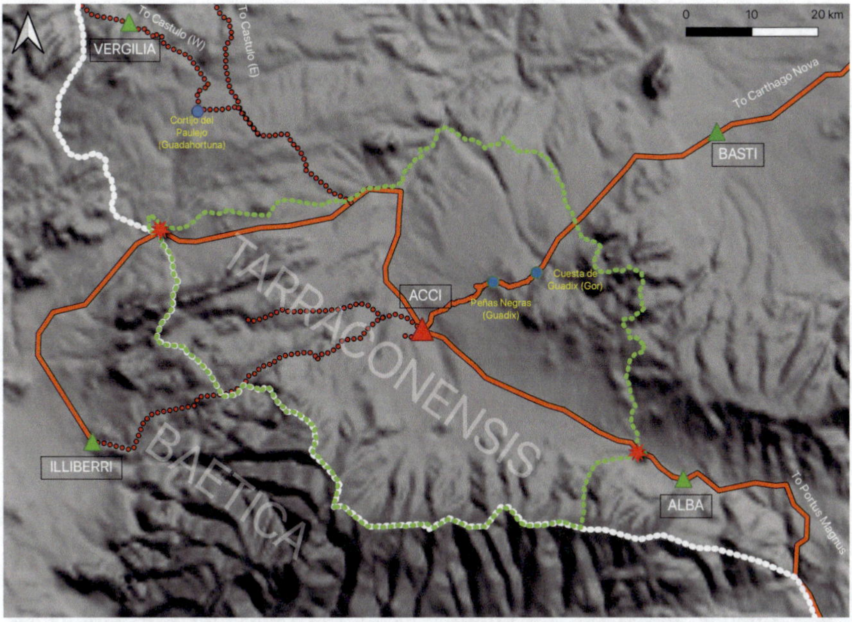


FIGURE 11.8 Main roads around *Acci* (in orange), possible secondary roads (in red dotted), boundary between provinces (in white dotted), and remains of ancient roads (blue dots)

detouring to the north through the current municipalities of Torre-Cardela and Guadarhortuna to Sierra Mágina. The path may have bordered Sierra Mágina on the eastern side and followed a straight route to Mengíbar. Finally, by following the Guadalimar River it would have been possible to reach *Castulo*.

To the west of *Acci* was the *municipium* of *Illiberris*, in present-day Granada, which was accessed mainly via a corridor through the Sierra Harana because the natural border of the Sierra Nevada mountains made such a journey to the city quite lengthy. It would have been possible to reach the central area of *Hispania Baetica* by taking such a route. A minor road crossed the Sierra Nevada mountains following a route that entered the Sierra de Huétor through the current towns of Graena and La Peza and continued until the Aguas Blancas River. Then, the road would have continued to the southwest to *Illiberris*. The difficulty of the terrain in this mountainous area possibly made the path inconvenient. Surely, it would have been easier to transport goods by using the corridor through the Sierra Harana to the Cubillas River.

The road that connected *Acci* with the southeast coast crossed through the Fiñana corridor towards *Urci* and the *Portus Magnus*, a port probably located in the current city of Almería. That connection would have taken advantage of the easy terrain between the eastern slopes of the Sierra Nevada mountains and the Sierra de Baza and Sierra de los Filabres. The route would have run through the municipalities of Fiñana, Abrucena, and *Alba* (Abla) towards the Andarax Valley and on to the *municipium* of *Urci*, which marked the border between *Hispania Baetica* and *Hispania Tarraconensis*.

## 6 Conclusion

The blurred boundaries between the provinces of *Baetica* and *Tarraconensis*, and the limits of the *territorium* of *Acci*, are clearly articulated through several orographic, economic, and social elements that distinguish this area from the surrounding *territoria*. Bastetan populations, included those mostly in *Baetica* at the end of the Republican period and the early years of the reign of Octavian, were likely an important element in such an unambiguous region comprising two very different types of landscapes. The mountainous orography of the southeastern part of *Hispania* favored the homogeneous Bastetan populations settled on the northern side of the *Mons Solorius* and the decision to reunite these peoples based on the boundaries of the *Conventus Carthaginiensis*. Economic resources were possibly the decisive element that led the Romans to incorporate this area into *Hispania Tarraconensis*. The mining area of *Castulo* was integrated within *Hispania Tarraconensis* due to a need to pacify local populations after having briefly been part of *Hispania Baetica* (a province that lacked the resources to exert military control). The *territorium* of *Acci*, a node of terrestrial communications surrounded by other mining resources, was similarly integrated into a province with military contingents. Only in this way could Rome oversee its resources and make possible the safe transport of goods. The importance of the colony of *Acci* is not only visible in the written sources, which mention it as the only city in the southeastern part of *Hispania* with *ius Italicum*, but also is visible in the massive area included in its *territorium*. This theory can be supported thanks to the reinterpretation of the lost epigraph of Fiñana as a high or late imperial donation of land in the *ager Accitanus* – which was considered false or republican. It can be also sustained thanks to the epigraph of Cortijo de Periate, which is evidence of the influence of *Acci* along the corridor or Sierra Harana – previously interpreted as the site of an unknown settlement called *Acci Vetus*. *Acci* was undoubtedly one of the most important settlements in southeastern *Hispania* during the high imperial era, only surpassed by the capital of the *conventus*. The reality on the other side of the border was completely different, and the cities of *Hispania Baetica* experienced the wealthier rhythms of agricultural production.

# General Bibliography


Abad, L. 'Estratigrafía de la Casa de las Columnas', in *Itálica (Santiponce, Sevilla)*, ed. P. León (Madrid 1982), 135–202.

Abascal Palazón, J. M. 'La fecha de la promoción colonial de *Carthago Nova* y sus repercusiones edilicias', *Mastia* 1 (2002), 21–44.

Abascal Palazón, J. M., Alföldy, G. and Cebrián Fernández, R. *Segobriga V. Inscripciones romanas 1986–2010* (Madrid 2011).

Abascal Palazón, J. M. 'El hábito epigráfico en Hispania entre Trajano y Adriano', in *De Trajano a Adriano*. Roma matura, Roma mutans, ed. A. Caballos Rufino (Seville 2019), 275–296.

Adroher Auroux, A. M. and López Marcos, A. 'El vertedero de un metalurgo del bronce final (excavación arqueológica de urgencia en el solar de la calle San Miguel, 39 de Guadix, Granada)', *Anuario Arqueológico de Andalucía 1997*, vol. 3 (2001a), 293–298.

Adroher Auroux, A. M., Caballero Cobos, A. and López Marcos, A. 'Excavación arqueológica de urgencia en la calle Palacio s/n (Guadix, Granada)', *Anuario Arqueológico de Andalucía 1997*, vol. 3 (2001b), 285–292.

Adroher Auroux, A. M., López Marcos, A. and Pachón, J. A. *Granada arqueológica. La cultura ibérica* (Granada 2002).

Adroher Auroux, A. M. 'Fortificaciones republicanas entre la Citerior y la Ulterior: en las tierras de Bastetania', in *Las Guerras Civiles romanas en Hispania. Una revisión histórica desde la Contestania*, ed. F. Sala and J. Moratalla (Alicante 2014), 169–182.

Adroher Auroux, A. M. 'Arqueología en torno al territorio romano de Abla (Almería)', in *El municipio romano de* Alba *(Abla, Almería). Administración, sociedad y economía*, ed. A. J. Ortíz Ocaña (Almería 2016), 39–78.

Asenjo Sedano, C. *De* Acci *a Guadix: aproximación a la protohistoria de una ciudad del sudeste peninsular hispánico, inserta en un fenómeno de mutación de topónimo: una hipótesis de reconstrucción urbana* (Granada 2002).

Alarcón Hernández, C. 'Una aproximación al culto imperial en Hispania: avances interpretativos', *Revista de Historiografía* 28 (2018), 183–212.

Albertini, E. 'La route frontière de Maurétanie Césarienne entre Boghar et Lalla-Maghnia', *Bulletin de la société de géographie et d'archéologie d'Oran* (1928), 33–48.

Albertini, E. 'Le réseau routier de la Numidie méridionale', *CRAI* 75, no. 4 (1931a), 363–370.

Albertini, E. 'Inscriptions d'El Kantara et de la région', *Revue africaine* 72 (1931b), 193–261.

Albertini, E. *Les divisions administratives de l'Espagne romaine* (Paris, 1932).

Alföldy, G. 'Notes sur la relation entre le droit de cité et la nomenclature dans l'Empire romain', *Latomus* 25 (1966), 37–57.

Alföldy, G. Fasti Hispanienses. *Senatorische Reichsbeamte und Offiziere in den spanischen Provinzen des römischen Reiches von Augustus bis Diokletian* (Wiesbaden 1969).

Alföldy, G. 'Bildprogramme in den römischen Städten des *Conventus Tarraconensis* – Das Zeugnis der Statuenpostamente', *Revista de la Universidad Complutense de Madrid* (1972), 177–276.

Alföldy, G. *Die römischen Inschriften von Tarraco* (Berlin 1975).

Alföldy, G. *Konsulat und Senatorenstand unter den Antoninen. Prosopographische Untersuchungen zur Senatorischen Führungsschicht* (Bonn 1977).

Alföldy, G. '*Epigraphica Hispanica* VIII. Eine kaiserliche Widmung in der Stadt *Tucci*', *ZPE* 59 (1985), 189–199.

Alföldy, G. 'Augusto e le iscrizioni: tradizione ed innovazione. La nascita dell'epigrafia imperiale', *Scienze dell'Antichità* 5 (1991a), 573–600.

Alföldy, G. *Tarraco* (Tarragona 1991b).

Alföldy, G. *Studi sull'epigrafia augustea e tiberiana di Roma* (Rome 1992).

Alföldy, G. 'Hispania bajo los Flavios y los Antoninos: consideraciones históricas sobre una época', in *De les estructures indígenas a l'organització provincial romana de la Hispania Citerior*, ed. M. Mayer, J. M. Nolla, and J. Pardo (Girona 1998), 11–32.

Alföldy, G. 'El Imperio romano durante los siglos II y III: continuidad y transformaciones', in *Tarraco christiana civitas*, ed. J. M. Macias, A. Muñoz Melgar (Tarragona 2013), 13–30.

Alföldy, G. 'Augustus und die Inschriften: Tradition und Innovation. Die Geburt der imperialen Epigraphik', in *Die epigraphische Kultur der Römer*, ed. A. Chaniotis and C. Witschel (Stuttgart 2018), 73–102.

Alföldy, G. *Nueva historia social de Roma* (Seville 2021).

Alonso, M. A. *Los médicos en las inscripciones latinas de Italia* (*siglos II a.C.–III d.C.*). *Aspectos sociales y profesionales* (Santander 2018).

Alquier, P. 'Épigraphie latine & libyque du département de Constantine (1926–1930)', *Recueil des notices et mémoires de la société archéologique, historique et géographique du département de Constantine* 59 (1928–1929), 361–400.

Alston, R. *Soldier and Society in Roman Egypt. A Social History* (London 1998).

Alvar, J. 'La sociedad y el culto a Isis en la Bética', in *La sociedad de la Bética. Contribuciones para su estudio*, ed. C. González Román (Granada 1994), 9–28.

Álvarez Melero, A. *Prosopographie de la parentèle féminine des chevaliers romains* (Seville 2021).

Amela Valverde, L. 'El *nomen Pompeius* en *Hispania*: algunos aspectos críticos', *Emerita* 69, no. 2 (2001), 241–262.

Amela Valverde, L. 'Las concesiones de ciudadanía romana: Pompeyo Magno e Hispania', *MHA* 21–22 (2000–2001), 47–107.

Amela Valverde, L. 'Q. Casio Longino, Cuestor de la Ulterior', *Minerva* 16 (2002–2003), 123–130.

Amores, F. and Becerra Fernández, D. '*Marmora* de la Casa Demetrio de los Ríos de Itálica (Santiponce, Sevilla)', in Tituli-Imagines-Marmora. *Materia y prestigio en mármol. Homenaje a Isabel Rodà de Llanza,* ed. A. Gutiérrez García-Moreno and D. Gorostidi Pi (Madrid 2022), 497–508.

Andermahr, A. M. Totus in praediis. *Senatorischer Grundbesitz in Italien in der Frühen und Hohen Kaiserzeit* (Bonn 1998).

Ando, C. *Imperial Ideology and Provincial Loyalty in the Roman Empire* (Berkeley–Los Angeles 2000).

Ando, C. 'Law and the Landscape of Empire', in *Figures d'empire, fragments de mémoire. Pouvoirs et identités dans le monde romain impérial (IIe s. av. n. è.–VIe s. de. n. è.)*, ed. S. Benoist; A. Daguet-Gagey and C. Hoët-van Cauwenberghe (Lille 2011), 25–47.

Ando, C. 'Colonialism, Colonization: Roman Perspectives', in *The Oxford Handbook of Literatures of the Roman Empire,* ed. D. L. Selden and P. Vasunia (Oxford 2015), 27–34.

Ando, C. 'Legal Pluralism in Practice', in *The Oxford Handbook of Roman Law and Society*, ed. P. J. du Plessis, C. Ando and K. Tuori (Oxford 2016), 283–296.

Ando, C. 'Self, Society, Individual, and Person in Roman Law', in *Self, Self-Fashioning, and Individuality in Late Antiquity. New Perspectives*, ed. M. R. Niehoff and J. Levinson (Tübingen 2019), 375–392.

Ando, C. 'Public Law in Roman North Africa', in *Law in the Roman Provinces*, ed. K. Czajkowski, B. Eckhardt and M. Strothmann (Oxford 2020), 346–357.

Ando, C. 'Local Citizenship and Civic Participation in the Western Provinces of the Roman Empire', in *Civic Identity and Civic Participation in Late Antiquity and the Early Middle Ages*, ed. C. Brélaz and E. Rose (Turnhout 2021), 39–64.

Andreu Pintado, J. Edictum, municipium *y* lex: *Hispania en época flavia (69–96 d.C.)* (Oxford 2004).

Andreu Pintado, J. and Blanco, A. (eds.), *Signs of Weakness and Crisis in the Western Cities of the Roman Empire (c. II–III AD)* (Stuttgart 2019).

Andreu Pintado, J. 'From *Splendidissima Ciuitas* to *Oppidum Labens*: on the Causes of the Financial Problems and Material Ruin of Roman Provincial Cities at the End of the High-Empire', in *From* Splendidissima Ciuitas *to* Oppidum Labens*: Financial Problems and Material Ruin in Roman Provincial Cities at the End of the High-Empire. The Hispanic Provinces. Archaeology and Economy in the Ancient World. Proceedings of the 19th International Congress of Classical Archaeology*, ed. J. Andreu (Heidelberg 2020), 7–16.

Antela-Bernárdez, B. and Ñaco del Hoyo, T. (eds.), *Transforming Historical Landscapes in the Ancient Empires. Area of Research in Studies from Antiquity Universitat Autònoma de Barcelona Proceedings of the First Workshop – December 16–19th 2007* (Oxford 2009).

Arce, J. 'Inestabilidad política en Hispania durante el siglo II d.C.', *AEA* 54 (1981), 101–116.

Arce, J. 'Epigrafía de la Hispania tardorromana de Diocleciano a Teodosio: problemas de historia y de cultura', in *La terza età dell'epigrafia*, ed. A. Donati (Faenza 1988), 211–227.

Arias, L. *Hispania en el siglo II d.C. Circulación y perduración de la moneda* (Oxford 2012), 203–212.

Arteaga, O., Barragán, D., Roos, A. M. and Schulz, H. D. 'El proyecto geoarqueológico "puerto de Itálica"', *Revista Atlántica-Mediterránea* 18 (2016), 75–109.

Atkins, J. W. *Cicero on Politics and the Limits of Reason. The Republic and Laws* (Cambridge 2013).

Atkinson, J. 'Valerius Maximus on *Coriolanus*', *AClass* 60 (2017), 1–21.

Aubert, J.-J. and Sirks, B. (eds.) Speculum Iuris. *Roman Law as a Reflection of Social and Economic Life in Antiquity* (Ann Arbor 2002).

Badian, E. *Foreign* Clientelae (*264–70 B.C.*) (Oxford 1958).

Bailón García, M. El papel social y religioso de la mujer romana. *Fortuna Muliebris* como forma de integración en los cultos oficiales, *Habis* 43 (2012), 101–118.

Baldassare, I. 'La nécropole dell'Isola Sacra', in Ostia, *port et porte de la Rome antique*, ed. J. P. Descœudres (Genoa 2001), 385–390.

Baldassare, I. 'La necropoli dell'Isola Sacra', in *Espacios y usos funerarios en el Occidente* Romano, ed. D. Vaquerizo (Cordoba 2002), 11–26.

Baldassarre, I. Bragantini, I., Dolciotti, A. M., Morselli, C. and Taglietti, F. 'Necropoli dell'Isola Sacra. Le ricerche 1968–89: ripercorrendo un'esperienza', in *Ricerche su* Ostia *e il suo territorio. Atti del Terzo Seminario Ostiense (Roma, École française de Rome, 21–22 ottobre 2015)*, ed. M. Cébeillac-Gervasoni, N. Laubry and F. Zevi (Rome 2019), 53–66.

Balil Illana, A. 'Riqueza y sociedad en la España romana (ss. III-I a.C.)', *Hispania* 99 (1965), 325–366.

Bandelli, G. *Ricerche sulla colonizzazione romana della gallia cisalpina: le fasi iniziali e il caso aquileiese* (Rome 1988).

Baradez, J. 'Inscriptions de la région du *limes* de Biskra à Tobna', *Libyca* 1 (1953), 151–165.

Barbati, S. 'Gli studi sulla cittadinanza romana prima e dopo le ricerche di Giorgio Luraschi', *RDR* 12 (2012), 1–46.

Barbati, S. 'Ancora sulle cosiddette "colonie latine fittizie" transpadane (Asc. *In Pis.* 3 Clark)', *Quaderni Lupiensi di Storia e Diritto* 3 (2013), 59–106.

Bartels, J. 'Der Tod des Germanicus und seine epigraphische Dokumentation: Ein neues Exemplar des *senatus consultum de Cn. Pisone patre* aus Genf', *Chiron* 39 (2009), 1–9.

Barton, I. M. 'The Effects of Imperial Favour. Septimius Severus and *Lepcis Magna*', *Museum Africum* 6 (1977–1978), 60–63.

Bauman, R. A. *Women and Politics in Ancient Rome* (London–New York 1992).

Becerra Fernández, D. '*Marmora* en *Itálica* sectilia italicenses', 1, no. 2 (2016), 205–222.

Becerra Fernández, D. '*Marmor* en Itálica. Un estado de la cuestión', *Romula* 16 (2017), 167–194.

Becerra Fernández, D. and Vargas Vázquez, S. '*Marmora* en pavimentos en *opus sectile* de *Italica* e *Hispalis*', in Marmora Baeticae. *Uso de materiales pétreos en la Bética romana*, ed. J. Beltrán, M. L. Loza and E. Ontiveros (Seville 2018), 203–213.

Becerra Fernández, D. *Los materiales marmóreos del* Traianeum *de Italica* (Ph.D. diss., University of Seville, 2019).

Becerra Fernández, D. and Beltrán, J. 'Sobre soportes epigráficos. A propósito de las inscripciones del *Traianeum* de *Italica*', *Lucentum* 39 (2020a), 269–294.

Becerra, D. 'Expolio y reutilización de materiales marmóreos del *Traianeum* italicense. Balance historiográfico y nuevas líneas interpretativas', in Exemplum et Spolia: *la reutilización arquitectónica en la transformación del paisaje urbano de las ciudades históricas*, vol. 2, ed. P. Mateos and C. Morán (Mérida 2020b), 603–611.

Becerra Fernández, D., Ontiveros-Ortega, E. and Beltrán-Fortes, J. '*Marmora* of the *Traianeum* of *Italica* (Santiponce, Seville, Spain): New Data Provided by Archaeometric Analysis', *Geoarchaeology* (2021), 1–29.

Beltrán, J. and Rodríguez Hidalgo, J. M. *Itálica. Espacios de culto en el anfiteatro* (Seville 2004).

Beltrán, J. 'Itálica en época adrianea', in *Adriano. Emperador de Roma*, ed. J. González Fernández and P. Pavón (Rome 2009), 27–47.

Beltrán, J. 'La escultura', in *Itálica-Santiponce.* Municipium *y* Colonia Aelia Augusta Italicensium, ed. A. Caballos Rufino (Rome 2010), 115–126.

Beltrán, J. *et al.*, 'La explotación y el empleo de *marmora* en la *Baetica*. Un proyecto de investigación de base arqueométrica', *Itálica* 1 (2011), 57–76.

Beltrán, J. 'Explotación y rutas de comercialización de los *marmora* béticos', in *Rome, Portus and the Mediterranean*, ed. S. Keay (London 2012), 281–292.

Beltrán, J. 'Mármoles en la Bética durante el reinado de Adriano. El protagonismo de Itálica', in Roma, Tibur, Baetica. *Investigaciones adrianeas*, ed. R. Hidalgo and P. León (Seville 2013), 225–250.

Beltrán, J. 'La arqueología de Itálica de época de Trajano y Adriano', in *El legado de los emperadores hispanos*, ed. M. Romero Recio (Seville 2018), 153–176.

Beltrán Fortes, J. and Rodríguez Hidalgo, J. M. 'Las primeras excavaciones oficiales en Itálica: Los trabajos de Ivo de la Cortina en el año 1839', *Itálica* 2 (2012), 31–52.

Beltrán Fortes, J. 'Monumentalizzazione urbana nella *Baetica* augustea: esempli e modelli', in *Augusto e la Campania. Da Ottaviano a Divo Augusto. 14–2014 d.C.*, ed. C. Capaldi (Naples 2020), 497–508.

Beltrán Lloris, F. 'Inscripciones sobre bronce: ¿un rasgo característico de la cultura epigráfica de las ciudades hispanas?', in *XI Congresso Internazionale di Epigrafia Greca e Latina* (Rome 1999), 23–25.

Beltrán Lloris, F. 'Identidad cívica y adhesión al príncipe en las monedas municipales hispanas', in *Religión y propaganda en el mundo romano*, ed. F. Marco Simón, F. Pina Polo and J. Remesal Rodríguez (Barcelona 2002), 159–189.

Beltrán Lloris, F. 'The "Epigraphic Habit" in the Roman World', in *The Oxford Handbook of Roman Epigraphy*, ed. C. Bruun and J. Edmondson (Oxford 2015), 131–151.

Benito Lázaro, E. A. 'Los pueblos líbicos en el imaginario grecorromano: percepción y representación de realidades autóctonas norteafricanas entre los siglos VIII a.C. y III d.C.', (Ph.D. diss., Complutense University of Madrid, 2018).

Benoist, S. 'Penser la limite : de la cité au territoire impérial', in *Frontiers in the Roman World. Proceedings of the Ninth Workshop of the International Network Impact of Empire (Durham, 16–19 April 2009)*, ed. T. Kaizer and O. Hekster (Leiden 2011), 31–48.

Benseddik, N. *Les troupes auxiliaires de l'armée romaine en Maurétanie Césarienne sous le Haut-Empire* (Algiers 1982).

Benseddik, N. 'Limes, Mauretania Caesariensis', in *Dizionario epigrafico* IV, 43.2, ed. E. De Ruggiero (Rome 1984–1985).

Bernard, G. 'Les prétendues invasions maures en Hispanie sous le règne de Marc Aurèle : Essai de synthèse', *Pallas* 79 (2009), 357–370.

Bernard, G. and Callegarin, L. 'La titulature des magistrats et le statut de la cité de Tanger d'après l'épigraphie monétaire', in *Le forme municipali in Italia e nelle province occidentali tra i secolo I a.C. e III d.C.*, ed. S. Evangelisti and C. Ricci (Bari 2017), 183–192.

Bernard, G. 'Las incursiones mauritanas en la Bética bajo el reinado de Marco Aurelio', in Fretum Hispanicum. *Nuevas perspectivas sobre el Estrecho de Gibraltar durante la Antigüedad*, ed. A. Álvarez Melero, A. Álvarez-Ossorio Rivas, G. Bernard and V. A. Torres González (Seville 2018), 205–224.

Berrino, N. F. Mulier potens. *Realtà femminili nel mondo antico* (Galatina 2006).

Bertrand, J.-M. 'À propos du mot *provincia* : étude sur les modes d'élaboration du langage politique', *JS* (1989), 191–215.

Bianchi, L. and Bonanno, M. 'Una tradizione di scultura funeraria microasiatica a Ostia', *Bollettino di Archeologia* 8 (1991), 1–32.

Biondi, B. *Successione testamentaria, donazioni, Trattato di Diritto Romano*, 9–10 (Milan 1943).

Birley, E. 'Senators in the Emperors' Service', *PBA* 39 (1953), 197–214.

Bispham, E. *From* Asculum *to Actium. The Municipalization of Italy from the Social War to Augustus* (Oxford 2007), 247–379.

Blanch Nougués, J. M. 'Nuevas consideraciones acerca de la fundación funeraria de *Iunia Libertas* en *Ostia*', *RIDA* 54 (2007), 197–218.

Blanco, A. and Luzón, J. M. *El Mosaico de Neptuno de Itálica* (Seville 1974).

Blanco, A. 'La Itálica de Trajano y Adriano', in *Itálica (Santiponce, Sevilla)*, ed. P. León (Madrid 1982), 291–298.

Blanco, A. 'Hallazgos epigráficos', in *Traianeum de Itálica*, ed. P. León (Seville 1988), 103–117.

Bloch, R. 'Une campagne de fouilles dans la vallée du Chéliff. Les *Tigava castra*', *MEFRA* 58 (1941–1946), 9–42.

Bloch, H. '*Ostia* – Iscrizioni rinvenute tra il 1930 e il 1939', *NSA* 7 (1953), 239–306.

Boatwright, M. T. 'Italica and Hadrian's Urban Benefactions', in *Italica MMCC*, ed. A. Caballos Rufino and P. León (Seville 1997), 115–136.

Boëls-Janssen, N. *La vie religieuse des matrones dans la Rome archaïque* (Rome 1993).

Bonjour, M. 'Les personnages féminins et la terre natale dans l'épisode de Coriolan (Liv., 2, 40)', *REL* 53 (1975), 157–181.

Borg, B. E. *Crisis and Ambition. Tombs and Burial Customs in Third Century* CE *Rome* (Oxford 2013).

Boube, E. 'La mort lente du forum dans les villes des provinces hispaniques à la fin de l'Antiquité ou le symbole d'une société en cours de profonde mutation', in *Le forum en Gaule et dans les régions voisines*, ed. A. Bouet (Bordeaux 2012), 335–406.

Brassloff, S. 'Die Grundsätze bei der Commendation der Plebejer', *JÖAI* 8 (1905), 60–70.

Brassous, L. 'Les édifices de spectacles d'Hispanie entre les IIe et IVe siècles', in *Urbanisme civique en temps de crise*, ed. L. Brassous and A. Quevedo (Madrid 2015a), 273–288.

Brassous, L. and Quevedo, A. (eds.), *Urbanisme civique en temps de crise. Les espaces publics d'Hispanie et de l'Occident romain entre le IIe et le IVe siècle* (Madrid 2015b).

Bravo, G. 'La otra cara de la crisis: el cambio social', in *Ciudad y comunidad cívica en Hispania (siglos II y III d.C.)*, ed. E. Ortiz de Urbina (Madrid 1993), 153–160.

Bravo, G. '¿Otro mito historiográfico? La crisis del siglo III y sus teóricos en el nuevo debate', *SHHA* 30 (2012), 115–140.

Broughton, T. R. S. *The Magistrates of the Roman Republic. Volume I (509 B.C.–100 B.C.)* (New York 1951).

Brown, R. 'Livy's Sabine Women and the Ideal of Concordia', *TAPhA* 125 (1995), 291–319.

Brundrett, N. 'Roman Tomb Gardens: The Construction of Sacred Commemorative Landscapes', *The Brock Review* 11, no. 2 (2011), 51–69.

Brunt, P. A. *Italian Manpower, 225 B.C.–A.D. 14* (Oxford 1971).

Bruun, C. and Edmondson, J. (ed.), *The Oxford Handbook of Roman Epigraphy* (Oxford 2014).

Bruun, C. 'Le donne di *Ostia* como proprietarie di immobili e schiavi', *MEFRA* 130, no. 2 (2018), 387–393.

Buendía Moreno, A. F. and Villada Paredes, F. E. 'Prospección arqueológica de superficie realizada en las cuencas de los ríos Fardes y Aguas Blancas (Granada)', *Anuario Arqueológico de Andalucía 1987*, vol. 2 (1990), 118–129.

Burnett, A. 'Latin on Coins of the Western Empire', in *Becoming Roman, Writing Latin? Literacy and Epigraphy in the Roman West*, ed. A. E. Cooley (Portsmouth 2002), 33–40.

Buzón Calderón, F. et al., 'Informe de las prospecciones arqueológicas superficiales en el pasillo de Fiñana (Almería). Campaña de 1988', *Anuario Arqueológico de Andalucía 1988*, vol. 2 (1990), 9–13.

Caballero Cobos, A. 'Vías de comunicación en las comarcas de Baza y Huéscar. Una aproximación histórico-arqueológica desde la Prehistoria Reciente a la Edad Media' (Ph.D. diss., University of Granada, 2014).

Caballero Cobos, A. *et al.*, 'Evolución del paisaje minero en las Sierras Andaluzas Orientales que orlan los altiplanos de Baza y Guadix. Desde los orígenes hasta inicios de la Edad Moderna', in *Presente y futuro de los paisajes mineros del pasado. Estudios sobre minería, metalurgia y poblamiento*, ed. L. J. García, L. Arboledas, E. Alarcón and F. Contreras (Granada 2017), 327–339.

Caballero Cobos, A. *et al.* 'Bastetania antes de Roma. El poblado fortificado íbero de La Calera (Dólar, Granada)', *Cuadernos de Prehistoria y Arqueología de la Universidad de Granada* 30 (2020), 339–424.

Caballos Rufino, A. *Los senadores hispanorromanos y la romanización de Hispania (siglos I–III)* (Écija 1990).

Caballos Rufino, A. 'Un nuevo *procurator Augusti* de la Bética', in *II Congresso Peninsular de Historia Antiga* (Coimbra 1993), 715–740.

Caballos Rufino, A. *Itálica y los italicenses: aproximación a su historia* (Seville 1994).

Caballos Rufino, A., Eck, W. and Fernández Gómez, F. *El Senadoconsulto de Gneo Pisón padre* (Sevilla 1996).

Caballos Rufino, A. and Rodríguez Hidalgo, J. M. 'Hadrien et sa patrie d'Italica', in *Hadrien. Trésors d'une villa imperiale*, ed. J. Charles-Gaffiot and H. Lavagne (Milan 1999a), 16–25.

Caballos Rufino, A., Marín, J. and Rodríguez Hidalgo, J. M. (eds.), *Itálica arqueológica* (Seville 1999b).

Caballos Rufino, A. 'Significación político-administrativa de la provincia en el alto imperio romano: la mistificación de un concepto', in Lavdes provinciarvm: *retórica y política en la representación del imperio romano*, ed. J. Santos Yanguas and E. Torregaray Pagola (Vitoria 2007), 77–88.

Caballos Rufino, A. 'Publicación de documentos públicos en las ciudades del Occidente romano: el ejemplo de la Bética', in *Selbstdarstellung und Kommunikation. Die Veröffentlichung staatlicher Urkunden auf Stein und Bronze in der römischen Welt*, ed. R. Haensch (Munich 2009), 131–172.

Caballos Rufino, A. 'Adriano, la *Colonia Aelia Augusta Italicensium* y una nueva inscripción del "*Traianeum*" de Itálica', in *Pluralidad e integración en el mundo romano*, ed. F. J. Navarro (Pamplona 2010a), 265–277.

Caballos Rufino, A. 'Hitos de la historia de Itálica', in Itálica-Santiponce. Municipium y Colonia Aelia Augusta Italicensium, ed. A. Caballos Rufino (Rome 2010b), 1–16.

Caballos Rufino, A. 'De *Hispania* a *Tibur*: elites imperiales en el entorno de Villa Adriana', in Roma, Tibur, Baetica. *Investigaciones adrianeas*, ed. R. Hidalgo and P. León (Seville 2013), 21–76.

Caballos Rufino, C. '*Monumenta fatiscunt*. Meaning and Fate of Legal Inscriptions on Bronze: The Baetica', in *Literacy in Ancient Everyday Life*, ed. A. Kolb (Berlin 2019a), 289–318.

Caballos Rufino, A. 'Trajano, Adriano e *Italica*: de cuna de emperador a patria imperial', in *De Trajano a Adriano*. Roma matura, Roma mutans, ed. A. Caballos Rufino (Seville 2019b).

Caballos Rufino, C. 'Un senadoconsulto del año 14 d. C. en un epígrafe bético', *ZPE* 219 (2021), 305–326.

Cagnat, R. 'Chronique d'épigraphie africaine', *BCTH* (1894), 344–363.

Cagnat, R. 'Chronique d'épigraphie africaine', *BCTH* (1895), 310.

Cagnat, R. '13 Novembre 1900. Séance de la Commission de l'Afrique du Nord', *BCTH* (1900), CLXXIV–CLXXV.

Cagnat, R. *L'armée romaine d'Afrique et l'occupation militaire de l'Afrique sous les empereurs* (Paris 1913).

Cagnat, R. '15 Juin 1919. Séance de la Commission de l'Afrique du Nord', *BCTH* 1919, CCXV.

Caldelli, M. L.; Zevi, F. and Cébeillac-Gervasoni, M. *Epigrafia Latina.* Ostia*: Cento iscrizioni in contesto* (Rome 2010).

Caldelli, M. L. 'Evergetismo femminile ad *Ostia* tra tarda repubblica ed età altoimperiale', in Matronae in domo et in re publica agentes. *Spazi e occasioni dell'azione femminile nel mondo romano tra tarda repubblica e primo impero*, ed. F. Cenerini and F. Rohr Vio (Trieste 2016), 257–275.

Camps, G. 'Essais de cartographie culturelle : À propos de la frontière de Numidie et de Maurétanie', in *Frontières et limites géographiques de l'Afrique du Nord antique. Hommage à Pierre Salama*, ed. C. Lepelley and X. Dupuis (Paris 1999), 43–70.

Cantarella, E. *Pandora's Daughters. The Role and Status of Women in Greek and Roman Antiquity* (Baltimore 1987).

Cantarella, E. *La mujer romana* (Santiago de Compostela 1991).

Cantarella, E. *Pasado próximo. Mujeres romanas de Tácita a Sulpicia* (Madrid 1997).

Canto, A. M. 'El mosaico del Nacimiento de Venus de Itálica', *Habis* 7 (1976), 293–318.

Canto, A. M. 'El acueducto romano de Itálica', *MDAI*(*M*) 20 (1979), 282–337.

Canto, A. M. 'Excavaciones en "El Pradillo" (Itálica): un barrio tardío', in *Itálica* (*Santiponce, Sevilla*), ed. P. León (Madrid 1982), 227–241.

Canto, A. 'Epigrafía romana de Itálica' (Ph.D. diss., Complutense University of Madrid, 1985).

Canto, A. M. '*Colonia Patricia Corduba:* Nuevas hipótesis sobre su fundación y nombre', *Latomus* 50 (1991), 145–182.

Canto, A. M. 'La *Vetus Urbs* de Itálica, quince años después. La planta hipodámica de D. Demetrio de los Ríos, y otras novedades', *CPAM* 25 (1999), 145–191.

Cairns, J. W. and du Plessis, P. J. (eds.), *Beyond Dogmatics. Law and Society in the Roman World* (Edinburgh 2007).

Capogrossi Colognesi, L. '*Ius commercii, conubium, civitas sine suffragio*. Le origini del diritto internazionale privato e la romanizzazione delle comunità latino-campane', in *Le strade del potere*. Maiestas populi Romani: imperium, coercitio, commercium, ed. A. Corbino (Catania 1994), 369–391.

Capogrossi Colognesi, L. *Cittadini e territorio. Consolidamento e trasformazione della* 'ciuitas Romana' (Rome 2000).

Capogrossi Colognesi, L. *Law and Power in the Making of the Roman Commonwealth* (Cambridge 2014).

Cardon, É. 'Le patronat municipal en Bétique et en Tarraconaise sous les premiers Julio-Claudiens. Un exemple de loyalisme dynastique', in *Hispanité et romanité*, ed. J. M. André (Madrid 2004), 39–58.

Carter, M. 'Gladiatorial Ranking and the "*SC de Pretiis Gladiatorum Minuendis*" (*CIL* II 6278 = *ILS* 5163)', *Phoenix* 57, no. 1 (2003), 83–114.

Castillo García, C. 'Los senadores béticos. Relaciones familiares y sociales', in *Epigrafia e ordine senatorio*: 2. (*Tituli* 5) (Rome 1982), 465–519 [=].

C. Castillo García, Vestigia antiquitatis. *Escritos de epigrafía y literaturas romanas. Scripta a sodalibus collecta in honorem Carmen Castillo* (Pamplona 1997) Castillo García, C. 'Sevirato y augustalidad: un estamento intermedio en la vida ciudadana', in *Sociedad y economía en el Occidente romano*, ed. C. Castillo García (Pamplona 2003), 73–90.

Ceballos Hornero, A. 'El coste de los espectáculos gladiatorios en las ciudades del Occidente romano', *AEA* 80 (2007), 107–118.

Cébeillac-Gervasoni, M. '*Octavia*, épouse de *Gamala* et la *Bona Dea*', *MEFRA* 85, no. 2 (1973), 517–553.

Cébeillac-Gervasoni, M. and Zevi, F. 'Pouvoir local et pouvoir central à Ostie. Étude prosopographique', in *Les élites municipales de l'Italie péninsulaire de la mort de César à la mort de Domitien entre continuité et rupture. Classes sociales dirigeantes et pouvoir central*, ed. M. Cébeillac-Gervasoni (Rome 2000), 1–27.

Cenerini, F. *Dive e donne. Mogli, madri, figlie e sorelle degli imperatori romani da Augusto a Commodo* (Bologna 2009).

Cenerini, F. *La donna romana. Modelli e realtà* (Bologna 2009).

Cepas, A. *Crisis y continuidad en la Hispania del siglo III* (Madrid 1997).

Charles-Laforge, M.-O. 'Patrimoines et héritages des femmes à Rome : l'exemple des princesses antonines', in Arcana Imperii. *Mélanges d'histoire économique, sociale et politique offerts au Professeur Yves Roman*, ed. C. Chillet, C. Courrier and L. Passet (Paris 2015), 233–274.

Chastagnol, A. 'L'onomastique de type pérégrin dans les cités de la Gaule Narbonnaise', *MEFRA* 102, no. 2 (1990), 573–593.

Chaves Tristán, F. 'Las monedas de la Casa del Planetario (Itálica)', *Habis* 5 (1974a), 205–211.

Chaves Tristán, F. 'Las monedas de *Acci*', *Numisma* 138–143 (1974b), 141–148.

Chaves Tristán, F. *Las monedas Hispano-Romanas de* Carteia (Barcelona 1979).

Chaves Tristán, F. 'El papel de los itálicos en la amonedación hispana', *Gerión* 17 (1999), 295–315.

Chérif, A. 'Le *Fundus Tapp*(*hugabensis*) – Henchir Chaïeb : Un domaine agricole de la Région de Bou Arada (Tunisie)', *AntAfr* 55 (2019), 97–126.

Cherry, D. 'The Minician Law Marriage and the Roman Citizenship', *Phoenix* 44, no. 3 (1990), 244–266.

Cherry, D. *Frontier and Society in Roman North Africa* (Oxford 1998).

Chic, G. 'Marco Aurelio y Cómodo: el hundimiento de un sistema económico', in *La Hispania de los Antoninos (98–180)*, ed. L. Hernández Guerra (Valladolid 2005), 567–586.

Chic, G. 'Aspectos fiscales y de tributación a partir de Marco Aurelio: indicios de cambio', in Oppida labentia: *transformaciones, cambios y alteración en las ciudades hispanas entre el siglo II y la tardoantigüedad*, ed. J. Andreu (Uncastillo 2017), 117–156.

Chiusi, T. J. 'Lo straniero come compartecipe dell'esperienza giuridica. A proposito dello stato giuridico dello straniero a Roma', in *I diritti degli altri in Grecia e a Roma*, ed. L. Gagliardi and A. Maffi (Sankt Augustin 2011), 30–44.

Christol, M. and Magioncalda, A. *Studi sui procuratori delle due Mauretaniae* (Sassari 1989).

Christol, M. 'Du nouveau sur les *Cerretani* et sur la Cerdagne à l'époque romaine', *Sources. Les Cahiers de l'âne rouge* 7 (2020), 54–55.

Ciampoltrini, G. Munere Mortis. *Complessi tombali d'età romana nel territorio di Lucca* (Pisa 2009).

Ciccotti, E. *Donne e politica negli ultimi anni della Repubblica romana* (Milan 1895).

Cid López, R. M. 'El *ordo matronarum* y los espacios femeninos en la Roma antigua. Las fiestas de *Matronalia* y *Fortuna muliebris*', in *Pautas históricas de sociabilidad femenina rituales y modelos de representación: Actas del V Coloquio Internacional de la Asociación Española de Investigación Histórica de las Mujeres*, ed. M. Nash, M. J. de la Pascua and G. Espigado (Cádiz 1999), 43–58.

Cid López, R. M. 'La educación de la niña romana: de *puella* a *matrona docta*', in *Bien enseñada: la formación femenina en Roma y el Occidente romanizado*, ed. V. Alfaro Bech and R. Francia Somalo (Málaga 2001) 21–44.

Cid López, R. M. 'Mujeres y actividades políticas en la República. Las matronas rebeldes y sus antecesoras en la Roma antigua', in *Mujeres en la Antigüedad Clásica: género, poder y conflicto*, ed. A. Domínguez Arranz (Madrid 2010), 125–152.

Cid López, R. M. 'Las matronas y los *agmina mulierum* en la Roma antigua. Del matriotismo a la protesta', in *Cartografías de género en las ciudades antiguas*, ed. C. Martínez López and P. Ubric Rabaneda (Granada 2017) 207–232.

Cid López, R. 'Mujeres y acción política en la República tardía: las conspiradoras. Imágenes nuevas de viejas prácticas femeninas', in *Lo viejo y lo nuevo en las sociedades antiguas: homenaje a Alberto Prieto. XXXVI Coloquio del GIREA*, ed. J. Cortadella i Morral, O. Olesti Vila and C. Sierra Martín (Besançon 2018), 619–641.

Cinque, P. 'Policromia marmorea nei rivestimenti pavimentali e parietali della Villa Adriana di Tivoli: Nuove scoperte e verifiche', *Romula* 11 (2012), 161–204.

Cisneros, M. *Mármoles hispanos: su empleo en la España romana* (Zaragoza 1988).

Cisneros, M. 'El mármol y la propaganda ideológica: El modelo del foro de Augusto', in *Religión y propaganda política en el mundo romano*, ed. F. Marco Simón, F. Pina Polo and J. Remesal Rodríguez (Barcelona 2002), 83–104.

Coltelloni-Trannoy, M. in *Encyclopédie berbère* 31, s. v. 'Maurétanie (Royaumes)', 4717–4737 (online): [https://journals.openedition.org/encyclopedieberbere/521].

Coltelloni-Trannoy, M. *Le royaume de Maurétanie sous Juba II et Ptolémée (25 av. J.-C.–40 ap. J.-C.)* (Paris 1997).

Conde Guerri, E. *La ciudad de Carthago Nova: la documentación literaria (inicios-Julioclaudios)* (Murcia 2003).

Conesa Navarro, P. D. 'La palabra concedida. Discursos y actitudes "transgresoras" femeninas en la antigua Roma monárquica y republicana', *Arenal* 27, no. 2 (2020), 437–462.

Cormarck, S. 'The tombs at *Pompeii*', in *The World of Pompeii*, ed. P. Foss and J. J. Dobbins (London 2007), 585–606.

Corbier, M. '"Le deuxième sexe" à Rome', in *Marginación y mujer en el Imperio romano*, ed. P. Pavón Torrejón (Rome 2018), 13–32.

Corrales Aguilar, P. 'La provincia romana de la *Baetica*: Notas para el establecimiento de su límite oriental y su compartimentación conventual', *Baetica* 19, no. 1 (1997), 415–429.

Cortés Bárcena, C. and Alonso, M. A. 'Reflexiones en torno a la epigrafía de los *patroni civitatis* en *Hispania* y el Norte de *Africa*: los ejemplos de *Baetica* y *Mauretania*', in *L'Africa Romana. Trasformazione dei paesaggi del potere nell'Africa settentrionale fino alla fine del mondo antico* (Sassari 2012), 2073–2092.

Cortés Bárcena, C. *Epigrafía en los confines de las ciudades romanas. Los* Termini publici *en* Hispania, Mauretania *y* Numidia (Rome 2013).

Corzo Sánchez, J. R. 'El anfiteatro de *Italica*', in *El anfiteatro en la Hispania romana*, ed. J. M. Álvarez Martínez and J. J. Enríquez (Badajoz 1994), 187–212.

Corzo Sánchez, R. and Toscano San Gil, M. *Las vías romanas de Andalucía* (Seville 1992).

Corzo, R. 'El anfiteatro de Itálica', in *El anfiteatro en la Hispania romana*, ed. J. M. Álvarez Martínez and J. J. Enríquez (Badajoz 1994), 187–212.

Corzo, R. 'Colonia Aelia Augusta Itálica' in *Hispania. El legado de Roma* (Zaragoza 1998), 405–410.

Corzo, R. and Toscano, M. *Excavaciones en el teatro de ltálica* (Seville 2003).

Crawford, M. *Roman Statutes* (London 1996).

Crook, J. Consilium Principis. *Imperial Councils and Counsellors from Augustus to Diocletian* (Cambridge 1955).

Crook, J. A. *Law and Life of Rome* (Ithaca, NY 1967).

Curchin, L. A. *The Local Magistrates of Roman Spain* (Toronto 1990).

Curchin, L. A. *A Supplement to the Local Magistrates of Roman Spain* (Waterloo 2015).

Czajkowski, K. *Localized Law: The Babatha and Salome Komaise Archives* (Oxford 2017).

Czajkowski, K. and Eckhardt, B., 'Law, Status and Agency the Roman Provinces', *P&P* 241 (2018), 3–31.

Czajkowski, K.; Eckhardt, B. and Strothmann, M. (eds.), *Law in the Roman Provinces* (Oxford 2020).

D'Arms, J. H. 'Notes on Municipal Notables of Imperial *Ostia*', *AJPh* 97, no. 4 (1976), 387–411.

Dąbrowa, E. Legio X Fretensis. *A Prosopographical Study of its Officers (I–III C.* A.D.) (Stuttgart 1993).

Dalla Rosa, A. 'Mauretania', in *Roma e le sue province. Dalla prima guerra punica a Diocleziano*, ed. C. Letta and S. Segenni (Rome 2015).

David, B. and Wilson, M. *Inscribed Landscapes: Marking and Making Place* (Honolulu 2002).

De Angelis, F. *Spaces of Justice in the Roman World* (Leiden 2010).

Déderix, S. 'Funerary Landscapes and GIS Applications: a Review', in *3rd ARCH_RNT Proceedings Archaeological Research and New Technologies*, ed. N. Zacharias (Kalamata 2014), 21–30.

Degrassi, A. '*Quattuorviri* in colonie romane e in municipi retti da *duoviri*', in *Scritti vari di antichità raccolti da amici e allievi nel 75° compleanno dell'autore I*, ed. A. Degrassi (Rome 1962a), 99–177.

Degrassi, A. '*Duoviri aedilicia potestate, duoviri aediles, aediles duoviri*', in *Scritti vari di antichità raccolti da amici e allievi nel 75° compleanno dell'autore I*, ed. A. Degrassi (Rome 1962b), 179–184.

Degrassi, A. 'Sul duovirato nei municipi italici', in *Scritti vari di antichità raccolti da amici e allievi nel 75° compleanno dell'autore I*, ed. A. Degrassi (Rome 1962c), 185–192.

Degrassi, A. *Inscriptiones Latinae liberae rei publicae: imagines* (Berlin 1965).

Degrassi, A. 'L'amministrazione delle città', *Scritti vari di antichità raccolti da amici e allievi nel 75° compleanno dell'autore IV* (Trieste 1971), 67–98.

De Haas, T. C. A. and Tol, G. (eds.), *The Economic Integration of Roman Italy: Rural Communities in a Globalising World* (Leiden–Boston 2017).

De la Escosura Balbás, M. C. *La población de* Carthago Nova *de la conquista al Principado. Epigrafía y onomástica* (Barcelona 2021).

De Paolis, M. '*Iura sepulcrorum* a *Ostia*: consuntivi tematici ragionati', *ArchClass* 61 (2010), 583–629.

Delgado Delgado, J. A. *Élites y organización de la religión en las provincias romanas de la Bética y las Mauritanias: sacerdotes y sacerdocios* (Oxford 1998).

Demaeght, L. 'Inscriptions inédites de la Maurétanie Césarienne', *Bulletin de la société de géographie et d'archéologie de la province d'Oran* 12 (1892), 273–279.

Desanges, J. *Catalogue des tribus africaines de l'antiquité classique à l'ouest du Nil* (Dakar 1962).

Des Boscs-Plateaux, F. *Un parti hispanique à Rome ? Ascension des élites hispaniques et pouvoir politique d'Auguste à Hadrien (27 av. J.-C.–138 ap. J.-C.)* (Madrid 2005).

Diarte, P. *La configuración urbana de la Hispania tardoantigua. Transformaciones y pervivencias de los espacios públicos romanos, ss. III–VI d.C.* (Oxford 2012).

Diarte, P. 'Redefining the Urban Landscape in Hispania: Entertainment Buildings and their Transformations in Late Antiquity', *Hortus Artium Medievalium* 20, no. 1 (2014a), 25–38.

Diarte, P. 'Un camino sin retorno: la desarticulación de la ciudad clásica en la Antigüedad Tardía (ss. IV–V d. C.)', in *Modelos edilicios y prototipos en la monumentalización de las ciudades de Hispania*, ed. M. Martín-Bueno and J. C. Sáenz (Zaragoza 2014b), 97–106.

Díaz Ariño, B. *Epigrafía latina republicana de Hispania* (Barcelona 2008).

Díaz Ariño, B. 'Epigrafía y gobernadores provinciales en *Hispania* durante la República romana', *Chiron* 41 (2011), 149–179.

Díaz de Cerio Erasun, M. 'Los senadores originarios de Lusitania (1982–2012)', *EEFT(hist)* 25 (2012), 327–354.

Díaz Fernández, A. 'Notas en torno a la posible identidad de *M. Iun[ius] pro[cos]* (*AE*, 1984, 615) y el nacimiento de la ciudad romana de *Emporiae*', *Klio* 100, no. 1 (2018), 195–223.

Díaz Fernández, A. 'When did a *Provincia* become a Province? On the Institutional Development of a Roman Republican Concept', in *Provinces and Provincial Command in Republican Rome: Genesis, Development and Governance*, ed. A. Díaz Fernández (Zaragoza 2021), 41–69.

Dittenberger, W. and Purgold, K. *Die Inschriften von Olympia* (Berlin 1896).

Dixon, S. *The Roman Mother* (London 1988).

Dixon, S. 'A Woman of Substance: *Iunia Libertas* of *Ostia*', *Helios* 19 (1992), 162–174.

Domergue, C. and Rico, C. 'Les itinéraires du commerce du cuivre et du plomb hispaniques à l'époque romaine dans le monde méditerranéen', in *La Corse et le monde méditerranéen des origines au Moyen-âge: échanges et circuits commerciaux, Actes du colloque de Bastia* (Bastia 2014), 135–168.

Dondin-Payre, M. and Raepsaet-Charlier, M. T. (eds.), *Noms, identités culturelles et romanisation sous le Haut-Empire* (Brussels 2001).

Du Plessis, P. J. (ed.) *New Frontiers. Law and Society in the Roman World* (Edinburgh 2013).

Dubosson-Sbriglione, L. '*Veturia* : négociatrice et ambassadrice de Rome', *EuGeStA* 11 (2021), 110–130.

Duncan-Jones, R. P. *The Economy of the Roman Empire: Quantitative Studies* (Cambridge 1982).

Duncan-Jones, R. 'Economic Change and the Transition to Late Antiquity', in *Approaching Late Antiquity. The Transformation from Early to Late Empire*, ed. S. Swain and M. Edwards (Oxford 2004), 20–52.

Dupuis, X. '*Cuicul*, la Confédération Cirtéenne et les Suburbures : Des limites ambiguës', in *Frontières et limites géographiques de l'Afrique du Nord antique. Hommage à Pierre Salama*, ed. C. Lepelley and X. Dupuis (Paris 1999), 129–137.

Dupuis, X. 'Les origines de la colonie de *Cuicul*', *BSAF* 2001 (2006), 151–161.

Dyson, S. L. 'The Distribution of Roman Republican Family Names in the Iberian Peninsula', *AncSoc* 11–12 (1980–1981), 257–300.

Dyson, S. L. *The Creation of the Roman Frontier* (Princeton 2014).

Eck, W., Caballos Rufino, A. and Fernández, F. *Das Senatus Consultum de Cn. Pisone patre* (Munich 1996).

Eck, W. and Navarro, F. J. 'Das Ehrenmonument der *Colonia Carthago* für *L. Minicius Natalis Quadronius Verus* in seiner Heimatstadt *Barcino*', *ZPE* 123 (1998), 237.

Eck, W. 'Emperor and Senatorial Aristocracy in Competition for Public Space', in *The Emperor and Rome. Space, Representation and Ritual*, ed. B. C. Ewald and C. F. Noreña (Cambridge 2010a), 89–110.

Eck, W. *Monument und Inschrift. Gesammelte Aufsätze zur senatorischen Repräsentation in der Kaiserzeit* (Berlin 2010b).

Eck, W. 'Statuendedikanten und Selbstdarstellung in römischen Städten', in Eck, W. ed. *Monument und Inschrift. Gesammelte Aufsätze zur senatorischen Repräsentation in der Kaiserzeit* (Berlin 2010c), 127–142.

Eckhardt, B. 'Law, Empire, and Identity between West and East: The Danubian Provinces', in *Law in the Roman Provinces*, ed. K. Czajkowski, B. Eckhardt and M. Strothmann (Oxford 2020), 417–435.

Edmondson, J. and Gimeno Pascual, H. 'Primer testimonio de evergetismo en el foro de *Valeria* (*conventus Carthaginiensis, Hispania Citerior*): una nueva placa opistógrafa', *MDAI*(*M*) 58 (2017), 321–372.

Ehmig, U. 'Ausschlussverfahren: Eine Gruppe italischer Grabinschriften als Beispiel sozialer überassimilierung in der römischen Kaiserzeit', *Epigraphica* 77 (2015), 193–205.

El Bouzidi, S. and Ouahidi, A. 'La frontière méridionale de la Maurétanie Tingitane : contribution à la carte archéologique de la région de Volubilis', *DHA* 40, no. 1 (2014), 97–108.

Elton, H. *Frontiers of the Roman Empire* (London 1998).

Erim, K. T. *et al.*, 'The Copy of Diocletian Edict on Maximum Prices from Aphrodisias in *Caria*', *JRS* 60 (1970), 120–141.

Erkelenz, D. 'Ehrenmonumente des *L. Minicius Natalis* in Rom und Africa', *ZPE* 123, 1998, 257–269.

Erkelenz, D. '*Ubique gentium quadriuges et seiuges currus*: Gespannmonumente für Angehörige der hohen *ordines* im römischen Reich', *JRA* 16, 2003a, 201–218.

Erkelenz, D. Optimo praesidi. *Untersuchungen zu den Ehrenmonumenten für Amsträger der römischen Provinzen in Republik und Kaiserzeit* (Bonn 2003b).

España Chamorro, S. '*Corpus Milliariorum Baeticae*. Miliarios y política viaria en la *Hispania Ulterior Baetica* en época imperial', *ArchClass* 70, no. 9 (2019), 397–450.

España Chamorro, S. Unde incipit Baetica. *Los límites de la* Baetica *y su integración territorial (s. I–III)* (Rome 2021).

España-Chamorro, S. and Moreno Escobar, M. C. (eds.), *Landscapes and the Augustan Revolution in the Western Provinces* (London 2024).

Espinosa Espinosa, D. *Plinio y los "*oppida *de antiguo Lacio". El proceso de difusión del* Latium *en* Hispania Citerior (Oxford 2014).

Espinosa Espinosa, D. 'Reflexiones sobre la probable promoción de *Cesse/Tarraco* a colonia latina', *Klio* 98, no. 2 (2016) 570–604.

Espinosa Espinosa, D. 'The Question of the *oppida veteris Latii* in Pliny the Elder's *Naturalis Historia*', *CQ* 68 (1) (2018), 232–245.

Estarán Tolosa, M. J. *Epigrafía bilingüe del Occidente romano: el latín y las lenguas locales en las inscripciones bilingües y mixtas* (Zaragoza 2016).

Evans-Grubbs, J. *Women and the Law in the Roman Empire. A Sourcebook on Marriage, Divorce and Widowhood* (London 2002).

Fasolini, D. 'La compresenza di tribù nelle città della Peninsola Iberica: il caso della *Tarraconensis*', in *Hispania y la epigrafía romana. Cuatro perspectivas*, ed. J. F. Rodríguez Neila (Faenza 2009), 179–238.

Fasolini, D. 'L'ascrizione tribale delle comunità iberiche: il caso della Tarraconense', in *Le tribù romane. Atti della XVI*e *Rencontre sur l'épigraphie*, ed. M. Silvestrini (Bari 2010), 89–93.

Fasolini, D. *Le tribù romane della Hispania Tarraconensis. L'iscrizione tribale dei cittadini romani nelle testimonianze epigrafiche* (Milan 2012).

Fear, A. T. *Rome and Baetica* (Oxford 1996).

Ferrary, J.-L. 'L'onomastique dans les provinces orientales de l'Empire à la lumière du dossier des mémoriaux de délégations de Claros', *CGG* 19 (2008), 246–278.

Ferrer i Jané, J., Velaza Frías, J. and Olesti Vila, O. 'II. Nuevas inscripciones rupestres latinas de Oceja y los IIIIviri ibéricos de *Iulia Lybica*', *DHA* 44 (1) (2018), 169–195.

Février, P.-A. 'Remarques sur les inscriptions funéraires datées de Maurétanie Césarienne orientale (II$^{e}$–V$^{e}$ siècle)', *MEFRA* 76 (1964), 105–172.

Février, P.-A. *Approches du Maghreb romain* I (Aix-en-Provence 1989).

Février, P.-A. 'Aux origines de l'occupation romaine dans les hautes plaines de Sétif', in *La Méditerranée de Paul-Albert Février* (Rome 1996).

Finley, M. I. *Uso y abuso de la historia* (Barcelona 1984).

Flohr, M. (ed.), *Urban Space and Urban History in the Roman World* (London 2020).

France, J. 'Normes douanières et réglementation des échanges. Trois questions simples sur le tarif de Zaraï (Numidie)', *AntAfr* 50 (2014), 93–110.

Francisci, D. 'Le sepolture come indicatori di centuriazione. Due casi di studio dal Trentino-Alto Adige/Südtirol (Italia)', in *Sistemi centuriali e opere di assetto agrario tra età romana e primo medioevo. Atti del convegno Borgoricco (Padova) – Lugo (Ravenna), 10–12 settembre 2009*, ed. P. L. dall'Aglio and G. Rosada (Pisa–Rome 2010), 283–288.

Faoro, D. 'Praefectus fisci Germaniae', *ZPE* 205 (2018), 250–252.

Franconi, T. V. (ed.), *Fluvial Landscapes in the Roman World* (Portsmouth 2017).

Fraschetti, A. (ed.), *Roman Women* (Chicago–London 2001).

Gagé, J. Matronalia. *Essai sur les dévotions et les organisations cultuelles des femmes dans l'ancienne Rome* (Brussels 1963).

Gagliardi, L. 'Droit romain et droits locaux dans les municipes italiques avant la "*lex Iulia de civitate*"', *RD* 94 (2016), 369–391.

Gallego Franco, M. H. 'La mujer hispanorromana y la actividad económica: las profesiones', *Minerva* 7 (1993), 111–128.

Galsterer, H. *Untersuchungen zum römischen Städtewesen auf der Iberischen Halbinsel* (Berlin 1971).

Galsterer, H. 'The *Tabula Siarensis* and the Augustan Municipalization in Baetica', in *Estudios sobre la* Tabula Siarensis, ed. J. González Fernández and J. Arce (Madrid 1988), 61–74.

Galsterer, H. 'La trasformazione delle antiche colonie latine e il nuovo *ius Latii*', in *Pro populo Arimenese*, ed. A. Calbi and G. Susini (Faenza 1995), 79–94.

Ganter, A. 'Decline and Glorification: Patron-Client Relationships in the Roman Republic', in *Foreign* Clientelae *in the Roman Empire. A Reconsideration*, ed. M. Jehne and F. Pina Polo (Stuttgart 2015), 43–54.

Garcés, I. and Reyes, T. Aeso, *d'*oppidum *ibèric a* municipium *romà. Isona, Pallars Jussà*, (Barcelona 2014).

García y Bellido, A. *Colonia Aelia Augusta Italica* (Madrid 1960).

García Fernández, E. *El municipio latino. Origen y desarrollo constitucional* (Madrid 2001).

García Fernández, E. 'Ni ciudadanos ni extranjeros: la condición jurídica de la población provincial', in *Ciudadanos y extranjeros en el mundo antiguo: segregación e integración*, ed. J. Mangas Manjarrés and S. Montero Herrero (Madrid 2007), 227–240.

García Fernández, E. 'Reflexiones sobre la latinización de Hispania en época republicana', in Hispaniae. *Las provincias hispanas en el mundo romano*, ed. J. Andreu Pintado, J. Cabrero Piquero and I. Rodà de Llanza (Tarragona 2009), 377–390.

García Fernández, E. 'Un comentario al discurso *pro Balbo* de Cicerón', in *Dialéctica histórica y compromiso social, vol. 1*, ed. C. Fornis, J. Gallego and P. López Barja (Zaragoza 2010), 151–169.

García Fernández, E. 'Movilidad, onomástica e integración en Hispania en época republicana: algunas observaciones metodológicas', in *Viajes y cambios de residencia en el mundo romano*, ed. J. M. Iglesias Gil and A. Ruiz Gutiérrez (Santander 2011), 47–66.

García Fernández, E. 'Sobre la condición latina y su onomástica. Los ediles de Andelo', *Espacio, tiempo y forma. Serie II, Historia antigua* 25 (2012), 423–436.

García Fernández, E. '*Clientela* y difusión onomástica en Hispania: algunas observaciones sobre la documentación de Sagunto', in *Los espacios de la esclavitud y la dependencia desde la antigüedad. (Homenaje a Domingo Plácido. Actas del XXXV coloquio del GIREA*), ed. A. Beltrán, I. Sastre and M. Valdés (Besançon 2015a), 589–605.

García Fernández, E. 'Client Relationships and the Diffusion of Roman Names in Hispania. A Critical Review', in *Foreign* Clientelae *in the Roman Empire. A Reconsideration*, ed. M. Jehne and F. Pina Polo (Stuttgart 2015b) 107–118.

García Fernández, E. '*L. Venidius Ennychus* (TH 89) y el acceso de los magistrados provinciales a la ciudadanía romana', in Gratias tibi agimus. *Homenaje al profesor C. González Román*, ed. J. Mangas Manjarrés and Á. Padilla Arroba (Granada 2021), 117–137.

García Riaza, E. 'Sobre los mecanismos de integración de los vencidos en el Occidente romano-republicano: ¡algunas observaciones', in Vae Victis! *Perdedores en el Mundo Antiguo*, ed. F. Marco Simón, F. Pina Polo and J. Remesal Rodríguez (Barcelona 2012), 161–176.

García Riaza, E. 'Foreign Cities. Institutional Aspects of the Roman Expansion in the Iberian Peninsula (218–133 B. C.)', in *Foreign* Clientelae *in the Roman Empire. A Reconsideration*, ed. M. Jehne and F. Pina Polo (Stuttgart 2015), 119–140.

Gardner, J. F. *Women in Roman Law and Society* (London 1986).

Gargola, D. J. *The Shape of the Roman Order. The Republic and its Spaces* (Chapel Hill 2017).

Garnsey, P. *Social Status and Legal Privilege in the Roman Empire* (Oxford 1970).

Garrido, P., Guisado, F. and Costa, M. E. 'Itálica y las minas: de la hegemonía ilipense al *municipium* augusteo (ss. III–I a.C.)', *Itálica* 2 (2012), 147–164.

Gascou, J. *La politique municipale de l'Empire romain en Afrique proconsulaire de Trajan à Septime Sévère* (Rome 1972).

Gascou, J. 'Duumvirat, quattuorvirat et statut dans les cités de Gaule Narbonnaise', in *Epigrafia. Actes du colloque international d'épigraphie latine en mémoire de Attilio Degrassi pour le centenaire de sa naissance* (Rome 1991), 547–563.

Germoni, P. 'La nécropole de *Portus* à l'Isola Sacra : la fouille récente sur le côté oriental de la route antique', in Ostia, *port et porte de la Rome antique*, ed. J. P. Descœudres (Genoa 2001), 385–390.

Germoni, P., De Gregorio, L. Pischedda, C. N. and D'Andrea, A. 'Indagini archeologiche preventive nell'area della necropoli di Pianabella (area 12): nuove acquisizioni per la ricostruzione del paesaggio extraurbano di *Ostia* Antica tra I e IV secolo d.C.', in *Ricerche su* Ostia *e il suo territorio. Atti del Terzo Seminario Ostiense (Roma, École française de Rome, 21–22 ottobre 2015)*, ed. M. Cébeillac-Gervasoni, N. Laubry and F. Zevi (Rome 2019), 227–230.

Girardet, K. M. *Die Ordnung der Welt. Ein Beitrag zur philosophischen und politischen Interpretation von Ciceros Schrift* De legibus (Wiesbaden 1983).

Giuliani, C. F. *Forma Italiae. Regio I – volumen septimum. Tibur, pars prima* (Rome 1970).

Gnoli, R. *Marmora Romana* (Rome 1971).

Gnoli, R. 'Introduzione', in *Marmi antichi*, ed. G. Borghini (Rome 2004), 13–56.

Goffaux, B. 'Promotions juridiques et monumentalisation des cités hispano-romaines', *Saldvie* 3 (2003), 143–161 [=].

B. Goffaux, *La vie publique des cités dans l'Occident romain* (Rennes 2016).

Gómez Araujo, L. 'Las termas de Itálica y la arquitectura termal adrianea', in Roma, Tibur, Baetica. *Investigaciones adrianeas*, ed. R. Hidalgo and P. León (Seville 2013), 293–318.

Gómez-Pantoja, J. L. and Madruga, J. V. 'Flaminica Provinciae Baeticae et Norbensium', in *De Roma a las provincias: Las élites como instrumento de proyección de Roma, Juan Francisco Rodríguez Neila* in honorem, ed. A. Caballos Rufino and E. Melchor Gil (Seville 2014), 247–272.

González Bordas, H. and France, J. 'A New Edition of the Imperial Regulation from the Lella Drebblia Site near Dougga (*AE* 2001, 2083)', *JRA* 20 (2017), 407–428.

González Bordas, H. 'Africa', in *The Emperor and his Properties in the Roman World (44 BC–284 AD). Geography, Economy, History*, ed. A. dalla Rosa and M. Maiuro (Bordeaux, forthcoming).

González Estrada, L. 'La mujer como *exemplum*. Subversión, desafío y resistencia en Valerio Máximo', *Panta Rei* 12 (2018), 73–91.

González Fernández, J. 'The First Oath *pro Salute Augusti* Found in *Baetica*', *ZPE* 72 (1988), 113–127.

González Fernández, J. *Tácito y las fuentes documentales.* SS.CC. De honoribvs Germanici decernendis (tabula Siarensis) *y* de Cn. Pisone patre (Seville 2002).

González Fernández, J. 'El origen del culto imperial en la Bética según la documentación epigráfica', in *Culto imperial: política y poder*, ed. T. Nogales Basarrate and J. González Fernández (Mérida 2006), 173–189.

González Fernández, J. '*Asido quae Caesarina*', in *Colonias de César y Augusto en la Andalucía romana*, ed. J. González and J. C. Saquete Chamizo (Rome 2011), 273–296.

González Fernández, J. 'Texto legal epigráfico de una colonia latina de César o Augusto en la *Hispania Ulterior Baetica*', *SDHI* 81 (2015), 307–311.

González Fernández, J. '*Monumenta Memoriae Germanici Caesaris*', in Monumenta et memoria. *Estudios de epigrafía romana*, ed. J. M. Iglesias Gil and A. Ruiz-Gutiérrez (Rome 2017), 117–142.

González Román, C. 'La colonia *Iulia Gemella Acci* y la evolución de la Bastetania', *Dialoghi di Archeologia* 10, no. 1–2 (1992), 155–164.

González Román, C., Adroher Auroux, A. M. and López Marcos, A. 'Prospecciones en la zona norte del Río Fardes y Río Guadahortuna, (Granada)', *Anuario Arqueológico de Andalucía* 2 1992 (1995), 145–152.

González Román, C., Adroher Auroux, A. M. and López Marcos, A. 'El Peñón de Arruta (Jerez del Marquesado, Granada): una explotación minera romana', *FlorIlib* 8 (1997), 183–213.

González Román, C. 'Ciudad y poblamiento romano en la provincia de Granada durante el Alto Imperio', *Habis* 32 (2001), 271–296.

González Román, C. 'La ciudadanía, un proceso histórico de integración en la Roma republicana', in *Ciudadanos y extranjeros en el mundo antiguo: segregación e integración*, ed. J. Mangas Manjarrés and S. Montero Herrero (Madrid 2007), 195–225.

González Román, C. '*Acci*, la *colonia* y sus *cives*', in *Andalucía romana y visigoda. Ordenación y vertebración del territorio*, ed. J. González Fernández and P. Pavón Torrejón (Rome 2009), 229–252.

González Román, C. '*Colonia Iulia Gemella Acci* (Guadix, Granada)', in *Colonias de César y Augusto en la Andalucía romana*, ed. J. González Fernández and J. C. Saquete Chamizo (Rome 2011), 299–341.

González Román, C. 'Homogeneidad y diversidad en las colonias romanas: reflexiones desde *Acci*', in Debita verba. *Estudios en homenaje al profesor Julio Mangas Manjarrés*, ed. R. M. Cid and E. B. Fernández (Madrid 2013), 31–51.

Gourévitch, D. and Raepsaet-Charlier, M.-T. *La femme dans la Rome antique* (Paris 2001).

Goyau, G. 'La *Numidia Militiana* de la liste de Vérone', *MEFRA* 13 (1893), 251–279.

Graham, E.-J. 'The Quick and the Dead in the Extra-Urban Landscape: the Roman Cemetery at Ostia/Portus as a Lived Environment', in *TRAC 2004: Proceedings of the Fourteenth Annual Theoretical Roman Archaeology Conference, Durham 2004*, ed. J. Bruhn, B. Croxford and D. Grigoropoulos (Oxford 2005), 133–143.

Gregori, G. L. '*Loca sepulturae publice data* e *funera publica* nel Lazio d'età romana: qualche considerazione sulla documentazione epigrafica', in *Sepolti tra i vivi. Buried among the Living. Evidenza ed interpretazione di contesti funerari in abitato. Atti del Convegno Internazionale (Roma, 26–29 Aprile 2006), Scienze dell'Antichità. Storia Archeologia Antropologia* 14, no. 2, ed. G. Bartolomi and M. G. Benedettini (Rome 2007–2008), 1067–1079.

Groag, E. 'Patricier und *IIIviri monetales*', *Archäologisch-epigraphische Mitteilungen aus Österreich-Ungarn* 19 (1896).

Gros, P. *L'architecture romaine : du début du III^e siècle av. J.-C. à la fin du Haut-Empire. 1, Les monuments publics* (Paris 2002).

Gruter, J. *Inscriptiones antiquae totius orbis romani* (Amsterdam 1602).

Gsell, S. 'Notes d'archéologie algérienne', *BCTH* (1901), 308–323.

Gsell, S. 'Observations géographiques sur la révolte de Firmus', *Recueil de la société archéologique de Constantine* 36 (1902), 21–46.

Gsell, S. 'Chapelle chrétienne d'Henchir Akhrib (Algérie)', *MEFRA* 23 (1903), 3–25.

Guantes García, J. 'Maternidad y filiaciones en la Roma primitiva. Una revisión del rapto de las Sabinas', in *Madres y familias en la Antigüedad: Patrones femeninos en la transmisión de emociones y de patrimonio*, ed. R. M. Cid López, A. Domínguez Arranz and R. M. Marina Sáez (Gijón 2021), 99–114.

Guédon, S. *La frontière romaine de l'Africa sous le Haut-Empire* (Madrid 2018a).

Guédon, S. 'La frontière de l'Afrique romaine à l'époque tardive : Le cas emblématique de Tobna et du *limes Tubuniensis* (Notitia Dignitatum, Occ., 25.25)', *Historia* 67, no. 3 (2018b), 366–387.

Guédon, S. 'Road Network and Roman Frontier in Numidia: The Region of Tobna', in *Roman Roads: New Evidence – New Perspectives*, ed. A. Kolb (Berlin and Boston 2019), 323–337.

Gurlitt, W. *Über Pausanias* (Graz 1890).

Hächler, N. and Horster, M. 'Le regard du vainqueur?', in *The Impact of the Roman Empire on Landscapes. Proceedings of the Fourteenth Workshop of the International Network Impact of Empire (Mainz, June 12–15, 2019)*, ed. M. Horster and N. Hächler (Leiden 2022), 3–17.

Haensch, R. Capita provinciarum. *Statthaltersitze und Provinzialverwaltung in der römischen Kaiserzeit* (Mainz 1997).

Halkin, L. *La supplication d'action de grâces chez les Romains* (Paris 1953).

Hallett, J. P. *Fathers and Daughters in Roman Society. Women and the Elite Family* (Princeton 1984).

Haley, E. W., Baetica Felix. *People and Prosperity in Southern Spain from Caesar to Septimius Severus* (Austin 2009).

Hänninen, M. L. 'Religious Agency and Civic Identity of Women in Ancient *Ostia*', in *Gender, Memory and Identity in the Roman World*, ed. J. Rantala (Amsterdam 2019), 63–88.

Haeussler, R. *Becoming Roman? Diverging Identities and Experiences in Ancient Northwest Italy* (London 2013).

Häussler, R. 'Writing Latin – from Resistance to Assimilation: Language, Culture and Society', in N. Italy and S. Gaul', in *Becoming Roman, Writing Latin? Literacy and epigraphy in the Roman West*, ed. A. E. Cooley (Portsmouth 2002), 61–76.

Heinzelmann, M. *Die Nekropolen von* Ostia. *Untersuchungen zu den Gräberstraßen vor der Porta Romana und an der Via Laurentina* (Munich 2000).

Heinzelmann, M. 'Les nécropoles d'Ostie : topographie, développement, architecture, structure social', in Ostia, *port et porte de la Rome antique*, ed. J. P. Descœudres (Genoa 2001a), 373–384.

Heinzelmann, M. 'La situazione di Roma', in *Römischer Bestattungsbrauch und Beigabensitten in Rom, Norditalien und den Nordwestprovinzen von der späten Republik bis in die Kaiserzeit*, ed. M. Heinzelmann, J. Ortalli, P. Fasold, and M. Witteyer (Wiesbaden, 2001b), 23–34.

Helttula, A. 'On *itum ambitum datum*: a Formula of *ius sepulchri*', *Arctos* 8 (1974), 9–17.

Hemelrijk, E. A. Matrona Docta. *Educated Women in the Roman Elite from Cornelia to Julia Domna* (London–New York 1999).

Henderson, M. I. 'Julius Caesar and *Latium* in Spain', *JRS* 32 (1942), 1–13.

Herrmann, C. *Le rôle judiciaire et politique des femmes sous la République romaine* (Brussels 1964).

Herrman, P. *Der römische Kaisereid: Untersuchungen zu seiner Herkunft und Entwicklung* (Göttingen 1968).

Hernández Fernández, J. S. 'Tito Livio XLIII, 3 y los *nomina* de los magistrados monetales de Carteia', *Faventia* 16, no. 2 (1994), 86–107.

Herrera Rando, J. *Cultura epigráfica y romanización en la Hispania meridional. La epigrafía pública entre la república y el imperio* (Vitoria 2020).

Herzig, H. E. 'Frauen in *Ostia*: Ein Beitrag zur Sozialgeschichte der Hafenstadt Roms', *Historia* 32, no. 1 (1983), 77–92.

Hidalgo, R. 'En torno a la imagen urbana de Italica', *Romula* 2 (2003), 89–126.

Hidalgo, R. 'Anfiteatros', in *Arte romano de la Bética. Arquitectura y urbanismo*, ed. P. León (Seville 2008), 222–231.

Hilali, A. 'Recherche sur les frontières de l'Afrique romaine : espaces mobiles et représentations', in *Frontiers in the Roman World: Proceedings of the Ninth Workshop of the International Network Impact of Empire (Durham, 16–19 April 2009)*, ed. T. Kaizer and O. Hekster (Leiden 2011), 97–111.

Hillebrand, S. '*Der Vigintivirat: Prosopographische Untersuchungen für die Zeit von Augustus bis Domitian*' (Ph. D. diss., University of Heidelberg, 2006).

Höbenreich, E. 'Andróginas y monstruos. Mujeres que hablan en la antigua Roma', *Veleia* 22 (2005), 173–182.

Hörster, M. *Bauinschriften römischer Kaiser: Untersuchungen zu Inschriftenpraxis und Bautätigkeit in Städten des westlichen Imperium Romanum in der Zeit des Prinzipats* (Stuttgart 2011).

Hörster, M. 'Coinage and Images of the Imperial Family: Local Identity and Roman Rule', *JRA* 26 (2013), 243–262.

Hörster, M. and Hächler, N. (ed.), *The Impact of the Roman Empire on Landscapes. Proceedings of the Fourteenth Workshop of the International Network Impact of Empire (Mainz, June 12–15, 2019)* (Leiden 2021).

Houten, P. *Urbanisation in Roman Spain and Portugal*: Civitates Hispaniae *in the Early Empire* (London 2021).

Isserlin, R. M. J. 'A Spirit of Improvement? Marble and the Culture of Roman Britain', in *Cultural Identity in the Roman Empire*, ed. R. Laurence and J. Berry (London–New York 1998), 125–155.

Jacques, F. '*Ampliatio* et *mora*: Evergètes récalcitrants d'Afrique romaine', *AntAfr* 9 (1975), 159–180.

Jacques, F. 'Propriétés impériales et cités en Numidie Méridionale', *CGG* 3 (1992), 123–139.

Jehne, M. and Pina Polo, F. (eds.), *Foreign* Clientelae *in the Roman Empire. A Reconsideration* (Stuttgart 2015).

Jiménez Sancho, A., Rodríguez Gutiérrez, O. and Izquierdo, R. 'Novedades arqueológicas adrianeas en el teatro de Itálica y su entorno', in Roma, Tibur, Baetica. *Investigaciones adrianeas*, ed. R. Hidalgo and P. León (Seville 2013), 286–291.

Jiménez Hernández, A. 'Errores de replanteo en el anfiteatro de Itálica', *Arqueología de la arquitectura* 15 (2018) 5–18.

Jiménez Sancho, A. 'Italica. La red de alcantarillado', in *La gestión de los residuos urbanos en Hispania*, ed. J. A. Remolà and J. Acero (Merida 2011), 145–156.

Jiménez Sancho, A. 'Nuevas aportaciones sobre la construcción y evolución del graderío del teatro de Itálica: los resultados de las campañas de excavación de 2009 y 2011', *Italica* 2 (2012), 99–126.

Jiménez Sancho, A. 'La *porticus* del teatro de *Italica* y su transformación en santuario de Isis', in *La* porticus post scaenam *en la arquitectura teatral romana*, ed. S. F. Ramallo and E. Ruiz Valderas (Murcia 2020), 83–100.

Johne, K. P., Koehn, J. and Weber, V. *Die Kolonen in Italien und den westlichen Provinzen des römischen Reiches* (Berlin 1983).

Johnston, D. 'Munificence and *Municipia*: Bequests to Towns in Classical Roman Law', *JRS* 75 (1985), 105–125.

Johnston, D. *Roman Law in Context* (Cambridge 2022).

Johnstone, S. *A History of Trust in Ancient Greece* (Chicago 2011).

Jongman, W. 'Gibbon was Right: the Decline and Fall of the Roman Economy', in *Crises and the Roman Empire*, ed. O. Hekster et al. (Leiden 2007), 183–200.

Julien, Ch. A. *Histoire de l'Afrique du Nord* I (Paris 1968).

Kaizer T., and Hekster, O. (eds.), *Frontiers in the Roman World. Proceedings of the Ninth Workshop of the International Network Impact of Empire (Durham, 16–19 April 2009)* (Leiden 2011).

Kajanto, I. *The Latin Cognomina* (Helsinki 1965).

Kantor, G. 'Property in Land in Roman Provinces', in *Legalism: Property and Ownership*, ed. G. Kantor, T. Lambert and H. Skoda (Oxford 2017), 55–74.

Kasdi, Z. 'P. *Aelius Peregrinus Rogatus* et le gouvernement de la province de Maurétanie césarienne', *CGG* 27 (2016), 325–360.

Keay, S. J. 'Early Roman *Italica* and the Romanisation of Western Baetica', in *Italica MMCC*, ed. A. Caballos Rufino and P. León (Seville 1997), 21–48.

Keegan, J. G. 'The Will of *Caius Longinus Castor*', *BASP* 31, No. 3/4 (1994), 101–107.

Knapp, R. C. 'The Origins of Provincial Prosopography in the West', *AncSoc* 9 (1978), 187–222.

Knapp, R. C. 'La "*Via Heraclea*" en Occidente: Mito, arqueología, propaganda, historia', *Emerita* 54 (1986), 103–122.

Kremer, D. Ius Latinum. *Le concept de droit latin sous la République et l'Empire* (Paris 2006).

Kremer, D. 'Un conflit de propriété à Ostie au milieu du IIe siècle de n.è. Nouvelles considérations sur la supposée fondation funéraire de *Iunia Libertas*', *Iura* 61 (2013), 25–45.

Krieckhaus, A. *Senatorische Familien und ihre* patriae *(1./2. Jahrhundert n. Chr.)* (Hamburg 2006).

Kubitschek, J. W. *Imperium Romanum tributim discriptum* (Rome 1972).

Kulikowski, M. *Late Roman Spain and its Cities* (Baltimore 2004).

Laffi, U. 'Sobre la organización administrativa de Italia después de la Guerra social', in *Sociedad y política en la Roma republicana (siglos III–I a.C.)*, ed. E. Gabba and U. Laffi (Pisa 2000a), 79–94.

Laffi, U. 'La Italia romana: ciudades y estructuras administrativas', in *Sociedad y política en la Roma republicana (siglos III–I a.C.)*, ed. E. Gabba and U. Laffi (Pisa 2000b), 25–40.

Laffi, U. 'Osservazioni sulla *lex municipii Tarentini*', *RAL* ser. IX, 15 (4) (2004), 618–620.

Laffi, U. 'La struttura costituzionale nei municipi e nelle colonie romane. Magistrati, decurioni, popolo', in *Gli statuti municipali*, ed. L. Capogrossi Colognesi and E. Gabba (Pavia 2006), 109–132.

Langslow, D. R. 'Approaching Bilingualism in Corpus Languages', in *Bilingualism in Ancient Society. Language Contact and the Written Word*, ed. J. N. Adams, M. Janse and S. Swain, (Oxford 2002), 23–51.

Laporte, J.-P. Rapidum, *Le camp de la cohorte des Sardes en Maurétanie Césarienne* (Sassari 1989).

Laporte, J.-P. 'La limite entre les Maurétanies Césarienne et Sitifienne', in *Frontières et limites géographiques de l'Afrique du Nord antique. Hommage à Pierre Salama*, éd. C. Lepelley and X. Dupuis (Paris 1999), 213–219.

Lapuente, M. P., Turi, B. and Blanc, Ch. 'Marbles and Coloured Stones from the Theatre of *Caesaraugusta* (Hispania): Preliminary Study', in *ASMOSIA VII Actes du VII*[e] *colloque international de l'ASMOSIA Thasos 15–20 septembre 2003*, ed. Y. Maniatis (Athens 2013), 509–522.

Lassère, J.-M. Ubique populus. *Peuplement et mouvements de population dans l'Afrique romaine de la chute de Carthage à la fin de la dynastie des Sévères (146 a.C.–235 p.C.)* (Paris 1977).

Laubry, N. 'La désignation de la postérité. Autour de la formule *libertis libertabusque posterisque eorum* dans les inscriptions funéraires romaines', in *Esclaves et maîtres dans le monde romain. Expressions épigraphiques de leurs relations*, ed. M. Dondin-Payre and N. Tran (Rome 2016), 67–79.

Laubry, N. '*Monumentum Cartilianum*. Droit des tombeaux et société locale à Ostie', *ZPE* 206 (2018), 225–233.

Laubry, N. '*Iura sepulcrorum* à Ostie: un supplément', in *Ricerche su* Ostia *e il suo territorio. Atti del Terzo Seminario Ostiense (Roma, École française de Rome, 21–22 ottobre 2015)*, ed. M. Cébeillac-Gervasoni, N. Laubry and F. Zevi (Rome 2019), 349–367.

Lázaro Pérez, R. 'Epigrafía del Municipio Romano de *Alba Bastetanorum* (Abla-Almería)', in *El municipio romano de* Alba *(Alba, Almería), administración, sociedad y economía*, ed. A. J. Ortíz Ocaña (Almería 2016), 137–152.

Le Bohec, Y. *Frontières et limites militaires de la Maurétanie Césarienne sous le Haut-Empire* (Algiers 1982).

Le Bohec, Y. 'Frontières et limites militaires de la Maurétanie Césarienne sous le Haut-Empire', in *Frontières et limites géographiques de l'Afrique du Nord antique. Hommage à Pierre Salama*, ed. C. Lepelley and X. Dupuis (Paris 1999), 111–127.

Lefebvre, S. 'Les migrations des *Africani* en Péninsule Ibérique : Quelle vérité?', in Migrare. *La formation des élites dans l'Hispanie romaine*, ed. A. Caballos Rufino and S. Demougin (Bordeaux 2006), 101–203.

Lenoir, M. *Le camp romain. Proche-Orient et Afrique du Nord* (Rome 2011).

León, P. 'Itálica: problemática de la superposición de Santiponce al yacimiento', in *Arqueología de las ciudades modernas superpuestas a las antiguas* (Madrid 1985), 213–230.

León, P. Traianeum *de Itálica* (Seville 1988).

León, P. *Esculturas de Itálica* (Seville 1995).

León, P. *Retratos romanos de la Bética* (Seville 2001).

León, P. 'La Itálica adrianea', in *Adriano Augusto*, ed. J. M. Cortés and E. Muñiz (Seville 2004), 125–138.

León, P. '*Italica* de la madurez trajanea a la mutación adrianea', in *De Trajano a Adriano*. Roma matura, Roma mutans, ed. A. Caballos Rufino (Seville 2019), 729–750.

León, P. '*Italica*. Génesis y desarrollo del proyecto adrianeo', in Adventus Hadriani. *Investigaciones sobre arquitectura adrianea*, ed. G. E. Cinque, R. Hidalgo, A. Pizzo and A. Viscogliosi (Rome 2020a), 279–295.

León, P. 'Restos de acrolitos del *Traianeum* de *Italica*', in *Escultura romana en Hispania IX: Actas de la Reunión Internacional celebrada en Yecla del 27 al 29 de marzo de 2019*, ed. J. M. Noguera and L. Ruiz Molina (Murcia 2020b), 369–378.

León, P. 'Nuevas consideraciones sobre el *Traianeum* de *Italica*', in Adventus Hadriani. *Investigaciones sobre arquitectura adrianea*, ed. G. E. Cinque, R. Hidalgo, A. Pizzo and A. Viscogliosi (Rome 2020c), 297–308.

León, P. *Italica. La ciudad de Trajano y Adriano* (Seville 2021).

León, P. 'La contribución del mármol al prestigio de la arquitectura y de la escultura en la Italica adrianea', in *Tituli-Imagines-Marmora. Materia y prestigio en mármol. Homenaje a Isabel Rodà de Llanza*, ed. A. Gutiérrez García-Moreno and D. Gorostidi Pi (Madrid 2022), 229–236.

Le Roux, P. 'Les sénateurs originaires de la province d'*Hispania Citerior* au Haut–Empire romain', in *Epigrafia e ordine senatorio* 2 (Rome 1982), [=].

Le Roux, P. 'Peut-on parler de la cité hispano-romaine aux II^e^–III^e^ s. ? Questions de forme et questions de fond pour une absence de synthèse', in *Ciudad y comunidad cívica en Hispania* (*siglos II y III d.C.*), ed. E. Ortiz de Urbina (Madrid 1993), 187–195.

Le Roux, P. 'Oriunda Mauretania', in Ubique amici. *Mélanges offerts à Jean-Marie Lassère*, ed. C. Hamdoune (Montpellier 2001), 239–248.

Le Roux, P. 'Magistrats locaux et pouvoirs dans les cités des provinces hispaniques au Haut-Empire romain', in *Magistrados locales de Hispania. Aspectos históricos, jurídicos, lingüísticos*, ed. E. Ortiz de Urbina Álava (Vitoria 2013), 229–251.

Le Roux, P. 'Les sénateurs originaires d'Espagne citérieure (2) : un bilan 1982–2006', in *Epigrafia 2006. Atti della XIV^e^ rencontre sur l'épigraphie in onore di Silvio Panciera con altri contributi di colleghi, allievi e collaboratori*, III, ed. M. L. Caldelli, G. L. Gregori and S. Orlandi (Rome 2008), 1003–1027.

Le Roux, P. 'L'émigration italique en Citérieure et Lusitanie jusqu'à la mort de Néron', in *Roma y el nacimiento de la cultura epigráfica en Occidente*, ed. F. Beltrán Lloris (Zaragoza 1995), 85–95.

Le Roux P. *Espagnes romaines. L'Empire dans ses provinces. Scripta varia* II (Rennes 2014).

Le Roux, P. *L'Empire romain. Histoire et modèles. Scripta varia III* (Rennes 2022).

López Fonseca, A. 'El viaje en la novela latina: El Satiricón de Petronio y El Asno de oro de Apuleyo', *Revista de Filología Románica* 4 (2006), 77–84.

López García, A. 'La ciudad andalusí: El caso de Guadix', *Péndulo: Papeles de Bastitania* 8 (2007), 21–50.

López García, A. and Reyes Martínez, A. 'Apuntes para una historiografía de la Arqueología en la ciudad de Guadix (Granada). Entre los mitos y la realidad', in *Colecciones, arqueólogos, instituciones y yacimientos en la España de los siglos XVIII al XX*, ed. S. España Chamorro, R. Arranz Santos and A. Romero Molero (Oxford 2018), 61–74.

López García, A. 'The Discovery of a Roman Road between *Carthago Nova* (Cartagena) and *Iulia Gemella Acci* (Guadix), Spain', in *Archaeologies of Roads*, ed. T. Kalayci (Grand Forks 2023), 123–145.

López Godoy, N. *et al.* 'Prospección en el pasillo de Fiñana (Almería)', *Anuario Arqueológico de Andalucía 1987*, vol. 2 (1990), 73–76.

López Marcos, A. and Adroher Auroux, A. M. 'Un asentamiento rural romano en las estribaciones septentrionales de Sierra Nevada. Cortijo Cecilio (Fiñana, Almería)', in *1ª Conferencia Internacional de Sierra Nevada. Conservación y desarrollo sostenible*, ed. J. Chacón and J. L. Rosúa (Granada 1996), 11–28.

López Marcos, A. 'La "*porticus post scaenam*" del teatro de Guadix', in *La* "porticus post scaenam" *en la arquitectura teatral romana*, ed. S. F. Ramallo Asensio and E. Ruíz Valderas (Murcia 2018a), 101–117.

López Marcos, A., García Tortosa, F.J, Díaz Herrero, A. and Arribas, A. 'Inundaciones históricas en el teatro romano de Acci (Guadix, Granada) a través del registro sedimentológico', in *Geomorfología del Antropoceno. Efectos del Cambio Global sobre los procesos geomorfológicos*, ed. C. García, L. Gómez Pujol, E. Morán Tejeda and R. J. Batalla (Palma de Mallorca 2018b), 61–64.

López Moreda, S., Harto Trujillo, M. L. and Villalba Álvarez, J. 'Introducción general: valor educativo de los *exempla*', in *Valerio Máximo, Hechos y dichos memorables: Libros I–VI* (Madrid 2003), 39–44.

López Sánchez, F. 'La crisis de las ciudades hispanas comenzó con Adriano: ¿decadencia interna o falta de estímulos externos?', in Oppida labentia. *Transformaciones, cambios y alteración en las ciudades hispanas entre el siglo II y la tardoantigüedad*, ed. J. Andreu (Uncastillo 2017), 157–176.

Lowe, B. 'Bilingualism and Language Contact in Republican Iberia', *Epigraphica* 76 (2014), 111–146.

Loza, M. L. 'El agua en los teatros hispanorromanos. Elementos escultóricos', *Habis* 25 (1994), 263–284.

Loza, M. L. *et al.*, '*Marmora* de *Italica*: Elementos arquitectónicos procedentes del solar de la calle Feria 19 (Santiponce, Sevilla)', in Italica. *Investigaciones arqueológicas en la* Vetus Urbs, J. Beltrán and J. L. Escacena (Seville 2021), 171–196.

Lozano Gómez, F. 'El surgimiento y desarrollo de la adoración imperial: la dicotomía explicativa imposición-espontaneidad', in *Jerarquías religiosas y control social en el mundo antiguo. Actas del XXVII Congreso Internacional GIREA-ARYS*, ed. L. Hernández Guerra and J. Alvar (Valladolid 2002), 433–439.

Luraschi, G. Foedus, ius Latii, civitas. *Aspetti costituzionali della romanizzazione in Transpadana* (Padua 1979).

Luzón, J. M. *Excavaciones en Itálica. Estratigrafía en el Pajar de Artillo* (Madrid 1973).

Luzón, J. M. *La Itálica de Adriano* (Seville 1975).

Luzón, J. M. 'Consideraciones sobre la urbanística de la ciudad nueva de Itálica', in *Itálica (Santiponce, Sevilla)*, ed. P. León (Madrid 1982a), 77–95.

Luzón, J. M. 'El teatro romano de ltálica', in *Actas del Simposio El Teatro en la Hispania Romana* (Badajoz 1982b), 183–201.

Machuca Prieto, F. *Una forma fenicia de ser romano: identidad e integración de las comunidades fenicias de la Península Ibérica bajo poder de Roma* (Seville 2019).

MacMullen, R. 'The Epigraphic Habit in the Roman Empire', *AJPh* 103 (1982), 233–246.

Madrid Balanza, M. J. and Noguera Celdrán, J. M. '*Carthago Nova* fases e hitos de monumentalización urbana y arquitectónica (siglos III a.C.–III d.C.)', *EFT* 7 (2014), 13–60.

Manni, E. *Per la storia dei municipi fino alla guerra sociale* (Rome 1947).

Manning, J. G. *The Open Sea. The Economic Life of the Ancient Mediterranean World from the Iron Age to the Rise of Rome* (Princeton–Oxford 2018).

Mañas, I. 'Pavimentos decorativos de Itálica. Una fuente para el estudio de la ampliación adrianea', *Romula* 8 (2009), 197–198.

Mañas, I. 'Arquitectura doméstica', in *Itálica-Santiponce.* Municipium *y* Colonia Aelia Augusta Italicensium, ed. A. Caballos Rufino (Rome 2010), 81–98.

Mañas, I. *Mosaicos romanos de Itálica (II): mosaicos contextualizados y apéndice* (Madrid 2011).

Marco Simón, F. 'Los inicios del culto imperial en la Hispania augustea', *Gerión* 35, no. 1 (2017), 773–789.

Marín Díaz, N. and Gorlat, J. C. 'Los orígenes de *Acci* y su configuración como importante centro urbano en la Antigüedad', in *Tres estudios sobre Guadix y su tierra*, ed. M. Espinar Moreno (Guadix 1990), 1–34.

Marinucci, A. Disiecta membra. *Iscrizioni latine da* Ostia *e Porto 1981–2009* (Rome 2012).

Marotta, V. 'Doppia cittadinanza e pluralità degli ordinamenti. La *Tabula Banasitana* e le linee 7–9 del Papiro di Giessen 40 col. I', *AG* 236 (3–4) (2016), 461–491.

Martín, F. 'Sobre el significado de provincia', in Vrbs aeterna. *Actas y colaboraciones del coloquio internacional, Roma entre la literatura y la historia: homenaje a la profesora Carmen Castillo*, ed. C. Alonso del Real, P. García Ruiz, A. Sánchez-Ortiz and J. B. Torres Guerra (Pamplona 2003), 177–186.

Martín-Bueno, M. 'La ciudad Julio-Claudia, ¿una estrella fugaz?', in *II Congreso de Arqueología Peninsular*, vol. IV, ed. R. de Balbín and P. Bueno (Zamora 1997), 117–122.

Martín-Bueno, M. 'La ciudad hispanorromana: deseo y realidad', in Oppida labentia. *Transformaciones, cambios y alteración en las ciudades hispanas entre el siglo II y la tardoantigüedad*, ed. J. Andreu (Uncastillo 2017), 3–35.

Martínez Chico, D. and González García, A. 'Análisis metalográfico e isotópico del « bronce de Tiberio », epígrafe jurídico bético del año 14 d. C.', *CPAM* 48, no. 2 (2022), 183–204.

Martínez López, C. 'Las mujeres y la paz en la Historia. Aportaciones desde el mundo antiguo', in *Historia de la paz: tiempos, espacios y actores*, ed. F. A. Muñoz Muñoz and M. López Martínez (Granada 2000), 255–290.

Mataix Ferrándiz, E. *Shipwrecks, Legal Landscapes and Mediterranean Paradigms. Gone under Sea* (Leiden 2022).

Mateos Cruz, P. and Picado Pérez, Y. 'El teatro romano de *Metellinum*', *MDAI(M)* 52 (2011), 373–410.

Mattingly, D. J. *Tripolitania* (London 1995).

Mawani, R. *Accross Oceans of Law. The Komagata Maru and Jurisdiction in the Time of Empire* (Durham–London 2018).

Mayer M. and Rodá I. 'The Use of Marble and Decorative Stone in Roman *Baetica*', in *The Archaeology of Early Roman Baetica*, ed. S. Keay (Portsmouth 1998), 217–234.

McGinn, T. A. J. '*Cui bono?* The True Beneficiaries of Roman Private Law', in *Ancient Law, Ancient Society*, ed. D. P. Kehoe and T. A. J. McGinn (Ann Arbor 2017), 133–166.

Meiggs, R. *Roman* Ostia (Oxford 1973).

Melchor Gil, E. 'La construcción pública en la Hispania romana: iniciativa imperial, municipal y privada', *MHA* 13–14 (1992–1993), 129–170.

Melchor Gil, E. and Pérez Zurita, A. D. 'La concesión de honores públicos a magistrados y decuriones en las ciudades de la Bética', *FlorIlib* 14 (2003a), 173–233.

Melchor Gil, E. 'Aportaciones pecuniarias de los notables locales a las finanzas municipales de las ciudades hispanas', in *Sociedad y economía en el occidente romano*, ed. J. F. Rodríguez Neila, C. Castillo, and F. J. Navarro (Pamplona 2003b), 199–230.

Melchor Gil, E. 'Las élites municipales hispanorromanas a fines de la República y en el Alto Imperio: ideología y conductas sociopolíticas', in Hispaniae. *Las provincias hispanas en el mundo romano*, ed. J. Andreu Pintado, J. Cabrero Piquero and I. Rodà de Llanza (Tarragona 2009a), 391–410.

Melchor Gil, E. 'La regulación jurídica del evergetismo edilicio durante el alto Imperio', *Butlletì Arqueològic* 31 (2009b), 145–169.

Melchor Gil, E. '*Quattuorviri* y *aediles* en los municipios de constitución cuatorviral a fines de la República y en época altoimperial', *RSA* 43 (2013a), 133–152.

Melchor Gil, E. 'Instituciones de gobierno de las comunidades hispanas no privilegiadas (s. III a.C.–s. I d.C.): *senatus* y *magistratus*', in *Magistrados locales de Hispania. Aspectos históricos, jurídicos, lingüísticos*, ed. E. Ortiz de Urbina Álava (Vitoria 2013b), 117–139.

Melchor Gil, E. 'Magistrados y magistraturas en la Carmona romana', in *El gobierno municipal de Carmona a lo largo de la historia. Actas VIII Congreso de Historia de Carmona*, ed. M. González Jiménez and A. Caballos Rufino, Seville [2013c], 39–58.

Melchor Gil, E. 'François Jacques tenía razón: sobre el no declinar de las élites locales y de la vida municipal durante el siglo II y el primer tercio del siglo III d.C.', in Oppida labentia. *Transformaciones, cambios y alteración en las ciudades hispanas entre el siglo II y la tardoantigüedad*, ed. J. Andreu (Uncastillo 2017), 217–244.

Melchor Gil, E. *El patronato cívico en la Hispania romana* (Seville 2018).

Mellado Rivera, J. A. Princeps Iuventutis. *La imagen monetaria del heredero en la época Julio-Claudia* (Alicante 2002).

Meyer, E. A. 'Explaining Epigraphic Habit in the Roman Empire: The Evidence of Epitaphs', *JRS* 80 (1990), 74–96.

Millar, F. *The Crowd in Rome in the Late Republic* (Ann Arbor 2002).

Milnor, K. 'Augustus, History, and the Landscape of the Law', *Arethusa* 40, no. 1 (2007), 7–23.

Mirón, M. D. 'Las sacerdotisas béticas del culto imperial: ciudadanía, movilidad y control territorial', in *El mundo religioso hispano bajo el Imperio romano: pervivencias y cambios*, ed. L. Hernández Guerra (Valladolid 2007), 167–178.

Modéran, Y. in *Encyclopédie berbère* 31, s. v. 'Maurétanies (Provinces)', 4737–4751 (online): [https://journals.openedition.org/encyclopedieberbere/523].

Modéran, Y. *Les Maures et l'Afrique romaine* (*IV*$^{e}$–*VII*$^{e}$ *siècle*) (Rome 2003).

Mommsen, T. *Römisches Straatsrecht* III$^{3}$ (Leipzig 1887).

Morbidelli, P. *et al.*, 'Roman Quarries of the Iberian Peninsula: "Anasol" and "Anasol"-type', *European Journal Mineralogy* 19 (2007), 125–133.

Morizot, P. 'La présence romaine dans le Djebel Amour (Algérie) : Apport des images Spot et de la photographie aérienne', in *Frontières et limites géographiques de l'Afrique du Nord antique. Hommage à Pierre Salama*, ed. C. Lepelley and X. Dupuis (Paris 1999), 185–212.

Mouritsen, H. 'Freedmen and Freeborn in the Necropolis of Imperial *Ostia*', *ZPE* 150 (2004), 281–304.

Mouritsen, H. 'Freedmen and Decurions: Epitaphs and Social History in Imperial Italy', *JRS* 95 (2005), 38–63.

Muñiz Grijalvo, E. and Lozano, F. 'Imperial Cult Processions and Landscape in the Greek Cities of the Roman Empire: The Case of the Demosthenia of Oenoanda', in *The Impact of the Roman Empire on Landscapes. Proceedings of the Fourteenth Workshop of the International Network Impact of Empire* (*Mainz, June 12–15, 2019*), ed. M. Horster and N. Hächler (Leiden 2022), 249–262.

Murciano, J. M. Monumenta. *Tipología monumental funeraria en* Augusta Emerita. *Origen y desarrollo entre los siglos I a.C. y IV d.C.* (Merida 2019).

Mustakallio, K. 'Women Outside their Homes. The Female Voice in Early Republican Memory: Reconsidering *Cloelia* and *Veturia*', *Index* 40 (2012), 165–174.

Navarro, F. J. 'La presencia del emperador en las ciudades de la Hispania romana', in *De Augusto a Trajano. Un siglo en la historia de Hispania*, ed. F. J. Navarro (Pamplona 2000), 33–55.

Navarro, F. J. 'La organización provincial de Hispania durante el Imperio Romano (Siglos I–III)', in Hispaniae. *Las provincias hispanas en el mundo romano*, ed. J. Andreu Pintado, J. Cabrero Piquero and I. Rodà de Llanza (2009), 345–360.

Navarro Caballero, M. Perfectissima femina. *Femmes de l'élite dans l'Hispanie romaine*, Bordeaux, 2017.

Nichols, J. *Civic Patronage in the Roman Empire* (Leiden 2014).

Nicolet, C. 'L'onomastique des groupes dirigeants sous la République', in *L'onomastique latine*, ed. H.-G. Pflaum and N. Duval (Paris 1977), 45–61.

Nogales Barrasate, T., Gonçalves, L. and Lapuente, P. 'Materiales lapídeos, mármoles y talleres en Lusitania', in *Marmora Hispana: explotación y uso de los materiales pétreos en la Hispania Romana*, ed. T. Nogales and J. Beltrán (Rome 2008), 407–466.

Ogilvie, R. M. *A Commentary on Livy. Books 1–5* (Oxford 1965).

Öğüş, E. 'Columnar Sarcophagi from Aphrodisias: Construction of Elite Identity in the Greek East' (Ph.D. diss., Harvard University, 2010).

Olivanti, P. and Spanu, M. 'Necropoli dell'Isola Sacra, scavo 1988–1989: alcune riflessioni su occupazione degli spazi, cronologia delle sepolture, corredi', in *Ricerche su* Ostia *e il suo territorio. Atti del Terzo Seminario Ostiense* (*Roma, École française de Rome, 21–22 ottobre 2015*), ed. M. Cébeillac-Gervasoni, N. Laubry and F. Zevi (Rome 2019), 67–77.

Olmo López, R. *El centro está en la periferia. Las competencias de los gobernadores provinciales romanos en Hispania durante el Principado* (Zürich 2018).

Ordóñez Agulla, S. and García-Dils de la Vega, S. '786. Pedestal en homenaje a un sacerdote y magistrado local procedente del entorno de Marchena (Sevilla)', *Ficheiro Epigráfico* 223 (2021a), 8–16.

Ordóñez Agulla, S. and García-Dils de la Vega, S. 'Un municipio romano en Marchena (Sevilla)', in *Arqueología y numismática. Estudios en homenaje a la profesora Francisca Chaves Tristán*, ed. E. Ferrer Albelda, M. Oria Segura, E. García Vargas, F. J. García Fernández and R. Pliego Vázquez (Seville 2021b), 777–790.

Orfila Pons, M., Castillo Rueda, M. A. and Casado Millán, P. J. 'Estudio preliminar de los elementos constructivos hidráulicos de época romana del río Cubillas (Tramo Deifontes-Albolote, Granada)', *AAC* 7 (1996), 83–114.

Orlin, E. 'Augustan Reconstruction and Roman Memory', in *Memory in Ancient Rome and Early Christianity*, ed. K. Galinsky (Oxford 2016), 115–144.

Ørsted, P. '*Quattuor publica Africae*: Custom Duties or Landtax?', in *L'Africa romana. Atti del IX convegno di studio su « L'Africa romana ». Nuoro, 13–15 dicembre 1991*, vol. II, ed. A. Mastino (Sassari 1992), 812–829.

Ortiz de Urbina, E. (ed.) *Ciudad y comunidad cívica en Hispania (siglos II y III d.C.)* (Madrid 1993).

Ortiz de Urbina, E. *Las comunidades hispanas y el derecho latino: Observaciones sobre los procesos de integración local en la práctica político-administrativa al modo romano* (Vitoria 2000).

Ortiz de Urbina Álava, E. 'Sobre los procesos de (re)organización institucional cívica en Hispania', in *Magistrados locales de Hispania. Aspectos históricos, jurídicos, lingüísticos*, ed. E. Ortiz de Urbina Álava (Vitoria 2013), 279–308.

Ozcáriz Gil, P. 'Organización administrativa y territorial de las provincias hispanas durante el Alto Imperio', in Hispaniae. *Las provincias hispanas en el mundo romano*, ed. J. Andreu Pintado, J. Cabrero Piquero and I. Rodà de Llanza (2009), 323–338.

Ozcáriz Gil, P. *La administración de la provincia Hispania Citerior durante el Alto Imperio Romano: organización territorial, cargos administrativos y fiscalidad* (Barcelona 2013).

Padilla Monge, A. '*Asido Caesarina*: consideraciones acerca de su status', *Habis* 16 (1985), 307–327.

Padilla Monge, A. 'El epígrafe *CIL* II, 1305', *Habis* 20 (1989), 185–192.

Padilla Monge, A. 'Algunos comentarios sobre las canteras de la Bética durante los siglos III–V', *HAnt* 23 (1999), 321–330.

Padilla Monge, A. 'Algunas cuestiones en torno a la elite de Carteia', *Gerión* 29, no. 1 (2011), 239–263.

Padilla Monge, A. '*Pagus Marmorariensis, mons Mariorum, statio serrariorum Augustorum* y canteras de Almadén de la Plata. Algunas precisiones', *BMAN* 3 (2018), 119–129.

Pallarés, F. 'Las excavaciones de la plaza de San Miguel y la topografía romana de Barcino', *Cuadernos de Arqueología e Historia de la Ciudad* 13 (1969), 5–42.

Panciera, S. *Epigrafi, epigrafia, epigrafisti: scritti vari editi e inediti (1956–2005) con note complementari e indici* (Rome 2006).

Parca, M. *The Franchetti Collection in Roma. Inscriptions and Sculptural Fragments* (Rome 1995).

Parker, A. J. *Ancient Shipwrecks of the Mediterranean and Roman Provinces* (Oxford 1992).

Parkin, T. G. and Pomeroy, A. J. *Roman Social History: A Sourcebook* (London 2007).

Paroli, L. *Scavi di* Ostia *12. La basilica di Pianabella 1* (Rome 1999).

Pastor Muñoz, M. 'Nueva inscripción latina de Piñar (Granada)', *HAnt* 24 (2000), 155–164.

Pastor Muñoz, M. 'Epigrafía y sociedad en la colonia *Iulia Gemella Acci*', in *Actas del I Congreso Internacional de Historia Antigua "La Península Ibérica hace 2000 años", Valladolid, 23–25 de noviembre 2000*, ed. L. Hernández Guerra, L. Sagredo San Eustaquio and J. M. Solana Sáinz (2002), 425–439.

Pastor Muñoz, M. 'Epigrafía y culto imperial en la Granada romana', *FlorIlib* 26 (2015), 105–137.

Pausanias. *Description of Greece, Volume II: Books 3–5 (Laconia, Messenia, Elis 1)*. Translated by W. H. S. Jones and H. A. Ormerod. Loeb Classical Library 188. (Cambridge, MA 1926).

Pausanias, *Guida della Grecia. 5, Libro V: L'Elide e Olimpia*. Testo e traduzione a cura di G. Maddoli. Commento a cura di G. Maddoli e V. Saladino (Milan 1995).

Pausanias, *Description de la Grèce. T. 5, Livre V: l'Élide (I)*. Texte établi par M. Casevitz, traduit par J. Pouilloux, commenté par A. Jacquemin (Paris 1999).

Pavón Torrejón, P. '*Feminae ab omnibus officiis civilibus vel publicis remotae sunt* (D. 50.17.2, Ulp. 1 Sab.): Ulpiano y la tradición a propósito de las mujeres', in *Marginación y mujer en el Imperio romano*, ed. P. Pavón Torrejón (Rome 2018), 33–62.

Pavón Torrejón, P. '*Infirmitas enim feminarum, non calliditas auxilium demeruit* (D. 16.1.2.3, Ulp. 29 ad ed.) o la "extrema dualidad" de la condición femenina en el senadoconsulto Veleyano', in Conditio feminae. *Imágenes de la realidad femenina en el mundo romano*, ed. P. Pavón Torrejón (Rome 2021), 127–150.

Pellegrino, A. 'Le culte des morts et les rites funéraires dans le monde romain', in Ostia, *port et porte de la Rome antique*, ed. J. P. Descœudres (Genoa 2001), 367–372.

Pellicer, M. 'Excavaciones en Itálica (1978–1979): muralla, cloaca y cisterna', in *Itálica (Santiponce, Sevilla)*, ed. P. León (Madrid 1982), 205–224.

Pena Gimeno, M. J. 'La tribu *Velina* en Mallorca y los nombres de *Palma* y *Pollentia*', *Faventia* 26, no. 4 (2004), 69–90.

Pena Gimeno, M. J. 'Problemas históricos en torno a la fundación de Valencia', in *Valencia y las primeras ciudades romanas de Hispania*, ed. J. L. Jiménez Salvador and A. Ribera (Valencia 2012), 267–278.

Pensabene, P. 'Considerazioni sul trasporto di manufatti marmorei in età imperiale a Roma e in altri centri occidentali', *Dialoghi di Archeologia* 6, no. 2 (1972), 317–362.

Pensabene, P. 'Amministrazione dei marmi e sistema distributivo nel mondo romano', in *Marmi antichi*, ed. G. Borghini (Rome 2004), 43–54.

Peppe, L. *Posizione giuridica e ruolo sociale della donna romana in età repubblicana* (Milan 1984).

Pérez Bareas, C., Lizcano Prestel, R., Casado Millán, P. J. and Burgos Juárez, A. 'Actuación arqueológica de urgencia realizada en el Cine Acci de Guadix, Granada', *Anuario arqueológico de Andalucía 1998*, vol. 3 (2001), 351–358.

Pérez Zurita, A. D. 'Reflexiones en torno al cuatorvirato en la *Hispania* romana', *Polis* 16 (2004), 133–168.

Pérez Zurita, A. D. 'El cuatorvirato y la promoción jurídica de los municipios hispanos', *Revista General de Derecho Romano* 5 (2005).

Pérez Zurita, A. D. 'La implantación de la edilidad en *Hispania*: adopción y adaptación del modelo romano-itálico', in *De Roma a las provincias: las elites como instrumento de proyección de Roma. Juan Francisco Rodríguez Neila* in honorem, ed. A. Caballos Rufino and E. Melchor Gil (Seville 2014), 495–521.

Periñán Gómez, B. 'Apuntes sobre la "*Lex Gellia Cornelia de civitate danda*"', in *Derecho, persona y ciudadanía. Una experiencia jurídica comparada,* ed. B. Periñán Gómez (Madrid 2010), 547–578.

Picard, G. Ch. *Castellum Dimmidi* (Paris 1947).

Pina Polo, F. 'Las comisiones senatoriales para la reorganización de Hispania', *DHA* 23, no. 2 (1997), 83–104.

Pina Polo, F. 'Hispania of Caesar and Pompey. A Conflict of *Clientelae*?', in *Del* imperium *de Pompeyo a la* auctoritas *de Augusto. Homenaje a Michael Grant*, ed. M. P. García-Bellido, A. Mostalac and A. Jiménez (Madrid 2008), 41–48.

Pina Polo, F. 'Las migraciones en masa y su integración en el Imperio romano', in *Pluralidad e integración en el mundo romano*, ed. F. J. Navarro (Pamplona 2010), 63–80.

Pina Polo, F. 'Los Cornelio Balbo: clientes en Roma, patronos en *Gades*', in *Identità e autonomie nel mondo romano occidentale. Iberia-Italia, Italia-Iberia III*, ed. A. Sartori and A. Valvo, (Faenza 2011), 335–354.

Pina Polo, F. 'Generales y clientelas provinciales: ¿qué clientelas?', in *Romanización, fronteras y etnias en la Roma Antigua: el caso hispano*, ed. J. Santos Yanguas, G. Cruz Andreotti, M. Fernández Corral and L. Sánchez Voigt (Vitoria 2013).

Pitts, M. and Versluys, M. J. (eds.), *Globalisation and the Roman World: World History, Connectivity and Material Culture* (Cambridge 2014), 161–206.

Pliny. *Natural History, Volume II: Books 3–7*, translated by H. Rackham. Loeb Classical Library 352 (Cambridge, MA, 1942).

Pococke, R. *A Description of the East and Some Other Countries*, vol. I (London 1743).

Pomeroy, S. B. *Goddesses, Whores, Wives and Slaves. Women in Classical Antiquity* (New York 1975).

Poulle, A. 'Inscriptions de la Numidie et de la Maurétanie sétifienne', *Recueil des notices et mémoires de la société archéologique du département de Constantine* 17 (1875), 417–422.

Price, M. *Decorative Stone: The Complete Sourcebook* (London 2007).

Quack, J. and Takacs, S. 'Serapis', in *Brill's New Pauly*, consulted online on 2 June 2021 http://dx.doi.org.libproxy.helsinki.fi/10.1163/1574-9347_bnp_e1109510.

Ramallo, S. and Quevedo, A. (eds.), *Las ciudades de la Tarraconense oriental entre los s. II–IV d.C. Evolución urbanística y contextos materiales* (Murcia 2014).

Randazzo, S. 'Gli equilibri della cittadinanza romana, fra sovranità e impatto sociale', in *Integration in Rome and in the Roman World*, ed. G. De Kleijn and S. Benoist (Leiden 2014), 21–42.

Rebuffat, R. 'Notes sur les confins de la Maurétanie Tingitane et de Maurétanie Césarienne', *Studi Magrebini* 4 (1971), 33–64.

Rebuffat, R. 'Nomadisme et archéologie', *L'Afrique dans l'Occident romain, Ier siècle av. J.-C.–IVe siècle apr. J.-C.* (Rome 1990), 231–247.

Rebuffat, R. 'La frontière de la Tingitane', in *Frontières et limites géographiques de l'Afrique du Nord antique. Hommage à Pierre Salama*, ed. C. Lepelley and X. Dupuis (Paris 1999), 265–293.

Rebuffat, R. 'Mobilité des personnes dans l'Afrique romaine', in *Mobilité des personnes en Méditerranée de l'époque antique à l'époque moderne, procédures de contrôle et documents d'identification*, ed. C. Moatti (Rome 2004), 155–203.

Redondo-Moyano, E. 'El encuentro de *Veturia* y Coriolano (D. H. *Antiquitates Romanae* 8.44–53)', *SPhV* 18 (2016), 335–342.

Remesal Rodríguez, J. *La Bética en el concierto del imperio Romano* (Madrid 2011).

Revell, L. 'The Written City: Political Inscriptions from Roman *Baetica*', in *Written Space in the Latin West, 200 BC–AD 300*, ed. G. Sears and P. Keegan (London 2013), 229–332.

Revell, L. *Ways of Being Roman: Discourses of Identity in the Roman West* (Havertown 2016).

Richardson, J. '*Imperium Romanum*: Empire and the Language of Power', *JRS* 81 (1991), 1–9.

Richardson, J. 'The Meaning of *imperium* in the Last Century BC and the First AD', in *The Roman Foundations of the Law of Nations. Alberico Gentili and the Justice of Empire* ed. B. Kingsbury and B. Straumann (Oxford 2010), 21–29.

Richardson, J. 'Fines provinciae', in *Frontiers in the Roman World: Proceedings of the Ninth Workshop of the International Network Impact of Empire (Durham, 16–19 April 2009)*, ed. O. Hekster and T. Kaizer (Leiden 2011), 1–12.

Ripollès, P. P. and Velaza, J. '*Saguntum*, colonia latina', *ZPE* 141 (2002), 285–291.

Ripollès, P. P. *Las acuñaciones provinciales romanas de Hispania* (Madrid 2010).

Rodà, I. 'Los mármoles de Itálica. Su comercio y origen', in *Itálica MMCC: Actas de las Jornadas del 2.200 aniversario de la fundación de Itálica (Sevilla, 8–11 noviembre 1994)*, ed. A. Caballos Rufino and P. León (Seville 1997), 155–180.

Roddaz, J. M. 'Agripa y la Península Ibérica', *Anas* 6 (1993), 111–126.

Rodero, S. 'Algunos aspectos de la decoración arquitectónica del *Traianeum* de Itálica', *Romula* 1 (2002), 75–106.

Rodríguez Gutiérrez, O. *El teatro romano de Itálica: estudio arqueoarquitectónico* (Madrid 2004a).

Rodríguez Gutiérrez, O. 'Programas decorativos de época severiana en Itálica', in *La decoración arquitectónica en las ciudades romanas de Occidente*, ed. S. F. Ramallo (Murcia 2004b), 355–377.

Rodríguez Gutiérrez, O. 'Los *marmora* en el programa arquitectónico y decorativo del teatro romano de Itálica: Antiguas hipótesis, nuevas propuestas y posibles certezas a la luz de las aportaciones de los análisis de microscopía óptica de polarización', in Marmora Hispana: *explotación y uso de los materiales pétreos en la Hispania Romana*, ed. T. Nogales and J. Beltrán (Rome 2008), 231–259.

Rodríguez Gutiérrez, O. 'Altar hexagonal del teatro', in *Itálica, cien años, cien piezas*, ed. J. R. López Rodríguez and J. Beltrán (Seville 2014), 56–57.

Rodríguez Hidalgo, J. M. 'Reflexiones en torno a la Itálica de Adriano', *Habis* 17–18 (1987–1988), 583–590.

Rodríguez Hidalgo, J. M. 'La nueva imagen de la Itálica de Adriano', in *Italica MMCC*, ed. A. Caballos Rufino and P. León (Seville 1997), 87–114.

Rodríguez Hidalgo, J. M, *et al.*, 'La Itálica de Adriano: resultados de las prospecciones arqueológicas de 1991 y 1993', *AEA* 72 (1999) 73–98.

Rodríguez Hidalgo, J. M. 'Historia de la investigación', in *Itálica-Santiponce.* Municipium y Colonia Aelia Augusta Italicensium, ed. A. Caballos Rufino (Rome 2010), 17–34.

Rodríguez Hidalgo, J. M. and Jiménez Sancho, A. 'Itálica, la Colina de los Dioses. De Augusto a Adriano', in Navigare necesse est. *Estudios en homenaje a José María Luzón Nogué*, ed. J. García, I. Mañas and F. Salcedo (Madrid 2015), 231–242.

Rodríguez Neila, J. F. 'Gestión administrativa en las comunidades indígenas hispanas durante la etapa pre-municipal', in *Actas del I Coloquio de Historia Antigua de Andalucía (Córdoba 1988), vol. 1*, ed. J. F. Rodríguez Neila (Córdoba 1993), 385–412.

Rodríguez Neila, J. F. 'Introducción histórica', in *Las capitales provinciales de Hispania, Córdoba. Colonia Patricia Corduba*, ed. X. Dupré Raventós (Rome 2004) 7–20.

Rohr Vio, F. 'La voce e il silencio: il dissenso delle matrone al tramonto della Repubblica', in *Lo spazio del non-allineamento a Roma fra Tarda Repubblica e Primo Principato. Forme e figure dell'opposizione politica*, ed. R. Cristofoli, A. Galimberti and F. Rohr Vio (Rome 2014), 95–115.

Rohr Vio, F. '*Matronae* nella tarda repubblica: un nuevo profilo al femminile', in Matronae in domo et in re publica agentes – *spazi e occasioni dell'azione femminile nel mondo romano tra tarda repubblica e primo impero: atti del Convegno di Venezia, 16–17 ottobre 2014*, ed. F. Cenerini and F. Rohr Vio (Trieste 2016), 1–21.

Rohr Vio, F. *Le custodi del potere. Donne e politica alla fine della repubblica romana* (Rome 2019).

Rohr Vio, F. *Powerful Matrons. New Political Actors in the Late Roman Republic* (Seville–Zaragoza 2022).

Roldán, L. 'La casa de la Exedra de Itálica (Santiponce, Sevilla). Un intento de valoración espacial a través de las técnicas constructivas', in *La casa urbana hispanorromana: ponencias y comunicaciones* (Zaragoza 1991), 303–311.

Roman, D. 'Aix-en-Provence et les débuts de la colonisation de droit latin en Gaule du Sud', *RAN* 20 (1987), 185–190.

Román, J. 'Transformaciones postadrianeas del ámbito doméstico en la Nova Urbs de Itálica: una aproximación a partir de la Terra Sigillata africana', *Romula* 9 (2010), 289–314.

Romanelli, P. *Storia delle province romane dell'Africa* (Rome 1959).

Romero Vera, D. *La ciudad hispanorromana en el siglo II d.C. Consolidación y transformación de un modelo urbano* (Ph.D diss., University of Cordoba 2016a).

Romero Vera, D. 'Espacios no construidos en la ciudad romana: problemas y perspectivas de estudio a partir de varios casos hispanos', *MDAI(M)* 57 (2016b), 393–408.

Romero Vera, D. 'Caracterizando a la ciudad hispanorromana de época antonina: muralla, viario y red de saneamiento', *Conimbriga* 58 (2019), 233–254.

Romero Vera, D. 'Edificios de espectáculos en la Hispania del siglo II d.C.: un análisis sincrónico', *Lucentum* 39 (2020a), 247–268.

Romero Vera, D. '138–192 d.C.: el punto de inflexión. Una aproximación a las transformaciones de las áreas forenses hispanas entre los reinados de Antonino Pío y Cómodo', in Exemplum et Spolia: *la reutilización arquitectónica en la transformación del paisaje urbano de las ciudades históricas*, vol. 2, ed. P. Mateos and C. Morán (Mérida 2020b), 707–714.

Romero Vera, D. 'Consideraciones sobre la arquitectura doméstica urbana de Hispania en el siglo II d.C.', *Spal* 29, no. 1 (2020c), 243–270.

Romero Vera, D. 'Termas públicas en la Hispania de época antonina: una aproximación a su secuencia evolutiva', *Pyrenae* 51 (2020d), 69–98.

Romero Vera, D. 'Continuidad y transformación en las ciudades hispanorromanas del siglo II d. C.: la fase trajano-adrianea (98–138 d. C.)', *Arqueología Iberoamericana* 47 (2021a), 31–40.

Romero Vera, D. 'Conjeturas en torno a la ruptura del modelo urbanístico altoimperial en Hispania: la fase tardoantonina y primoseveriana (138–211 d. C.)', *Arqueología Iberoamericana* 47 (2021b), 41–52.

Romero Vera, D. 'Notas sobre topografía y costumbres funerarias en las necrópolis urbanas de Hispania del siglo II d.C.', *Ágora. Estudos Clássicos em Debate* 23 (2021c), 169–188.

Romero Vera, D. 'Los foros de Hispania en el siglo II d.C.: intervenciones arquitectónicas, escultóricas y epigráficas', *Latomus* 80 (2021d), 82–112.

Roselaar, S. T. *Public Land in the Roman Republic. A Social and Economic History of* Ager Publicus *in Italy, 396–89 BC* (Oxford 2010).

Roselaar, S. T. 'The Concept of *Commercium* in the Roman Republic', *Phoenix* 66 (2012), 381–413.

Roselaar, S. T. 'The Concept of *Conubium* in the Roman Republic', in *New Frontiers: Law and Society in the Roman World*, ed. P. du Plessis (Edinburgh 2013), 102–122.

Rowe, G. *Princes and Political Cultures. The New Tiberian Senatorial Decrees* (Ann Arbor 2005).

Rudich, V. *Political Dissidence under Nero: The Price of Dissimulation* (London 2014).

Rudolph, H. *Stadt und Staat im römischen Italien: Untersuchungen über die Entwicklung des Munizipalwesens in der republikanischen Zeit* (Leipzig 1935).

Ruiz Bueno, M. D. *Dinámicas topográficas urbanas en Hispania: el espacio intramuros entre los siglos II y VII d. C.* (Bari 2018).

Ruiz Castellanos, A. *Ley de las Doce Tablas* (Madrid 1991).

Ruiz de Arbulo Bayona, J. 'Tarraco, Carthago Nova y el problema de la capitalidad en la Hispania citerior republicana', in *Miscel.lània arqueològica a Josep M. Recasens* (Tarragona 1992), 115–130.

Ruiz Gutiérrez, A. 'El paisaje epigráfico de la ciudad romana: concepto y perspectivas de estudio', in *Paisajes epigráficos de la Hispania romana. Monumentos, contextos, topografías*, ed. J. M. Iglesias Gil and A. Ruiz Gutiérrez (Rome 2013), 13–28.

Ruiz Osuna, A. B. 'Arquitectura funeraria en la Bética: el ejemplo de las capitales conventuales', *AAC* 17 (2006), 157–194.

Russell, A. *The Politics of Public Space in Republican Rome* (Cambridge 2016).

Salama, P. *Carte du réseau routier de l'Afrique romaine* (Algiers 1949).

Salama, P. *Les voies romaines de l'Afrique du Nord* (Algiers 1951a).

Salama, P. 'Les bornes milliaires de Djemila-Cuicul et leur intérêt pour l'histoire de la ville', *Revue africaine* 95 (1951b), 213–272.

Salama, P. 'La voie romaine de la vallée de la Tafna', *Bulletin d'archéologie algérienne* 2 (1966–1967), 183–217.

Salama, P. 'Un point d'eau du *limes* maurétanien', in *Maghreb et Sahara, Mélanges*, ed. J. Despois (Paris 1973), 336–357.

Salama, P. 'Un chapiteau inscrit d'époque chrétienne à Aïn Touta (Algérie)', in *Mélanges d'antiquité tardive*. Studiola in honorem Natalis Duval, ed. C. Balmelle, P. Chevalier and G. Ripoll (Turnhout 2004), 37–45.

Salazar Ortiz, N., Pàmies, D. and Moreno, I. 'De Sigarra a Prats de Segarra: noves descobertes arqueològiques al Municipium Sigarrense (els Prats de Rei, Anoia) entre l'ibèric antic i l'edat mitjana', *Tribuna d'arqueologia* (2013–2014), 115–134.

Salazar Revuelta, M. 'Estatus jurídico y social de la *materfamilias* en el marco de la ciudadanía romana', in Mulier. *Algunas historias e instituciones de derecho romano*, ed. R. Rodríguez and M. J. Bravo (Madrid 2013), 199–222.

Salcedo Garcés, F. 'Indigenismo y aculturación en la frontera de la Tripolitana romana', *RdA* 44 (2020), 145–168.

Saller, R. P. and Shaw, B. D. 'Tombstones and Roman Family Relations in the Principate: Civilians, Soldiers and Slaves', *JRS* 74 (1984), 124–156.

Salmon, J. and Shipley, G. (eds.), *Human Landscapes in Classical Antiquity. Environment and Culture* (London-New York 1995).

O. Salomies, *Die römischen Vornamen: Studien zur römischen Namengebung* (Helsinki 1987).

Salomies, O. *Adoptive and Polyonymous Nomenclature in the Roman Empire* (Helsinki 1992).

Salvadore, M. *Il nome, la persona. Saggio sull'etimologia antica* (Genoa 1987).

Salvador Oyonate, J. A. 'La Bastitania romana y visigoda: Arqueología e historia de un territorio' (Ph.D. diss., University of Granada, 2011).

Salway, B. 'What's in a Name? A Survey of Roman Onomastic Practice from c. 700 B.C. to A.D. 700', *JRS* 84 (1994), 124–145.

Sánchez-Ostiz, A. Tabula Siarensis. *Edición, traducción y comentario* (Pamplona 1999).

Sánchez Quirante, L. and Fernández Sanjuan, L. 'Prospección arqueológica superficial de la Sierra de Baza y Altiplano de Baza-Caniles', *Anuario Arqueológico de Andalucía 1987*, vol. 2 (1990), 48–50.

Sánchez Quirante, L. 'Prospección arqueológica superficial del sector occidental de la Sierra de Baza, Campaña de 1990', *Anuario arqueológico de Andalucía 1990*, vol. 2 (1992a), 124–127.

Sánchez Quirante, L. 'Investigación Arqueológica en la Sierra de Baza-Gor', in *Investigaciones arqueológicas en Andalucía: 1985–1992. Proyectos*, ed. J. M. Campos Carrasco and F. Nocete Calvo (1992b), 329–340.

Santero, J. M. 'Colonia Iulia Gemella Acci', *Habis* 3 (1972), 203–222.

Saquete Chamizo, J. C. and Iñesta Mena, J. 'Un fragmento de ley municipal hallado en la *Baeturia Turdulorum* (*conventus Cordubensis, provincia Baetica*)', *ZPE* 168 (2009), 293–297.

Saquete Chamizo, J. C. and Guerra Millán, S. 'Una inscripción constructiva procedente de *Metellinum* (provincia Lusitania)', *ZPE* 196 (2015), 303–306.

Saquete Chamizo, J. C. 'Colonias en la *Hispania Ulterior* entre César y Augusto. Balance y perspectivas de estudio', in *Le strutture locali dell'Occidente romano: Stato dell'arte e prospettive di ricerca*, ed. S. Sisani, E. García Fernández, and E. Melchor Gil (Rome) (2023).

Schnabel, P. 'Die Weltkarte des Agrippa als wissenschaftliches Mittelglied zwischen Hipparchen und Ptolemaeus', *Philologus* 90 (1935), 405–440.

Schultz, C. E. *Women's Religious Activity in the Roman Republic* (Chapel Hill 2006).

Schumacher, L. 'Die vier hohen römischen Priesterkollegien unter den Flaviern, den Antoninen aund den Severern (69–235 n. Chr.)', in W. Haase (eds.), *Aufstieg und Niedergang der römischen Welt. Geschichte und Kultur Roms im Spiegel der neueren*

*Forschung*. II. *Principat*. Volume 16, no. 1, *Teilband Religion* (*Heidentum: Römische Religion, Allgemeines*) (Berlin–New York 1978), 777–780.

Scott, M. *Space and Society in the Greek and Roman Worlds* (Cambridge 2012).

Senatore, F. '*Quattuorviri aediles* nella colonia romana di Pompei?', *ZPE* 1997, 283–291.

Sherwin-White, A. N. *The Roman Citizenship* (Oxford 1973).

Sillières, P. *Les voies de communication de l'Hispanie méridionale* (Paris 1990).

Sisani, S. 'Le magistrature locali delle comunità municipali di ambito provinciale: uno studio sulla diffusione del quattuorvirato e del duovirato tra l'età tardo-republicana e l'età imperiale', *Gerión* 36 (1) (2018a), 41–77.

Sisani, S. 'Latinità non latina: lo *ius Latii* come strumento di integrazione delle comunità provinciali in età repubblicana', *Gerión* 36 (2) (2018b), 331–378.

Sisani, S. 'Il duovirato nei municipia italici: contributo allo studio della fase finale del processo di municipalizzazione nell'Italia centrale e meridionale', *Gerión* 39 (1) (2021), 41–93.

Slimani, S. and Kherbouche, V. 'Les formes d'occupation antique dans le Hodna : état des lieux', in *La frontière méridionale du Maghreb : approches croisées* (*Antiquité-Moyen Âge*), ed. S. Guédon (Bordeaux 2018), 193–206.

Slootjes, D. and Peachin, M. (eds.), *Rome and the Worlds beyond its Frontiers* (Leiden 2017).

Smadja, E. 'Culte impérial et religion en Afrique du Nord sous le Haut Empire romain', *Dialogues d'histoire ancienne. Supplément 1. Hommage à Pierre Lévêque* (Besançon 2005), 225–237.

Smith, P. J. *The Archaeology and Epigraphy of Hellenistic and Roman Megaris, Greece* (Oxford 2008).

Solin, H. and Salomies, O. *Repertorium nominum gentilium et cognominum Latinorum*, editio nova (Olms 1994).

Solin, H. *Studi storico–epigrafici sul Lazio antico* (Rome 1996).

Solin, H. 'Abuso dell'onomastica nella ricerca epigrafica', in *Usi e abusi epigrafici. Atti del Colloquio Internazionale di Epigrafia Latina*, ed. M. G. Angeli Bertinelli and A. Donati (Rome 2003), 279–286.

Speidel, M. P. 'A Thousand Thracian Recruits for *Mauretania Tingitana*', *AntAfr* 11 (1977), 167–173.

Spencer, D. *Roman Landscape: Culture and Identity* (Cambridge 2010).

Squarciapino, M. F., Gismondi, I., Barbieri, G., Bloch, H. and Calza, R. *Scavi di* Ostia *III: Le Necropoli 1. Le tombe di età repubblicana e augustea* (Rome 1958).

Stefanile, M. *Dalla Campania alle* Hispaniae. *L'emigrazione dalla Campania romana alle coste mediterranee della Penisola Iberica in età tardo-repubblicana e proto-imperiale* (Naples 2017).

Steiner, A. P. '*The vigintivirate during the Empire. A Study of the Epigraphical Evidence*' (Ph. D. diss., University of Ohio, 1974).

Stevenson, T. 'Women of Early Rome as "*Exempla*" in Livy, "*Ab Urbe Condita*", Book 1', *Classical World* 104, no. 2 (2011), 175–189.

Stolte, B. 'Jurisdiction and the Representation of Power, or the Emperor on Circuit', in *The Representation and Perception of Roman Imperial Power. Proceedings of the Third Workshop of the International Network Impact of Empire (Roman Empire, c. 200 B.C.–A.D. 476), Rome, March 20–23, 2002*, ed. P. Erdkamp, O. Hekster, G. de Kleijn, S. T. A. M. Mols and L. de Blois (Leiden 2003), 261–268.

Strabo, Geography, Volume II: Books 3–5. Translated by Horace Leonard Jones. Loeb Classical Library 50. (Cambridge, MA 1917).

Strada, J. *In tabulis xilographicis adiectis ad … praeterea addidimus omnes antiquitates quae passim in tota Hispania* (Frankfurt 1575).

Straumann, B. *Roman Law in the State of Nature. The Classical Foundations of Hugo Grotius' Natural Law* (Cambridge 2015).

Strong, A. K. *Prostitutes and Matrons in the Roman World* (Cambridge 2016).

Stylow, A. U. 'El *municipium Flavium V*(---) de Azuaga (Badajoz) y la municipalización de la *Baeturia Turdulorum*', *SHHA* 9 (1991), 11–27.

Stylow, A. U. 'Apuntes sobre las tribus romanas en Hispania', *Veleia* 12 (1995), 105–124.

Stylow, A. U. 'Las estatuas honoríficas como medio de autorrepresentación de las élites locales de Hispania', in *Élites Hispaniques*, ed. S. Demougin, M. Navarro and F. Des Boscs-Plateaux (Bordeaux 2001), 141–155.

Stylow, A. U. 'Una aproximación a la Carmo romana a través de su epigrafía. Nuevas aportaciones y revisión crítica', in *Carmona Romana, vol. 1*, ed. A. Caballos Rufino (Seville 2012), 133–148.

Stylow, A. U. 'Die *Accitani veteres* und die Kolonie *Iulia Gemella Acci*. Zum Problem von *veteres*, Alt-Stadt und Kolonie in der *Hispania Ulterior*', *Chiron* 30 (2017), 775–806.

Suárez, P. *Historia del Obispado de Guadix y Baza* (Guadix 1696).

Syme, R. 'Hadrian and Italica', *JRS* 54 (1964), 142–149 [=].

Syme R. *Roman Papers* II (Oxford 1979).

Syme, R. 'Rival Cities, Notably Tarraco and Barcino', *Ktèma* 6 (1981), 271–285.

Syme, R. 'Clues to Testamentary Adoption', in *Epigrafia e ordine senatorio* 1 (Rome 1982), 397–410.

Syme, R. 'Spaniards at Tivoli', *AncSoc* 13–14 (1982–1983), 241–263 [=].

R. Syme, *Roman Papers* IV (Oxford 1988).

Symonds, M. *Protecting the Roman Empire. Fortlets, Frontiers, and the Quest for Post-Conquest Security* (Cambridge 2017).

Taglietti. F. 'Ancora su incinerazione e inumazione: la necropoli dell'Isola Sacra', in M. Heinzelmann, J. Ortalli, P. Fasold and M. Witteyer (eds.), *Römischer Bestattungsbrauch und Beigabensitten in Rom, Norditalien und den Nordwestprovinzen von der späten Republik bis in die Kaiserzeit — Culto dei morti e costumi funerari romani. Roma, Italia settentrionale e province nord-occidentali dalla tarda Repubblica all'età imperiale* (Wiesbaden 2001), 149–158.

Takács, S. A. *Vestal Virgins, Sibyls, and Matrons: Women in Roman Religion* (Austin 2008).

Tarpin, M. 'Strangers in Paradise. Latins (and some other non-Romans) in Colonial Context. A Short Story of Territorial Complexity', in *Roman Republican Colonization. New Perspectives from Archaeology and Ancient History*, ed. J. Pelgrom and T. D. Stek (Rome 2014), 160–191.

Taylor, T. S. 'Social Status, Legal Status and Legal Privilege', in *The Oxford Handbook of Roman Law and Society*, ed. P. J. du Plessis, C. Ando and K. Tuori (Oxford 2016), 349–361.

Tersptra, T. *Trading Communities in the Roman World: A Micro-Economic and Institutional Perspective* (Leiden 2013).

Tersptra, T. *Trade in the Ancient Mediterranean: Private Order and Public Institutions* (Princeton 2019).

Thomas, Y. *« Origine » et « commune patrie ». Étude de droit public romain (89 av. J.-C.–212 ap. J.-C.)* (Rome 1996).

Thomasson, B. E. *Praesides provinciarum Africae* (Lund 1969).

Thommen, L. *An Environmental History of Ancient Greece and Rome* (Cambridge 2012).

Thouvenot, R. *Essai sur la province romaine de Bétique* (Paris 1940).

Tran, N. and Loriot, X. '*Vettius Anicetus, quinquennalis* des charpentiers de marine', *MEFRA* 121, no. 1 (2009), 241–253.

Tucci, P. *et al.* '*Italica* (Seville. Spain): Use of Local Marble in Augustan Age', *Periodico di Mineralogia* 79 Special Issue (2010), 113–129.

Tweedie, F. C. 'The *Lex Licinia Mucia* and the *Bellum Italicum*' in S. T. Roselaar (ed.), *Processes of Integration and Identity Formation in the Roman Republic* (Leiden–Boston 2012), 123–139.

Tuori, K. 'Legal Pluralism and the Roman Empire', in *Beyond Dogmatics: Law and Society in the Roman World*, ed. J. W. Cairns and P. J. du Plessis (Edinburgh 2007), 39–52.

Tuori, K. 'The Savage Sea and the Civilizing Law: The Roman Law Tradition and the Rule of the Sea', in *Thalassokratographie: Rezeption und Transformation antiker Seeherrschaft*, ed. H. Kopp and C. Wendt (Berlin 2018), 201–2018.

Uggeri, G. 'Minturnae', in *Brill's New Pauly*, consulted online on 2 June 2021 http://dx.doi.org.libproxy.helsinki.fi/10.1163/1574-9347_bnp_e805900.

Valentini, A. *Donne e politica a Roma tra III e II secolo a.C.* (Milan 2010).

Valette, E. 'Les "discours" *de Veturia, Valeria* et *Hersilia* : Les mises en scène de la parole matronale dans la tradition historiographique romaine', *Mondes anciens* 3 (2012), http://journals.openedition.org/mondesanciens/782.

Vanhove, D. *Roman Marble Quarries in Southern Euboea and the Associated Road Networks* (Leiden-New York-Cologne 1996).

Vaquerizo, D. *Necrópolis urbanas en* Baetica (Tarragona–Seville 2010).

Vargas, S. 'La techumbre marmórea del *Traianeum* de *Italica*', in Marmora Baeticae. *Usos de materiales pétreos en la Bética romana. Estudios arqueológicos y análisis arqueométricos*, ed. J. Beltrán, M. L. Loza, M. L and E. Ontiveros (Seville 2018), 215–222.

Verboven, K. 'Professional *Collegia*: Guilds or Social Clubs?', *AncSoc* 41 (2011), 187–195.

Verboven, K. and Hekster, O. 'Introduction', in O. Hekster and K. Verboven (eds.), *The Impact of Justice on the Roman Empire* (Leiden 2017), 1–17.

Vittinghoff, F. *Römische Kolonisation und Bürgerrechtspolitik unter Caesar und Augustus* (Wiesbaden 1952).

Vives Escudero, A. *La moneda hispánica* (Madrid 1924).

Von Hesberg, H. Monumenta. *I sepolcri romani e la loro architettura* (Milan 1994).

Walsh, J. P. *Consumerism in the Ancient World: Imports and Identity Construction* (London 2014).

Ward-Perkins, J. B. 'Severan art and architecture at *Lepcis Magna*', *JRS* 38 (1948), 59–80.

Watson, A. *The Spirit of Roman Law* (Athens, GA 1995).

Webb, L. M. '*Exaequatio* and *aemulatio*: Regulation of Elite Female Status Competition in Mid-Republican Rome', in *Gender and Status Competition in Pre-Modern Societies* (Turnhout 2021), ed. M. Bayless, J. Liliequist and L. M. Webb, 43–78.

Webb, L. M. 'Female Interventions in Politics in the *libera res publica*: Structures and Practices', in *Leadership and Initiative in Late Republican and Early Imperial Rome*, ed. R. M. Frolov and C. Burden–Strevens (Leiden–Leiden 2022) 151–188.

Whittaker, C. R. *Frontiers of the Roman Empire: A Social and Economic Study* (Baltimore–London 1994).

Williamson, C. 'Monuments of Bronze: Roman Legal Documents on Bronze Tablets', *ClAnt* 6, no. 1 (1987), 160–183.

Williams-Thorpe, O. and Potts, P. J. 'Geochemical and Magnetic Provenancing of Roman Granite Columns from Andalucía and Extremadura, Spain', *OJA* 21 (2002), 167–194.

Wilson, A. J. N. *Emigration from Italy in the Republican Age of Rome* (Manchester 1966).

Wilson, A. 'The Mediterranean Environment in Ancient History: Perspectives and Prospects', in *The Ancient Mediterranean Environment between Science and History*, ed. W. V. Harris (Leiden 2013), 259–276.

Witcher, R., Tolia-Kelly, D. P. and Hingley, R. 'Archaeologies of Landscape: Excavating the Materialities of Hadrian's Wall', *Journal of Material Culture* 15, no. 1 (2010), 105–108.

Witschel, C. 'Hispania en el siglo III', in Hispaniae. *Las provincias hispanas en el mundo romano*, ed. J. Andreu et al. (Tarragona 2009).

Woolf, G. 'Monumental Writing and the Expansion of Roman Society in the Early Empire', *JRS* 86 (1996), 22–39.

Woolf, G. *Becoming Roman: The Origins of Provincial Civilization in Gaul* (Cambridge 1998).

Woolf, G. 'The Rulers Ruled', in *Reconsidering Roman Power*, ed. K. Berthelot (Rome 2020), 76–99.

Zablocka. M. 'Il *ius trium liberorum* nel diritto romano', *BIDR* 91 (1988), 361–390.

Zanker, P. *The Power of Images in the Age of Augustus* (Ann Arbor 1990).

Zevi, F. 'Brevi note ostiense', *Epigraphica* 30 (1968), 89–95.

Zucca, R. 'Fruizioni idroterapiche e culti idrici nel Viterbese', in Usus veneratioque fontium. *Atti del Convegno Internazionale di Studio su « Fruizione e Culto delle Acque Salutari in Italia »*, ed. L. Gasperini (Rome 2006), 146–160.

Zuiderhoek, A. 'The Ambiguity of Munificence', *Historia* 56, no. 2 (2007), 196–213.

Zuiderhoek, A. *The Politics of Munificence in the Roman Empire. Citizens, Elites and Benefactors in Asia Minor* (Cambridge 2009).

# Index of Names

# Index of Toponyms

# Index of Ancient Sources

Printed in the United States
by Baker & Taylor Publisher Services